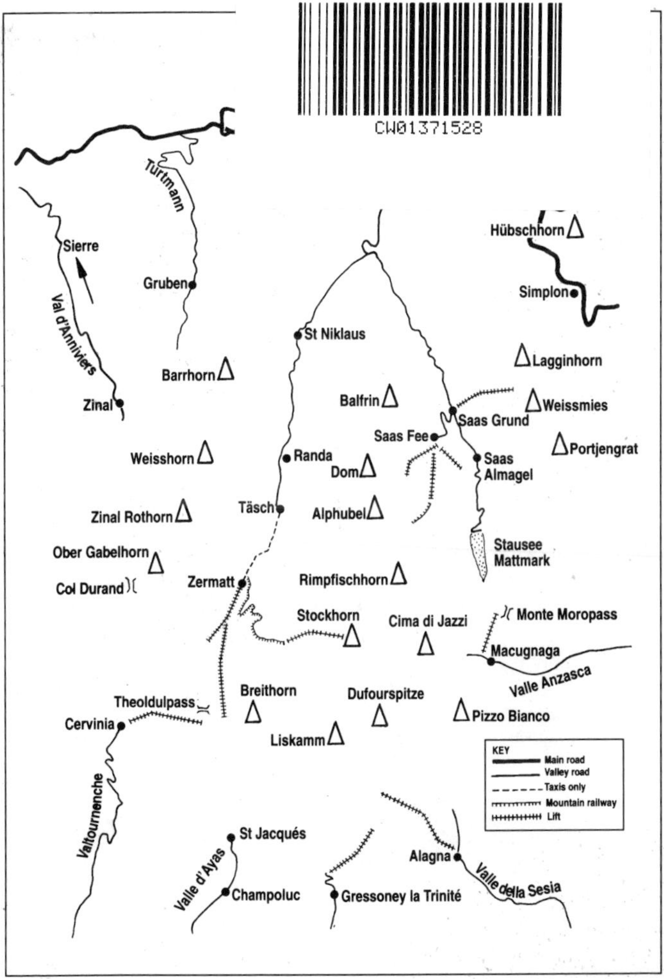

Türtmann
Sierre
Gruben
Val d'Anniviers
Barrhorn
Zinal
Weisshorn
Zinal Rothorn
Ober Gabelhorn
Col Durand
Hübschhorn
Simplon
St Niklaus
Lagginhorn
Balfrin
Weissmies
Saas Grund
Saas Fee
Portjengrat
Randa
Saas Almagel
Dom
Täsch
Alphubel
Stausee Mattmark
Zermatt
Rimpfischhorn
Stockhorn
Cima di Jazzi
Monte Moropass
Macugnaga
Valle Anzasca
Breithorn
Dufourspitze
Theoldulpass
Pizzo Bianco
Cervinia
Liskamm
KEY
Main road
Valley road
Taxis only
Mountain railway
Lift
Valtournenche
St Jacqués
Alagna
Valle d'Ayas
Valle della Sesia
Champoluc
Gressoney la Trinité

Valais Alps East *Selected Climbs*

Valais Alps East

SELECTED CLIMBS

By Les Swindin and Peter Fleming

General Editor: Les Swindin

ALPINE CLUB . LONDON
1999

Valais Alps East *Selected Climbs*

First published in Britain by the
Alpine Club 55/56 Charlotte Road London EC2A 3QT

Copyright © 1999 by the Alpine Club

Replaces Pennine Alps East (Collomb) 1979
and part of Pennine Alps Central (Collomb) 1975

Produced by the Alpine Club Editorial and Production Board

Sketch maps drawn by Peter Fleming and Rod Powis

Cover photographs
Front The view E from the Triftjigrat on the Breithorn
    Les Swindin

Back The Grand Gendarme on the ENE ridge of the Lenzspitze
    Wil Hurford

Typeset in Plantin from the authors' word processor by
Tony Welch, Forest View Consultancy, Gloucester

Black and white and colour reproductions by
Bordercolour, Carlisle

Printed in England by
The St Edmundsbury Press, Bury St Edmunds

British Library cataloguing in Publication Data. A catalogue
record for this book is available from the British Library

ISBN 0-900523-62-x

Contents

Disclaimer *front end papers*

Area map *front end papers*

List of photographs 7

General Editor's and Authors' preface 10

General information 13

Using this guide(13) Using huts(17) When to climb(19) Maps(20) Other guide books(21) Equipment(22) Language(22) Weather Forecasts(22) Rescue and insurance(24) Indices(25) Valley bases(25) International comparison of grades(32)

Introduction 33

Huts 37

Multi-day walking tours 59

Valley rock climbing areas 63

Weisshorn Chain 71

Mont Durand, Ober Gabelhorn, Wellenkuppe, Trifthorn, Zinal Rothorn, Besso, Blanc de Moming, Schalihorn, Weisshorn, Bishorn, Brunegghorn, Barrhorn

Breithorn - Liskamm Chain 113

Klein Matterhorn, Breithorn, Pollux, Castor, Liskamm

Monte Rosa Group and the Weissgrat 165

Punta Giordani, Piramide Vincent, Corno Nero, Ludwigshöhe, Parrotspitze, Signalkuppe, Zumsteinspitze, Dufourspitze, Nordend, Cima di Jazzi, Monte Moro, Pizzo Bianco, Riffelhorn, Stockhorn

The Saas peaks and the Mischabel 221

Strahlhorn, Rimpfischhorn, Allalinhorn, Egginer, Mittaghorn, Alphubel, Täschhorn, Leiterspitzen, Dom, Lenzspitze, Nadelhorn, Hohbärghorn, Dirruhorn, Ulrichshorn, Balfrin, Gross Bigerhorn

East side of the Saas Valley 275
Joderhorn, Sonnighorn, Mittelrück, Portjengrat, Portjenhorn, Dri Horlini, Weissmies, Lagginhorn, Fletschhorn, Jegihorn. Jegigrat, Senggchuppa, Hübschhorn

Enchaînements 319
List of climbs 323
General index 333
Photographs 337
Alpine Club information *back end papers*
Mountain rescue procedures *back end papers*

List of photographs

1 Ober Gabelhorn and Mont Durand W Flanks
2 Ober Gabelhorn S Face
3 Ober Gabelhorn N Face
4 Wellenkuppe and Trifthorn E Flanks
5 Zinal Rothorn from the SE *Peter Fleming*
6 Zinal Rothorn W Flank
7 Trifthorn and Zinal Rothorn (part) W Flanks
8 Zinal Rothorn E Face
9 Mammouth SE Face SW Sector
10 Mammouth SE Face NE Sector
11 Besso and Blanc de Moming S Flanks
12 Zinal Rothorn and Schalihorn E Flanks
13 Weisshorn SE Flank *Bob Chubb*
14 Weisshorn W Face
15 Weisshorn NE Face
16 Bishorn and Weisshorn from the N
17 Brunegghorn and Bisjoch N Flanks
18 Schölihorn and Barrhorn E Flanks
19 Klein Matterhorn N Flank *Peter Fleming*
20 Breithorn S Flank from the SW
21 Breithorn Central Summit from the SE
22 Breithorn N Flank
23 Breithorn W Summit NNW Face
24 Breithorn Central Summit N Flank
25 Roccia Nera and Breithorn E Summit N Flanks
26 Breithorn E Summit and Roccia Nera from the SE
27 Pollux, Liskamm and Castor from the W
28 Castor and Pollux N Flanks
29 Liskamm W Summit NNE Face

30 Liskamm E Summit NE Face
31 Liskamm S Flank
32 Piramide Vincent and Punta Giordani S Flanks *Gino Buscaini*
33 Piramide Vincent SW Flank
34 Sperone Vincent
35 Piramide Vincent, Parrotspitze and Signalkuppe E Flanks
     Gino Buscaini
36 Nordend and Dufourspitze W Flanks
37 Dufourspitze S Face
38 Monte Rosa E Face *Peter Fleming*
39 Nordend and Cima di Jazzi from the N
40 Nordend NW Flank
41 Nordend E Face *Peter Fleming*
42 Cima di Jazzi E Flank
43 Pizzo Bianco W Flank
44 Riffelhorn N Side
45 Strahlhorn and Cima di Jazzi from the W
46 Strahlhorn N Flank
47 Strahlhorn E Face *Gino Buscaini*
48 Rimpfischhorn and Strahlhorn W Flanks
49 Rimpfischhorn SW Flank
50 Rimpfischhorn W Flank
51 Rimpfischhorn and Allalinhorn from the NE
52 Allalinhorn N Flank
53 Mittaghorn and Egginer W Flanks
54 Alphubeljoch and Allalinhorn W Flanks
55 Alphubel E Flank
56 Alphubel W Flank
57 Dom and Täschhorn from the SW
58 Leiterspitzen S Flank
59 Täschhorn W Flank
60 Dom NW Flank

61 Lenzspitze and Nadelhorn from the E
62 Nadelhorn, Stecknadelhorn and Hohbärghorn NE Flanks
63 Hohbärghorn, Nadelhorn and Lenzspitze W Flanks
64 Hohbärghorn and Dirruhorn NE Flanks
65 Nadelhorn N Side
66 Gross Bigerhorn W Flank
67 Joderhorn from the W   *Peter Fleming*
68 Joderhorn E Face   *Renato Armelloni*
69 Sonnighorn N Flank
70 Mittelrück and Portjengrat E Flanks   *Renato Armelloni*
71 Portjengrat W Side
72 Lagginhorn and Fletschhorn E Flanks   *Renato Armelloni*
73 Dri Horlini SE Face SW Sector
74 Dri Horlini SE Face Central Sector
75 Weissmies W Flank
76 Weissmies from the SW
77 Fletschhorn and Lagginhorn W Flanks
78 Fletschhorn N Face   *Peter Fleming*
79 Jegihorn S Flank
80 Jegigrat
81 Hübschhorn NW Flank   *Peter Fleming*

All unaccredited photographs are by *Les Swindin*

General Editor's and Authors' preface

This guide book forms the companion volume to *Valais Alps West* and describes an area which has the greatest concentration of the highest peaks in Western Europe. Within it are nine of the twelve highest peaks in the Alps.

Amongst the mountains described there are 27 separate ones over 4,000 metres clustered around the Swiss resorts of Saas Fee, Zermatt and Zinal and their ascents are much sought-after. Whilst none of these mountains is so well-known as the Matterhorn, which is described in the other volume, many have very familiar names, having featured prominently in the long history of mountaineering and even today provide the setting for some notable adventures.

Many of the peaks are predominantly snow covered with rock showing through principally on the ridges. Where faces have exposed rock this is often loose and unsuitable for climbing on except in exceptional conditions, especially in summer, so most face routes will involve climbing snow and ice to a large extent. As a consequence you will find very few routes of extreme difficulty described in this guide compared to what you might expect in a guide to the Mont Blanc massif. It is a region for classical alpinism where fitness and good rope technique will pay dividends. Great satisfaction will be had by moving quickly and efficiently over various types of terrain. The mountains lend themselves to traverses many of which are classic outings that can often be extended into multi-day affairs. Some suggestions are given in the text.

Many British climbers will, like the two authors, spend their first alpine season in one of these resorts. Whilst many of the mountains are high there are some lower peaks suitable for novices to cut their alpine teeth. Even some of the higher summits are easily attainable by almost anyone with some winter climbing experience in Britain, provided they have the necessary level of fitness.

GENERAL EDITOR'S AND AUTHORS' PREFACE

We have attempted in this guide book to include something for everyone. Rudimentary information is provided for folks interested in sports climbing on valley crags which are often suitable for a visit if the higher peaks are not in condition. On the other hand many popular climbs are described as well as many much less frequented routes. In this region of mass tourism it is still possible to find a route that you will have to yourself, even on the most popular mountain. You will find that the vast majority of people follow the easiest route to the summit both in technical difficulty and in physical effort. Choose an alternative way and you can enjoy peace and tranquillity.

In describing routes we have been conscious of the fact that conditions on these mountains can vary dramatically from one year to the next to such an extent that a route might be predominantly on rock one year and snow another. We have tried to allow for this to some extent in our descriptions but in general routes are described in what might be considered normal conditions. It is up to the user to determine whether or not there is an abundance or a dearth of snow and to allow for this in their choice of route. The grading of routes is somewhat subjective since the difficulties encountered depend very much on the conditions at the time. Since these are so variable the grades quoted tend to be those of the concensus view and apply to routes as they are described. If you find a route undergraded it might be that the conditions are adverse or alternatively that you have not followed the best line. Whilst we indicate the general line of a route and individual sections of it, climbers must exercise their own judgement as to the precise line to take in any particular conditions encountered.

Remember that when there is a lack of snow, rockfall, which is ever present in the Alps, is increasingly likely to occur. Care should be exercised in this respect when studying the photo-diagrams since quite a large proportion of these photographs were taken during the summers of 1996 and 1997 both of which, and particularly the latter, had copious amounts of snow. If you are in any doubt make enquiries at the local tourist

GENERAL EDITOR'S AND AUTHORS' PREFACE

office or at the guides' bureau. Other objective dangers such as avalanche, serac falls and crevasses should never be taken lightly. Slides of wet snow can be particularly dangerous and even apparently safe glaciers may just have a hidden crevasse. Rock can tumble into the valley. The editor recollects a particularly disturbing incident when a large rock landed in the Atermenzen campsite.

The format used in this guide book is similar to that used in all the more recent Alpine Club guide books with one or two modifications. Details are given in the General Information section which you are recommended to read carefully and take heed of any advice given.

The authors have both climbed extensively in the region over many years but whatever their first-hand knowledge is, the writing of the guide book has required input from many other people, some are known to the authors whilst others are correspondents who have sent information. Inevitably there will be errors, alterations to routes and discrepancies. Should you find any you feel are significant or you have any other useful information or comments, please address them to the General Editor at the Alpine Club. Corrections and updated information for Alpine Club guide books is periodically published in the *Guide Books* section of the Alpine Club Web site (http://www.alpine-club.org.uk).

Our special thanks go to the following people who have been of great assistance in the preparation of this guide book: Renato Armelloni, Gino Buscaini, Rob Collister, Wil Hurford, Lindsay Griffin, Peter Ledeboer, Alan Lyall, Martin Moran, Jeremy Whitehead, the Swiss Alpine Club, some of its members and hut guardians and all the people whose brains we have picked in campsites and in mountain huts. In addition we would like to thank John Slee-Smith and Peter Hodgkiss of the AC Guide Book Editorial and Production Board for getting the book into print and Rod Powis for his fine work on the sketch maps.

Les Swindin and Peter Fleming 1999

General Information

USING THIS GUIDE

Route Numbers

In this guide book we use the same system that was used in *Valais Alps West*. Each mountain is given a unique numerical identity with the various routes on the mountain being differentiated by a unique letter. Thus the Breithorn is numbered 23 and its SSW Flank Route is identified by the number 23a. The letter 'a', as here, is usually used to identify the 'ordinary' route of ascent of the particular mountain.

Mountain Route Introduction

The route introduction, found in italics, gives a brief overview of the route and sometimes includes important information, both historical and practical, that would not normally be appropriate in the route description that follows. The height of the route is generally found at the end of the introduction. Unless otherwise stated this is the vertical interval from the base (perhaps the bergschrund) to the top of the route. The actual climbing involved may be much greater.

Mountain Route Descriptions

Route descriptions vary considerably in detail from short explanations to detailed accounts. As the vast majority of routes found in the Valais are of a mountaineering nature, topo diagrams have not been used. Common British usage in naming routes and features has generally been maintained. The terms L and R or Lwards and Rwards are always used with reference to the direction of movement of the climber. Occasionally, with features such as couloirs or glaciers the orographical reference to the L or R bank is applied when viewed in the direction of flow (ie looking downwards). At the end of the route description is the total time proposed for the ascent. This will give a good indication as to the time needed for a rope of two climbing competently at the standard and experiencing no delays due to route finding and extended rests, other parties, weather etc. However, these figures give no more than an indication; the timing of routes is a pretty inexact science. In the many years that the authors have climbed in this region they have usually bettered the times given and have rarely if ever exceeded them.

The Alps are in a constant state of flux. Glacial recession, warm winters with less than 'normal' amounts of snow, hot summers, rockfall, all can dramatically alter the character of a route. Although every effort has been made to ensure accuracy, absolute accuracy can never be guaranteed. It may be that changing conditions have affected the route, or the route itself has had very few ascents, or even that the authors or their correspondents have simply got it wrong. Unlike a pure rock climbing guide to a crag in Britain or the USA, which will describe a line with some intimacy, alpine route descriptions give direction, allowing parties to use their experience, route finding abilities and most of all sound judgement to follow the correct course. The basic information is all there, but when using this guide responsible mountaineers at whatever standard will assess the current conditions and employ common sense.

First Ascent

Brief details of the first ascensionists have been included both to supplement information on the climb and so that history is not lost. The climbers involved in the first ascent are listed in alphabetical order, irrespective of the roles played by the various members during the course of the ascent. In the case of older routes the guides names are listed after those of the clients.

First Winter Ascent

The first winter ascent (FWA) of a route, where known and considered relevant or historically significant, has been recorded as it is believed that its inclusion will supplement information on the climb. As noted elsewhere, the UIAA recommendation which is now widely accepted is that the dates for winter ascents should fall between the 21st Dec and the 20th March.

GENERAL INFORMATION

Valley Base

This gives an indication of the most popular and most convenient valley base from which to attempt the climb. However, it is not suggested that the climb cannot be done from a different location if so desired.

Grade

The overall grade of the climb is indicated in the margin. In this guide unless the route in question is fairly short and purely a rock climb a French Adjectival Grade is used. In order of rising difficulty: F (Facile or easy), PD (Peu Difficile or not very difficult), AD (Assez Difficile or quite difficult), D (Difficile or difficult), TD (Très Difficile or very difficult) and ED (Extrêmement Difficile or extremely difficult). Further refinement is possible by adding a plus or a minus sign to the grades of TD and below but the ED grade is open-ended in a numerical fashion ie ED1, ED2 etc. The overall grade reflects not only the technical difficulty of the route but also its seriousness and the commitment needed to complete it. Length, altitude and objective danger play an important part in this grading and certain climbs, while they may not be technically demanding by modern standards, receive a high overall grade due to their inherent seriousness. This will generally be discovered in the introduction to the route.

Climbs have been graded for a completely free ascent unless otherwise stated. A number of ice/mixed routes described in this book are generally only feasible in the winter/spring and their overall grade reflects the added problems with climbing at this time of year.

An attempt has been made to introduce a simple grading system for those excursions that are suitable for a walker as opposed to the alpinist. W1 refers to walks on good footpaths with little in the way of objective danger and suitable for any reasonably fit person. W2 refers to routes more suitable for experienced mountain walkers who can find their way when paths become indistinct or non-existent; rough ground, easy snow slopes and/or dry glaciers may have to be traversed and there may be steeper sections where a fall could prove fatal. Snow covered glacial crossings, where crevasses may be present, or exposed mountain scrambles with rock moves of I/II, will be F or above.

Free climbing on rock is graded according to the UIAA system as this is the rating that has always been used throughout the region and is still widely employed by Swiss and German protagonists operating on mountain crags, as opposed to sports climbing where French grades have been almost (but not quite) universally accepted. The technical difficulty is graded numerically in Roman numerals ie I, II, III etc and is open ended. Further refinement is achieved by adding a plus or minus sign. A table of grading comparisons has been included but should only be used as a general indication. Aid climbing is graded A0, A1, A2 etc. A0, a popular alpine grade, occurs when a bombproof peg/bolt/nut is used as a handhold to aid progress. On A1 and above climbers will need to stand in slings/étriers and use progressively sophisticated gear (hooks and copperheads etc) with the prospect of increasingly long falls should a piece fail. Short rock routes may sometimes be given an overall numerical UIAA rock grading. This rating is that of the hardest section and the route description will reveal whether the climb is sustained at the grade.

With climbs that involve technical difficulties on snow and ice the grading is less precise due to the variable conditions from season to season and from year to year. On routes involving hanging glaciers or ice slopes with serac formations (eg certain routes on the Liskamm) there are constant changes in the difficulties and objective dangers. Certain glacier approaches have become extremely tortuous in recent dry summers and formerly classic snow arêtes at medium altitude can now be exposed crumbling shale by mid-July. The average angle of a mixed/ice face is often quoted in the introduction. The difficulty of certain sections on the route is also generally indicated by angle but on a few occasions by using the Scottish technical ice grade of 1, 2, 3 etc.

Photograph Numbers

If the route is marked on any of the photographs assembled in the back of this guide then the number of that photograph appears inside a shaded rectangle in the margin. Some routes may be visible and marked on more than one photograph. If this is the case the photograph which best shows the route has its number displayed in the shaded rectangle whilst the other photograph number(s) is shown below this in a smaller font size. A dashed line indicates that this section of the route is not visible on the picture. Routes on the photographs are identified by route number. On some photographs the lines of routes referred to in the text but not described in detail have been added, usually with a 'note' caption, as dotted lines.

Abbreviations

These are used for points of the compass (N, S, E and W), left (L), right (R), hours (hr), minutes (min), circa (c) and metres/kilometres (m/km). Others frequently used are CAS (Swiss Alpine Club), CAI (Italian Alpine Club), Pt (Point, Pointe and Punta) as used on the map for a summit, Pt is also used for a spot height marked on the relevant map. 4WD generally signifies an unmade road in the mountains. In some cases these may be quite driveable by ordinary cars when conditions are good. The abbreviation 'var' appears on photographs indicating a variation or alternative line of ascent. Throughout the guide book the French word rappel is used as opposed to the German word abseil, meaning to rope down. At the same time the German word bergschrund is used rather than the French word rimaye.

USING HUTS

The network of mountain huts allows time to be spent in the heart of the range close to proposed ascents and without the burden of a heavy rucksack. Several routes can sometimes be accomplished from a single base before returning to the valley. Although relatively expensive, hut fees can be significantly reduced on production of a reciprocal rights card (such as those

GENERAL INFORMATION

from national clubs such as the Alpine Club, Austrian and Swiss Alpine Clubs or the UIAA/BMC etc.) However, there is no reduction in private huts. In Swiss huts during the height of the season it is generally necessary for groups (generally four or more people) to pre-book bed space several days in advance and in the more popular huts it is often quite advisable for individuals to do this. If unsure, aim to get there early. Most huts are now on a telephone link and their numbers are noted in the huts section. Unfortunately not all hut guardians speak English. If you have a problem communicating by telephone the local Tourist Office will usually make a booking on your behalf or you can ask campsite or hotel staff to do the same. On arrival the first priority, whether one has pre-booked or not, should be to report to the guardian (after changing boots for hut slippers provided). Tell the guardian your proposed route for the following day and what time you wish to rise (although you will often find that there is a 'standard' time to rise). To minimise early morning disturbance you will probably be given a room with others who wish to depart at the same time. It is possible that very late arrivals may find their reserved bed space has been allocated to someone else. Please remember to telephone and cancel if you know you are not going to be able to take up your booking.

Most huts offer a restaurant service. In CAI huts there will normally be some provision for self catering as long as a stove and cooking utensils have been brought. No such facility exists in most Swiss huts and here the resident hut staff will cook food that parties bring up themselves. There is normally a charge for this service covered by the 'wood tax'. Simple fare, that can be cooked quickly in a single pan, is preferred. Jugs of hot water can usually be bought at a reasonable price in order to make your own drinks etc. Some Swiss huts will now allow you to use the kitchen after they have finished preparing food for paying guests - this facility is noted in the *Huts* section as - self catering possible. Most huts will offer bunk beds or continuous 'matrazenlager' with mattresses, blankets and pillows. Some unguarded bivouac huts can have quite good facilities but it is always best to assume little more than blankets and mattresses.

Despite the benefits of hut facilities, during the high season, noise, overcrowding and increasing costs have led to a number of parties electing to camp or bivouac near by. Discreet wild camping/bivouacking is tolerated in the mountains, though officially tents should only be erected from dusk to dawn and should be a suitable distance away and preferably out of sight of a hut. Above the snowline there is very little problem. The Swiss have a much stricter approach to wild camping than the Italians. Whether camping, bivouacking, staying in huts or travelling through the mountains there is absolutely no excuse for not taking all refuse back down to the valley for proper disposal or recycling.

WHEN TO CLIMB

The alpine summer season may extend from mid-June to late Sept, although at the beginning of this period there can still be copious amounts of spring snow, while towards the end of the season the nights can be cold and a heavy snowfall possible. Alpine huts do not usually open until their approaches are clear of spring snows. They tend to close by the middle of Sept when most holiday makers have gone home (15th June -15th Sept is often the normal opening period for wardened huts). July and Aug are the busy months with the peak period generally the last two weeks in July and the first two in Aug. Climbers searching for tranquillity on other than the more esoteric routes should come outside these times. Summers, especially in more recent years, have been hot and characterised by violent thunderstorms. More stable conditions tend to occur in late spring - an ideal time for ice/mixed climbs - and in Sept/Oct, when the colours can be brilliant, the atmosphere free from haze and the mountains almost empty.

Winter climbing as opposed to ski-mountaineering is not practised here to anything like the same extent as in the Mont Blanc Massif and documentation of this aspect of the sport is imprecise. The lack of téléphérique systems giving easy access to high mountain winter venues leads to long, complicated and often avalanche-prone approaches, especially on the Italian side. Although the accepted period for a winter ascent to be valid is from the 21st Dec to the 20th March inclusive, ascents outside of that period can be equally, if not sometimes more, demanding. April and May are usually very popular months with ski-tourers and the region, especially around Zermatt and Saas, will be very busy. May and June can also be excellent months for the big mixed or ice faces, which now appear so barren during the summer. Those able to visit the region during the autumn over the last few years will have enjoyed both excellent weather and conditions for ice or mixed climbing, and for alpinists keen on attempting the more difficult lines of this nature, Oct and Nov appear to be shaping up as the prime months.

MAPS

The Swiss Federal Topographic Service publish a set of Carte Nationale de la Suisse (CNS)/ Landeskarte (LK) to the whole of the country and this guide is primarily designed to be used in conjunction with these maps. All altitudes and nomenclature are taken from these maps and it is pointless to attempt using this guide without them.

In the 1:50,000 series a full coverage of the region described in *Valais Alps East* would require sheets 274 (Visp), 284 (Mischabel), and 294 (Gressoney). A composite map (assemblages) at the same scale 5006 (Matterhorn-Mischabel), covers almost all of the Swiss side of the range and most of the Italian side. Sheets on a scale of 1:25,000 are also available for the Swiss side of the range, four sheets are needed for the region covered by 284 (Mischabel) etc. Although these large-scale maps can be very useful, many are simple enlargements of the 1:50,000 editions and the latter series is perfectly adequate for the job.

Very useful for those visiting the Italian valleys are the products of Studio FMB Bologna who produce a fairly cheap Euro Carte - Carte de Sentieri at 1:50,000 entitled *Cervino Monte Rosa* which covers parts of the Valpelline and the

Valtournenche as well as the Ayas, Gressoney, Sesia and upper part of the Anzasca valleys. Kompass produces 1:50,000 scale Carta Touristica maps covering part of the region, the relevant ones being 87 (Breuil-Cervinia Zermatt) and 88 (Monte Rosa). Cheap local maps to valley footpaths etc are often available from tourist offices.

OTHER GUIDE BOOKS

There are fairly up to date entirely definitive guides to the Valais. The Swiss Alpine Club *Alpes Valaisannes* series, Volumes 3, 4 and 5 (Col Collon to the Theodulpass, Theodulpass to Monte Moro and Strahlhorn to the Simplon, all by Maurice Brandt) are comprehensive works to the Swiss side of the region. Gino Buscaini's *Monte Rosa* (CAI) is the definitive guide to the Italian side and also to parts of the Swiss side (including the Mischabel peaks). There are many guides of a 'Selected Climbs' format, notably *Les 100 Plus Belles Courses dans les Alpes Valaisannes* by Michel Vaucher, part of the well-known Rébuffat 'coffee table' series. Although published in 1979, this is still a must due to its many splendid photographs. The SAC publish *Hochtouren im Wallis/Guide du Valais* (Hermann Biner) which describes in a single volume routes up to D standard in the areas covered by Brandt's comprehensive guide books. This volume is available on CD rom in German. There are many books covering the 4,000m peak of the Alps; notably, in the English language, *The Alpine 4,000m Peaks* by the Classic Routes (Richard Goedecke).

Those who want to investigate more of the valley cragging in the area are advised to purchase a copy of *Escalade en Valais Central* by Daniel and Eric Blanc, which describes 400 routes in topo format that lie on both sides of the Rhone valley above Sion. There is also Beat Ruppen's *Kletterführer Oberwallis* which has topo diagrams for crags in the Turtmann, Zermatt and Saas valleys, on the Simplonpass and N of the Rhone. Also covering the area described in this guide book is the well-known *Schweiz Plaisir West* by Jürg von Känel.

EQUIPMENT

Many of the standard routes on the snowy peaks will require little more than an axe and crampons plus the ability to judge snow conditions and extricate a member of the party from a crevasse. On middle grade climbs where lengthy rappels are not anticipated most parties will nowadays use a single 10mm or possibly 11mm rope, carry a small selection of wires and Hexentrics, and several long slings for spikes and flakes. A couple of ice screws may also prove useful, even for glacier travel. On the harder routes a double rope, full set of rock and ice gear (quickdraws, Friends and rock pegs) and possibly bivouac equipment will be needed. There are many manuals on the craft of alpinism for the less experienced and by the time parties are attempting the routes in the upper grades, they should have gathered all the requisite know-how to judge for themselves exactly what gear will be needed.

LANGUAGE

In most of the E part of the Valais German is the principal language of the valley people although in the Zinal and Turtmann valleys French is the predominant language used. On the Italian side of the range it is not uncommon to find that French is widely understood but becomes progressively less so as you move E. English is understood in many of the Swiss villages, especially in big hotels and some shops, but will often not get you very far in the Italian valleys. However, the local populace of the Italian mountain valleys is well-known for its hospitality and friendliness, and consequently any language barrier seems less of a problem than would perhaps be experienced in some other parts of the Alps.

WEATHER FORECASTS

Some centres post weather bulletins, usually at the local tourist office. These are generally updated once a day in the season and often give the forecast for several days hence. In the Valais and in Switzerland in general a telephone service can be used to obtain weather information. Dial 162 to hear a recorded message (which is updated at 06.15, 08.00, 12.45, 18.15 and 22.15) giving the weather forecast in the language of the region for the whole of the country. You need to insert at least 90c (rp). In German-speaking Switzerland it should still be possible to get this forecast in French by prefacing the number with 022 or 027 whilst in French speaking Switzerland it should be possible to obtain the forecast in German by prefixing the number with 01 or 033. This number can also be obtained from other countries by using the international code for Switzerland (0041) followed by 22 for French or 1 for German. For the Italian language the prefix is 91.

Another number giving a recorded mountain weather forecast in the Valais is 157 12 62 60 (costs c90c/min), this is a premium rate line. Another premium rate line (c2fr/min) connects you to a weather forecaster to whom you can ask specifics; dial 157 52 72 0. A forecast given by English-speaking operators at the Swiss Meteorological Society in Zürich can be obtained after 2pm by dialling 157 52 620 (also a premium rate line). If all else fails an English language forecast for Chamonix, which should give some indication of what might be in store, can be obtained by dialling the international code for France (0033) then 450 53 17 11.

In the Aosta region of Italy local weather information can be obtained (in Italian) by telephoning 0165 77 63 00 or 0165 44 11 3 otherwise, including the Piemonte region, telephone the Swiss 162 service (see above). In winter an avalanche bulletin can be heard by dialling 187 in Switzerland or 0165 312 10 in Italy.

Telephone numbers are changed from time to time and visitors should ask locally for the updated number if they are experiencing problems. At the time of writing, the last change to telephone numbers in Switzerland was in 1996. With effect from Sept 1998 it is necessary when making local telephone calls in Italy to include the local code. The 157 and 187 lines can only be dialled within Switzerland.

A further source of weather forecasts is local and national newspapers which can usually be consulted in local bars.

Some weather information can be obtained on the Internet:
French speaking TV in Switzerland: http://www.tsr.ch/meteo/site/meteo.html

German speaking TV in Switzerland: http://www.sfdrs.ch/sendungen/meteo/

France: http://www.meteo.fr/

Meteostat Service Homepage: http://www.tscupna.es/Meteostat/Meteostat en.html

RESCUE AND INSURANCE

In the event of rescue being necessary, readers are referred to the back page of this guide. Rescues will invariably be expensive, especially in Switzerland, and normal holiday insurance will not cover medical expenses for those injured when mountaineering. It is most sensible for all climbers to have some sort of insurance policy that adequately covers the potential cost of mountain rescue, subsequent hospitalisation in Switzerland and repatriation. There are now many policies from which to choose depending on your country of origin.

In Switzerland the REGA organisation operate a rescue and medical emergency service which anyone can use. They claim to be able to reach any point in Switzerland within 15min of notification. They can be contacted by radio on a free emergency frequency or by telephone (see details inside rear cover). REGA works on the same principles as the Red Cross which means that in an emergency it will rescue without first asking who will pay. It depends on voluntary donations. In return for donations (there is a minimum) REGA's assistance is free to donors in cases of emergency. You will often find donation slips in huts. They can be contacted by post at Swiss Air-Ambulance, GAC, Postfach 1414, CH-8058 Zürich-Flughafen, Switzerland. By e-mail: info@rega.ch or by telephone 0041 1 654 33 11

GENERAL INFORMATION

INDICES

At the back of this guide are two 'indices': a general index in conventional form and a tabulated list of routes. The tabulated list includes the valley base from which the route is normally attempted, the style of the climb (rock, ice, mixed etc), an indication of the route length and the overall grade. This should assist parties at a particular base to choose a route according to weather, conditions and ability.

VALLEY BASES

No one valley base covers the whole area described in this guide, but most are quite well developed to accommodate tourist trade. There are large and small resorts which provide all kinds of accommodation from five star hotels to dortoirs. Many camp sites, noted in the description to each valley, are becoming increasingly full during the high season, especially so on the Italian side, and in the future pre-booking will probably become essential if one is to ensure tent space on a popular site. Switzerland Tourism (in the UK at Swiss Centre, Swiss Court, London, W1V 8EE. Tel: 0171 734 1921. e-mail CompuServe 100610,1746) is the best source of information about valley accommodation and public transport in Switzerland. Information on the Italian valleys can be obtained from the addresses given below.

Swiss Valleys

THE MATTERTAL is surrounded by no less than 24 peaks of over 4,000m. It has therefore always been regarded as one of the foremost mountaineering centres in the Alps and as a result has been developed commercially to exploit this. Zermatt is the undisputed tourist capital of this German speaking valley. The Matterhorn in all its splendour dominates the town and ensures the prosperity of its future. This mountain is described, along with the Dent d'Herens and the Dent Blanche, in the companion volume for the *Valais Alps West*.

GENERAL INFORMATION

Zermatt lies at the southern end of the Mattertal at an altitude of 1,600m. From the Rhone valley it is reached by rail from Visp or Brig. The public road terminates 5km short of Zermatt which is out of bounds to motor cars other than those belonging to residents. There is a large car park at the village of Täsch from where the short remainder of the journey can be completed by rail or taxi.

Zermatt has all modern facilities, a huge choice of hotels, apartments, supermarkets, restaurants, bars, equipment suppliers, a guides' bureau, tourist office and banks, etc. There is a small camp site at the northern end of the town, quite close to the station, and nearby is another station for the rack and pinion railway to the Gornergrat, which connects with the cable car to the Stockhorn.

The cable car to Schwarzsee and the Klein Matterhorn is at Furi at the southern end of the town. The intermediate station of Trockenersteg provides access to summer skiing via tows on the Theodule glacier. The underground metro to Sunnegga, completed in 1980, also starts from Zermatt and this connects with a cable car to the Unterrothorn 3,103m.

7km down the valley, midway between Täsch and Randa, is Atermenzen. This is the most popular camp site in the valley, with full facilities including a restaurant and bar. 'Freddy' taxis provide a regular and reasonably priced service between the campsite and Zermatt. There is a smaller, quieter campsite at Täsch close to the railway station.

From this village a steep narrow road winds up to Täschalpen. At the time of writing there is no restriction on the road, which saves a lot of leg work for climbers going to the Täsch hut.

THE SAASTAL branches off the Mattertal 7km S of Visp, just beyond the small town of Stalden. The Saastal provides access to the eastern side of the whole Mischabel chain of peaks and also to the Portjengrat, Weissmies, Fletschhorn group. There are several villages in the valley, including Saas Balen, Saas Grund, Saas Almagell, and on a higher shelf below the Fee glacier is Saas

Fee, the main resort. Saas Fee, like Zermatt, is out of bounds to car traffic. There is a variety of accommodation, hotels, chalets and apartments, etc. Each village has several shops, at least one bank and a guides' bureau. Four camp sites are available in the valley. Most convenient for climbers are the ones at Saas Grund and Saas Fee. Cars may be taken as far as the Mattmark Dam 2,200m, which is useful for walkers and climbers visiting the Monte Moropass area.

The whole valley is served by Swiss Postal coaches with the usual efficiency. Several cable car systems provide useful lifts for the alpinist, notably to Hohsaas for the Weissmies, to the Längfluh for the Alphubel, etc., and the Felskinn/Mittelallalin metro for the Allalinhorn or the newly rebuilt (1997) Britannia Hut. The Saastal is a major mountaineering centre, second only to Zermatt, in the Valais Alps.

ZINAL at 1,675m is an important mountaineering centre at the head of the Val d'Anniviers in the French speaking area of the Valais and gives access to the western approaches of the Ober Gabelhorn-Weisshorn chain. It was from Zinal that Leslie Stephen made the first ascent of the Zinal Rothorn on 20th August 1864 with the guides Melchior and Jacob Anderdegg. A good road rises steeply from Sierre in the Rhone valley. On reaching Vissoie the road divides going one way to Grimenz and to St Luc and Chandolin the other. For Zinal the road goes on up the valley via Ayer and after 28km ends at Zinal, with the "fish tail" rock peak of Besso in full view. Whilst this is not as commercialised as the valley bases described previously, it is amply provided with all facilities, hotels, restaurants, bars, shops and bank, etc. and the campsite is just beyond the village near the end of the road. The valley is well served with buses.

Halfway between Visp and Sierre, a steep and narrow road climbs from Turtmann into the Turtmanntal 1,900m. Whilst this valley is not recommended as a base it is a popular starting point from the Turtmann hut for the Bishorn 4,153m, the Brunegghorn 3,883m and the Barrhorn 3,610m.

GENERAL INFORMATION

TOURIST OFFICE TELEPHONE NUMBERS - Dial 0041 for Switzerland.

Zermatt	027 967 01 81	Fax 027 967 01 85
Internet	zermatt.ch/	
Zinal	027 475 13 70	Fax 027 475 29 77
Internet	zinal.ch/	
Saas Fee	027 958 18 58	Fax 027 958 18 60
Internet	saas-fee.ch/	
Saas Grund	027 957 24 03	Fax 027 957 11 43
Internet	saastal.ch/	

MOUNTAIN GUIDE OFFICE TELEPHONE NUMBERS

Zermatt	027 966 24 60	Fax 027 966 24 69
Zinal	027 475 13 73	
Saas Fee	027 957 44 64	Fax 027 957 12 49
Saas Grund	027 957 14 44	Fax 027 957 14 43

Italian Valleys

VALTOURNENCHE is not a particularly attractive valley within the autonomous region of Aosta. It has the town of Breuil/Cervinia at its head. This has been developed principally for the ski-ing fraternity and so the slopes above the town are littered with lifts and drags. There are few attractions for the summer visitor. For the purposes of this guide book it is of interest only as a means of access to the Theodulpass and Testa Grigia (Plateau Rosa) from the Italian side. Camping in the valley is very limited, the only sites being down the valley, with one site just below the town of Valtournenche and another at Buisson. Otherwise the valley has all the usual facilities that one expects to find in a tourist area such as tourist office, banks, shops, hotels, guest houses, bars, restaurants, a guides' office and local bus services. For further information contact: Azienda del Turismo, Piazza Emiglio Chanoux 8, 1-11100 Aosta, Italy.

VALLE d'AYAS is also part of the autonomous region of Aosta and is a relatively undeveloped valley (although there are some ski-installations) but with all the tourist facilities that one might require in Ayas and Champoluc. Camping facilities are very limited with what sites there are (between the village of Brusson and Ayas) largely occupied by permanently fixed caravans. The hamlet of St Jacques (St Giacomo) marks the roadhead and is an overnight stopping place on the Tour of Monte Rosa walk. It has hotel and hut-type accommodation. The road does extend beyond St Jacques but is rough and not open to the public at large and is followed by visitors heading for the Mezzalama and Valle d'Ayas Guides huts. For further information contact: Azienda del Turismo, Piazza Emiglio Chanoux 8, 1-11100 Aosta, Italy.

VALLE di GRESSONEY is also known as the Lys Valley and inhabited by the descendents of the Walsers, folks of German origin who came here from the Valais in the 13th century and who account for the local dialect. As part of the autonomous region of Aosta it is highly developed for tourism with an emphasis on ski-ing in the upper part of the valley above Gressoney la Trinité. Consequently you will find everything you might need in the main resorts, Gressoney St Jean and Gressoney la Trinité. Camping space is extremely limited with permanently sited caravans occupying much of the available space. The only place that tents might find space is in Gressoney St Jean. The site is on the W side of the river but is not signposted. The Swiss (Gressoney) map shows the roadhead at Gressoney la Trinité but this is out of date and it now extends as far as Staffal (or Tschaval: Staval on the Swiss map) where some of the ski-installations are to be found and can be reached by a local bus service or car. The Italian map shows a camp site at Staffal but this no longer exists. Gressoney is an overnight stopping place (hotels) on the Tour of Monte Rosa. Approaches to the Quintino Sella, Città di Mantova and Gnifetti huts start from the valley. For further information contact: the regional tourist office in Aosta (see above) or the local office Azienda del Turismo, Villa Margherita 11025 Gressoney St Jean, Italy.

VALLE della SESIA, which is in the Piemonte region of Italy has

at its head the unattractive town of Alagna, starting point of the
lift system to Punta Indren. There are all the facilities of a tourist
resort including a campsite. The road extends N of Alagna, rising
to a car park at c1,500m, but this is closed to all but authorised
local traffic during the summer season. There is a bus service.
Alagna is the starting point for access to the Città di Mantova,
Gnifetti, Gugliermina and Resegotti huts. For further information contact: Azienda Promozione Turistica della Valsesia, Corso
Roma 38, 1-13019 Varollo-Vercelli, Italy.

VALLE ANZASCA, which is also in the Piemonte region, is a
long and attractive valley with the resort of Macugnaga at its
head. This is made up of three separate villages: Borca, Staffa
and Pecetto, of which Staffa is the largest and most developed.
The area attracts visitors in summer and in winter (for ski-ing)
and is worth a visit for a close-up view of the Monte Rosa E face
if for nothing else. There are all the facilities of a modern tourist
resort including two campsites. The most useful of these is
situated between Borca and Staffa, although, like most campsites
in these valleys, much of the space is occupied by permanently
sited caravans. The other site is some way down the valley.
Macugnaga is the starting point for access to the Zamboni and
Zappa, Marinelli, Gallarate, Belloni, Eugino Sella, and Oberto
huts. For further information contact: IAT-UFFICIO
Informazioni Turistiche, Piazza Municipio, 28030 Macugnaga,
Italy.

TOURIST OFFICE TELEPHONE NUMBERS - Dial 0039
for Italy

Aosta	0165 23 66 27	Fax 0165 34 65 7
This is the regional office.		
Champoluc	0125 30 71 13	
Gressoney la Trinité	0125 36 61 43	
Gressoney St Jean	0125 35 51 85	Fax 0125 35 58 95
Alagna	0163 82 29 88	
Macugnaga	0324 65 11 9	Internet infosquare.it/ servizi/Macugnaga

MOUNTAIN GUIDE OFFICE TELEPHONE NUMBERS

Breuil-Cervinia	0166 94 81 69	Fax 0166 94 98 85
Champoluc	0125 30 71 13 (Tourist office)	
Gressoney la Trinité	0125 36 61 43 (Tourist office)	
Gressoney St Jean	0125 35 51 85 (Tourist Office)	
Magugnaga	0324 65170	

INTERGUIDE - Societa Cooperativa Aosta 0165 40 93 9
  Fax 0165 44 44 8
  Internet guidealpine.com

GRADING COMPARISONS

UIAA	FRENCH	UK		USA	AUS
IV	4			5.5	12
V−	4+	MS	4a	5.6	13
V	5−	S			
V+	5 5a	VS	4b	5.7	14
VI−	5+ 5b	HVS	4c	5.8	15
VI	5c		5a	5.9	16
					17
VI+	6a	E1	5b	5.10a	18
VII−	6a+			b	19
VII	6b	E2		c	20
				d	21
VII+	6c		5c	5.11a	22
		E3		b	
VIII−	7a		6a	c	23
VIII	7a+	E4		d	24
VIII+	7b		6b	5.12a	25
IX−	7b+	E5		b	26
			6c	c	27
IX	7c	E6		d	28
IX+	7c+	E7			29
	8a				30

Introduction

This area of the Valais has the greatest concentration of the highest peaks in western Europe. Within it there are nine of the twelve highest peaks in the Alps.

The area covered by this guidebook contains 27 separate mountains over 4,000 metres, many of which are linked by high ridges of mixed terrain, allowing splendid traverses to incorporate several peaks in one expedition. For these reasons the Valais Alps are the focus of middle grade, classic style mountaineers.

The SE part of the main range follows the international frontier between Italy and Switzerland and also forms the natural watershed, the long valleys of the N carrying off the melt water to the great rift of the Rhone valley to flow away to the Mediterranean. To the S the Italian valleys feed the waters to the River Po and then out to the Adriatic.

The Monte Rosa Massif consists of ten summits of over 4,000m. One of these is the Dufourspitze, the second highest summit in the Alps at 4,634m and the highest summit in Switzerland, the Italian frontier being 180m to the E. Viewed from the Swiss side, usually from the Gornergrat, the Monte Rosa group presents itself as a bulky but relatively benign massif and this aspect is much photographed. This contrasts sharply with the E face of Monte Rosa viewed from Macugnaga in the Italian Anzasca valley where it presents a vast wall of steep rock and ice almost 10km long and is nowhere less than 2,000m above the meadows in the valley below. It is of almost Himalayan proportions and offers the mountaineer some of the longest and most difficult routes in the Alps. As the cols between the peaks do not fall below 4,000m Monte Rosa is the largest mountain massif in the Alps. The Margherita hut, perched at 4,556m on the summit of the Signalkuppe, is the highest hut in western Europe.

From the Lisjoch, an important pass between Valle Sesia and the Zermatt valley, the frontier continues W along the ridge of the two summits of Liskamm (4,527m). This ridge was formerly notorious for double cornices. These have seldom formed in recent years, but Liskamm remains an important snow mountain, providing an excellent ridge traverse, and has a fine route on its NE face direct to the E summit. The twin peaks of Castor and Pollux rise to the W of the Felikjoch. These are often climbed together, usually from the Italian side. The approach from the N or Swiss side is more serious due to the crevassed nature of the glaciers and the lack of convenient huts.

The huge bulk of the Breithorn dominates the skyline from the Schwarztor to the Klein Matterhorn. Viewed from the Gornergrat it presents a 2½km long wall of rock and ice, providing at least two classic routes up the N face. The Italian side by contrast consists of relatively easy snow slopes.

The Breithorn is probably the easiest 4,000m peak in the Alps. The approach from the lift station on the Klein Matterhorn involves an ascent of only 350m.

The Theodulpass and Testa Grigia area nearby are served with uphill transport from both sides of the frontier, providing access to the high summer skiing facilities from which both Zermatt and Breuil (Cervinia) derive substantial income. The Theodulpass has been an important and easy pass since at least Roman times.

N of the Monte Rosa Massif the frontier runs along the Weissgrat for several km, dividing the sunny and fertile Macugnaga valley to the E from the high and extensive snowfields on the Swiss side which feed the Gorner and Findel glaciers to the W. This section, when viewed from the W, does not have any notable summits, only the Cima di Jazzi and the Jägerhorn thrust their tops over 3,800m above the snowfields. Ascents are rarely undertaken from the Swiss side on account of the long distances from huts. On the Italian side, however, which is much more precipitous, there are several huts quite close to the ridge.

From the Schwarzberg Weisstor the frontier turns to the E but rising to the N along the main ridge, the watershed between the Saastal and the Mattertal is reached. The high mountains contained in the first half of this group are separated by glaciers and form four independent transverse ridges running from SE to NW each with an important peak. The first is the Strahlhorn 4,190m, followed by the Rimpfischhorn 4,199m and then the Allalinhorn 4,027m. These three summits have long rocky ridges facing SE. The last is the Alphubel 4,206m. Its rocky countenance is on the W side. This group of independent peaks has easy access from several huts. In addition, since 1985, the highest underground funicular in the world, the Metro Alpin, starts at Felskinn (Saas Fee) and climbs up to Mittelallalin 3,500m, bringing the Allalinhorn within easy reach. Each of these mountains are popular training grounds for the higher and more serious ascents in the district.

N of the flat topped Alphubel the character of the range changes dramatically and, from the Mischabeljoch, becomes a series of sharp rocky ridges linking many high summits. First is the Täschhorn, a magnificent peak and one of the most difficult in the Valais. It is linked to the Dom by a high ridge which enables a classic traverse of the two peaks to be made. The Dom 4,545m is the highest mountain entirely in Switzerland and is therefore a popular climb via its relatively easy northern flanks from the Zermatt side. The slope on the Saas, or E sides of these peaks consists of one of the longest and most continuous slopes in the Alps, frequently raked by avalanches down the many couloirs to the Fee glacier, whilst on the Zermatt side, several secondary ridges contain narrow glaciers between them. Viewed from the N, these Mischabel peaks present a snowy aspect which is a contrast to the decidedly rocky appearance from Zermatt to the S.

N of the Dom, sharp rock arêtes are found on the Lenzspitze, Nadelhorn sections of the ridge, which provide sporting expeditions from both sides of the range.

From the Nadelhorn the ridge divides. The NW branch continues over the Hobärghorn and the Dirruhorn, the last 4,000-er at the northern end of the Mischabel group. The NE branch provides a link with the more modest area of lower peaks known as the Balfrin group which terminates at the confluence of the Mattertal and the Saastal. The Ried glacier is a prominent feature and flows from the main ridge past the Bordier hut down towards the town of Grächen.

The E side of the Saastal is bounded by a chain of peaks some 25km long, equal in length to the western chain already described. That, however, is where the similarity ends. The Monte Moropass defines its southern limit and this has become a popular objective from the Swiss side due to the opening of the road up to the Mattmark dam. There is a cableway station on the S side. The pass is noted for the outstanding view of the Macugnaga face of the Monte Rosa. The first 15km of the ridge consists of several relatively unimportant rocky summits of between 3,000m and 3,500m. The Swiss flanks are made up of rather monotonous, high, scree filled valleys, some containing small glaciers. The Italian side by contrast boasts green alpine pastures and several lakes.

Further N at the Sonnighorn, the quality of the rock improves and the ridge becomes of more interest to the mountaineer. Perhaps the most popular rock climb in the district is the traverse of the Portjengrat, which is made more easily accessible since the construction of the Almageller hut was completed. The highest point of the Portjengrat, Pizzo d.Andolla is where the national frontier diverges to the E. Just above the hut the Zwischbergenpass marks another change in the character of the ridge. The next section includes the three highest peaks E of the Saastal, the Weissmies 4,023m, the Lagginhorn 4,010m and the Fletschhorn 3,993m. These summits by contrast are generally snow-covered and have large glaciers. The SE sides have high rock walls which dominate the Laggin valley where there is a bivouac hut.

Most, by far, of the ascents of these popular peaks are made from the two huts on the Saas side. One can be reached by gondola lift. In the mid-1980's the local communities in the Saastal considered the ambitious project of artificially raising the summit of the Fletschhorn to make it a 4,000-er, with the idea of attracting more climbers to the area and boosting the hotel trade, etc.

The traverse of all three peaks has been done several times but usually only the Lagginhorn and Fletschhorn are combined, and the Weissmies is traversed on its own. The Simplonpass road provides access to the more serious stuff on the N face of the Fletschhorn and the E faces of all three peaks. N of this high trio the ridge includes several smaller peaks before terminating above the town of Brig in the Rhone valley.

The high chain of mountains bounding the W side of the Mattertal includes some of the finest sculpted ideal mountain forms to be found in the Alps, with sharp summits and exposed ridges. For mountaineering 'par excellence', it would be difficult to equal elsewhere.

There are no mechanical means of gaining height in this range and one must start from the valleys. The southern section from the Col Durand begins with a small peak, Mont Durand, which is a popular training peak from the Schönbiel hut, affords spectacular views of the greater giants nearby, the Matterhorn, Dent d'Herens and the Dent Blanche.

Beyond the Arbenjoch the fine granite ridge of the Arbengrat rises to the summit of the Ober Gabelhorn 4,063m. By contrast the N approach to this mountain is mainly on snow. It is normally traversed in conjunction with the Wellenkuppe. Since the construction of the bivouac hut on the S side above the Arben glacier, it can be done comfortably in either direction depending on the snow conditions on the ENE ridge. The view from the Wellenkuppe provides the best view of the Zinal Rothorn 4,221m, the sharpest peak in the range and probably the most popular. It has splendid ridges, the longest being the Rothorngrat starting at the Triftjoch and including the Trifthorn, a good training peak in itself. If this ridge is combined with a descent of the N ridge on the Zinal side it becomes one of the finest expeditions in the Alps. Generally the rock is very good, but due to the recession of the glaciers and snow fields over several years, care must be taken on the ordinary route from the Rothorn hut, which crosses the S flank of the summit pyramid.

N of the summit a high subsidiary ridge extends W over the Blanc de Moming and terminates at the Besso, a rock peak prominent from the Val d'Anniviers. The main ridge continues in a NNE direction to the Schalihorn 3,974m, a somewhat isolated peak which tends to be neglected and is very much overshadowed by the Weisshorn 4,505m. One of the most striking mountains in the Alps, it rises like a huge pyramid with three long ridges culminating in a pointed summit. The N ridge with its distinctive gendarme, if combined with the E ridge in descent, provides a most magnificent expedition. Since the Ar Pitetta hut was built on the W flank of the Weisshorn interest has revived in the old W face approach known as the Younggrat. It is in this area of the range that the watershed changes on the W from the Val d'Anniviers to the Turtmanntal, the valleys being divided by the ridge spur running NW to the Tête de Milon and Les Diablons. The N ridge of the Weisshorn descends to the Weisshornjoch then rises again to the Bishorn 4,153m, which is somewhat dwarfed by its mighty neighbour.

Beyond the wide Brunegg glacier to the NW rises the Brunegghorn 3,833m. This mountain dominates the view from the lower reaches of the Mattertal, whilst travelling S from St Niklaus and is a worthy objective on its own, either from the Topali hut or the Turtmann hut. Other minor peaks can also be climbed from these huts and form the northern limit of the range described in this guide. One of them is the Barrhorn with a characteristic rounded dome shaped summit when seen from the W. The other is the Stellihorn, which is comprised mainly of poor limestone.

HUTS

The huts are listed in the same order that ascents from them are described in this guide. These are divided between five distinct mountain groups: (i) Rothorn-Weisshorn Chain, (ii) Breithorn-Liskamm Chain, (iii) Monte Rosa Group, (iv) Mischabel Chain and (v) Weissmies Chain

Where the position of a hut is not indicated on the map a Grid Reference is quoted where this is known accurately. Other huts that can be reached and mountains that can be climbed from each hut are listed under the heading 'ASCENTS'. Winter room indicates that only a part of the hut is open in the winter months and when no guardian is present.

H1 **Schönbiel Hut** 2,694m (Schönbielhütte) CAS. *A medium sized*
W1 *hut which has recently (1996) been improved. It is situated on a grassy spur below the Schönbiel, just above the junction of the Zmutt and Schönbiel glaciers. It can be visited by parties on the classic High Level Route. The expensive téléphérique to Furi shortens the approach by 1hr but is perhaps hardly worth the financial outlay. Open with a resident warden from April to mid-May and late June to late Sept. Room for 80: self catering possible: winter room.* TEL: 027 967 13 54.

(i) From Zermatt the path is clearly signposted and follows the river up to Zmutt (1,936m: 1¼hr). This point can be reached from Zermatt by following alternative paths further up the hillside. It continues in the same direction, taking the R fork at a bridge and passing the picturesque waterfall section of the river, to the moraine on the R side of the debris-covered Zmutt glacier. Follow the moraine past Hohle Bielen (2,429m), finally zigzagging up R to the hut. **4hr** from Zermatt

(ii) From the midway station of Furi on the Zermatt to Schwarzsee téléphérique follow an excellent path through the woods on the L side of the river to Stafel (2,139m). Now continue on a good track to join the previous route near to the Arben re-entrant. **3hr** from Furi

ASCENTS: Mont Durand, Ober Gabelhorn, Mountet hut via the Col Durand. Other routes from this hut are described in *Valais Alps West*.

H2 **Mountet Hut** 2,886m (Cabane du Mountet) CAS. *A large and*
W1 *well-frequented hut that has recently (1996) been improved and enlarged. It is situated below the Mammouth on a rocky area above the junction of the Mountet and Zinal glaciers. The approach, entirely on the E side of the Zinal glacier, is clearly signposted and has cables etc on one section. Open from April to late May and late June to late Sept. Places for 125: winter room.* TEL: 027 475 14 31

Less than 1km S of Zinal the road ends at a bridge over the main Navisence river (1,675m) where parking is possible. Continue on the path that follows the W side of the river, passing the Vichiesso chalet (1,862m) to reach and cross the bridges at 1,907m. The path now leads on to the moraine on the E side of the Zinal glacier and then climbs up to and traverses the grassy flanks W of the Besso, crossing a couloir to finally reach the base of the SW ridge of the Besso. From here the path rises gradually across stony ground passing below the SW ridge of the Mammouth to reach the hut. **4½hr** from Zinal village

ASCENTS: Mont Durand, Ober Gabelhorn, Mammouth, Besso, Blanc de Moming, Zinal Rothorn, Trifthorn, Schönbiel hut via Col Durand. Other routes from this hut are described in *Valais Alps West*.

H3 **Arben Bivouac Hut** 3,224m (Arben Biwak) SAC. *A very*
F *superior bivouac hut provided with all the requirements for DIY*
2 *cooking which is situated on a rock island in the middle of the Arben glacier below the S face of the Ober Gabelhorn. Places for 15.*

From Zermatt follow Route H1 to the stream issuing from the Arben valley. Cross the bridge then follow the rough roadway into the valley to reach the moraine named Arbengandegg. Climb this to a height of c2,890m where it meets the rock barrier below the glacier. A cairned route leads on to the glacier and further waymarks indicate the line of approach to the hut. **c4hr**

ASCENTS: Ober Gabelhorn

HUTS

H4 **Rothorn Hut** 3,198m (Rothornhütte) SAC. *A large, popular hut
W2 situated high above the Trift gorge at the foot of a rock rib which
5 separates the Trift and Rothorn glaciers. Open from early July to mid-
4 Sept. Places for 90: winter room.* Tel 027 967 20 43

From the centre of Zermatt follow the path to Trift (signposted).
Turn R just past the Berggasthaus Trift and, after crossing a
stream, climb more steeply for a few min to the point where a R
fork leads towards the Mettelhorn. Keep L here and cross the
fairly level ground of Vieliboden before rising again to reach, after
crossing another stream, the foot of the E lateral moraine of the
Trift glacier. Enjoy, if you can, the climb up the moraine to the
hut. **4-5hr**

ASCENTS: Ober Gabelhorn, Wellenkuppe, Trifthorn, Zinal
Rothorn, Schalihorn

H5 **Ar Pitetta Hut**, 2,786m (Cabane d'Ar Pitetta) SAC. *Situated
W2 high in the Ar Pitetta combe directly W of the Weisshorn summit and
14 SSE of the Col de Milon. Open from late June to late Sept. Places for
24: self catering possible.* Tel 027 475 40 28

From Zinal follow Route H2 to the crossing of the Navisence
river at 1,907m. The path now turns N to pass Pt 2,082m before
reaching a stream below Louchelet. Turn R here and, after
passing a small tarn, head ESE and then E below the Pt d'Ar
Pitetta to the hut. **4-5hr**

An alternative and more exciting start to the route follows the E
bank of the Navisence river to the bridge at 1,731m. Just beyond
this the path climbs the hillside on the L. Traverse R to some
rocks marked, in blue, 'Pas de Chasseur'. Climb the rocks
making ample use of the fixed chains and then follow the
continuation path through the woods to join the route described
above.

ASCENTS: Weisshorn, Schalijoch, Tracuit hut via Col de Milon

H6 **Tracuit Hut** 3,256m (Cabane de Tracuit) SAC. *A large hut
W2 frequently occupied by large groups of youths. It is situated c300m SE
6 of the Col de Tracuit, the lowest point between the Diablons des Dames*

39

HUTS

and the Tête de Milon. Open from early July to mid-Sept. Places for 110: self catering possible: winter room. Tel 027 745 15 00

(i) From the S extremity of Zinal follow a path heading SE to Combautanna (2,578m). From here the path continues roughly ENE towards the Col de Tracuit. A little way below the col it swings R before climbing on to the ridge SE of the low point. The hut is a few m further SE. **4hr**

(ii) From the Turtmann hut follow Route 17a to a little way beyond Gassi. Before following the path to the edge of the Brunegg glacier it's a good idea to scramble up the rocks on the R and examine the best way of crossing the glacier (usually above an ice-fall) to reach, close to the top, the massive rock island below Pt 2,913.4m separating it from the Turtmann glacier. On these rocks a path and light coloured ramp lead to the cairn at the top. Descend on to the Turtmann glacier and go down this (heading W) on to the level section at c2,800m. Cross to the L bank and climb this side of the glacier, eventually reaching a poorly marked path leading to the Col de Tracuit. The hut is c200m away. **3-4hr**

ASCENTS: Bishorn, Weisshorn, Tête de Milon, Ar Pitetta hut via Col de Milon

H7 **Weisshorn Hut** 2,932m (Weisshornhütte) SAC. *A relatively
W2 small hut which is never thronged with day-trippers. It is situated on the S side of the Wisse Schijen c500m from the E edge of the Schali glacier. Open mid-July to mid-Sept, dates depending on the climbing conditions on the Weisshorn. Places for 30: self catering possible: winter room.* Tel 027 967 12 62

There are a number of starting places in the vicinity of Randa which all link up by the time they reach Jatz at 2,246.3m. From Randa village cross the bridge over the Mattervispa then follow the path heading roughly SW. From Wildi cross the bridge over the Mattervispa opposite the sports field and pick up a path heading SW. From the camp site of Atermenzen cross the Mattervispa by one of the bridges N or S of the site and follow paths to the farm at 1,618m. All the routes signpost the hut and each one provides a sustained up hill walk. From Jatz the path is less steep but still quite sustained as it heads roughly WSW to the hut. **4-5hr**

ASCENTS: Schalijoch, Weisshorn

H8 **Schalijoch Bivouac Hut** c3,780m (Biwak Schalijoch) SAC. *A*
14 *smart little hut situated at the foot of the Schaligrat on the Weisshorn,*
13 *c30m above and NE of the Schalijoch itself. Places for 8.* Emergency telephone only.

There is no easy access to the hut. See Routes 11a and b. The safest and the recommended means of reaching it is by a traverse of the Schalihorn (see Route 10a).

ASCENTS: Weisshorn, Schalihorn

H9 **Turtmann Hut** 2,519m (Cabane Tourtemagne) SAC. *A*
W1 *delightful, quite small hut situated on a rocky shoulder a little way N*
16 *of the snout of the Brunegg glacier and below the W ridge of the Barrhorn. It is very easy to access. Open from mid- June to late Sept. Places for 50: self catering possible.* Tel 027 932 14 55

Park at the roadhead at Sänntum (1,901m) in the Turtmanntal. Walk up the roadway beyond this point (restricted access by car) to the lakes at 2,174m. Cross the valley and follow an easy path to the hut. **2hr**

ASCENTS: Bishorn, Barrhorn, Brunegghorn, Tracuit hut, Topali hut via the Schölijoch

H10 **Topali Hut** 2,674m (Topalihütte) SAC. *A small hut situated at*
W2 *the end of the Distulgrat on the E side of the Barrhorn. Always open*
18 *with resident warden at week-ends during the summer season or on demand. Places for 24: self catering possible.* Tel 027 956 21 72 (Guardian's home: 027 956 13 23)

From St Niklaus drive to Ze Schwidernu then follow the path steeply upwards to a split at c1,360m. Turn R and follow a most impressive path steeply up to Bode at 1,905m. Things ease off a little now as the path leads on to the chalet at Walkerschmatt

HUTS

(2,139m). Continue more easily to Scheidchrommo where the hut comes into view. Keep on the same path all the way to the hut. **4-5hr**

ASCENTS: Brunegghorn, Barrhorn, Bishorn, Turtmann hut

H11 **Gandegg Hut** 3,029m (Gandegg). *Private. Situated on the rocky*
W1 *spine separating the Ob and Unt Theodule glaciers. Although this is a private hut, dortoir rates are similar to members' rates in SAC huts, the overnight fee includes breakfast or demi-pension. The guardian is very welcoming but will not cook your food or provide hot water and there are no self catering facilities. Open from July to Sept. Places for 30.* Tel 077 28 39 96 (a mobile)

From Trockenersteg, which is the intermediate station of the Klein Matterhorn lift out of Zermatt, follow a marked path to the hut. **½hr**. Trockenersteg itself can be reached from Zermatt on foot in about 4 hr.

ASCENTS: Kl Matterhorn, Breithorn, Theodule hut, Cervinia guides' hut

H12 **Theodule Hut** 3,317m (Rifugio del Teòdulo) CAI. *Situated on a*
F *rocky shoulder overlooking the Theodulpass from its N side and just on the Italian side of the border. Open from late March to late Sept (but closed in June). Places for 86: no self catering facilities: winter room.* Tel 0166 94 94 00 (Italy: 0039)

Approaches are the same as for the Theodulpass (Routes 21a and b). The hut is on the N side of the pass and is reached in a few minutes by a path and steps.

ASCENTS: Breithorn, Pollux, Castor, Cervinia guides' hut, Gandegg hut, Rossi and Volante bivouac hut, Valle d'Ayas guides' hut

H13 **Cervinia Guides' Hut** c3,470m (Rifugio Guide del Cervino).
F *Grid ref 620,40/83,60. Private. Situated close to the lift station on the Testa Grigia (the usual means of approach from the Italian side). Operated like a hut in summer (with bar, restaurant and solarium!) but only as a restaurant in winter. There are no self cooking facilities. Places for 40.* Tel 0166 94 83 69 (Italy: 0039).

From the Klein Matterhorn lift station follow Route 21b(ii) towards the Theodulpass. ½-**1hr**

ASCENTS: Breithorn, Pollux, Castor, Theodule hut, Gandegg hut, Rossi and Volante bivouac hut, Valle d'Ayas guides' hut

H14 **Mezzalama Hut** 3,004m (Rifugio Ottorino Mezzalama) CAI.
W2 *Situated at the top of the moraine separating the Grande and Piccolo Verra glaciers. Open from late June to mid-Sept. Places for 38 (winter room).* Tel 0125 30 72 26 (Italy: 0039)

From San Giacomo (St Jacques) follow a poor road to Alpe Pian di Verra Sup (possible taxi service). Above Pt 2,382m a path leads on to the moraine crest on the E bank of the Grande Verra glacier. Follow this to the hut. **4hr**.
From Alpe Pian di Verra Inf, a track leads N and gains the crest of the moraine which can be followed to the hut.

ASCENTS: Breithorn, Pollux, Castor, Valle d'Ayas guides' hut, Rossi and Volante bivouac hut

H15 **Rossi and Volante Bivouac Hut** c3,750m (Bivacco Rossi e
F Volante, or Bivacco Cesare e Giorgio) CAI. *Situated on a rock*
26 *island on the snow spur descending SSW from the Roccia Nera and E*
20 21 *of the Schwarztor. A typical small Italian metal bivouac hut which is very cramped if full. Places for 6 maximum. At the time of writing a new hut was being installed nearby with a capacity of 12.*

(i) From the Klein Matterhorn lift station follow the snow crest to the broad saddle at 3,796m and then cross the glacier bowl ESE to the Breithornpass. From the pass head NE, descending a little, to pass below a rock island and the SSE spur of the Breithorn central summit. Just beyond this latter point slant up on to the higher glacier terrace (c3,650m) on the S side of the Breithorn. Curve round, maintaining height, to where the terrace starts to peter out below Roccia Nera. Slant down SE for a few m and then traverse across to the outcrop on which the hut is sited. **2hr**

If crevasses are a problem on the glacier terrace take a lower line from below the Breithorn central summit, used on the approach to Pollux, and up to the top of the rognon on which the hut stands on its L side.

(ii) From the Valle d'Ayas guides' hut follow Route 24a to the Schwarztor and then contour W to the hut. **c1hr**

(iii) From the Monte Rosa hut follow Route 24b to the Schwarztor. PD: **4hr**

ASCENTS: Breithorn, Pollux, Castor

H16 **Valle d'Ayas Guides' Hut** c3,420m (Riffugio Lambronecca or
F Nuova Mezzalama). *Grid ref 625,70/84,55. Private. Telephone booking essential. A new hut (1991) situated at the top of the long rock rib which continues above the moraine separating the Grande and Piccolo Verra glaciers. Open late June to late Sept. Places for 80.* Tel 0125 30 80 83 (Italy: 0039)

From the Mezzalama hut follow a path NNW to get on to the Grande Verra glacier. Climb NE up the glacier to a height of c3,200m where, on the R, you should see a stony combe (fairly obvious on the map). Now either climb the combe (path to a ramp slanting up from R to L) to reach the hut or, turn NW on the glacier and, avoiding crevasses, reach the glacier ramp leading to the Zwillingsjoch. Climb the ramp to the height of the hut then traverse R to reach it. **1½-2hr**

Many parties will reach this hut from above, approaching from the direction of the Breithorn, Castor or Pollux. It is important to start the descent from the SW foot of Pollux from where Route 24a is reversed.

ASCENTS: Breithorn, Pollux, Castor, Theodule hut, Cervinia guides' hut, Rossi and Volante bivouac hut

H17 **Quintino Sella Hut** 3,858m (Cappana Quintino Sella) CAI.
F *Situated on a short level spur on the W edge of the Felik glacier and S of Castor and Punta Perazzi. A relatively new hut built alongside the old one (which has 30 places for winter use). Open from late June to late Sept. Places for 140.* Tel 0125 36 61 13 (Italy: 0039)

HUTS

(i) From San Giacomo (St Jacques) take a taxi or walk to Alpe Pian di Verra Sup and then climb grassy slopes ESE to the small lake at 2,775m (poorly marked track). Climb the combe on the E side of the lake to the ridge at its lowest point. This is the Sup Bettolina pass (c3,100m). Follow the ridge Nwards, just on the E side. The route becomes quite exposed and there are chains for security before the crest is reached at 3,490m. Follow the narrow crest, equipped with ropes, to the hut. **3hr** using a taxi

(ii) From Gressoney-la-Trinité drive or take a bus to Staffal (Staval on the Swiss map) further up the valley and use the two stage lift to the Colle di Bettaforca. Follow the path Nwards on the E side of the ridge to join with the route from San Giacomo. **2½-3hr** from the Colle di Bettaforca. On foot from Staffal a more direct path leads via Alpe Bettlino to the Passo di Bettolina where the ridge mentioned above is joined. Add 2-3hr if you use this approach

ASCENTS: Castor, Liskamm, Gnifetti hut, Monte Rosa hut

H18 **Monte Rosa Hut** 2,795m (Monte Rosahütte) SAC. *A massive*
F *hut which is frequently overcrowded. It is situated at Unt Plattje above*
36 *the R lateral moraine of the Grenz glacier at the bottom of the NW flank of the Dufourspitze. The guardian will not cook your food but there is a small self catering facility with running water at a trough. Take a stove etc. Open from mid-March to mid-Sept (but closed in June). Places for 150; winter room.* Tel 027 967 21 15

From the Rotenboden station on the Gornergrat railway follow the path, at first S then just S of E to reach the Gorner glacier at a height of c2,660m. Head SSW straight across the usually dry glacier towards the lateral moraine on the R bank of the Grenz glacier. The moraine is supported by slabby rocks with two ramps slanting up L to R. Climb the uppermost of these ramps to gain the crest of the moraine and then follow this to the stairway leading to the hut. **2-2½hr**

ASCENTS: All the Monte Rosa peaks, Liskamm, Castor, Pollux, Britannia hut, Città di Gallarate bivouac hut, Margherita hut, Gnifetti hut, Quintino Sella hut

HUTS

H19 Città di Mantova Hut c3,470m (Rifugio Città di Mantova).
F *Grid ref 631.80/82.70. Situated below the Gnifetti hut on the E side*
32 *of the rock rib separating the E branch of the Lis glacier and the Garstelet glacier (the latter is not named on the map) and close to the foot of the latter. Private (Gressoney guides). Hut fees are the same as in CAI huts and it is a little more comfortable than the Gnifetti hut. Open late June to mid-Sept. Places for 85: winter room.*
Tel 0163 781 50 (Italy: 0039)

(i) Access from Alagna Valsesia is by way of the téléphérique to Puntra Indren. From the lift station follow a marked trail NW on the Indren glacier (used for skiing) until below a rock barrier separating this glacier from the Garstelet glacier (unnamed on the map: this is the small glacier just S of the Gnifetti hut) and a fork in the trail. Take the L branch and reach the hut above the barrier after crossing some patches of névé. **1hr**

(ii) From Gressoney-la-Trinité drive or take a bus to Staffal (Staval on the Swiss map) further up the valley and then use the lift system to the Passo dei Salati (via Alpe Gabiet). From the pass (2,936m: not marked on the map) follow the broad ridge N to Punta Indren. From there follow the route described above. **c2hr**

From either of these valley bases it is possible to walk to the hut but very few people actually do so. Allow **5hr**

ASCENTS: Liskamm, Monte Rosa peaks except Nordend, Gnifetti hut, Quintino Sella hut, Margherita hut, Monte Rosa hut, Balmenhorn bivouac hut

H20 Gnifetti Hut 3,611m (Capanna Giovanni Gnifetti) CAI. *A big*
F *hut with the highest chapel in the Alps built alongside it. Situated near*
33 *the top of the rock rib separating the E branch of the Lis glacier and*
32 *the Garstelet glacier (the latter is not named on the map). Open from Easter to late Sept. Places for 270: winter room.* Tel 0163 780 15 (Italy: 0039)

Approach as for the Città di Mantova hut (Route H19). At the fork on the glacier take the R branch and climb the rock barrier on to the Garstelet glacier. Walk up the uncrevassed glacier, before turning L to reach the hut. **1½hr**

ASCENTS: Liskamm, Monte Rosa peaks except Nordend, Città di Mantova hut, Quintino Sella hut, Margherita hut, Monte Rosa hut, Balmenhorn bivouac hut

H21 **Balmenhorn Bivouac Hut**, 4,167m (Bivacco Felice Giordano)
F CAI. *A small wood-built hut situated on the Balmenhorn, a rognon on the E side of the Lis glacier. A large (3.6m) statue of Christ stands on the rocks above the hut. A typical small Italian bivouac hut. Places for 6.*

33

Follow Route 30b towards the Lisjoch and when almost level with the rognon contour under it and climb the rock (II) to the hut from the R. **1½hr** from the Gnifetti hut

ASCENTS: Liskamm, Monte Rosa peaks except Nordend

H22 **Margherita Hut** 4,554m (Rifugio Regina Margherita) CAI. *The highest refuge in Europe: situated on the summit of the Signalkuppe, it also serves as an observatory and research centre and is constructed so as to dissipate the effects of lightning strikes. No self-cooking facilities. Open mid-June to mid-Sept. Places for 80 (winter room).*
Tel 0163 910 39 (Italy: 0039)

F
35
36

See Route 37a. **1½hr** from the Lisjoch

ASCENTS: Liskamm, Monte Rosa peaks except Nordend, Gnifetti hut, Balmenhorn bivouac hut, Monte Rosa hut

H23 **Città di Gallarate Bivouac Hut** c3,690m (Bivacco Città di Gallarate) CAI. *A quite small, typical Italian bivouac hut, constructed in wood and sheet metal and situated against the S summit of the Jägerhorn. Places for 9.*

40
39 41

See Route 43a: AD- from Belloni bivouac hut, PD from Monte Rosa hut and F from Stockhornpass.

ASCENTS: Nordend

H24 **Gugliermina Bivouac Hut** 3,212m (Capanna Fratelli Gugliermina or Capanna Valsesia) *CAI. A wooden construction situated on the massive rock promontory SE of the Parrotspitze which separates the Sesia and E branch of the Piode glaciers. Places for 12.*

F
35

HUTS

From Alagna Valsesia walk or take the bus to the parking area at the roadhead (c1,500m). Follow the track on the N side of the river (Acqua Bianca) to the chalets at Pt 1,603m. Continue heading NW to the head of the valley. Cross two streams descending from Alpe Vigne and then climb a steep path to the L end of a rock barrier. A fork R here leads to the Barba - Ferrero hut at Alpe Vigne sup (not named on the map). Keep L and cross a stream to get onto the crest of the moraine. Follow this until a sort of ramp leads off on its L side. Follow this (some snow patches) to its end and then climb directly up to the hut at the top of a rock step. **c6hr** from the roadhead

ASCENTS: Parrotspitze, Sperone Vincent, Piramide Vincent, Punta Giordani

H25 **Resegotti Bivouac Hut** c3,660m (Refugio Luigina Resegotti)
F CAI. *A wooden bivouac hut, painted red and situated on the Cresta Signal, the E ridge of the Signalkuppe, 825m E of the Passo Signal and 5m below the snow crest on rocks on the S side. Places for 10 maximum.*

From Alagna Valsesia follow Route H24 to the path leading R to the Barba - Ferrero hut at Alpe Vigne sup. Take this path and reach this hut at c2,230m above the R end of the rock barrier. From the hut climb the path leading up the grassy L lateral moraine of the Sesia glacier. Climb to the crest of the moraine then follow this to reach a small depression. From here move R on to the S Locce glacier and climb it Nwards to where it steepens to the R of a massive rognon having the appearance of a horse (the cavallo). Now slant up L and, after crossing the bergschrund, follow a sort of valley until below and L of the hut. Cross another bergschrund then climb rocks to the hut (chains and risk of stonefall). Alternatively, instead of slanting L, slant R and climb to the crest of the ridge on the W side of the Pt Tre Amici and then follow the crest W to the hut. Allow **6-7hr** from Alagna

It is possible to reach this hut from Macugnaga.

ASCENTS: Signalkuppe

H26 Marinelli Bivouac Hut 3,036m (Capanna Damiano Marinelli)
F CAI. *Situated on the Crestone Marinelli on the N side of the well-known Marinelli couloir (Canalone Marinelli). Stone built with a wooden floor and cut into the rocks behind. Rather superior to most bivouac huts. It has been made very conspicuous having been painted with diagonal red and white stripes. Places for 12*

41
38

From Macugnaga (Pecetto) follow Route H27 on to the R lateral moraine of the Belvedere glacier. Follow the crest for a little way towards the Zamboni and Zappa hut but at a fork in the track about 20min from Belvedere (signpost) turn R on to the glacier. Cross it (paint flashes) to the L bank and follow this S to pass below the Nordend glacier before reaching the moraine below the Crestone Marinelli. Climb the moraine crest then turn the Crestone Marinelli on the N side via névé and scree before reaching its broad crest at a grassy saddle. A path now leads up grassy slopes and a few easy rock steps to the hut. **3½-4hr** from Belvedere

ASCENTS: Dufourspitze, Nordend

H27 Zamboni and Zappa Hut 2,065m (Rifugio Zamboni e Zappa)
W1 CAI. *Situated below very attractive grassy slopes NE of Pizzo Bianco on the E side of the R lateral moraine of the Belvedere glacier. It is ideally situated for observing the E face of Monte Rosa. A short distance from the hut is a very large, cubic boulder with a number of bolted routes. Open from late June to mid-Sept. Places for 85 (winter room).* Tel 0324 653 13 (Italy: 0039)

From Macugnaga (Pecetto) take the chairlift to Belvedere (1,904m). A 5-10min walk leads to the edge of the Belvedere glacier. Descend moraine on to the rubble covered glacier and cross it S to the R lateral moraine (waymarked with paint flashes). Follow the crest to a block and cairn (about 20min from Belvedere) then take the lower track to the hut. **45min** from Belvedere

ASCENTS: Signalkuppe, Pizzo Bianco, Marinelli hut

HUTS

H28 Belloni Bivouac Hut 2,509m (Bivacco Valentino Belloni) CAI.
W2 *Another typical, wood built Italian bivouac hut situated near the bottom of the E ridge of the Gr Fillarhorn. Places for 9.*

From Macugnaga (Pecetto) take the chairlift to Belvedere (1,904m). From the top of the lift climb a short, steep rise then descend on to the Belvedere glacier. Cross the glacier (cairns and poles) WSW to a break in the L lateral moraine below Alpe Fillar. A track leads to some ruined buildings (1,974m) and from there continues towards the first step on the E ridge of the Gr Fillarhorn. Take this track to the step then slant up L in a big couloir down which the stream from the Piccolo Fillar glacier flows. Cross below steep walls before it is possible to slant back R to reach a steep couloir which leads to the hut. **2hr** from Belvedere

ASCENTS: Jägerjoch, Altes Weisstor

H29 Euginio Sella Hut 3,029m (Rifugio Euginio Sella) CAI. *A*
W2 *small, old hut situated on a rocky promontory orientated E-W which*
42 *separates the Jazzi and Roffel glacier (the former is not named on the map and has its origins close to the Neues Weisstor). The hut is protected from avalanches by the wall against which it is built. Open at all times with a guardian present from mid-July to end-Aug. Places for 28.* Tel 0324 654 91 (Italy: 0039)

(i) From Macugnaga (Pecetto) follow Route H28 as far as the ruined buildings at Alpe Fillar. Now take a steep path Nwards to where it contours the hillside and, at c2,350m joins a steep path leading directly up towards the hut. Below the hut reach névé and follow this Lwards beneath the rocks of the promontory to a passage which in turn leads back R across slabs to the hut. **3½-4hr**

(ii) From the lift station on the Italian side of the Monte Moropass follow a marked path, at first N then W, which leads, on the S side of Monte Moro, to Pt 2,906m on the ridge crest. Move on to the Swiss side and follow scree and névé to a rock band which is crossed to give access to the Seewjinen glacier.

Almost immediately climb a steep slope on the N side of the
Seewjinenhorn and then contour the glacier slopes below the
Rothorn before slanting up to reach the crest of the frontier ridge
close to the summit of the Steinchalchhorn (3,333m). Continue
on the crest past Pt 3,345m to reach the Steinchalchlücke
(c3,360m: not named on map) which is marked with a pole and
is at the foot of the steep rise to the E summit of the Roffelhorn
(3,478m). Descend fairly steeply down rocks and then snow on
the S side of the ridge to reach easy terraces which are followed
to the foot of a 30m couloir. Climb this (fixed ropes) to a
horizontal terrace on the S side of Pt 3,478m. Easier going across
terraces and ramps interspersed with couloirs gives access to the
E side of the Roffel glacier. Cross the fairly uncrevassed glacier in
an arc, descending gradually, to the hut. **4hr**: PD

ASCENTS: Cima di Jazzi, Strahlhorn, Città di Luino bivouac hut

H30 **Città di Luino Bivouac Hut** c3,570m (Bivacco Città di Luino)
PD CAI. *A small, yellow painted metal bivouac hut with a wooden*
45 *interior wonderfully situated close to the crest on the Italian side of the*
48 *E ridge of the Schwarzberghorn (Pt 3,609m: not named on map)*
c100m from the summit. Worthy of a visit in its own right. Places for 8
maximum.

(i) From the Eugenio Sella hut follow a marked route from its E
side up the rocks above the hut. Move R on to the glacier and
climb steeply up to the snow shoulder SSE of Pt 3,639m. A
more interesting way is to keep to the rocks all the way. This
involves climbing a small chimney (II+) and some pleasant
scrambling to reach the snow shoulder. Above the shoulder is a
band of rock about 100m high. Start climbing this by a small
couloir on the R for a few m then follow a ramp Lwards until it is
possible to get on to another, higher ramp which is followed for
c20m to the bottom of another small couloir. Climb this (II) to a
small terrace on the R then slant L up a slab (II+) to a final
small terrace which gives easy access to the crest of the ridge at
the Passo Jacchini c3,520m (not named on the map: 1½hr).

Head N on the Swiss side, descend slightly, and contour at

c3,500m until below Pt 3,609m (the Schwarzberghorn). Climb snow slopes to the crest then contour across the S side to reach the E ridge a little above the hut which is on the Italian side of the ridge. **2½hr** in total

(ii) From the Monte Moropass lift station follow Route H29(ii) to the Steinchalchlücke. From here contour round the Roffelhörner on the N side and regain the crest of the ridge at Pt 3,517m (some crevasses) or a little higher towards Pt 3,609m (the Schwarzberghorn). Follow the snowy crest to the hut. **4hr**

(iii) From Mattmark the hut can be reached by climbing the Schwarzberg glacier. Take the R fork on the track on the W side of the reservoir to Schwarzbergalp. A path leads off L to Chäste, take this path to Pt 2,693m and then continue along the crest of the moraine to a height of c2,800m. Move on to the glacier and climb it to reach the crest of the frontier ridge at or W of Pt 3,517m. Go up the ridge to the hut. **4-5hr**. This approach is F

(iv) From Berghaus Flue head E past two small lakes and then follow the moraine crest for a further km before getting onto the Findel glacier. Continue on the R bank of the glacier to below the Strahlchnubel. Pass a difficult crevassed part of the glacier and, still on the R bank, reach the S foot of the Adlerhorn above some large crevasses. Now head out further on to the glacier towards Pt 3,321m and in roughly the same line reach the Neues Weisstor or join (i) above at the snow slope leading to the crest. From the former, traverse Pt 3,609m (the Schwarzberghorn) and descend the E ridge to the hut. **c5hr**

ASCENTS: Cima di Jazzi, Strahlhorn

H31 **Berghaus Flue** 2,618m (Flue). Private. *Situated at Fluealp above*
W1 *the R bank of the Findel glacier. Similar rates to that paid by members in SAC huts for demi-pension. Places for 50.* Tel 027 967 25 51

From the lift station at Blauherd follow the path leading past the Stellisee and continue on the same path to the hut. **45 min**. Walking from Zermatt takes 3-4hr

ASCENTS: Stockhorn, Strahlhorn, Rimpfischhorn, Britannia hut

HUTS

H32 **Täsch Hut** 2,701m (Täschhütte) SAC. *A popular hut of medium*
W1 *size easily accessible from Täsch. It is situated on a grassy terrace close to the foot of the Alphubel's Rotgrat. Open from early Apr to mid-May and late June to late Sept. Places for 65 (winter room).*
Tel 027 967 39 13

From Täsch drive or walk to Ottavan (2,214m: parking). From here walk up the roadway (suitable for authorised 4WD vehicles) to the hut. **1-1½hr** from Ottavan

ASCENTS: Mischabeljoch, Täschhorn, Alphubel, Allalinhorn, Rimpfischhorn, Britannia hut, Längfluh hotel

H33 **Britannia Hut** 3,030m (Britanniahütte) SAC. *Extended and*
F *completely rebuilt internally, it was re-opened in 1997. It is situated*
51 *close to a col at the E end of the Hinter Allalin ridge which separates the Hohlaub and Chessjen glaciers and is at the end of an almost horizontal track leading from the upper Felskinn lift station. Open from March to May and from late June to late Sept. Places for 134 (winter room).* Tel 027 957 22 88

(i) From Felskinn follow a wide track which climbs SE on to the Chessjen glacier. From here a pisted track rises gradually until just S of the Egginerjoch (ski-tow) and then contours the upper part of the glacier to reach the hut. There is a slight danger from seracs at the start. **c½hr**

(ii) From the upper lift station at Plattjen (2,570m), which can be reached on foot or by lift from Saas Fee, follow the path leading round the E side of the Mittaghorn and the Egginer. A path from Zer Meiggern just S of Saas Almagell, another potential starting point, joins this path. The path leads to the Chessjen glacier N of the hut. Climb it to the hut. **2hr** from Plattjen

An approach, on foot, can also be made from the Mattmark barrage. Follow the road alongside the reservoir before turning R to pass Schwarzbergalp before crossing the Allalin and Hohlaub glaciers. **4hr**

HUTS

ASCENTS: Strahlhorn, Rimpfischhorn, Allalinhorn, Alphubel, Längfluh hotel, Täsch hut via Allalinpass, Monte Rosa hut via Adlerpass

H34 **Mischabeljoch Bivouac Hut** 3,851m (Mischabeljoch biwak)
57 SAC. *Grid ref 633.060/102.600. A newly constructed hut (1996), standing on stilts near the foot of the N ridge of the Alphubel. The old hut has been destroyed. There is a resident guardian at times but there is no booking system although he will provide meals. Places for 24. Emergency telephone only. Guardian's home Tel 022 757 61 17*

See Routes 61a.

ASCENTS: Täschhorn, Alphubel

H35 **Längfluh Hotel** 2,870m. *A private establishment much more akin*
W1 *to a hut than a hotel. The hotel (possibility of self-catering - ask when booking) itself is situated a few m S of the upper lift station at Längflue (map spelling), a rocky rib projecting into the Fee glacier to the SW of Saas Fee. It is administered by the lift operators but meals and accommodation are usually taken at the lift station. Open during the ski-ing season and from July-Sept. Places for 130. Booking at the lift station in Saas Fee or telephone the top lift station.*
Tel 027 957 21 32

Use the lift or walk from Saas Fee using the path starting at Chalbermatten and passing the lower station of the Felskinn lift. **c3hr** on foot

ASCENTS: Aphubel, Allalinhorn, Britannia hut, Täsch hut

H36 **Dom Hut** 2,940m (Domhütte) SAC. *A splendid hut with a*
W2 *magnificent view of the Weisshorn from its position just N of the snout of the Festi glacier. Open from early July to late Sept. Places for 75: self catering possible: winter room.* Tel 027 967 26 34

From the main road through the centre of Randa village take the narrow road then path through meadows leading to a bridge across the Dorfbach. Once across the bridge follow the steep path through the forest to reach the open alpine slopes above it at 2,016m. Continue steeply up the fields to meet the Europaweg at c 2,280m. Cross this and continue up the rock barrier of

Festiflue. Follow the path Rwards under this until it is possible to scale the barrier. The route up the rocks has steps, fixed ropes etc and a bit of scrambling to relieve the grind. Eventually it breaks out on to stony terrain not far below the hut. **4-5hr**

ASCENTS: Dirruhorn, Hohbärghorn, Nadelhorn, Lenzspitze, Dom, Täschhorn

H37 **Mischabel Hut** (Mischabelhütte) AAC Zurich. *Run on the same*
W2 *lines as SAC huts and gives reciprocal rights. This fine, modern hut*
61 *has a reputation of having a very stiff approach walk, situated as it is at the top of the steep rock promontory overlooking Saas Fee on the S side of the Hohbalm glacier. Some people like to use the gondola lift to Hannig to shorten the walk but the expense seems difficult to justify. Open from late June to late Sept. Places for 130: self catering possible: winter room.* Tel 027 957 13 17

From the church in Saas Fee take a path heading W. Pass through a wooded section before reaching a river. Cross this then start the steep grind. High up there is some easy scrambling but the steepness is maintained almost all the way. **c4hr**

ASCENTS: Lenzspitze, Nadelhorn, Hohbärghorn, Dirruhorn, Ulrichshorn, Balfrin, Bordier hut

H38 **Bordier Hut** 2,886m (Bordierhütte) SAC. *A relatively small hut*
W2/F *situated on a terrace near the foot of the WSW ridge of the Klein Bigerhorn and overlooking the Ried glacier. Open most of July and Aug. Places for 56: self catering possible: winter room.*
Tel 027 956 19 09.

From Gasenried (parking at the entrance to the hamlet) walk along the road until a little way past a chapel. A path branches off L (signpost to Grat) and then contours the hillside parallel to a water channel (bise). Cross a bridge and then a little further on keep L at a fork before starting the steep climb through the forest to Alpja. There is a welcome water source towards the top of the steepest part of the path. An alternative route starts across the road from the car park and follows a path heading roughly SE. Cross four water channels before reaching Pt 1,930m below

Grefzug. Beyond the block of forest take a path leading R and cross the old bed of the Ried glacier before joining the path to Alpja described above.

Beyond Alpja the path starts to climb quite steeply up the L lateral moraine of the Ried glacier as far as Pt 2,600m. It then cuts up the flank of the hillside (cairns; snow patches) before making a short descent on to the glacier at c2,760m. Cross the mainly dry glacier following marker poles, more or less at the same height and then rising to reach the R bank of the glacier at c2,820m. Scramble up a few rocks and then follow the path easily to the hut. **3-4hr**

ASCENTS: Gr Bigerhorn, Balfrin, Ulrichshorn, Nadelhorn, Hohbärghorn, Dirruhorn, Mischabel hut

H39 **Oberto Hut** 2,796m (Rifugio Gaspare Oberto). *A private hut*
W1 *but run by the CAI. Situated just E of and below the top of the téléphérique lift station on the Italian side of the Monte Moropass. Open at all times when the lift is operating (summer: usually end-June to end-Sept, and winter: Dec to end-April). Places for 32.*
Tel 0324 655 44 (Italy: 0039)

(i) On the Italian side, most people will approach from Macugnaga by lift: walking from Staffa takes c4hr.

(ii) From the Swiss side follow Route 48b from Mattmark to the Monte Moropass. Scramble down from the statue to the lift station.

ASCENTS: Monte Moro, Joderhorn, Città di Luino bivouac hut, Euginio Sella hut

H40 **Città di Varese Bivouac Hut** c2,640m (Bivacco Città di
W2 Varese) CAI. *A small hut situated on the first level section of the E*
70 *ridge of the Mittelrück. Places for 10.*

(i) From Antronapiana a narrow road leads to Alpe Cheggio (1,497m). Cross the dam and follow a path on the W side of the reservoir to reach the Alpe del Gabbio. Keep on the path leading into the Loranco valley and follow it to Alpe Corone. The wardened Andolla hut is situated on the N side of the valley and you will see this signposted. Continue heading E up stony ground to reach the N side of the Mittelrück E ridge close to its foot. Slant up L up the first rise in the ridge to reach the hut. **c4hr**

(ii) Climbers based in Switzerland can reach the hut by crossing the Sonnigpass (see Route 74b(i)).

ASCENTS: Mittelrück, Portjengrat (Pizzo d'Andolla)

H41 **Almageller Hut** 2,894m (Almagellerhütte) SAC. *An attractive,*
W1 *modern hut situated below the S side of the Dri Horlini in the NE*
76 *sector of the Almagellertal. Open from mid-June to late Sept. Places for 120 (winter room).* Tel 027 957 11 79

From the carpark close to the bridge across the Almagellerbach in Saas Almagell, follow a path climbing through the forest on the E side of the valley which crosses the river c1km W of Stafel. Keep on the path on the N side of the river to reach the Almagelleralp hotel (accommodation: 2,194m). Follow the path upstream and keep on it where it turns into the Wysstal. The hut comes into view as the slope relents. **c3½hr**

ASCENTS: Sonnighorn, Mittelrück, Portjengrat, Portjenhorn, Weissmies, Dri Horlini, Città di Varese bivouac hut

H42 **Weissmies Hut** 2,726m (Weissmieshütten) SAC. *Two huts, a*
W1 *smallish old one and a reasonably large and modern one, situated*
77 *c2km W of the Lagginjoch below the frontal moraines of the glacier forming the flank of the col on this side. Open from Mid-June to Sept. Places for 135: winter room.* Tel 027 957 25 54

(i) Most parties will use the lift system from Saas Grund to Chrizbode (or walk to here starting from the lift station and passing Trift on the way). From here follow the path WNW to the hut. The last section is quite steep. **c1hr**

(ii) Some parties may wish to access the hut from Hohsaas. Follow the path W and then NE down moraine slopes. At c3,030m the path turns NW before reaching a roadway. Walk down this a few m then follow a path to the hut. **½hr**

ASCENTS: Jegihorn, Jegigrat, Fletschhorn, Lagginhorn,
Weissmies, Hohsaas hut

H43 **Hohsaas Hut** 3,098m (Hohsaashütte). *A mountain restaurant*
75 *with dortoir accommodation situated close to the lift station at*
77 *Hohsaas. Open when the lift is operating in the ski season and from*
June to mid-Oct. Places for 40 (meals have to be bought).
Tel 027 957 17 13

From Saas Grund take the télécabin lift almost to the door and
from the Weissmies hut reverse Route H42(ii) (1hr)

ASCENTS: Lagginhorn, Weissmies, Weissmies hut

H44 **Laggin Bivouac Hut** 2,438m (Laggin biwak) SAC. *A small,*
W2 *prefabricated hut situated near the foot of the R lateral moraine of the*
Sibiluflue glacier on the E side of the Fletschhorn. Places for 10.

Waymarked from Simplon village, a bridleway heads S across the
Lauigrabe torrent. Follow this track which climbs steeply
through woods at first and then contours the hillside before
climbing again to Pt 2,059.2m (Antonius oratory). The path
then crosses almost horizontally the steep slopes of Goldweng
before rising steeply again to a commemorative cross. Keep on
the path past Färicha (avoid a lower path) before a last steep
ascent leads to the hut. In places the path is rather faint but is
cairned. **c3½hr**

ASCENTS: Fletschhorn, Lagginhorn

H45 **Fletschhorn Bivouac Hut** 3,040m (Bivouac des Pères de
W2 Bethléem). *Property of the Centre de Vacance Bethléem at the old*
Simplon hospice. Situated NE of the Senggchuppa at the N foot of the
Mattwald glacier. Places for 10.

Approach from Saas Balen via a road (car access) to Greube
(2,300m). Follow the roadway from here to a horseshoe bend at
c2,380m where a path leads off towards Sattel (Pt 2,813) further
N. The climb to Sattel involves some scrambling up slabs and a
few rock steps (1hr). From Sattel a wide, stone covered terrace
leads ENE. Follow the terrace along the 2,800m contour line,
turning N along this line to pass the locality called

Gletscherweng. Once across the Mattwaldbach head NE up moraine slopes and areas of exposed rock to the hut (c1½hr). **2½-3hr**

ASCENTS: Senggchuppa, Fletschhorn

Multi-day Walking Tours

There is less opportunity in the region described in this guide book for this type of activity compared to the walks outlined in *Valais Alps West*; nevertheless there is one outstanding tour suitable for any determined walking party which is prepared to do some glacier crossing. This is the *Tour of Monte Rosa*. In addition the classic *Haute Route* between Chamonix and Zermatt can be extended by a crossing to Saas Fee but this is more demanding of some mountaineering skills. There is a long distance footpath route starting in Chamonix and terminating at the Simplonpass which traverses the hills N of the mountains described in this guide. Brief details of this are listed below. Apart from those used by the *Tour of Monte Rosa* there are a number of paths traversing the ridges separating the Italian valleys to the S of the region which could be combined to give a multi-day walk. Switzerland Tourism provide a useful booklet entitled *Wandertouren/Les Tours - Sentier Valaisans/Walliser Wanderwege* which outlines various multi-day walks.

Italian Tourist Offices supply free maps but the *Carte di Sentieri* are better.

Tour of Monte Rosa
There are many variations to this tour but outlined here is what might be described as the classic itinerary. This walk is quite comparable to the *Tour of Mont Blanc*, with equally spectacular scenery and taking approximately the same time. A recent development and a vast improvement to the tour is the opening (in 1997) of a high level path on the E side of the Mattertal linking Grächen with Zermatt.

MULTI-DAY WALKING TOURS

The tour is circular so it can be started at any point along the circuit and it can be undertaken in either direction. If you want to avoid the use of uphill transport in the form of ski-lifts and cable cars you need to consider carefully which is the preferred direction. Travelling anti-clockwise will involve the steep ascent from Macugnaga to the Monte Moropass but probably takes the new path from Grächen to Zermatt in the prefered direction. The tour can generally be undertaken from about mid-June to mid-September. Overnight accommodation can be had in hotels, dortoirs or mountain huts

Assuming a start from Zermatt and travelling anticlockwise:

Stage 1. From Zermatt to St Jaques (St Giacomo) in the Valle d'Ayas crossing the Theodulpass and the Colle Sup delle Cima Blanche. This is the stage involving glacier crossing and is also the most time consuming. Probably the ideal starting point for this stage is the Gandegg hut (or use an early lift out of Zermatt to Trockenersteg) so that the Theodule glacier can be crossed early in the day whilst it is still frozen. The glacier can be crevassed and the use of a rope is recommended although crampons can probably be dispensed with. You should allow c12hr walking from Zermatt and 8hr from the Gandegg hut.

Stage 2. St Jaques (St Giacomo) to Gressoney. The shortest route is via the Colle di Bettaforca but to enjoy the scenery more follow the Vallone di Verra to the Piano di Verra before climbing to the Passo Sup di Bettolina. From here head S along the ridge to the Passo di Bettolina before descending to the Gressoney valley at Staffal via Alpe Bettolina. This should take c6hr.

Stage 3. Gressoney to Alagna. From Staffal follow paths via Alpe Gabiet to the Colle d'Olen before descending to Alagna. This takes roughly 7hr.

Stage 4. Alagna to Macugnaga. A steep climb from the head of the Valle della Sesia leads to the Colle del Turlo and a steep descent into the delightful Valle Quarazza. Follow the valley past the old gold mine to Staffa. This will take the best part of 8hr.

Stage 5. Macugnaga to Saas Fee. The path is signposted from Staffa to the Monte Moropass and is a steep pull up through the woods at first after which it relents a little. The frontier ridge is crossed some way W of the lowest point. Follow waymarks from the lift station leading to the statue of the Madonna. When descending on the Swiss side take great care with navigation if it is foggy (which it frequently is). See Route 48b which describes the approach to the pass from Mattmark. From the dam you can follow the road to Saas Almagell but a path on its E side is a far better alternative. A km S of the village the path crosses the road and the river. Follow this route or walk through the village and rejoin the same path just W of the village. A rough road, or a path above the road can be followed into Saas Fee. The walk to the Monte Moropass should take c4hr and it will take a further 4-5hr to get to Saas Fee.

Stage 6. Saas Fee to Grächen. A much easier day with far less ascent than on the previous few but still quite delightful with super views of the high peaks above Saas Grund. The footpath is sign-posted. The easiest start is to walk through the village to Wildi and then follow the rough road (avoid two lower foot-paths) to the first hairpin bend. Take the higher path from here which contours the mountain side at a height of c2,000m. The path rises eventually to a little over 2,300m on the E side of the Lammenhorn. This altitude is then more or less maintained until the ridge separating the Saastal and Mattertal is reached although there is something of a sting in the tail as you need to climb up to the ridge. The more adventurous walkers might like to cross the ridge via the Seetal combe which has a crossing point close to 3,000m. Various paths or lifts lead down to Grächen. This is a 6-7hr day.

Stage 7. The best is saved to the last. The Swiss authorities have developed a new high level footpath linking Grächen to Zermatt and referred to as either the Höhenweg or the Europaweg (a free map is available from the local Tourist Offices). It climbs to a height of c2,600m on the E side of the Mattertal and allows walkers stunning views of the great 4,000m peaks on the W side of this valley that had previously been denied them. From Grächen follow a footpath S which climbs to the highest watercourse. Follow this through the woods before climbing to the moraine below the Reid glacier. A path crosses the bed of the former glacier to the moraine on the W side of the glacier stream. Turn R here but very soon, once back in the woods, turn L and make the pleasant climb up to Grat. The newly engineered path starts here. Take care with stream crossings after rain but otherwise enjoy the walk and the views. Above the village of Randa the path leading to the Dom hut is crossed. A diversion to the hut is recommended, although some easy scrambling is involved, and an overnight break can be made at the hut. The path continues into the Wildikin gorge before descending to cross scree slopes above Täsch via a sheltered walkway. Here it joins the old path leading up to Ottavan and a welcome bar (with overnight accommodation). Two paths lead on, via Tufteren, to Sunnegga above Zermatt. For the very best views take the higher one crossing the Ober Sattla. From Sunnegga there is an Alpine Metro into Zermatt. This will be an 8-10hr day.

Chamonix to the Simplonpass

Starting in Chamonix this route follows footpaths all the way to the Simplonpass. To reach Zinal, at the W of the region described in this guide, it crosses the Col de Balme and Fenêtre d'Arpette to Champex. It then follows the Val Ferret to reach the Col du Grand St Bernard and then Bourg St Pierre. It next crosses the Col de Mille to reach the Panossiere hut and then the Mauvoisin barrage. The route then heads N to reach the Cabane de Louvie where it turns E again towards the Dixence barrage. The next objective is Arolla and then Les Haudères. From here the way is via the Col de Torrent to the Moiry barrage and on to Sorebois and then either direct to Zinal or go via the Petit Mountet.

From Zinal a path leads N to the Hotel Weisshorn above St Luc and then on over the Meidpass to Gruben. St Niklaus is reached next by crossing the Augstbordpass. The best bet now is to take the post bus to Grächen. From here you do a stage of the *Tour of Monte Rosa* via Hannigalp to Saas Fee. Another bus ride (walking is a possibility) will take you to Gspon before the final stage of the walk leads you over the Gebidumpass and the Bistinepass to the Simplonpass.

Valley rock climbing

British climbers visiting alpine valleys for the first time are often astounded to see acres of rock on which, were it located in Britain, they would expect to find a network of routes. It is only in relatively recent years that there has been any substantial development of climbing on such crags, especially the smaller ones close to the main resorts. Routes on these crags are usually well equipped with 10mm stainless steel bolts and offer the visitor climbing of all standards suitable for the odd day spent in the valley or when the weather is unsuitable for ascents of the high peaks. All the crags described are of relatively easy access either by road, lift or train. Some rock climbing guide books are listed in the *General Information* section of this volume but for readers requiring more information than is supplied here you are recommended to enquire at local tourist offices where topo guides may be available, otherwise try local sports shops or the local mountain guide bureau (see below for the Zermatt valley).

Switzerland

ZINAL VALLEY
Little has been developed here apart from the cliffs of the Mammouth which are described in the main section of the guide. Closer to the village, about 1.8km S of the campsite and on the W side of the river there are two areas of boulders with marked routes. Across the river from the village centre is Belvédère. It is reached by crossing the bridge close to the campsite and following the signposts. The crag is 30m high and is split into an upper and lower section by a terrace. The E and N

sides of the lower tier have c12 routes in the range III and IV whilst the S and E sides of the upper tier have fewer but harder climbs

TURTMANNTAL
Brunegg: A number of crags have been developed around the Turtmann hut with routes ranging in grade from III to IX. They are mostly one pitch climbs but there is one good 3-pitch climb at IV. All the routes are equipped: ask at the hut for details.

ZERMATT VALLEY
St Niklaus: S of the village there are literally acres of steep rock on both sides of the valley awaiting the development of potentially multi-pitched routes. What have been developed are climbs on a number of small crags on the hillside on the W side of the village. These can be reached by crossing the railway track near the station. One group of crags is almost directly above the station parking area and has 1 to 3 pitch routes in the III+ to VI range. Another small crag lies further N just above a path from the station whilst further crags are to be found uphill from here. These have routes in the V-/V+ range. Further up the valley there are climbs on crags scattered around Täsch and Zermatt. Details of the Täsch and Zermatt climbs can be found in the cheap, Robert Andenmatten booklet of climbs entitled *Zermatt Free Climbs* which is available from the Zermatt Guides' Office. All the climbs are named at their foot and none of the routes cross so the lines are easy to follow. The booklet has a star rating but this is unhelpful since all the routes are given at least two stars except those at Tossen where only one star routes are available and at Gornerflüe where there are some with three stars. Very brief details are given below of the various sites.

Gornerflüe: This is undoutedly the major crag in the Zermatt area. It is SSE facing and situated at a height of c2,500m overlooking the snout of the Gorner glacier below the W ridge of the Riffelhorn. It is reached from the Rotenboden station on the Gornergrat railway. Walk W, passing two small tarns, towards Gakihaupt (Gagenhaupt on the map) following the line of the stream issuing from the tarns. Where the stream turns sharply L take a path heading L. Leave this path before the first bend and scramble down to a rappel point. A 20m rappel and some easy scrambling gives access to the majority of the climbs. These range in difficulty from IV to VII- and in length from 2 to 4 pitches. It is worth carrying some wedges.

A few harder climbs (VII and VII+) are reached by turning towards the glacier after passing the two small tarns. c150m after leaving the path you reach a rappelling area.

Gakihaupt: Named as such on the 1:25,000 map but as Gagenhaupt on the 1:50,000 map, the crag is not far from that of Gornerflüe. It is probably best approached from the Riffelberg station on the Gornergrat railway. Head towards the Matterhorn and in c15min, where the path descends you find the climbing area. Climbs range in difficulty from VI+ to VIII but are only 10m in length.

Gandegga: A few relatively easy 1 and 2 pitch climbs are located fairly close to the Gandegg hut. The crag can be clearly seen from the Trockener Steg lift station looking towards the Monte Rosa and is reached in c20min from there. Routes are graded III and IV.

Furi: A few crags are scattered around and easily approached from the lift station at Furi.

Grawflüe: is a two tier crag with 1 and 2 pitch climbs in the VI- to VIII range, the lower tier providing a warm-up route to the more difficult climbs above. Head towards Hermettji and then along a ski piste to a path leading towards the Gorner glacier. 100m beyond a bridge turn uphill towards the hydroelectric installations. You soon arrive at the foot of the crag.

Tossen: has a number of short routes (10m) and 3 longer ones (20-50m) in the range VI to VII+. From the lift station head E along the Zermatt road. Cross a bridge and then turn R and reach the N sector of the crag above the U bend. The E sector is a little higher.

Further along the same road two boulders are visible c50m apart above the road. This is Schweigmatten where you might enjoy some short climbs (8m) from grade III upwards.

Eschelbalmen: Just a few minutes walk from the centre of Zermatt, this 18m high crag has a dozen routes in the range VI to IX although these grades are reported to be 'Stiff'. From the catholic church head up the street and turn R after the dry cleaners. A steep path leads to the crag.

Fuxtei: This small crag is c5min walk from the campsite in Täsch on the W side of the valley. There is one relatively easy route (IV), the rest are much stiffer, up to VIII+.

Resti: A 40m slab on the roadside where the Täschalpen road crosses the gorge. Limited parking near the bridge. Although the slab is not steep there are few holds and the degree of friction is low. Grades are in the range III to V+.

Springlbode: There is what appears to be a completely undeveloped, large crag high on the hillside above the Atermenzen campsite N of Randa. It is steep slabby rock up to c100m high and 150-200m wide. It can be approached in c1hr by a steep path starting on the S side of the Wildibach, reached by walking up the field at the top end of the campsite. This path meets the new Europaweg at 2,230m. Turn R along this path and reach an area of large boulders. The crag is just up the hillside.

Schönbiel: Hardly a valley crag. Beyond the Schönbiel hut and towards the Dent Blanche is a 30m high crag with six routes in the range V to VII

There are further possibilities for rock climbing near Grächen.

Hohtschuggen: a 35m high crag immediately below the Hohtschuggen Restaurant. Follow the road from Grächen through Egga to the roadhead. From the parking area a 10min walk leads to the crag. There are 9 routes graded from III to VII.

Gabelhorn: This peak is located on the ridge above Grächen which is easily reached by utilising the Seetalhorn lift from the village. Walk to the pass above the top lift station and then head SSE along the ridge, turning any obstacles on the E side. The Gabelhorn can be easily recognised as it has two distinctive gendarmes forming a sort of fork on the summit. The N most of these gendarmes, which was first climbed in 1904 with the aid of a rope placed over the top by throwing a stone tied to string, has two equipped routes. Photographs obtained of a later ascent (1923) have been widely used to illustrate the history of alpinism.

The L-hand route (1972) starts at the foot of the monolith on the W side and climbs over a roof to a shoulder L of the summit. The R-hand route (1983), which is more direct, starts at the col between the gendarmes. Both routes are TD.

SAASTAL

The major crag is the SE face of the Dri Horlini situated above the Almageller hut. This crag is described in the main section of the guide book. A number of smaller crags in and around Saas Fee have equipped routes.

Biele: This crag is situated just below the top part of the Kapellenweg, the path linking Saas Grund and Saas Fee. From Saas Fee, alongside the bus station, descend the Kapellenweg to a short distance before the Kapelle Maria. A path leads off R to the Feevispa. Follow this path and after the first bend take a horizontal path leading R to the foot of the crag. Grades of routes are marked at their base, the easier routes are on the R. Grades of climbs vary between II and VI+.

Feekin: Close to the Feevispa (in fact the routes start almost in the river bed), this crag has 8 routes ranging in difficulty from V- to VIII-. The best approach is from the bridge leading into the Mischabel campsite. Follow the path up the L bank of the river to a concrete water course. Follow this for a few paces then take a path through undergrowth to the edge of the river and the crag.

Mittags Platte: Just S of Saas Almagell a bridge crosses the river. SSW of the bridge is the Brandgrabe. The crag forms the base of the Brandgrabe on the L side. One four pitch route (135m) has been equipped and follows the crest of the rib L of the obvious ramp (used for descent) and the big roof. The grade is IV to V and is on agreeably sound rock. Avoid damp conditions since there is some lichen. To descend, make two rappels to the ramp and then follow its grassy slopes to the bottom.

Hischer Flie: NE of Furggstalden is a steep rock wall roughly 200m high. One good but quite difficult route has been climbed and equipped on this wall (1987). The start is located a little way R of the anti-avalanche wall. White paint flashes show the way to the start, first up R then a long traverse L. Pitches vary in difficulty from III to VII (an overhang is VII+ free but can be aided: A0). Descend the route by rappel.

Italy

VALTOURNENCHE

Singlin: S of Cervinia on the road to Valtournenche and a few hundred m below the second set of hairpin bends, is a series of S facing crags. They are reached from a lay-by above the hamlet of Singlin. The longest route is 70m but many are much shorter and grades range from III/IV to VIII. The rock is good and the routes are well equipped.

Le Chateau: A small crag close to Cervinia and in view from the sports ground. Well equipped but a bit friable with grades of V/VI.

VALLE d'AYAS

Extrapieraz: S of the village of Extrapieraz, on the W side of the river there are two prominent, E facing buttresses. The larger one, well seen from the road has some well-equipped routes from V+ to VIII. Use a small metal bridge to cross the river.

Palestra di Champoluc: A 25m high crag N of Champoluc on the W side of the valley with about 10 routes in the range IV to VIII-, all equipped and on quite good rock. From Champoluc follow the main valley road and park at the Ostava lift station. Cross the bridge over the river and the fields beyond.

VALLE di GRESSONEY

Palestra di Lysbalma: 1km S of Gressoney la Trinité, on the E side of the valley is an isolated crag with an electricity pylon on top. There are a few routes at about VI and one aid route. The rock is not altogether perfect, routes are equipped but some wedges will be found handy.

Gaby: Between the village of Gaby and the bridge at Trèntaz are two massive blocks. They are not far from the road c500m SE of the bridge. There is a small parking area on the roadside. Routes range in grade from V to IX.

VALLE della SESIA

Fun d'Scotte: A SW facing crag of compact gneiss N of Alagna and close to the remains of an old gold mine. There are numerous routes from one to four pitches and with a range of difficulty varying from IV to VIII. All routes are well equipped. c2.5km N of Alagna there is a small parking space on the R. Take the track crossing the river and reach the crag in c10min.

Acqua Bianca: A little way above the roadhead in Valsesia, on the R side of the cascade is a crag with some equipped climbs.

MACUGNAGA

Gildo Burgener: Up the hillside from the sports complex in Pecetto is a steep crag with several one pitch routes. All are VI to VII+ except one which is grade IV. The rock is compact but fully equipped.

Luciano Bettineschi: Just W of Pecetto, reached by following the path out of the village centre which follows a stream. Where the path reaches the steep hillside on the R, just after it crosses the stream, you will see the crag above. There are c15 routes with difficulties ranging from VI- to IX.

Weisshorn Chain
Col Durand to the Barrhorn

The Col Durand at the southern end of the range provides a crossing point, mainly on glacial terrain, between the Zermatt and Zinal valleys. Rising to the N of the col, Mont Durand (3,713m) is a relatively unimportant peak but it is often either climbed from the Schönbiel hut in conjunction with the nearby and more popular Pointe de Zinal (3,789m) as a training climb, or traversed as a means of approach to or descent from the Arbengrat of the Ober Gabelhorn.

The Arbenjoch marks the foot of the Arbengrat, a splendid rock ridge, formed mainly of granite, which rises steeply to the summit of the Ober Gabelhorn (4,063m). Since the construction of the Arben bivouac hut in 1977 this route has become more popular, the ridge being joined a third of the way up. The mountain is frequently traversed in both directions using the ENE ridge, via the Wellenkuppe, from the Rothorn hut. This way of approach is largely on snow but the Grand Gendarme adds to the character of the route.

The Wellenkuppe (3,903m) is worthy of an ascent in its own right, if only for views which must rank among the finest in the Alps. Directly opposite and to the S is the N face of the Matterhorn, and in the opposite direction the Zinal Rothorn presents its most spectacular aspect, its summit forming the sharpest of any 4,000er in the Alps, with magnificent ridges falling steeply away on both sides. Beyond is the great pyramid of the Weisshorn. Closer to hand is the snowy N face of the Ober Gabelhorn.

The next peak in the chain is the Trifthorn (3,728m). This provides a good rock scramble when the bigger peaks are not in condition. It stands at the foot of the long rock ridge of the Rothorngrat, rising ever steeper to the summit of the Zinal Rothorn (4,221m), an imposing mountain and one of the most popular in the district. Fine gneiss ridges offer scope for a combination of superb traverses of this peak. Climbing the

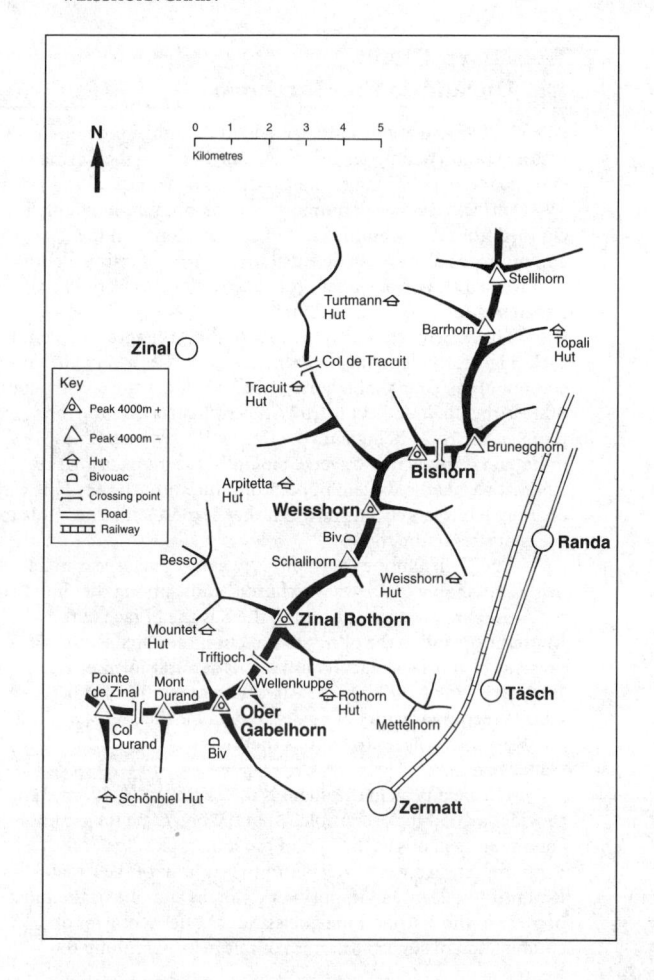

WEISSHORN CHAIN

N ridge from the Mountet hut and descending the SE ridge to the Rothorn hut or vice versa is one possibility, but an equally rewarding traverse, using only the Rothorn Hut and travelling light, can be made via the Rothorngrat descending the SE ridge. Purists may wish to start at the lowest point, the Triftjoch, and include the Trifthorn. This ridge, in its entirety, involves two kilometres of rock scrambling and climbing of no great difficulty and can be completed by a competent team in under 12hr, hut to hut. The views from the summit are second only to those of the Wellenkuppe. ½km N of the summit a high ridge branches W to the small summit of the Blanc de Moming, then turns NW to the Besso, a sharp rock peak well seen from the Zinal valley. Several worthwhile but relatively short routes are to be found here when the higher peaks are not in condition. In addition a 200m high band of rock known as Mammouth provides good rock climbing quite close to the Mountet hut.

Returning to the main chain of peaks the next one of note to the N of the Zinal Rothorn is the Schalihorn (3,974m). This mountain is overshadowed by superior neighbours and is difficult of access. It is not often climbed, but can be traversed in order to reach the bivouac hut on the Schalijoch (3,750m). From here rises the Schaligrat, the SW ridge of the Weisshorn (4,505m), one of the most striking and beautiful mountains in the Alps. Only the Matterhorn could be more magnificent. Like the ideal mountain, the Weisshorn rises in pyramid form, three faces and three soaring ridges culminate in a sharp peak, one of the highest in the Valaisian Alps. The N ridge, with its prominent Grand Gendarme descends to the Weisshornjoch. From here to the N it rises gently, and only a little higher are the twin summits of the Bishorn (4,135m), the last 4,000m peak in this range. Probably the most rewarding ascent of the Bishorn is via the E ridge which is half rock and half snow. It has spectacular views of the Weisshorn's NE face and N ridge.

The Brunegghorn (3,883m) is a worthy secondary peak. Below its steeply rising E face, in the Mattertal, sits the village of Randa, to its cost when, in 1991, a shoulder of the mountain some 700m high, collapsed into the valley, burying the railway and road and blocking the river, which caused extensive flooding in the lower part of the village. Some of the best routes on the Brunegghorn are via its three ridges starting from the Topali hut or the Turtmann hut.

Further N the mountains diminish in size and where the rock becomes limestone its quality declines. However, the Barrhörner (3,610m) with its twin summits is worthy of attention. When viewed from the W it resembles the glacially formed 'Half Dome', and provides an enjoyable excursion from either the Turtmann or Topali hut.

Col Durand 3,451m

First tourist crossing: G and W Matthews with M Charlet, J-B Croz and J Vianin, 17 Aug 1859

Situated between the Pointe de Zinal and Mont Durand it provides a crossing point between the Mountet hut and the Schönbiel hut and ultimately Zinal and Zermatt. The N side is quite steep towards the top and is often icy, as in the summer of 1998 when there was a c50m of grey ice. There may also be a difficult bergschrund on this side but a way past this can usually be found.

1a   SOUTH SIDE
F   Valley base: Zermatt

From the Schönbiel hut follow the path leading NNW for a few min. Take the first branch R which climbs a steep grassy slope into the combe named Kumme. Climb the combe (cairned track) in a fairly direct line towards the L end of a ramp leading to the col at its head. Follow the ramp to the col and on its E side follow a continuation track slanting down on to the Hohwäng glacier at Pt 3,150m. Climb the R (W) bank of the glacier passing close to the bottom of the rock rib marked Pt 3,312m before turning NNE to reach the col. There may be some large crevasses near the rock rib. **2½-3hr** and **650m**

1b NORTH SIDE

PD Valley base: Zinal

1/3

From the Mountet hut follow a track S on to the Mountet glacier. The aim is to climb the Durand glacier combe but to avoid crevasses do this by moving in an arc, at first heading SSE and finishing by heading SW. In this way reach the snow rib which extends SSW from the Roc Noir and climb this to the upper plateau of the glacier. Now head as direct as possible to the col, the actual direction being dictated by the position at which the bergschrund can be crossed. The slope above the bergschrund is usually quite steep for a few m and can be icy. **2½-3hr** and **780m**

Mont Durand 3,713m

Not an important summit and so rarely climbed for its own sake. It is however quite frequently crossed by parties ascending or descending the Ober Gabelhorn, from which it is separated by the Arbenjoch. The NNW flank may attract some climbers. There are two routes on the face, one of which is relatively safe (M Brandt and party, 9 Sept 1957: TD).

2a SOUTH-WEST RIDGE

PD Valley base: Zinal/Zermatt

From Col Durand follow the ridge crest easily on snow and then stony ground before a final steep snow slope leads to more easy ground and the summit. Approaching Col Durand from the Schönbiel side it is possible to join the ridge some way above the col. **1hr** and **260m**

2b NORTH-EAST RIDGE

PD Valley base: Zinal/Zermatt

1/3

From the Arbenjoch, which is the lowest point on the ridge between the Ober Gabelhorn and Mont Durand, follow the snow crest to the rocky point at Pt 3,678m. Beyond this make a steep

descent back on to snow and follow easy ground to the summit.
30-45min and **145m**

Ober Gabelhorn 4,063m

A Moore and H Walker with J Anderegg, 6 July 1865 via the E flank

One of the most attractive looking mountains in the Alps, especially when viewed from the N from where its beautifully sculptured N face is seen to best advantage. There can be few better views of the mountains than that of this peak seen from the Zinal Rothorn. It is a classically, pyramid shaped mountain with four ridges and faces. There are good to excellent climbs on all the ridges and on two of the faces and it is not unusual to combine two of these routes to make a traverse of the peak.

3a EAST-NORTH-EAST RIDGE
AD L Norman-Neruda with C Klucker, 1 Aug 1890
3 Valley base: Zermatt
1 2

Although it was the last of the four ridges to be climbed, this is the ordinary route from the Rothorn hut and involves a traverse of the Wellenkuppe. The ridge itself is mostly snow with rock in its upper part. The amount of rock showing through the snow cover seems to vary from year to year and can, on occasions, be quite considerable. The main obstacle on the climb is the Grand Gendarme which is at the foot of the ridge. This is very steep on the Wellenkuppe side but has fixed ropes to ease the ascent. **c900m**

From the summit of the Wellenkuppe (reached by Route 4a) descend the broad snow ridge leading W to where it narrows and becomes corniced. Keep on the R side here and reach the foot of the Grand Gendarme. Climb snowed-up slabs and some easy rocks to the bottom end of the fixed rope and use this to climb to the top of the gendarme (c20m, strenuous). Descend easily along the crest of the gendarme then along the continuing snow ridge to a low point. Now climb the ridge, generally keeping on the R side on snow then rock to the summit. If a lot of rock is exposed there will be sections of III (rappel on descent). 3hr from the Wellenkuppe: **6hr** from the hut

3b SOUTH FACE
D
2
E Oliver with A and A Aufdenblatten, 29 Aug 1923 by the route described
Valley base: Zermatt

The S face is almost entirely rock which is steep and of good quality gneiss. Its S facing aspect and its steepness ensures that it dries quickly and holds little snow. However, it does catch the sun early and routes on the face are exposed to the risk of stonefall so an early start is essential. A feature to look for is the Grand Gendarme on the WSW ridge, this can be picked out from the Arben bivouac hut. It is the largest step on the ridge below which is a gap and then a small, sharp gendarme. A couloir descends from the Grand Gendarme to the foot of the face. A good climb with several pitons in place. **c600m**

Head N from the Arben bivouac hut to reach the snow ramp leading R across the foot of the face. Follow this ramp to the foot of the couloir mentioned above which has a rock rib on each side. Either rib can be climbed but it is probably better to climb the one on the R. Move up the rib (III, IV) to where it steepens into a vertical pillar. Climb this (IV) for 50m to reach a black ramp (Vire de Charbon) and follow it R into a snowy couloir. Climb up this or the rocks on the L side (R bank) for three pitches (III+) to another ramp. From the ramp a dièdre leads up between the twin summits. Climb c40m up this (IV+) then traverse L for a pitch (III) before easy climbing leads to the top. **5-7hr**

A fairly direct line known as the Überkinger Pillar, finishing at the 'Gabel', was climbed solo by J Straub on 19 Aug 1984. It was graded D+ and has pitches of IV and V. Some stonefall danger.

3c WEST-SOUTH-WEST RIDGE - ARBENGRAT
AD H Hoare and E Hulton with J von Bergen, J Moser and P Rubi,
2 23 Aug 1874
1 Valley base: Zermatt

A very fine climb, up or down. The ridge starts at the Arbenjoch which can be reached by a traverse of Mont Durand. Climbed in its entirety, this makes for a long day out from the Mountet or Schönbiel huts so most parties climbing the ridge will start from the Arben bivouac hut and join the ridge some way above its lowest point. The majority of parties traversing the mountain ascend this ridge and descend the ENE ridge but really there is little to choose between doing it in this direction or in reverse. **840m** *from the hut*

From the Arben bivouac hut climb N across rock and névé to reach the foot of the S face where a rocky nose pokes out from the face and above which a long and partly snow-covered ramp slants up L to the ridge. Climb a couloir to the top of the nose and so gain access to the ramp. Follow this to the ridge which is joined at a small notch. This point is reached in c½hr from the Arbenjoch if approaching via Mont Durand. In descent it is important to locate this point. It is at roughly half-height between the lowest point and the Grand Gendarme and its most obvious feature is the top of the ramp on the S side which is almost horizontal for c15m and resembles a path.

Continue up the ridge, turning any difficulties on the L (maximum difficulty III-) to reach a pointed gendarme. Turn this on the R side (III-) and continue along the ridge to the base of the Grand Gendarme. Slant down on its L into a dièdre and climb this to where it steepens abruptly. Now move L until it is possible to climb back to the crest (III+) just beyond the gendarme. In descent a single rappel of 40m from the near top of the gendarme or two rappels using an intermediate piton overcome the step.

Keep on the crest now until you reach snow on the L side. Cross this to the bottom of the final rise which is turned on the L by traversing across slabs for c40m and climbing a couple of short steps (III) which lead to a little wall on the L and the summit. **3½-4hr**

3d NORTH-NORTH-WEST RIDGE - COEURGRAT
AD
F Douglas with P Taugwalder and J Vianin, 7 July 1865
Valley base: Zinal

Climbed one day after the first ascent of the mountain. This is the ridge descending towards the Mountet hut and forms the ordinary route from that hut. In normal conditions the route is mostly on snow, the upper snow ridge being quite pleasant but steep. Don't be too late in the day if you intend descending this way, soft snow can be quite dangerous. The alternative, if returning to the Mountet hut, is to descend the Arbengrat and traverse Mont Durand to reach the Col Durand before reversing Route 1b.

For some time the lower part of this route was abandoned in favour of a more direct line on the L of the lowest part of the ridge; however, recent changes have made that route much less appealing. The present day route via the Coeur is not too inviting, especially when there is little snow cover and has never appealed to the authors.
1,260m

Approach from the Mountet hut as for Route 1b before heading SE towards Le Coeur, the heart-shaped rock island at Pt 3,090m. Pass this on the N or S side to its upper edge and then climb up to a break line, partly snow covered, slanting up R to L across the ridge. Follow this line all the way across the ridge, descending a little on the E side on to a steep snow slope above a narrowing couloir. Climb the slope bearing slightly L to the lower edge of the glacier plateau below the N face. More steep snow and probably a band of rock leads back to the crest of the ridge. If snow cover is poor it may be necessary to continue towards the N face before climbing steeply Rwards up to the ridge. Once on the ridge, it is followed to the summit. **5-6hr**

3e NORTH FACE

TD- H Kiener and R Schwarzgruber, 30 July 1930
3 FWA: P Sala and B Steulet, 1 March 1969
1 First ski descent: M Burtscher and K Jerchke, 16 July 1977
Valley base: Zinal

*A straightforward snow/ice slope comparable with the NE face of the Lenzspitze, except that in this case the final 100m is much steeper and is mainly rock: most parties avoid this section. This is a wonderful symmetric face standing above a tormented glacier basin. The first ascent party climbed the route in a day from Zermatt, crossing the Triftjoch and descending into this basin from where they climbed to the foot of the face. The approach to the face today from the basin is less sure and although a way might be negotiated up a glacier ramp running parallel to the NNW ridge, a route followed by one of the authors many years ago, nowadays almost every party approaches from the Mountet hut via Route 3d. The face itself is c**450m** high and has an angle of c55°*

Follow Route 3d to the lower edge of the glacier plateau below the face then follow this SE to below the bergschrund. Cross this where possible, often the most difficult bit of the climb, then take a direct line towards the summit. Below the final rocks exit on to the NNW ridge or the ENE ridge. 2½-4hr for the face, allow **6hr** from the hut

3f SOUTH-EAST RIDGE - GABELHORNGRAT

AD+ E Davidson and J Hartley with J Jaun and P Rubi, 3 Sept 1877
2 Valley base: Zermatt

A route which is becoming better known since the opening of the Arben bivouac hut. Well worth some attention. **840m**

From the Arben bivouac hut head NE across the E branch of the Arben glacier to reach the rock wall below the Obergabeljoch (Pt 3,597m). Terraces slant down L from the col across this wall. Utilise these terraces which are gained on the extreme L and climb to the col (1hr). Just above the col cross a bergschrund (sometimes awkward) then climb rocks above bearing R. A nice snow crest leads to a square-cut gendarme. Traverse it or turn it on the R then follow the ridge which is in parts snow and in parts rock. Eventually the ridge steepens. Climb two big steps easily and reach a red-coloured tower. Turn this on the R (delicate and a bit loose, IV) then continue along the fine, exposed crest to the Gabel (a gendarme which forms a sort of fork with the summit rocks, well seen from Wellenkuppe).

Beyond the Gabel is a snow crest, cross this to the slabs of the summit block. Turn these by a traverse R and so reach the summit (3½-4hr). Allow **5-6hr**

If the Arben glacier is impassable it should be possible to reach the ridge at a higher point by following Route 3b on to the ramp below the S face and then following this Rwards to reach the ridge.

Wellenkuppe 3,903m

F Douglas with P Inäbnit and P Taugwalder, 1 July 1865 on an attempt to climb the Ober Gabelhorn

An easily recognised mountain on account of the distinctive snow crest which forms its summit. Frequently climbed in its own right as well as being a means of reaching the NNE ridge of the Ober Gabelhorn.

4a   EAST FLANK AND EAST-NORTH-EAST RIDGE
PD   First ascent party
4   Valley base: Zermatt
5

A fairly pleasant climb with some nice rock near the top. **705m**

From the Rothorn hut climb NW up the glacier combe until a little way short of the rock wall below Pts 3,658m and 3,790m. Turn SW and climb the glacier slope whilst gradually turning S to reach a snowy shoulder, clearly indicated on the map, which extends across the E face of the mountain. Climb the ridge above the shoulder, turning the first steep section on the L. Back on the ridge continue for c100m to a small buttress which is also turned on the L. Return immediately to the ridge and reach the final steep section which is quite impressive looking but easily climbed. A snow crest leads to the summit. **2½hr**

Trifthorn 3,728.3m

M Béreneck, 1872. No further details available. See *Alpine Journal* Volume 61 p 348

A popular mountain, climbed frequently from both the Rothorn hut and the Mountet hut. It makes a good training peak. Parties wishing to cross between the two huts are recommended to traverse this peak rather than to cross the Triftjoch which is quite dangerous on the W side.

5a SOUTH RIDGE
AD First ascent party
4 Valley base: Zermatt

An enjoyable climb in a fine situation. Keep to the crest of the ridge for the best rock. **530m**

From the Rothorn hut follow Route 4a to the point where it heads SW. Follow this line until you see the snowy couloir leading to the Triftjoch. Climb the couloir, taking to the rocks on the R (N) side towards the top. From the col follow the crest of the ridge all the way except for a step at about mid-height which is climbed by a chimney on the Mountet side. **3hr**

5b NORTH-EAST RIDGE
F Valley base: Zinal
7
3

The ridge itself is very short and entirely snow, falling to the Col du Mountet (Pt 3,658m). Any difficulties encountered will be on the glacier approach to this col. **c800m**

From the Mountet hut follow a slightly rising path to the moraine of the Mountet glacier. Climb the moraine to the first cairn and then slant down a poor path to the glacier. Take as direct a line as possible to the Col du Mountet (Pt 3,658m) avoiding crevasses as necessary (usually a trail). The steep section below the col is turned on the R. From the col climb the ridge in a few min to the summit. **2½-3hr**

Zinal Rothorn 4,221.1m

L Stephen and F Grove with J and M Anderegg, 22 Aug 1864

For the climber, this is one of the finest mountains in the Valais. The rock is as good as any that will be found in the region. The main spine of the mountain runs roughly N to S along the rocky N and SW ridges. Butting up to the spine is a third ridge, the SE ridge, which is steep and rocky at the top but quickly levels out into what is called the Schneegrat. Each of the ridges provides an excellent climb and in addition there is the steep, 800m high E face. When the mountain is viewed from the N, its upper part appears to be a gigantic, thin blade of rock slightly inclined to the E which emphasises the steepness of the E face. The ridges are well worth combining to give a traverse of the peak. Probably the best combination is to ascend the SW ridge and descend the N ridge. This can be started from either the Mountet hut or the Rothorn hut. From the latter a return to the hut would necessitate a second day, ideally crossing the Trifthorn. The views N and S from the summit are stunning.

6a SOUTH-EAST RIDGE VIA THE GABEL

AD
5
4 6
8

C Dent and G Passingham with F Andenmatten, A Burgener and F Imseng, 5 Sept 1872

Valley base: Zermatt

The ordinary route on the mountain, much more interesting than most climbs of this category and a classic route. It avoids the upper part of

the SE ridge (Kanzelgrat) and climbs a couloir to a notch on the SW ridge known as the Gabel, finishing by the upper part of this ridge.
c1,020m

From the Rothorn hut climb the slopes of the Rothorn glacier close to the rocks of the rib which dominates the hut. As the angle eases bear more to the R until snow slopes lead to a higher snow terrace. Follow this back L a little way until it is possible to climb the rocks on the R, which dominate the terrace, to reach a further snow slope S of Pt 3,786m. Now either, climb up to this point and follow the rocky ridge NW to reach the quasi-horizontal Schneegrat or, contour below the rocks of the SE ridge and reach the Schneegrat beyond the point at which the rocks terminate. Continue along the ridge, sometimes delicate and with a couple of rock outcrops to the next section of rock (1½-2hr).

The rocks ahead steepen and straight ahead can be seen a deep couloir. Climb a couple of steps on the ridge then, where the ridge rears up Rwards, make a rising traverse (difficult when snow covered) on the S flank to reach the foot of the couloir. The couloir may have a lot of snow in it or may be quite dry, depending on the season. In either case climb it to the notch in the ridge above (the Gabel). The couloir is rigged for rappel descent so belays are easy to arrange.

From the notch climb the ridge crest to a step and turn this on the L, passing through a slot before descending a little and traversing on to a slab (Biner slab). Climb this making use of a slanting crack (III-: pitons, much more difficult if it is icy, in which case it is better to move further L and climb snow to reach the ridge) and more slabs above (III-) back to the crest. Rappel in descent unless conditions are perfect. Keep on the crest to a small gendarme and turn this on the L to reach the Kanzel (pulpit): a fine rock tower. Turn this by a very exposed yet easy traverse on the E side and a little further attain the summit (2-2½hr). **4-5hr** but other parties might cause delay

6b SOUTH-WEST RIDGE - ROTHORNGRAT

AD+ C Gross with R Taugwalder, Aug 1901. Previously descended by
5 J Robinson with A Kronig and P Perren, 16 Sept 1898
6 7 FWA: R Arnold and M Scherbaum, 10 Jan 1976
Valley base: Zermatt/Zinal

Perfect slabby gneiss which dries quickly and makes for a splendid climb. It can be started equally well from either the Mountet hut or Rothorn hut; both approaches lead to the same starting point on the ridge. This is some way above the lowest point of the ridge but misses none of the best climbing. The one detracting feature of the climb is that it joins the ordinary route and the crowds at the Gabel. **c480m**

(i) From the Rothorn hut follow Route 6a to the last snow hump of the Schneegrat. Descend L into the glacier bowl then cross the bowl horizontally to the foot of the snowy couloir leading up to the Ober Rothornjoch (not named on map). This is the col immediately N of Pt 3,877m (Pt du Mountet, an obvious spiky gendarme on the ridge). Climb the couloir, with a few rocks, to the col (2½-3hr).

(ii) From the Mountet hut follow Route 5b but instead of climbing into the combe below the Col du Mountet, pass to the N of the rock island SW of the Pt du Mountet. Follow a snow ramp ENE to reach the foot of the couloir leading to the Ober Rothornjoch. Climb rocks on the N side of the couloir and at the top traverse R to the col (3hr). If this particular route looks uninviting, it is simple enough to reach the same point by climbing the ridge from the Col du Mountet.

From the Ober Rothornjoch climb the ridge via a series of gendarmes, some fairly small others large. Although it is possible to turn some of them the best climbing is almost always to be had by traversing them. The first gendarme is easy and the top of the second is reached via a chimney on the L (III+). Cross a third without difficulty to a little saddle (often snow) and a little higher reach the crux gendarme which is c15m high. A slab leads to a belay (several pitons). Now either (i) traverse R (Zermatt side) for 2m and make some airy moves straight up to a small ledge (IV) then easily to the top, or (ii) climb direct to the top (two moves of V), or (iii) turn the gendarme on the Mountet side by the slab forming its base (III). The final split gendarme immediately S of the Gabel is turned on the L side. Continue to the summit by Route 6a (3-4hr). **6-7hr**

6c NORTH RIDGE
AD First ascent party
6 Valley base: Zinal

8 11
12

The ridge itself is quite short, terminating at a bifurcation where one ridge slants NNW before turning W at l'Epaule to form the fine snow crest of the Arête du Blanc and another ridge heads off NNE towards the Pt S de Moming. Continuing N between these two ridges, the slope rapidly steepens (50°) and falls dramatically to the upper basin of the Moming glacier forming in effect the N face of the mountain. A direct route up this face to l'Epaule (P Bonnant and Miss L Boulaz, 2 Aug 1940) is graded D and can be approached by crossing the lowest point of the Arête du Blanc from the Mountet hut (short, steep descent on the N side). The ridge is almost entirely rock but the approach route climbs the Arête du Blanc which can be icy and delicate. On the ridge there are several distinctive gendarmes, all of excellent gneiss, which provide plenty of interest. A superb climb which, on the first ascent, was climbed in a day from Zinal. **c460m**

From the Mountet hut follow a slightly rising path to the moraine of the Mountet glacier. Walk up the moraine crest to the second cairn. Leave the crest here and follow a cairned route through boulders to regain the crest where the angle eases. From here continue in roughly the same direction to reach the Mountet glacier and follow its R bank below the rocks of the E ridge of the Blanc de Moming. Eventually climb on to the crest of the Arête du Blanc where the bergschrund permits. Climb the crest to the rocks of l'Epaule, Pt 4,017m (3hr).

Continue easily up the ridge to the first gendarme (Gendarme du Déjeuner) and turn this on the Zermatt side to reach the next one which has the appropriate name of the Rasoir.

Traverse this (III) then turn the next gendarme (Sphinx) on the Mountet side. If there is any verglas it may be necessary to traverse the Sphinx (III). The next section of the ridge is very narrow (the Bourrique) and is best negotiated by a semi hand-traverse, first on one side of the ridge then the other. The final obstacle is the Bosse, c40m high and quite imposing from below. Climb this direct with the aid of a fixed cable (III: pitons). This is the most difficult pitch if there is any snow or ice on the rocks. From the top of the Bosse the summit is reached easily and quickly (1½-2hr). **c5hr**

6d EAST FACE DIRECT
TD
8
12
R Gréloz, A Roch and R Schmid, 6 Aug 1945
FWA: P Etter, U Gantenbein and A and E Scherrer, 27-28 Dec 1971
Valley base: Zermatt

A number of routes have been climbed on the face but only two, this one and what might be considered a variation of it, climb to the summit. Although the rock, especially in the upper part, is quite good the face is subjected to stonefall as it catches the sun very early in the day. This particular route is comparatively well sheltered but is best done in cool weather. **c800m**

From the Rothorn hut cross the Rothorn glacier NE to the col marked Pt 3,562m (Unt Äschjoch) and from there climb over the Ob Äschhorn to reach the glacier bowl below the E face. Slanting down the face from the vicinity of the Sphinx gendarme on the N ridge is a couloir which terminates on the glacier. Head for the foot of this couloir (1½-2hr).

Cross the bergschrund and climb its L side before slanting L in another couloir after c50m. Continue in this line towards the massive headwall up gradually steepening rocks (and snow) keeping on the R of any difficulties (III and IV). Below the steep headwall move up Rwards along a ramp and reach a steep pillar which bounds the R side of the wall.

The next section is the crux. c25m L of the pillar climb a

steep chimney-crack, which is rather loose: (three 12m pitches and one 40m pitch: V and V+: pitons). At the top traverse R (V) on to the crest of the pillar. Easier climbing follows up the broad crest via slabs and short walls (III and IV) to an icy terrace at the top of the wall. Move up L on easy ground to a steep chimney on the R. Climb this and exit through a hole a few m from the summit (7-8hr). Allow **10-12hr**

6e KANZELGRAT
D
5
E-R Blanchet with K Mooser, 5 Sept 1933 by the route described
Valley base: Zermatt

In essence this is the upper part of the SE ridge which the ordinary route avoids. Short but worth climbing although the difficulties are more severe than on any of the other ridge routes on the mountain. Mainly rock and quite sound. The first ascent party made three attempts by various lines starting on 31 July 1928 but were not satisfied with their efforts until the third attempt. **280m**

From the Rothorn hut follow Route 6a to the end of the Schneegrat (2hr). Climb two rock steps then, instead of traversing towards the couloir of the ordinary route, climb up, slanting L on snow and slabs (III), towards the crest of the ridge. After c30m traverse horizontally L on to a snow ramp and follow this to the ridge crest. Move a little way along the ridge then L to a 15m chimney. Climb the chimney (IV) and continue below the crest on the S side across steep slabs (IV) to reach a poorly defined chimney of light coloured rock which leads back to the crest just below the overhang of the Kanzel itself. Climb the chimney using a slab on the R (c15m: V: piton). Now make a few easier moves up L to a crack splitting an impending wall. Climb the wall (crux: c10m: V) to a small terrace and then a slab (III) to join the ordinary route just below the Kanzel (2hr). **4-5hr**

Mammouth 3,215m

This can hardly be described as a mountain, it is more of an extension of the SW ridge of the Blanc de Moming. It is situated N of the Mountet hut and provides the site for some very pleasant climbing on good rock on its SE wall, which varies in height from c180-200m. The routes were developed between 1970 and 1977 and reported in the SAC magazine *Les Alpes* in 1978. The routes were all marked with a number at the base and were equipped at the time. The original number is included in the list below in parentheses. Information about the routes has been difficult to find and reality on the ground has not always coincided with the information passed to the authors. Proceed with caution! Take a good selection of gear.

Many of the original paint marks have weathered away and only a few have been replaced. Sometimes the name of the route is painted on the rock and sometimes only an arrow is used and occasionally a letter. Some new routes have been established but at the time of writing no details of these are available and have not been included here. The guardian of the Mountet hut has only sketchy information. For the purposes of this guide book the crags have been divided into two sectors, SW and NE. Descent for Routes 1-7 is via a grassy ramp marked with painted arrows with a 40m rappel to finish (see photograph), otherwise descend by following Route 7a to the col at Pt 3,188m. No attempt has been made to show all the route lines on the photographs.

Valley base: Zinal

South-West Sector

0 (0)   Ancient easy route
1 (1a) Le Dièdre   IV+ and V
2 (1b) Caroline   V and V+ Clearly marked
3 (1c) L'Arnica   IV+
4 (2a) Le Génépi   IV and IV+
5 (2b) Les Gerbeurs   Mostly IV and IV+, moves of V and one of VI

WEISSHORN CHAIN

    6 (2c) Voie des aspirants-guides VI
    7 (2d) Les Chardons V
    8 (3)   Directe Sommitale III-IV with delicate traverse V+ and an overhang IV+. An arrow marks the start
    9 (4)   Voie Alaine Mostly IV, one step of V. Marked with an arrow and letter A at c20m above the start

10 North-East Sector
   10 (5)   Les Dalles IV
   11 (6)   L'Envol   IV with finishing moves of V
   12 (7)   La Dalle rouge   IV with a short section of A1
   13 (8)   Les Surplombs   IV but with a V+ finish
   14 (8a) Les doigts dans le nez   V+
   15 (9)   Les Choucas   V
   16 (10) Voie des guides   IV Named on the rock above the approach ramp
   17 (11) L'Araignée   V with a harder variation

7a   **TRAVERSE**
AD   Valley base: Zinal

11
9 10

The route follows the ridge from SW to NE, terminating at the col marked Pt 3,188m. It provides a very enjoyable outing and a fine alternative when the higher peaks around the Mountet hut are out of condition. Climbing difficulties are no more than III. **c250m**

From the hut walk back along the path NW to the foot of the ridge. Climb the ridge along the crest all the way to the col at its NE end. From the col reach the path back to the hut by crossing some bouldery ground towards the SE. **4hr** hut to hut

Blanc de Moming 3,663m and 3,657m

A relatively insignificant mountain but its traverse, coupled with that of the Besso makes a fine outing. It has two summits, the Smost and lower summit is entirely snow whilst the Nmost is rock.

8a SOUTH-WEST RIDGE

PD

11

Valley base: Zinal

Generally used as a means of descent and described here for that purpose. **780m**

From the S summit descend the ridge easily as far as a snowy shoulder on the R after descending c300m in height. Follow the snowy shoulder down until easy terraces (marked with cairns) lead S to the col marked Pt 3,188m. From here head SE across bouldery ground to quickly reach the path back to the Mountet hut. **1½hr**

8b NORTH-WEST RIDGE

AD

11

H King with A Anthamatten and A Supersaxo, 28 July 1886

Valley base: Zinal

This ridge forms part of the recommended traverse and starts at the low point on the ridge separating the Besso and the Blanc de Moming.

From the summit of the Besso descend, quite easily, the ridge leading SE to its lowest point. From this point the ridge has numerous gendarmes and each of these is climbed, ideally on the crest. Any difficulties can be turned on the E side but always on less sound rock than is found on the crest itself. Eventually a snow crest leads to the final rocks of the N summit. Continue SE to the S summit. **2-2½hr**

Besso 3,667.8m

Guides J Epiney and J Vianin, 1862 or earlier

An impressive peak, especially when seen from Zinal from where its NW flank appears all dark, rocky and very steep. There are at least three routes on this flank, climbed by S Albasini and C Portmann, two are rock climbs and the other is a steep icy couloir (an early season route). The classic outing on the mountain is a climb up its SW ridge. Combining this with the NW ridge of the Blanc de Moming makes an excellent expedition.

9a SOUTH-WEST RIDGE
AD   Valley base: Zinal

11

A very good climb on quite sound rock. There are two possible approaches to the foot of the climb the first of which is preferable provided there is a reasonable amount of snow but this is rare after early summer. The best means of descent is to continue the traverse over the Blanc de Moming via its NW ridge. A descent of the Ladies Route should only be attempted if you can be sure there is no ice or if it is well snowed up. **780m**

(i) From the Mountet hut follow the path NW round the foot of the Mammouth. Once round its SW foot, climb NE alongside the Mammouth, starting with a boulder field, and higher up turn more NE to reach the tiny Besso glacier (not named on map).

(ii) From the Mountet hut follow Route 6c to about the height of the col at Pt 3,188m. Turn L and cross more bouldery ground to the col. Descend the other side on to a snow slope which can be icy and which leads in turn down on to the tiny Besso glacier.

Now cross the glacier and climb stony or névé slopes up to the rocks SW of the summit. On the L close to the highest reaches of névé is a chimney-couloir which gives easy access to the crest of the SW ridge at a point close to an inclined gendarme. Once on the crest follow it in its entirety to the final step. One steep gendarme can be turned on the R by making a slight descent and return to the crest via a chimney. A direct ascent of the final step is IV/IV+ but it is easier to turn this on the R to reach the summit. **4-5hr**

9b LADIES ROUTE
PD   First ascent party

11   Valley base: Zinal

Of no particular merit and much easier to ascend than descend as it is all rather sloping and belays are not easy to arrange. Desperate when verglassed and subjected to stonefall when other parties are on the route. The line of the route is often picked out by a narrow band of snow in a couloir running below and parallel to the SW ridge. The couloir leads to the SE ridge of the mountain at a small shoulder not too far below the summit. ***780m***

Approach as for Route 9a(i) or (ii). Climb the chimney-couloir until it is possible, at about half-height to traverse horizontally R to the foot of the couloir running parallel with the SW ridge. Climb up the couloir keeping on its L (NW) side as far as the SE ridge. Climb this ridge, keeping on the E side to the summit. **3½hr**

Schalihorn 3,974.5m

T Middlemore with C and J Lauener, 20 July 1873

This is the highest point on the ridge linking the Zinal Rothorn and the Weisshorn. It is infrequently climbed in its own right on account of its difficulty of access but a traverse of the peak does provide the safest approach route to the Schalijoch bivouac hut. This route is described below from the Rothorn hut. However, some people recommend an approach from the Mountet hut, traversing from l'Epaule on the Zinal Rothorn over both the Pts S and N de Moming as well as the Schalihorn (AD: 10-15hr). The E and W flanks of the mountain are of little interest to the climber although routes have been established on them. The two principal ridges are those orientated SSW and N, whilst a third ridge, the SE ridge, is said to give a pleasant climb (AD) with access from the Weisshorn hut via Stockji.

10a TRAVERSE SOUTH-NORTH
PD Valley base: Zermatt

12

The SSW ridge is mostly snow and is only F. The rest of the traverse down the jagged N ridge is on quite poor rock and is very time consuming. It might be advantageous to rappel at least one of the steps (bits of II and III). When standing on the S summit the N summit has the appearance of being higher. This is not the case, it is c20m lower. ***1,050m***

From the Rothorn hut follow Route 6d into the glacier combe below the Zinal Rothorn E face. Contour round the upper slopes of this combe then climb a steepish snow slope Nwards (some large crevasses) to the SE foot of Pt N de Moming. Continue up the glacier bay on the E side of this peak to the col at Pt 3,731m (Hohlichtpass: 3hr). Climb the broad but fairly steep snow ridge NNE to the S (main) summit, finishing on a narrower snow crest and a few rocks (1hr).

Continue N by climbing down to the gap on the N side of the summit block. Follow a weakly defined gangway on the E side of the ridge to a deep couloir. On the other side of the couloir climb up 10m then turn a tower, supporting a cairn, via a stony terrace. Continue on the ridge almost to the N summit (Pt 3,955m). Pass this on the E side to reach the gap beyond and then follow the crest for a few m to a formidable looking gendarme. Descend on the E side to pass this and the next few gendarmes before returning to the crest just before a Sphinx-like gendarme. Pass this on the E side to reach easier terrain and some snow which takes you to the last gendarme. Turn this on the E side as well via a stony terrace which is followed to where it peters out. Descend from here directly to rubble-strewn ledges which lead easily to the Schalijoch (3-5hr). Allow **8-10hr**

Schalijoch 3,750m

J Hornby and T Philpott with C Almer and C Lauener, 10 Aug 1864

Of no practical value as a crossing point, the only reason for visiting this isolated spot is to climb the Schaligrat on the Weisshorn. Conveniently a bivouac hut has been placed on the first rocks N of the col. There are three possible routes to the hut (excluding a descent of the Schaligrat); the route described above (10a), one from the Ar Pitetta hut and one from the Weisshorn hut.

11a WEST SIDE

AD Valley base: Zinal

14

This route should be avoided if there is any risk of avalanche. There is always risk of stonefall. **965m**

From the Ar Pitetta hut head E and cross the moraine on to the Weisshorn glacier. Continue in the same direction towards Pt 3,281m and reach a couloir on its N side. Climb this and reach the glacier bay above a zone of seracs. Cross the bay SE then cross the bergschrund and follow a slabby ramp (possibly snow covered) slanting up R below a steeper wall. This leads to a steep snow slope which is climbed to the col. **4-5hr**

11b EAST SIDE

AD Valley base: Zermatt

13

At the time of writing this route is quite impractical due to the state of the glacier. The route is described in case conditions improve.

It is a long and quite complicated approach especially after the walk to the Weisshorn hut from where the route starts. It crosses the Schali glacier which is split into two parts by the vast rock promontory falling from the E ridge of the Weisshorn. The route avoids the worst parts of the glacier but it is exposed to the stonefall from the SE face. This starts early in the morning so a very early start is advisable. It is worth examining the rock promontory beforehand: look for a wide couloir at about half-height which is the key to crossing the promontory. **c800m**

From the Weisshorn hut follow Route 12a across the rock rib by Pt 3,145m. Leave the route to the Weisshorn E ridge here and climb W up steepening slopes (crevasses) to pass below the rib projecting into the glacier below Pt 3,916m. Reach the rock barrier splitting the glacier at c3,400m in the region of the couloir mentioned above.

Cross the barrier by starting c50m L and below a tongue of snow slanting up from the glacier and which appears to offer a line of ascent. Climb the rocks straight up for c40m then cross a couloir on the L to some slabs which are usually running with water. Cross the slabs (with difficulty if verglassed) then climb straight up steep but easy rock to regain the glacier. Now climb up the glacier for c100m before traversing L and descending gradually and, after crossing a bergschrund, reach the rocks below Pt 4,057m at c3,600m. From here traverse broad stony terraces towards the col which is reached c50m above its low point. **c5hr**

Weisshorn 4,506m

J Tyndall with J Bennen and U Wenger, 19 Aug 1861

Considered by many to be the finest mountain in the Alps on account of its size and regular shape - three principal ridges and three faces, each of similar dimensions - and its relative isolation. Leslie Stephen in his masterpiece *The Playground of Europe* describes it as 'an almost faultless mountain'. The peak can be seen and instantly recognised from many distant viewpoints. The best climbing is along the ridges, the faces are exposed to objective dangers although the much neglected NE face is worth attention. Undoubtedly the most satisfying way of climbing the peak is to ascend one of the ridges and descend another, usually the E ridge will be chosen for descent. A not unpopular expedition is to make a double crossing of the summit - the Croix du Weisshorn. This involves climbing the Schaligrat (SSW ridge) and descending the NNW ridge (usually refered to as the N ridge) to the Tracuit hut. From there cross to the Ar Pitetta hut and climb the Younggrat and N ridge back to the summit before descending the E ridge to the Weisshorn hut. A and A Salamin completed this circuit in an astonishing 7½hr on 19 Aug 1981 although they missed out visiting the first two huts.

12a EAST RIDGE

AD First ascent party
13 Valley base: Zermatt
15

This is the ordinary route if any route on the mountain can be described as such. Parties attempting the route need to be physically fit and well acclimatised: it is a long and tiring climb. **1,575m**

From the Weisshorn hut follow the path NW to the E edge of the Schali glacier. Cross this almost horizontally towards a little snowy couloir cutting through the long rock rib close to Pt 3,145m. Now climb the snow slope on the W side of the rib to the rocks at the top. Move R across snow and slabs (II) on to a shoulder which may be scree or snow covered and forms the end of a short, broad rib. This rib lies at the bottom of a broad buttress originating at Pt 3,916m. The continuing line of ascent is further L up another fairly prominent rib: it is not via the couloir on the R. Climb up the shoulder to the foot of the wall a little higher. Climb straight up the wall for a few m then descend slightly L wards to a terrace (cairn). The whole of this section can be snow covered, as it was in summer 1997. Near the foot of the rib turn a steep wall on the L and then zigzag up the rib surmounting loose but short steps (well marked) as far as the lower rocks of the E ridge (beware stonefall from other parties: 3hr).

The first section of ridge has a succession of small towers. Follow the crest, which is slabby and possibly verglassed, to the first of these and turn it on the N side but after this traverse all the teeth except one of the early ones which is particularly steep and is turned on the S side (stakes). Franz Lochmatter, the famous guide, fell from here in 1933. The very last tooth is turned on the R (1hr).

The next section of ridge starts as a narrow and sometimes corniced snow ridge and then broadens and steepens. Climb the ridge without difficulty, passing Pt 4,178m to reach a bergschrund at c4,300m (½hr). The slope continues to steepen and is followed more or less directly to the summit where a few rocks may be encountered. Late in the season the upper slopes may be icy, in which case it is probably better to climb the rocks on the S side of the ridge, especially close to the summit (1-1½hr). **6-8hr**

12b SOUTH-SOUTH-WEST RIDGE - SCHALIGRAT

D E Broome with J Biner and A Imboden, 2 Sept 1895
14 Valley base: Zinal/Zermatt
13

An excellent climb on sound rock and in a wonderful setting: you are likely to have it to yourself. It is mainly a rock climb, at least in normal conditions. Fairly sustained with a few pitches of IV. 755m

From the Schalijoch bivouac hut climb the ridge, turning the first group of gendarmes on the R (E) side. Just above a particularly pointed gendarme return to the ridge at a snowy gap. From here keep to the ridge, traversing gendarmes (III and IV) or turning them on the R as seems appropriate until the ridge appears to peter out into the SSE face at about three-quarter height.

    On the L is a couloir leading down the W face. Cross the top of this couloir and climb directly up the SE face of the tower beyond. The remaining gendarmes are all linked by exposed snow crests and are all traversed. **5-7hr**

12c WEST FACE - YOUNGGRAT

D- G Young with B and L Theytaz, 7 Sept 1900
14 FWA: Probably S Albasini and C Portmann, 20 Jan 1989
Valley base: Zinal

The W face (or flank) of the Weisshorn appears to be nearly always in the shade. It is massive and seamed with ribs and couloirs which would suggest the possibility of a reasonable number of routes. Unfortunately it is a dangerous place and so there has been relatively little climbing activity, and what there is has been concentrated around the centre of the face, below the summit. One route in particular on this face stands out above all the others and it is the one described here. The most prominent feature on the N ridge is the

Grand Gendarme. Projecting W from this is a long rock rib which has become universally known amongst alpinists as the Younggrat (after Geoffrey Winthrop Young who pioneered the route and was otherwise particularly active on this mountain, making first ascents of four routes and descent of three others, apart from his efforts in other parts of Valais). It is a good climb on steep, slabby rock and although some of it is loose this occurs where the climbing is easy. At one time Zinal guides tried to popularise the route and placed a large number of stakes and fixed rope. Much of this equipment was removed in 1965 but some of the stakes remain in place and are particularly useful in descent. Only attempt the route after a spell of dry weather otherwise verglas will be a problem.

The route is thought to be a quick means of descent from the summit but the point where the N ridge is abandoned is not easy to locate without prior knowledge and so the route should only be considered for this purpose if you need to get off the N ridge quickly in a storm. ***1,720m*** *from the hut*

From the Ar Pitetta hut head up stony moraine slopes to reach the Weisshorn glacier on the N side of the continuation of the rib. Climb up the glacier passing Pt 3,575m and higher still cross the bergschrund. Reach the top of the snow slopes and the start of the rib (2½-3hr). Climb up easy but loose rock close to the edge of the rib which begins to steepen as the rock improves and the first of the stakes are found. Somewhat higher one is obliged to move L c20m by an imposing step in the ridge. Climb a steep wall c5m high (IV+ if done free) and then move back R (possibly snow) above the step. Now, for c200m, follow a series of slabs interspersed with easy ground. The slabs lead to the crest of the ridge. Here a fault line (chimney) leads R in 5m to the slabby couloir bordering the S side of the rib. Don't miss it! From the couloir make a rising traverse R for c70m (poor protection) to below the col immediately S of the Grand Gendarme. Climb more or less directly up to the col (3-4hr). Continue to the summit via Route 12d (1hr). **7-8hr**

Other West Face Routes

Various routes have been climbed on the face since the first in 1883. The easiest line (D) appears to be a combination of the three earliest ones. It starts high in the glacier bay N of Pt 3,281m and climbs on to the buttress on the R. Above this it follows a vague rib and then a couloir descending from the N ridge, c100m from the summit.

R Dittert, L Flory and F Marulaz, 26 July 1945, reached the rib above Pt 3,281m from the L. They followed the rib to where it joins the central snowfield. Here they slanted L to a second rib, and followed this until it steepened. They finished by slanting L again to join the N ridge about halfway between the Grand Gendarme and the summit (TD: sound rock but threatened by stonefall).

Another, more direct route, climbs the same rib at the start, but reaches this by a line starting up the couloir in the centre of the face, before accepting the challenge of the steep upper part of the face. It was climbed in winter by F and R Theytaz, 28/29 Feb and 1 March 1968. It has difficulties on rock up to V+ and is probably undergraded at TD. S Albasini and C Portmann, 20 Jan 1989, followed the same route but finished by a line to the L of the Theytaz route (TD).

The most recent and by far the most difficult route on the face was climbed by the Slovenians Z Petric and B Pockar, June 1996. It takes a fairly direct line up the stoneswept snowfield and mixed ground to the R of the 1968 Direct Route. It is 1,150m in height and has rock pitches of VI+ and ice between 60° and 75°. Unfortunately the pair disappeared later in the year whilst acclimatising on Kabru.

12d NORTH RIDGE
AD+ H Biehly with H Burgener, 21 Sept 1898
14 Valley base: Zinal
15 16

In reality this is the NNW ridge but all (at least all British) alpinists refer to it as the N ridge. It has to be one of the best climbs in the Alps and is definitely a classic. It is long (2km) and maintains a height of over 4,000m along its whole length from the summit of the Bishorn. It is not technically difficult (no more than III+), with what difficulties there are concentrated into the rock section which is about one quarter of the total length of the climb, but it should not be undertaken lightly. Escape from the ridge in poor conditions is not an appealing prospect so only set off on the crux section if you are convinced that the weather is going to remain fine. **450m** *from the Bishorn*

From the summit of the Bishorn, reached via Route 13a in c3hr, follow the snow ridge SSW down to the Weisshornjoch and then continue along the ridge to the flat rocks at Pt 4,203m and the start of the crux section. If there is a lot of snow on the rocks, serious consideration should be given to abandoning the climb here (½hr).

Descend the first step which is easy enough to down climb then follow the ridge, close to the crest, to a second step which can also be down climbed without much difficulty. A little further along the ridge reach a large tower which has to be turned. Do this on the L (E) side by a 10m traverse and then climb a dièdre-chimney for 20m (III+) to regain the crest. Continue to the saddle before the Grand Gendarme (Pt 4,331m). This can be turned fairly low on the E side across smooth slabs but this is not easy and any snow makes it particularly uninviting. It is better to climb it (or contour across its E face at about half-height). To do this traverse L for c5m then climb a dièdre and continuation chimney (III+) and then the ridge to the top. It is possible to traverse from the top of the chimney. Descent to the col on the S side by rappel (3-3½hr).

The ridge now turns to snow, is quite narrow in places and may be corniced. Climb it (brilliant!) to the summit cross (1hr). **7-9hr** from the Tracuit hut

12e NORTH-EAST BUTTRESS

TD O Smith and G Young with J Knubel, 31 Aug 1909
15 FWA: P Etter, U Gantenbein and A and E Scherrer, 29/30 Dec 1969
Valley base: Zermatt

The NE face of the Weisshorn, which has a height of almost 1,000m at its highest point, is divided into two parts by an ill-defined buttress descending from the summit. Most of the routes that have been climbed on the face are concentrated around this buttress since it provides the best protection from the bands of seracs which threaten the greater part of the face. The climb itself is quite elegant but at the same time rather tedious and is probably best ascended early in the season when snow conditions are likely to be at their best. It is always a serious undertaking. The approach to the foot of the route can be impossible on account of crevasses and seracs. The mean angle is 48°. **c1,000m**

From the Weisshorn hut follow the path NW to the edge of the Schali glacier. Head N up this, passing W of Pt 3,240m, to the saddle at Pt 3,468m. Further N is a ridge descending NE from Pt 3,782m. Cross this ridge by climbing the lower of two stony couloirs and have a good look from here to see if it is possible to reach the foot of the buttress. Cross the Bis glacier to the start of the climb at the foot of the buttress on its N side (3hr). This point can also be reached by crossing the Bisjoch from the Turtmann hut or from the Topali hut. In years of meagre snow cover the lower part of the buttress will be almost bare rock.

Climb the snow slope which is steep and broad at first but gradually narrows to a crest. Reach an icy nose which can be difficult and then continue at a gentler angle up a more open slope, avoiding any seracs as appropriate. Finish on the E ridge or continue by a direct line to the summit. **4-7hr** from the foot: up to **10hr** from the Weisshorn hut

12f EAST FACE OF NORTH-EAST BUTTRESS
TD G Bonfanti and R Quagliotto, 17 July 1983
15 Valley base: Zermatt

This route climbs the E flank of the buttress so the approach to the start is not usually a problem. It was considered at the time of the first ascent, done under cold and snowy conditions, to be a major ice climb. There are objective dangers on the first half of the climb which should be completed in the dark or very first light. It is a bit steeper than the previous route with a slope reaching c60°. The lower part of the buttress on the E flank is formed by a series of rock ribs separated by icy couloirs. The route starts up the L-hand couloir which is R of the broadest rib. ***c1,000m***

Approach the face as for Route 12e (3hr). Climb the couloir (mixed) to the snow/ice slope above and then slant up Rwards to reach the R side of the low profile rock rib which extends up the whole of the E flank of the buttress. Continue straight up to the crest of the buttress and join Route 13e to the summit. **6-8hr** from the foot: up to **11hr** from the Weisshorn hut

12g NORTH-EAST FACE DIRECT
D+/TD H Rouquette, P Gabarrou and P-A Steiner, 16 Sept 1980
15   although the route had previously been descended on skis:
M Burtscher and K Jeschke, 6 July 1978
Valley base: Zermatt

Essentially an ice climb with a slope varying in steepness between 45° and 55° and taking a very direct line to the summit, starting from the point on the L (N) side of the NE buttress where it merges into the rest of the face. Threatened by seracs from below the E ridge. ***c1,000m***

Reach the foot of the climb as for Route 12e. Start at the foot of the central avalanche runnel close to a rock wall on its L bank. Cross the bergschrund then slant R towards the edge of the rock wall and climb up alongside this and out of the line of fire of serac fall. Continue in a direct line, above the rocks, to the summit. There is the possibility of a steep pitch to pass a final serac barrier close to the summit. **c7hr** climbing: allow **10hr** from the Weisshorn hut

Bishorn 4,153m

G Barnes and R Chessyre-Walker with J Chanton and
J Imboden, 18 Aug 1884

In some ways the Bishorn appears no more than an elongation of the N ridge of the Weisshorn, to which it is linked by its short

SSW ridge above the Weisshornjoch, and thus a part of that mountain. From some viewpoints however, it can be seen to have a character and identity of its own. It has twin tops separated by a short snow crest with the lower one being a rocky point (Pt 4,135m) ENE of the true summit. Mrs E Burnaby (later to become Mrs Le Blond, founder of the Ladies' AC) climbed to this lower summit on 6 Aug 1884 with her guides J Imboden and P Sarbach and should probably receive the plaudits for the first ascent of the mountain. This lesser summit is now known as Pt Burnaby. For some reason they appear not to have visited the true summit. Of particular interest is the fact that this is one of very few mountains in which a female was seriously involved in the early exploration. The summit is a tremendous viewpoint, especially for the N ridge of the Weisshorn. Of interest to the alpinist are the NW flank, a gentle glacier slope, the E ridge which is worthy of much greater attention and the NE face.

13a NORTH-WEST FLANK
F First ascent party
16 Valley base: Zinal

One of the easiest routes to the summit of a 4,000m peak and climbed by all and sundry. **900m**

From the Tracuit hut walk on to the Turtmann glacier and cross this heading E to the reach the snowy saddle WNW of Pt 3,591m. Take care to avoid crevasses which lie in the direction of travel. From the saddle climb straight up the glacier SE to the saddle between the two summits. Now follow the crest steeply to the summit (possible cornice). **2½-3hr**

It is possible to climb this route from the Turtmann hut by following Route 17a towards the Bruneggjoch. Shortly before reaching the Bruneggjoch cross the Brunegg glacier to the foot of the rock rib E of Pt 3,591m (shown on the map as the point where the 3,200m contour line meets the rock). Climb this rib (marked at half-height by a vein of light coloured rock) to reach the Turtmann glacier and join the route from the Tracuit hut leading to the summit. The rib is quite unpleasant in descent! **5-6hr**

13b NORTH-EAST FACE

D E-R Blanchet with K Mooser and R Lochmatter, 21 Sept 1924
15 FWA: M Gamma, J Henkel and G Leutenegger, 23 Jan 1969
Valley base: Turtmanntal

This is an attractive yet complex snow/ice face c700m high. Its detail has changed quite markedly over the years with the relative lack of winter snow. It is basically a fairly even angled face, steepening towards the top (50°-55°) but distorted by a profusion of seracs, the principal band of which form a protective barrier across the foot of the face. The key to the route is in overcoming this serac band which can require the climbing of vertical ice. Parties wishing to climb the face must make their own judgement as to the best line. **670m**

From the Turtmann hut follow Route 17a towards the Bruneggjoch. Just before reaching this col slant across the Brunegg glacier to the foot of the face (3hr). Cross the serac band at the most convenient point and then climb the face above as direct as possible to the rocky E summit. **7-9hr** from the hut

Two routes have been climbed, solo, on the rocky R side of the face and avoiding the seracs, in both cases when the rocks were quite snowy. C Lukes, 4 June 1983, made an ascending traverse R on to the second rib R of the edge of the serac band. He climbed this until about level with the serac band and then made an ascending traverse back L to reach NW ridge at c4,000m. L Pigeau, 14 Aug 1987, took a more direct but exposed line following a couloir leading up towards the serac band which he turned by a straightforward snow slope.

13c EAST RIDGE

AD Mrs E Burnaby with J Imboden and P Sarbach, 6 Aug 1884
15 Valley base: Zermatt/Turtmanntal
16

This fine ridge descends E from the rocky E summit as far as Pt 3,939m where it splits. The major branch from the split leads ENE to the Bisjoch. An ascent of the ridge is a very worthwhile objective although it receives relatively little traffic on account of its remoteness. **610m**

From the Bisjoch, reached by Route 15a climb the ridge, which is part rock and part snow to Pt 3,939m. Above this point a fine snow crest leads to the foresummit at Pt 4,135m. Descend the crest on the other side to a snow saddle and continue on the steepening crest to the summit. **2½-3½hr** from the Bisjoch

Col de Milon 2,990m

This col facilitates the crossing between the Tracuit hut and the Ar Pitetta hut but is otherwise of little interest to the alpinist other than being a fine viewpoint. Recently the path linking the two huts has been upgraded.

14a SOUTH SIDE
F Valley base: Zinal

From the Ar Pitetta hut contour NW, at hut height, and cross a moraine then a stream to reach another moraine which leads N and is followed to the col. **45min-1hr** and **200m**

14b NORTH SIDE
W2 Valley base: Zinal

From the Tracuit hut descend the hut approach path towards Zinal. At a height of c3,000m turn S to pass Pt 2,794m and cross the stream S of this point. Beyond the stream continue more or less S to the col, finishing up steep slopes with a fixed chain. **2hr** and **290m**

Tête de Milon 3,693m

C Cannon and W Kippen with J and P Truffer, 23 Aug 1887

Valley base: Zinal

This peak is of no great interest except that it makes a good viewpoint and a reasonable training route. It can be climbed by its rocky WSW ridge from the Col de Milon (see Route 14a). The ridge has a number of gendarmes interspersed with slabs. The first gendarme can be passed on the L otherwise climb them all (III and IV). The last gendarme is descended on the R. Return to the valley by descending the snowy NW ridge (some big crevasses) to the Tracuit hut. **c10hr** round trip from the valley

Bisjoch 3,543m

Count de Burges and Baron de St Joseph with F Andenmatten and F Devouassoud, 31 July 1862

The col links the Brunegg glacier on its N side with the Bis glacier to the S and is the low point in the ridge connecting the Bishorn with the Brunegghorn. It is of little use as a crossing point but gives a possible means of connection between the Weisshorn hut and the Turtmann or Topali huts if the Bis glacier is passable (see Route 12e).

NORTH SIDE

15a Valley base: Zermatt/Turtmanntal
PD
17
16

Reach the Brunegggjoch from the Turtmann hut by Route 17a or from the Topali hut by Route 17b. From the col follow the snow slope between the NW ridge of the Brunegghorn and some rocks parallel to it just to the W then descend SW into the glacier bowl below the Bisjoch. Contour across the bowl and climb up a little glacier valley to the col. **4hr** from the Turtmann hut, **3½hr** from the Topali hut and **c1,000m** or **770m** respectively

Brunegghorn 3,833m

J and F Tantignoni with H Brantschen, 1853

A most impressive looking peak when viewed from the N or NE and a very fine viewpoint itself. It has three ridges which each provide enjoyable routes. Of the three faces, only the NNE provides any interest although a direct ascent of the W face is

SOUTH-WEST RIDGE

16a First ascent party
F Valley base: Zermatt/Turtmanntal
17

Although the ridge rises from the Bisjoch it is most often reached at a higher point, just E of the snow dome of Pt 3,671m. **470m**

From the Bruneggjoch climb the névé slopes on the W side of the NW ridge then contour round until directly N of the saddle in the ridge E of Pt 3,671m. Cross the bergschrund and climb up to the saddle. Continue up the ridge, keeping on its N side to avoid the cornice, to the summit (which will almost certainly have a cornice). **1½-2hr** from the Bruneggjoch: **c5hr** from either the Turtmann or Topali huts

NORTH-WEST RIDGE

16b A Cust, F Gardiner and F Wethered with H and P Knubel and
PD+ L Proment, 29 July 1876 in descent
17 Valley base: Zermatt/Turtmanntal

A quite narrow ridge which is mostly snow but there are three rock steps to overcome in an exposed position high up. The ridge is much harder when icy conditions prevail and the best line of ascent of the rock steps is not at all obvious. **470m**

From the Bruneggjoch climb straight up the ridge, which steepens as you progress, to the first step. Climb this and the two further steps on the SW side of the ridge and so reach the summit. **1½-2hr** from the Bruneggjoch: **c5hr** from either the Turtmann or Topali huts

NORTH-NORTH-EAST FACE

16c E-R Blanchet with K Mooser, 14 Aug 1925
TD Valley base: Zermatt
17

The route described here climbs only the upper, steeper (56°-58°) part of the face. The lower part lies E of the rocks below Pt 3,419m and was climbed by M Brandt and A and R Voillat, 24 July 1957 (AD). It is

entirely snow but usually turns to ice quite early in the season. **c250m**

From the Topali hut follow Route 17b towards the Bruneggjoch. Above the ice-fall on the upper plateau of the Abberg glacier head SE and follow a sort of glacier ramp, which slants up W to E below the face, until directly below the summit. Climb the face to the summit. **4-5hr** from the hut

NORTH-EAST RIDGE

16d Valley base: Zermatt

AD 17

The route described here is for the upper part of the ridge, that is above the point where the ridge bifurcates at Pt 3,590m. The ridge comes dramatically into view as you drive up the Zermatt valley road towards St Niklaus, taking the form of a beautiful but irregular snow crest. Considering its aesthetic appearance, it receives few ascents. This is probably because it appears on a relatively minor summit, were it on a 4,000m peak it would be much sought after. **c250m** *on the ridge*

From the Topali hut follow Route 16c on to the glacier ramp. Continue up the ramp to the point where it joins the NE ridge at a shoulder at c3,600m. Climb the ridge from here taking care to avoid any problems with cornices. There is one fairly steep section of c50m and a cornice might guard the summit. **4-5hr** from the hut

Bruneggjoch 3,365m

J Hornby and T Philpott with C Lauener and J Vianin, 30 July 1864

The col links the Abberg glacier on its E side with the Brunegg glacier to the W and lies between the Brunegghorn and Schöllihorn.

WEISSHORN CHAIN

17a WEST SIDE
F   Valley base: Turtmanntal

17
From the Turtmann hut follow a path SE to a rock barrier split by a narrow couloir (Gässi). Climb the couloir then continue on the path along the moraine on the R bank of the Brunegg glacier. Leave the moraine and move R to pass below Pt 3,071.9m and follow the E side of the glacier to reach the col. There are some large crevasses just prior to the col. If these are impassable climb the rocks above the E bank. **3hr** and **845m**

17b EAST SIDE
PD   Valley base: Zermatt

18
From the Topali hut follow a path S then turn up the Chella combe (small cairns and snow patches) aiming for the saddle at Pt 3,020m which is marked by a large block straddling the ridge. Descend a little on to the névé of the lower part of the Schölli glacier and contour round to the moraine E of Pt 3,182m. Now, keeping as high as possible, descend on to the edge of the Abberg glacier. Follow the L bank to the foot of the ice-fall and then climb this, usually without difficulty on to the upper plateau of the glacier. Easy slopes lead to the col. If the ice-fall is difficult (maybe late in the season), pass it via the broken rocks on the R side (there is a marked route). **2½hr** and **690m**

An alternative route (and this appears to be the preferred route by most parties in any conditions) is to climb to the Schöllijoch (see below) and contour the W side of the Schöllihorn to the pass. Same time

Schöllijoch 3,343m

Marked on the map by a spot height but no name, it lies between the Schöllihorn and the Inners Barrhorn. A useful crossing point for connecting the Turtmann and Topali huts and also gives easy access to the summit of the Schöllihorn by way of its NW ridge and the Inners Barrhorn by its SSW ridge.

18a WEST SIDE
F Valley base: Turtmanntal

From the Turtmann hut follow Route 17a to the point where it descends on to the Brunegg glacier. Then climb the R bank of the névé slopes leading towards the col, which is reached by a snowy couloir and a few rocks. **2-2½hr and 825m**

18b EAST SIDE
F Valley base: Zermatt

From the Topali hut follow Route 17b to the Schölli glacier. Climb the glacier and a steep snow slope to the col. **2hr and 670m**

Barrhörner 3,583m and 3,610m

Mrs E Jackson with A Pollinger and M Truffer, 1 Sept 1883

Twin peaks separated by a c700m interconnecting ridge. The Inners Barrhorn to the S is the lower of the two. Fairly uninteresting in appearance when viewed from the W where they present stone and snow covered slopes that can be climbed almost anywhere. The traverse of the peaks is a pleasant enough excursion that can be undertaken from either the Turtmann hut or the Topali hut and is worth climbing for the views alone.

19a TRAVERSE NORTH-SOUTH
PD Valley base: Zermatt/Turtmanntal

The climb is only F from the Turtmann hut. **c1,200m** *from the Turtmann hut:* **1,025m** *from the Topali hut*

(i) From the Turtmann hut follow Route 17a to the top of the Gässi couloir. Just beyond this climb NNE to Pt 3,057m and then follow the rounded ridge all the way to the summit of the Üssers Barrhorn (3hr).

(ii) From the Topali hut the aim is to reach the Barrjoch (not named on map) which lies between the Üssers Barrhorn and the

Gässispitz and can be clearly seen from the hut. Head W from the hut along vague tracks on to the Unt Stelli glacier. Climb the glacier towards the couloir descending from the Barrjoch, passing R of the ice-fall. Either climb the couloir (easy in good snow conditions but some stonefall) or continue SSW up the edge of the glacier to the foot of a ramp starting at c3,200m which slants up to the col. Climb the ramp to the col. From the col climb the steep snow slope of the N face to the summit (2½-3hr).

Follow the broad ridge SSE to the summit of the Inners Barrhorn (½hr) and then descend the SSW ridge to the Schöllijoch (Pt 3,343m). Return to the Turtmann hut via Route 18a or to the Topali hut via Route 18b. **c6hr** hut to hut

Mettelhorn 3,406m

This peak overlooks Zermatt from the NNW and is a wonderful view point. Frequently ascended as a training walk (beware of blisters).

20a FROM THE TRIFT GORGE
W2 Valley base: Zermatt

From the centre of Zermatt follow the path up the Trift gorge to the Berggasthaus Trift (Pt 2,337m). Continue along the route towards the Rothorn hut but turn R off this by the path leading into Triftchumme. Climb this path all the way to the snow just E of Pt 3,166m. Cross easy névé slopes Ewards, passing a subsidiary peak on its W side to join a path leading steeply to the summit. **4-6hr** and **c1,800m**

Breithorn - Liskamm Chain
Theodulpass to the Lisjoch

This group of high and snowy peaks provides an impressive frontier between Switzerland and Italy and is well seen from the Gornergrat and the Stockhorn.

The 3km long summit ridge of the Breithorn (4,165m) dominates the view. There are five distinct high points, all exceeding 4,000m. The impressive N face gives several routes of high standard on steep, mixed terrain. Two of these are classics which can be approached from the Gandegg hut.

Since the construction of the cable car lift to the Klein Matterhorn (3,883m) in 1979, the Breithorn has become the easiest 4,000er in the Alps. However one should not be too complacent. Lives have been lost due to the sudden onset of white-out conditions even on the easy SSW flank.

The southern aspect of the mountain is in sharp contrast to the northern side, being of relatively easy snow slopes. The Mezzalama and Valle d'Ayas guides' huts provide access from the Italian side. Also on the S side the Quintino Sella hut may be used for ascents of Castor (4,228m) and Pollux (4,092m) - the 'twins'. Though small by comparison to their near neighbours an ascent or traverse of these peaks demands more commitment, skill and attention. The glaciers to the N, the Zwillings and the Schwärze glaciers are badly crevassed, therefore this line of approach is not often used, but the long N ridge of Pollux, which divides these glaciers, may be ascended from the Monte Rosa hut. Otherwise, for climbers based in Zermatt, the southern flanks of the Breithorn must be crossed from the Klein Matterhorn to reach the peak.

To the SE of Castor is the Felikjoch. The frontier then follows the SW ridge of the Liskamm to its western summit (4,527m). This huge mountain has been variously described over the years as 'beautiful', 'magnificent', 'gothic', 'a man-eater', 'feared', and so on, but it no longer 'devours fearful climbers', at least not so frequently as in times past when the

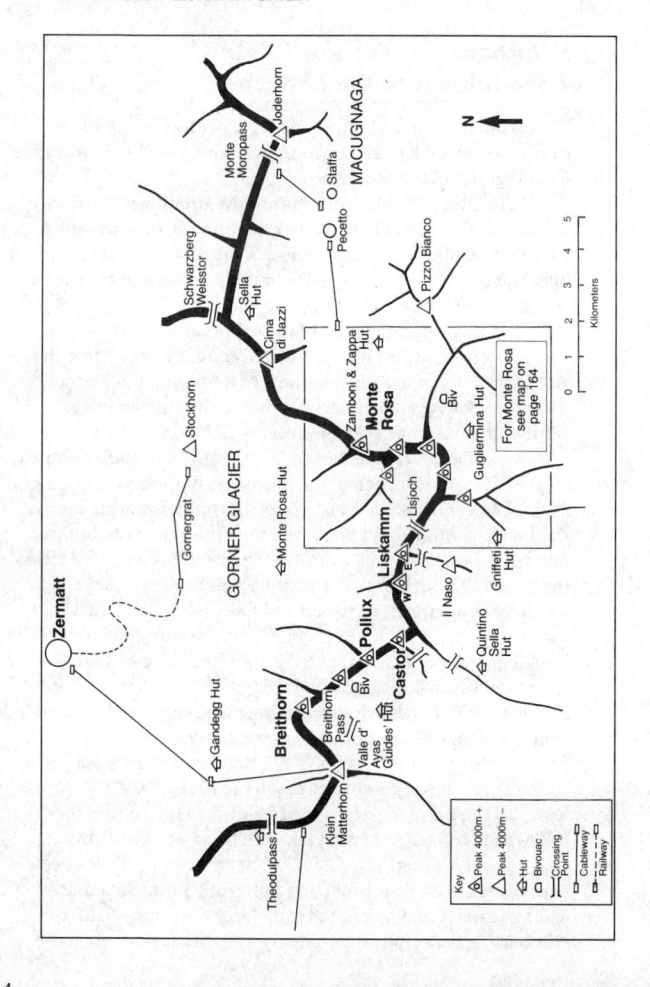

BREITHORN - LISKAMM CHAIN

E ridge was notorious for double cornices which were very difficult to avoid. Such dangerous snow structures no longer seem to form. The mountain, however, remains a serious and prized objective. The traverse of its two summits, usually from E to W, is by far the most popular and is a very fine expedition. The impressive and lengthy Swiss flanks overlooking the Grenz glacier offer serious ice routes, some of which are exposed to avalanche from seracs and are for experienced alpinists only.

At the foot of the E ridge of the Liskamm is the Lisjoch (4,151m) an important pass over the frontier, providing a direct connection between the Monte Rosa hut and the Gnifetti hut. During the Second World War this pass together with the Theodulpass, served as an escape route for refugees fleeing from Italy to seek shelter in neutral Switzerland. Unfortunately, the dangerous and extensive Grenz glacier claimed many victims, particularly during the winter months.

Theodulpass 3,301m

Used as a crossing point for many centuries, possibly as far back as Neolithic times. Roman coins and weapons have been found in the glacier.

The easiest crossing point of the frontier ridge between the Grand St Bernard pass and the Monte Moropass. The Theodule hut is situated just above the pass on its N side.

21a ITALIAN SIDE
F Valley base: Cervinia

(i) Most people will use the téléphérique from Cervinia (Breuil) to the Testa Grigia (3,479m) and walk more or less N wards down to the pass utilising the Theodule glacier, joining a ski piste part way down. ¼**hr** or less

(ii) On foot from Cervinia follow footpaths passing first of all the Albergo Monte Cervino and then Plan Torette. Continue ENE and then E to the Cappella Bontadini. Almost the whole of the route follows the line of some ski-installations. Keep below the last ski-tow and reach the small glacier on the W side of the pass, crossing some stony terrain in the process, and climb this to the pass. It should also be possible to follow the line of the last ski-tow to reach the ridge a little way above the Theodule hut. **c4hr** and **c1,300m**

21b SWISS SIDE
F Valley base: Zermatt

(i) It is possible to make use of the téléphérique from Zermatt to Trockener Steg and from there go on foot to the pass. From the lift station a marked path leads S to the Gandegg hut. From here a path leads SSW as far as the Oberer Theodule glacier. Cross the possibly crevassed glacier heading SW before following the line of a ski-tow or the adjacent piste. Finally reach the pass after skirting round the E side of the Theodulhorn. Allow **2hr** from Trockener Steg: **c380m**

The Gandegg hut can be reached on foot from Zermatt by following the roadway or footpaths to Furi and then the footpath leading first to Furgg and then the hut. c3½hr to the hut and a further 1½hr to the pass

(ii) Affluent people might prefer to use the téléphérique from Zermatt to the Klein Matterhorn and walk to the pass from there. From the lift station walk down to the saddle at Pt 3,796m. From here descend SW to a steepening of the glacier slope which can then be descended almost in the fall-line (crevasses) until the slope eases. Alternatively, where the slope steepens, follow a prepared piste which makes a long, sweeping curve to reach the foot of the slope. From here turn NW and continue the descent to the Testa Grigia alongside a ski-tow. Continue more or less N down the glacier to the pass. **1-1½hr**

Klein Matterhorn 3,880m

H de Saussure with J-M Couttet, J-B Erin and five other guides, 13 Aug 1792

A fairly insignificant summit although its appearance from the Zermatt side is quite distinct. Its value as a climbing venue has been spoiled by the development of the téléphérique station on its flanks. Nevertheless two routes, although infrequently climbed, appear to be worthwhile.

22a NORTH-WEST RIDGE

AD B Neuhaus with A and O Supersaxo, 27 July 1904
19 FWA: A Biancardi and G Gandolfo, 11 Jan 1948
Valley base: Zermatt

An interesting mixed route somewhat spoiled in its upper part by the construction of the lift station which has effectively ruined the final part of the ridge. **1,000m**

From the Gandegg hut descend the cliff path to the Unterer Theodule glacier then head more or less S to the rock island at Pt 3,095m. Turn the island on its W side and then follow snow slopes above, heading SSE to gain the rocks at the NW end of the snow ridge descending NW from Pt 3,758m. Climb the rocks on the R to gain the snow crest. Continue to the summit by following the easy ridge which is littered with construction materials. **3½-4hr**

22b NORTH-EAST FACE

D B Bich and G Gandolfo, 28 July 1948
19 Valley base: Zermatt

This is said to be a good climb on sound rock with pitches of IV and V. The first ascent party used numerous pitons, only one remains in place so several need to be carried. **1,000m**

From the Gandegg hut follow Route 22a to a height of c3,450m before traversing L to the foot of the face. Start up slabs, possibly interspersed with bands of snow or ice, to reach a break line slanting up L. Follow this weakness for 50m and then cross a snow/ice couloir. This is the couloir clearly indicated on the map immediately N of the lift station. Follow a ramp line, which may be snow or ice covered, leading up to the steep headwall and climb this free (exposed). Complete the climb up an icy couloir. The first ascent party, in poor conditions, took **7hr** from the foot of the wall

Breithorn 4,164m

H Maynard with J-M Couttet, J-B and J-J Erin and J Gras, 13 Aug 1813

A big mountain with a long crest running roughly E - W and which is continually above 4,000m. At the E end of the ridge is the Roccia Nera (4,075m) and between this and the main summit are three other identifiable tops. These are Gendarme 4,106m, Breithorn E (4,139m) and Breithorn central (4,159m).

There is a great contrast between the N and S flanks of the mountain. The S flank is predominantly snowy and not very high, rising only 250m-350m above a glacier terrace. Climbing on this flank should be avoided after about mid-day when it can become quite soft and dangerous. The N flank in contrast is high, steep and a complex of snow, ice and rock.

23a SOUTH-SOUTH-WEST FLANK

F First ascent party
20 FWA: A Bürcher, J Seiler and M Stockalper, 21 Jan 1888
21 Valley base: Cervinia/Zermatt

One of if not the most frequented route in the Alps, made easy by the availability of mechanical aids on both Italian and Swiss sides of the mountain. Most people make use of the lift systems and climb the mountain in a day from the valley but the purist will start from either the Theodule hut, the Cervinia guides' hut or the Gandegg hut. In summer there is usually a well worn piste from the Breithornplateau which is easy to follow. However, care must be taken in misty conditions in these parts since the terrain is fairly featureless and, if the trail is lost or becomes obscured in any way, relocation is not easy. The summit slopes are quite steep, sometimes icy and there may be an occasional crevasse. **370m** *from the snow saddle*

(i) From the Gandegg hut follow Route 21a to the Theodulpass and then reverse Route 21b to the broad snow saddle at Pt 3,798m. **c2½hr**

(ii) From the Theodule hut join the same route at the pass. **c1½hr**

(iii) From the Cervinia guides' hut at the Testa Grigia lift station join the same route by a short descent on to the glacier. **c1hr**

(iv) From the Klein Matterhorn lift station walk out of the tunnel and along the ridge to the snow saddle. **10min**

From the broad snow saddle walk E towards the Breithornpass but before reaching it turn NE up the steepening S flank of the mountain. As the angle increases turn NW and head for the SW ridge which is followed to the summit. To avoid crowds, instead of turning towards the SW ridge it is just as easy to slant up NE to reach the ESE ridge close to Pt 4,076m from where the summit is easily attained. **c1½-2hr** from the snow saddle

23b NORTH-WEST AND SOUTH-WEST FLANKS

AD G Prothero with G Taugwalder, 27 July 1888

23
22 Valley base: Zermatt

A much more sporting approach from the Gandegg hut is to climb by way of the buttress that forms the R bank of the upper part of the Unterer Theodule glacier. This route avoids the seracs of the upper part of the Triftji glacier but it would be prudent to have an inspection of the route beforehand to ensure that the passage above the last rocks is itself free from serac danger. The line of ascent can be clearly seen from the Gandegg hut. **c1,300m**

From the hut descend the cliff path on to the glacier and cross it SE to the snow slope below Pt 3,167m. Climb the narrowing snow slope to gain the crest of the buttress. Follow it on both rock and snow, the final steep snow/ice slope leads up to the glacier below Pt 3,696m. Cross the glacier Swards and then climb to a snow shoulder at the foot of the SW ridge. Join Route 23a for the climb to the summit. **5-6hr**

Breithorn: North and North-North-West Face of the Main Summit

A large and complex face with both rock and ice features with a mean angle of 51°. Much of it is threatened by seracs. The lower part of the face, on the R (W), is formed by the much crevassed upper arm of the Triftji glacier above which there is an irregularly shaped rock buttress. The buttress itself is separated from a higher rock band by a slanting snow/ice ramp, the rock band itself being overhung by seracs. On the L side the Triftji glacier is bounded by a steep rock wall which is separated from the rock buttress by a steep snow/ice couloir. The bounding rock wall is topped by a glacier slope with a multitude of seracs below half-height. The upper part of this slope is more even snow/ice interspersed with rocks. The E boundary of the face is the Triftjigrat, the line of a justifiably classic route. Most of the routes on the face have probably had more winter ascents than summer ones.

23c BETHMANN-HOLLWEG ROUTE
TD D von Bethmann-Hollweg with O and O Supersaxo, 3 Sept 1919
23
22 Variation start: Fr Bachschmidt, F Rigele and W Welzenbach, 1 Aug 1926
FWA: C Mauri and E Peyronel, 20 March 1955
Valley base: Zermatt

Probably the route on the face least exposed to falling ice but nevertheless the danger still exists. Good ice climbing with some difficulties on sound rock. **c1,100m**

From the Gandegg hut follow Route 23b to the crest of the buttress above Pt 3,167m before finding a way to cross the upper part of the Triftji glacier to the bounding wall on its E side. Depending on the state of the Triftji glacier it may be safer to follow the Welzenbach variation which climbs the R bank of the glacier below the E bounding wall to reach the couloir by which it is climbed. Surmount this wall by means of a couloir to the L of the steep snow/ice couloir separating this wall from the rock buttress on the R or climb the snow/ice couloir itself. The latter alternative may be subjected to some stonefall. The route continues up fairly steep snow/ice slopes to a bergschrund. Cross this and reach the final obstacle which is the rock band guarding the summit. Climb this or, more easily, the mixed ground further L before snow slopes lead to the top. **8-10hr**

23d BETHERMIN-GABARROU ROUTE
TD-/TD M Bethermin and P Gabarrou, 29 Sept 1979

23 Valley base: Zermatt

A very direct line up the face but seriously exposed to the dangers of seracs. The first ascent party experienced 'quasi' winter conditions. **c1,100m**

From the Gandegg hut follow Route 23e to the glacier bowl below the Triftjisattel. On the R is a rock buttress below Pt 3,335m. Climb the buttress by the rib on its L (E) side, thus avoiding the seracs, to gain the glacier slopes above. Higher up is a band of overhanging seracs. Climb up to this serac band via snow and mixed terrain before moving L to find a way past or through the seracs. Higher up the slope is a rock barrier. Climb it on its R side (mixed) and then trend Lwards to reach easier mixed ground and the summit snow slopes. **8-9hr**

Other routes on this face include two which climb the irregularly shaped rock buttress below the slanting snow/ice ramp. The rock is quite sound and provides some good mixed climbing but is seriously threatened by the serac band below the summit. R Arnold and M Ineichen, 29 July 1974, climbed a wandering line R of centre on the buttress before following the slanting ramp L to breach the uppermost rock barrier (TD/TD+). On 5 Aug 1994 the Slovenians Z Petric and B Pockar took a more direct line. They had dry rock and were able to climb the buttress in rock boots. They called the route Black Panther (ED2: VII-: 85°: 12hr). A few weeks earlier (on 25 June) Pockar, this time with P Meznar, climbed a route, entitled Karatanska (ED1:VI-), which climbs above the E bounding wall of the Triftji glacier, reached low down, and with an 80° ice pitch at the top of the initial seracs. It then skirts the L edge of the main buttress, this section giving some sustained climbing to join the finish of the Arnold/Ineichen Route.

23e TRIFTJIGRAT

D R Fowler with P Knubel and G Ruppen, 15 Sept 1869

23 FWA: G Airoldi, G Brignolo, A Mellano and R Perego, 18 March
22 24 1962

Valley base: Zermatt

Although the name suggests a ridge, a lot of the climbing is on quite open slopes. It is a classic route with varied climbing and some very fine situations, but not entirely free from objective dangers. Although longer, it has been compared with the N buttress of the Aig du Chardonnet. **920m** *from the Triftjisattel*

From the Gandegg hut descend the cliff path on to the Unterer Theodule glacier. Head SE across the glacier towards the rocks of Pt 2,982m. Pass the rocks on the R and then descend the Triftji glacier to a height of c2,880m before crossing it to reach the E branch of the glacier which descends in a NWerly direction from the Triftjisattel. (Note that both seracs and the state of the glacier make it easier and safer to descend after Pt 2,982m rather than taking a higher traverse line). Climb up this branch on its R (N) bank until below the Triftjisattel (not named on the map) which is situated to the S of Pt 3250.6m (Triftji: 2-2½hr)

Keep on snow on the W side of the rocky ridge before getting on to the ridge at the first break in the rocks. Follow it to the first snow shoulder. Climb this on the L or R on steep snow or ice. Continue to a steepening snow slope and climb this on the L to rocks which allow further easy progress. Continue easily to a snow crest which in turn leads to a glacier terrace (Triftjiplateau). Above are the summit slopes (2-2½hr).

Move R on the terrace, cross the bergschrund and climb the steep snow/ice slope (55°) to the most prominent rock rib. Climb this, on excellent holds, then more snow to a higher rock band. This can be climbed direct but it is usually simpler to pass it on the L and reach the easier summit snow slopes (2-3hr). **7-9hr** in all

If the final slopes are found to be too icy it may be possible to make an alternative finish further E. The Triftjiplateau is dominated by a zone of seracs and the route finds its way round these to their L (E). Instead of moving R along the terrace continue more or less S to reach their bounding L edge. Climb a sort of ramp which slants up Rwards until above the seracs (some steep steps) and continue to the summit up steep, E facing snow slopes. 2-3hr

Breithorn: Central Summit 4,159m

A snowy summit separated from the main summit to the W by the saddle at 4,076m. Although the summit itself, its W ridge and its SW face are snowy, its N face is of steep rock interspersed with icy couloirs above a very steep glacier slope. A number of mixed and ice routes have been climbed on the face, all quite serious. The SE face of this top is also mostly rock and presents at least one worthwhile climb. Its E ridge is mostly rock rising in three main steps. The highest of these forms a sort of rock summit to complement the higher snow summit and is given the name 'Torrione Maggiore'. The ascent of the E ridge is described in the Traverse of the Breithorn (Route 23w).

23f SOUTH-SOUTH-WEST SPUR

PD E-R Blanchet and R Chaubert with K Mooser, 17 Aug 1925
21
20 Valley base: Cervinia/Zermatt

A straightforward snow climb leading directly to the summit up the spur forming the S boundary of the SE face. **350m**

Reach the foot of the spur by following Route H15. Cross the bergschrund and climb the snow slope keeping to the L of the rocks. **2-2½hr** from the Breithornpass

North Face of Central Summit

There are two possible approach routes to the face which rises above the upper part of the Breithorn glacier. The first starts from the Gandegg hut and crosses the Triftjisattel before descending on to the W side of the glacier. This is the longer approach and is probably favoured by Swiss based climbers. The alternative and favoured approach is from the Rossi and Volante bivouac hut via the Schwarztor and requires less effort. It joins the E side of the Breithorn glacier from the Kl Triftjisattel. Most routes on the face involve c800m of climbing. The lower half of the face is a steep glacier slope interrupted by crevasses and serac bands which at times can be almost impossible to climb directly. Above this is a steep rock wall which has a complex of icy goulottes and steep buttresses and is often capped by a cornice.

23g ORIGINAL ROUTE

D+ F Serbelloni with E and O Frachey, Aug 1953
24 FWA: G Ferrari and A Sioli, 21/22 March 1970
22 Valley base: Champoluc/Zermatt/Cervinia

Although this is one of the less difficult routes on the face it is typical of each of them in that there is a long, steep and crevassed glacier slope to climb to reach the head-wall. On the head-wall this particular climb is predominantly mixed in nature. Take care with the rock, which may well be verglassed. **c850m**

Reach the upper part of the Breithorn glacier as for Route 23m(i) or (ii). High above the W side of this glacier are the seracs forming the base of the Triftjiplateau (see Route 23e). Climb the steepening, crevassed glacier slope, keeping well L of the bounding rocks of the Triftjigrat, until level with and L of the seracs of the Triftji plateau. Move up Rwards on to the upper, E edge of the Triftjiplateau. Directly above is a steep, snowfilled couloir. Climb this to a break in the rocks on the L and then follow the break, slanting up Lwards for 2 pitches (mixed). Finish the route by climbing up steepish rocks and the snow slope above, finally finding an appropriate way through or past the cornice at the top. **6-8hr** according to conditions from the foot of the glacier slope

23h DESSERT SEMI-FREDDO
D+
24
22

L Bordoni and G Grassi, 18 July 1985
Valley base: Champoluc/Zermatt/Cervinia

One of Grassi's many routes on the N side of the mountain. There are several variations to the route described. Similar in nature to Route 23g, which it crosses in its upper part and is sometimes finished via that route, except that on the head-wall the climbing is mostly on ice. There is always some danger from falling ice. **c850m**

Follow Route 23g on to the Triftjiplateau. Climb directly up the rocks on the L to a steep, icy ramp which slopes up Rwards. Cross the ramp by moving up Lwards and then, from its upper edge, climb more rocks to a second icy ramp. Cross this in the same way and gain a steep, snowy area further L. Climb up this (60°-65°) and then head Rwards to the foot of a narrow, little icy couloir. Climb the couloir as far as a snowy rib and then get into another couloir slanting up R and follow this until it narrows into a goulotte. Continue up this to its end (60/70°) and then climb up to some rocks below a higher rock rib. Climb these for a few m then slant L across ice (55°) to the last rocks above which a snow rib leads to the top. **c8hr** from the foot of the glacier slope

23i VIAGGIO DI ORDINARIA FOLLIA

TD G Grassi, B Maihot and E Tessera, 24 May 1984
24 Valley base: Champoluc/Zermatt/Cervinia
22

Another Grassi route and almost entirely on ice. The line is quite complicated but essentially it follows the narrow goulotte R of the Gabarrou-Steiner Route (23j). **c850m**

Follow Route 23g to just below the E edge of the Triftjiplateau. Slant up L close to the rocks to the foot of an icy ramp slanting up to the R (crossed higher up by Route 23h). Climb the slope above the ramp to a steep ice slope. Cross this Lwards before traversing horizontally to reach a goulotte which cuts through a smooth rock-band. Climb the goulotte (70°) then move back Rwards until directly above the start of the initial ramp. Now climb straight up, at first on icy rocks, then a steepening ice slope (up to 70°) and finally a narrow and very steep goulotte (80°).

Now, on less steep ground, reach an ice slope interspersed with rocks. Head up Rwards to the main goulotte and climb this (70°) then a short, steeper section before moving up a Rward slanting snow ramp which leads to a branch of the main goulotte. The route from here is up a short couloir, blocked off at its top, and not up the goulotte. At the top of the couloir an icy slab leads L (70°) to the R edge of the main goulotte's continuation. Climb the edge to a good belay and then get back into the goulotte and follow it Rwards to the final snow slope. Climb this and exit where the cornice is most easily surmounted. **8-10hr** from the foot of the glacier slope

23j GABARROU-STEINER ROUTE

TD P Gabarrou and P-A Steiner, 17 Sept 1979
24 FWA: C Portmann and P Torrents, 5 Jan 1993
22 Valley base: Champoluc

A very direct line to the summit and more or less safe from serac fall. Gabarrou's first of two new routes on the mountain in 12 days. Mostly snow/ice climbing. **c850m**

Reach the upper part of the Breithorn glacier as for Route 23m(i) or (ii). Start directly below the summit up relatively easy snow slopes which are interrupted by short steep steps and reach the bergschrund. Cross this, with some difficulty, and continue straight up into a couloir at the head of the slope which is directly below a compact and slightly overhanging rock wall and R of the lowest rocks. Climb the couloir, ice at first and then mixed, before slanting up R on icy slopes to pass the rock wall (crux). Carry on up snow/ice slopes and then a major goulotte with some steep steps to the final slope. Two pitches lead to the summit. **8-10hr**

23k GOULOTTE SPETTRO GLAUCO
TD/TD+ G Grassi, V Ravaschietto and A Siri, 24 July 1985
24
22
Valley base: Champoluc/Zermatt/Cervinia

This was Grassi's third route on the face and was undertaken only six days after he climbed Desert Semi-Freddo. Compared with that route however it is of quite different character. The terrain here, at least in the difficult sections, is more mixed. Protection is difficult to place and thus the climbing is quite committing. c850m

Reach the upper part of the Breithorn glacier as for Route 23m(i) or (ii). Climb the steepening glacier slope towards the lowest rocks of the upper face. There may be some steep steps to overcome before reaching the main difficulties. Cross the last bergschrund below and L of the couloir at the head of the slope referred to in Route 23j and climb steeply up ice to an icy ramp leading up Lwards through rocks. Follow the ramp for two pitches (55/65°) then move back R and climb a series of steps to a steeper and larger one. Climb this via a narrow goulotte (70°) and then slant up L to a snow/ice slope. Climb this and cross a slight barrier before continuing straight up snow/ice to reach the L side of a small crag.

    Climb a narrow goulotte (60/65°) on the left to the base of a steep snow/ice slope. Climb this slope directly to the foot of a major goulotte which is then followed for three pitches up its twisting bed. On the last pitch it may be necessary to use the rocks on the R. All this is between 60° and 75°. Now leave the goulotte on rock, at first traversing horizontally Rwards and then straight up to a large detached block (IV and IV+).

Above is another snow/ice slope which is climbed slanting up R to a rock rib. From here keep traversing R across mixed rock and ice to a belay on the ice slope beyond: all quite hard. Next descend gradually Rwards (55°) before traversing further R on difficult mixed ground (V) to a big rift. On the R of this is the goulotte of Route 23j. Climb to the top of a parallel goulotte further L (60/70°) and then get on to the rocks on the R. Traverse almost horizontally to gain the goulotte just mentioned and climb this for 40m. Reach the summit by climbing another pitch up the goulotte and a final pitch up a short crest. Allow at least **12hr**

Another route (Manera Route), thought to be good value, climbs to the rocky fore-summit (Torre Maggiore). Climbed by L Castiglia, P Crivellaro, U Manera, C Persico and L Pezzica, 7 Sept 1980 and graded TD/TD+. It climbs the glacier slope to pass on the E side of a rognon, above which it gains the foot of a rib which is sheltered from icefall. The rib has rock difficulties up to V+ and A1 as well as some mixed climbing.

Despite the congestion of routes on the face parties still manage to find new lines. In the very snowy summer of 1997 the Slovenians T and U Golob and D Polenik climbed a route they entitled Nektar: ED2: 28 July 1997. The line of the route is not known but is reported to have difficulties up to the modern ice grade of V/6 with mixed/rock of IV+. It was probably only due to the exceptionally snowy conditions that the line was climbable.

231 CENTRAL SPUR OF SOUTH-EAST FACE
AD E Cavalieri, G Cerri, G Dagnino and G Migliorino, Aug 1964
21 Valley base: Cervinia/Zermatt

Pleasant climbing on good rock. **250m**

Reach the foot of the face by Route H15. The route starts up the

Descending the Arbengrat on the Ober Gabelhorn
(Route 3c) Les Swindin

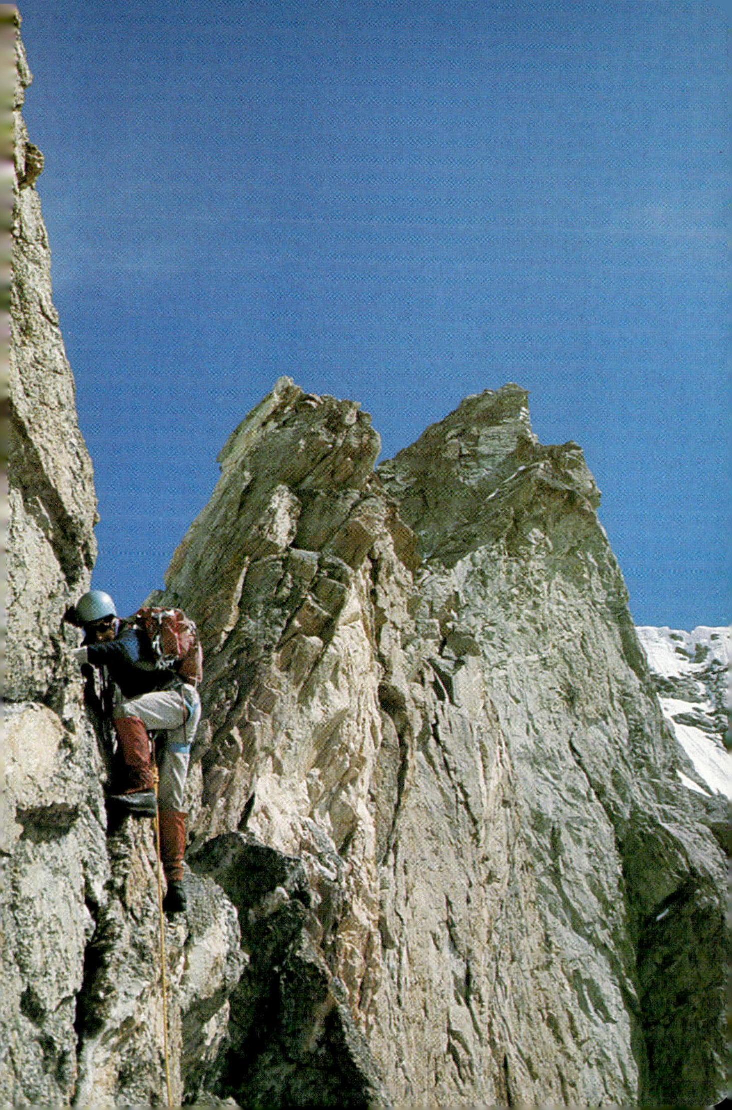

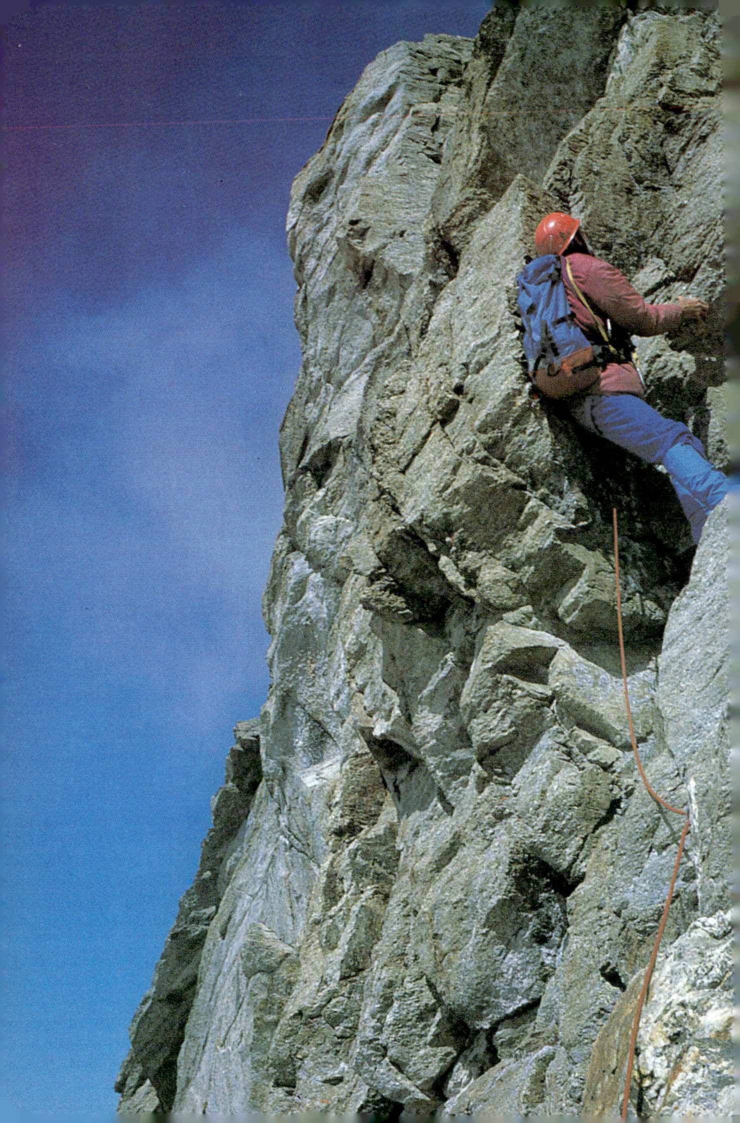

large buttress in the middle of the face whose R side sits at the foot of the longest snow ramp slanting up to the SSW spur. Cross the bergschrund and steep snow slope above to the rocks. Climb these to reach the snow slope above the buttress. Cross the snow slope by slanting up steeply Lwards to the main spur above, which lies directly in line with the summit. Climb this to a short dièdre and exit from this by a delicate move R (III). Continue up the rib on slabby rock to a steeper step which is passed on the R via a small rib. Broken rocks now lead up to the final snow slope, climbed by a snow crest. **c4hr** from the Breithornpass

Breithorn: East Summit 4,139m

The S flank is almost entirely snow with just a short rock buttress forming the summit and can be climbed almost anywhere. The WNW ridge forms part of the Breithorn traverse route, as does the short SE ridge. Most dramatic is the N flank which is mostly of rock split by a massive snow filled couloir which is clearly indicated on the map. Projecting from the face is a long ridge terminating c2km N on the Gorner glacier. The upper part of this ridge is the line of the Younggrat route. Several routes and variations to these have been climbed on this flank and three of these are described here.

23m YOUNGGRAT

D   R Mayor, C Robertson and G Young with J Knubel and
25 M Ruppen, 18 Aug 1906
22 FWA: P Aredi and V Lazzarino, 24/28 Feb 1963
Valley base: Zermatt/Champoluc/Cervinia

A long and serious classic climb with the main difficulties near the top. Mainly snow and ice but with some enjoyable rock as well as some difficult mixed climbing. **c640m** *from the Kl Triftjisattel*

(i) From the Gandegg hut follow Route 23e to the Triftjisattel. From the saddle descend c120m (it used to be c70m) in the

Crux pitch of the Kanzelgrat on the Zinal Rothorn
(Route 6e) Peter Fleming

couloir on the E side which is not quite as bad as it at first appears but requires one 10m rappel. Head SE across the upper basin of the Breithorn glacier, taking a high line to keep well above some large crevasses whilst at the same time keeping well clear of the seracs on the N face, and so reach the Klein Triftjisattel at 3,498m (neither named or marked on the map: 4hr)

(ii) Coming from the Italian side, the Klein Triftjisattel can also be reached from the Schwarztor by descending the L bank of the Schwärze glacier keeping close to the rocks of the Roccia Nera and passing below Pt 3,512m to a height of roughly 3,400m to gain a snowy ramp on the L which leads to the saddle. The glacier may be tricky just before the ramp (c1hr).

Follow the arête, at first on snow and then on rock, turning most of the difficulties on the L (E) side. Eventually reach the, so-called, Grand Gendarme which is not at all obvious when you are on the ridge. It is turned on the L by a 10m horizontal hand traverse followed by a slightly descending traverse for another 10m (III) to reach a brèche. Continue on snow and rock to another delightful rock pitch up the crest of yet another gendarme. From its top descend 10m on easy rock on the E side to a horizontal ledge which is used to avoid a sharp and steep-sided snow crest. Once back on the crest a pitch of difficult mixed climbing leads to easier angled snow. Continue to the summit rocks which are turned by a traverse to the R, usually on steep ice, to reach more mixed ground which in turn leads to the summit ridge. The traverse referred to above can be undertaken just below the summit rocks or c75m below these, depending on conditions. The higher traverse is shorter (c35m) and leaves less difficult climbing to the summit (8hrs). **c12hr** in total

It is possible to climb the summit rocks direct but this is considerably more difficult than any of the climbing that has gone before: 40m IV+.

23n NORTH-EAST COULOIR

TD-/TD L Graf, K Kubiena and E Vanis, 24 July 1954

25 Variation start: E Cavalieri, A Mellano and R Perego, 29 July 1960

FWA: E Boreatti and A Sioli, 20 Mar 1972

Valley base: Champoluc/Zermatt/Cervinia

The most obvious line on this side of the mountain, situated between the N ridge (Younggrat) and the NE spur. It is broad and fairly evenly angled (55°) except for the lowest part which is steeper and narrower than the rest and mostly rocky. This part is somewhat exposed to stonefall and so the variation start is described. This avoids the lower part of the couloir by the rocks on the L (E). The orientation of the face on this part of the mountain ensures that the rock dries quite quickly and that snow quickly consolidates into good névé.
640m

Reach the start from the Rossi and Volante bivouac by traversing to the Schwarztor and following Route 23m(ii) from there. Pass below Pt 3,512m to the foot of the couloir. Cross the bergschrund directly below the couloir and climb up to the foot of the rock spur on the L of a small icy couloir. Climb several pitches by the easiest line before ascending a smooth 5m slab. Continue up the L side of a small couloir for c25m (IV) before moving into the couloir and following it delicately for a further 20m (piton). A slab on the R (V, piton) leads to easier terrain. Follow the crest of the spur over two short steps to a ledge below two narrow chimneys. Climb the L-hand chimney for a few m and then transfer to the R-hand one (15m, IV+) before easy rocks lead up to the snow of the main couloir.

Climb in the centre of the couloir, gaining this by a snow crest leading L from the top of the spur. Continue up the couloir as far as possible before exiting on to the Younggrat and finishing up that route. **7-10hr** from the hut

23o NORTH-EAST SPUR
TD E Cavalieri and P Villaggio, 31 July 1961
25 Valley base: Champoluc/Zermatt/Cervinia

A very fine mixed climb with difficulty increasing as height is gained. Situated to the L (E) of the NE couloir, it climbs a steepish snow slope (50°-55°) for c150m and continues up slabs (III and IV) for another 150m before reaching the upper mixed section which extends for a further 350m. **c650m**

Start from the Rossi and Volante bivouac hut and reach the foot of the climb by following Route 23m(ii). After passing below Pt 3,512m cross the bergschrund where possible, usually to the R of the foot of the spur and climb the snow slope towards its foot. This will involve crossing deep grooves created by stonefall. Continue up the L side of the rocks until a broken rock ramp above an overhang can be followed to the crest of the spur. To avoid stonefall it is as well to reach this point before sunrise.

   Climb easily just L of the crest following a couloir and then a narrow chimney to overcome a steeper section. A few m higher, leave the couloir at a break leading R. Traverse for c12m with one delicate move (III+) to some steep slabs. Climb the slabs to regain the crest of the spur above some overhangs. Continue on the crest up excellent slabby rock (III and IV).

   Higher up the slabs become interspersed with bands of snow and the slope becomes steeper. Reach the bottom of a dièdre slanting up Lwards. Climb its L side and then a short and slightly overhanging wall (V, with 2 pitons) before leaving the dièdre and continuing straight up on mixed terrain. The slope steepens again and all the ledges become banked out with snow or ice. Head towards a triangular grey tower split by a dièdre and climb this, avoiding an overhang on the R (V, with 1 piton). Two delicate pitches up frequently verglassed rock (2 pitons in place) lead to a steep couloir breaking through some overhangs. Climb the couloir, which is usually icy and quite difficult, for several pitches. One pitch in particular is often icy and delicate. Pitons are in place for belays. Towards its top the couloir curves L. Here keep to rocks on its L and continue to a final steepening. Two pitches up a chimney (IV) lead to the summit crest. **c12hr** from the foot of the climb

Breithorn: Gendarme 4,106m

A distinctive pinnacle on the ridge between the Roccia Nera and the E summit. Its NE and ENE faces provide the line of two worthwhile climbs. In fact the two climbs share some common ground in their middle parts.

23p **NORTH-EAST FACE**
TD+ B Mailhot and G Grassi, 30 June 1984
25 Valley base: Champoluc/Zermatt/Cervinia

Another of the prolific Grassi's routes on the mountain and given the name Immaginando l'Inimmaginabile. The route climbs the lower part of the face via a difficult goulotte before moving L to join the line of ENE Wall Route (23q). The routes follow the same line to the steep upper rock wall where the Grassi route takes a system of icy couloirs and ledges towards the col W of the highest point. **c500m**

The obvious starting point is the Rossi and Volante bivouac hut. From here follow Route 23m(ii) to the foot of the wall. To the E of the Pt 3,512m is a long steep and narrow couloir (the NE couloir and the line of 'Primorska Smer', P and P Podgornik, 22 Aug 1980, TD) and to the E of this is a chimney-couloir easily seen from below. Climb the snow/ice slope below the couloir and one pitch up into the narrower part of it (good belay point). Continue with difficulty up the narrow icy goulotte. This is taken on the L side at first then on the R by a vertical wall, to pass an obstruction, before returning to the L side again and finally exiting by the R wall (75°-80° with one section of 90°). Short steps lead to a rib which in turn leads to a big icy ramp slanting L.

Three pitches up the ramp lead to easier ground (common with Route 23q) as far as the upper rock wall. Reach this, via a snow slope, at an icy chimney-couloir which slants steeply R. An initial narrow and vertical section of the chimney leads on to some mixed terrain and subsequently a steep and narrow rocky section (IV+). This is followed by a further icy chimney (90°) before easier climbing leads to a snow crest. Move Rwards now over mixed ground to a snow slope below a steep wall. Cross the snow slope Rwards for c25m to where a belay can be taken below a peculiar overhang. Keep moving R to an icy ramp and climb it, with difficulty at the start on mixed terrain, to its end and a belay. Keep on the snow slopes just R of the rocks above and climb to a small but very steep couloir which is used to exit the route. **c8hr** climbing

23q EAST-NORTH-EAST WALL
D+ A Molinari with O Frachey, 23 Sept 1951
25 Valley base: Champoluc/Zermatt/Cervinia

The first route climbed on the N side of the Breithorn on the section between the Roccia Nera and the Younggrat and achieved by the well known Italian female alpinist Anna Molinari with one of the famous Frachey brothers. The lower part of the route is somewhat exposed to stonefall. There are some pitons in place. **c500m**

Approach as for Route 23p but after crossing the bergschrund, start the climb further L than that route at a slabby rock face L of a conspicuous snow patch. The route slants slightly Rwards to a short wall, which is climbed, and then a short ice crest is followed to reach the foot of a steep rock step. Cross an ice slope Rwards to gain a fairly steep icy couloir. Climb this for c50m using holds on the R wall and then a rock couloir for a further 40m to a jammed block. Leave the couloir here, moving R with the aid of the block, and get on to a ramp slanting up from R to L (cairn: possibly snow covered). Follow the ramp to its end and then climb the wall that confronts you on its L side. The line now follows a series of little couloirs and ledges slightly Lwards to flat ledge. From here short rock steps and icy grooves lead to the summit. **c6hr** climbing

Breithorn: Roccia Nera 4,075m

The most easterly summit of the Breithorn overlooks the Schwarztor to its SE. It is mostly rock, providing some pleasant sunny routes on its S side but much more austere and demanding ones on compact rock on the N face.

23r SOUTH-WEST FLANK
F

Valley base: Cervinia/Zermatt/Champoluc

Used as an approach for the Traverse of the Breithorn and as an easy descent route from the climbs on the faces. 325m

From the Rossi and Volante bivouac hut climb to the top of the rognon on which the hut stands and then straight up the snow slope to the crest of the ridge (possibly a cornice) and then follow this E to the summit. **c1hr**

23s NORTH WALL - VIA DEL GRAN DIEDRO GHIACCIATO
TD+

M Bernardi and G Grassi, 11 May 1980
FWA: A Jaccod and R Nicco, 12 March 1982
Valley base: Champoluc/Zermatt/Cervinia

Another fine climb by Grassi with some very demanding mixed terrain. The route follows the line of the massive dièdre formed by the N face of Roccia Nera and the NE face of Pt 4,106m. c450m

From the Rossi and Volante bivouac hut contour to the Schwarztor and descend the Schwärze glacier before contouring L under the N face. Start somewhat R of the fall-line from the dièdre, cross the bergschrund and climb the steep snow and ice slope above to reach mixed ground at its top. Slant Lwards up this for c70m (65°) to the edge of an ice slope (60°) leading in turn, in about 1 pitch, to the bottom of the massive dièdre. Climb the bed of the dièdre with difficulty (VI) for 30m to a belay below a steep goulotte. Climb this (1 pitch, mostly 65°-70° with steps of 80°). Next climb some icy blocks before a delicate Lwards traverse and a steep ice slope lead to a belay in 35m.

Now slant up L to below a very steep goulotte. Climb it (70°, difficult mixed climbing) to its termination and then move Rwards to a detached block and belay (c70m). Further mixed climbing leads L now to the foot of the final section. Climb this for 40m (80°) to the less steep ground and exit through the (usually easy) cornice. **c10hr** climbing

23t NORTH WALL
TD F Cerbelloni with E and O Frachey, 8 Aug 1952
25 Valley base: Champoluc/Zermatt/Cervinia

A very notable ascent for the time considering the equipment available to climbers of that epoch. A very exposed route with difficulties on both ice and rock. Take care to note the state of the cornice at the top since this can prevent exit from the route. **c450m**

Start as for Route 23s. Cross the bergschrund and climb the steep snow and ice slope to reach the face a little to the R of the summit fall-line where a shallow ice couloir slants up L. Get into the couloir via snowy rocks and a traverse L and then climb it steeply until it narrows. Climb the narrow section with some difficulty and then follow the rocks forming a crest on the side of the couloir as far as a system of slabs. Climb these more easily for a few pitches to reach a snowy ledge and move L into the centre of the wall. Climb two pitches more or less straight up to finally reach the short snow slope below the cornice. Cross this and overcome the cornice, possibly by tunnelling. Allow **8hr**

23u NORTH-EAST WALL
TD L Castiglia, P Giglio and R Rosso, 11/12 July 1982
25 Valley base: Champoluc

The first ascent party used artificial aid to climb the lower overhanging wall but the route was free climbed one day later by G Grassi and I Meneghin and the description given is for the climb to be done in this mode. The upper part follows a rounded rib. **c450m**

Reach the start as for Route 23s and climb the steep snow and ice slope to reach the face just R of the overhanging part. Start up some slanting slabs to the foot of a dièdre (40m, IV-). Climb the dièdre for 15m (V), move L on to ice and then follow snow and rock to a belay at the bottom of a very steep crack on the L at the top of the dièdre.

Now traverse L and climb another dièdre/chimney (V) by bridging or back and footing. Continue on mixed terrain from the top of the dièdre moving Rwards at first and then straight up an ice slope before finally moving L again across a very steep slope, thus avoiding a prominent rock band. Large blocks form a belay point. Continue the Lwards traverse for a few more m and then climb a narrow, icy goulotte (70°) to cross a rock barrier. Now climb Rwards in a small couloir until a traverse L across an ice slope leads to the crest of the rib overlooking the lower part of the face.

Climb the rib (IV and IV+) to some terraces and then a pitch up easier ground at first (III) and then a vertical crack (IV and IV+) to reach a vertical wall. Cross a short couloir Lwards and climb a secondary narrow rib (III, IV and V) to gain a small icy couloir. Climb this to reach the top of the vertical wall. Next climb a rib to gain the bottom of a narrow goulotte. Climb this (65°-70° at its steepest) before moving Rwards to another couloir which leads back L towards the crest of the rib. Climb the couloir for 30m before making a delicate traverse L over mixed ground to regain the crest.

Another step in the rib is avoided on the R, by snow and then a slab, before continuing on the crest to a belay on the R. Climb this (IV+) and continue on the crest until it steepens again. A traverse L across icy slabs gives access to some easy ramps which lead in about a rope's length to the final short snow slope. The cornice should be easy to overcome. **7-8hr** climbing

Further L, starting in the angle between the main wall and a large flying buttress, G Grassi and E Tessera, 3 July 1983, climbed a route (Via Peraice) with a first pitch steepening to 90°. It is only likely to be climbable in winter or early in the summer season.

23v SOUTH-EAST RIDGE
D+ G Crespi with E and G Frachey, 28 July 1941
26 Valley base: Cervinia/Zermatt/Champoluc

An attractive (mostly) rock climb at high altitude, another product of the Frachey brothers. The route described starts on the SE face and gains the ridge at a prominent, usually snowy shoulder. It has pitches of IV and V with the odd pull on a peg. Carry some pitons in case of verglas. **c400m**

From the Rossi and Volante bivouac hut contour to the Schwarztor and descend the Swiss side until below the snowy shoulder on the SE ridge. Start c50m R of the short couloir with a rock rib on its E side and climb 3 pitches more or less straight up (IV). Alternatively climb the rib on the E side of the couloir for 3 pitches (III and IV). Some easier but possibly mixed terrain now leads to the crest of the ridge close to the snowy shoulder.

    Continue up the ridge over some short overhangs (steps of IV+) until below a more distinctive overhang. This is climbed on the R (V, several pitons in place) usually with a bit of aid. Above, some short slabs (IV+) lead to a final snow crest. **c4hr**

23w TRAVERSE OF THE BREITHORN
AD J Anderson with U Almer and A Pollinger, 16 Aug 1884
20 FW traverse: G Dondeynaz and M Gaillard, 26 Feb 1959
21 22 Valley base: Cervinia/Zermatt/Champoluc
24 25
26 *The first traverse party avoided the central summit on the S side and in so doing avoided the best of the climbing. It wasn't until 1900 that it was completed in its entirety (E Hahn and party). It is usually done from E - W but is no more difficult in the reverse direction.*

    The ridge is c2.5km long and gives some quite varied climbing on both rock and snow and has some outstanding view points. Highly recommended. Some parties like to include it in a much longer traverse which starts at the Margherita hut and crosses the Liskamm, Castor and Pollux en route to the Breithorn. One should be aware that the crest of the ridge can have some large cornices. Despite its length and altitude it is a far safer and less demanding proposition than say a traverse of the Weisshorn or the Täschhorn-Dom traverse, since there are several points on the ridge where it is possible to reach or abandon the route by ascending/descending the S side from/to the Grande Verra glacier. Often guided parties climb a truncated version of the route using one or other of these points.

The obvious starting point is the Rossi and Volante bivouac hut but the climb can be started from various other bases. Most obvious are the Mezzalama hut or the Valle d'Ayas guides' hut, the Cervinia guides' hut at Testa Grigia, the Theodule hut or from the Klein Matterhorn lift. However, from wherever you start make it early if you contemplate doing the entire traverse. **690m**

From the Rossi and Volante bivouac hut follow Route 23r to the summit of Roccia Nera (1 hr). (It is not essential to visit this summit since the route from here turns back on itself). Follow the crest of the ridge W and then NW (cornices on the N side). The ridge is fairly level at first then steepens and leads to the rocky gendarme of Pt 4,106m (½hr). Descend exposed rock (quite delicate) on the S side to reach a snow col c50m below from where an easy climb to the E summit of the mountain is made (c½hr).

Descend starting NW but a little way below the summit turn to the S. There is a rappel point (20m rappel) but it is not too difficult to down climb (exposed) to reach the steep snow slope (possibly icy) below. Descend now to the saddle at Pt 4,022m (½hr). At this point the route can be abandoned but this misses the best of the climbing.

To continue, keep on the crest to the first rocks of the central summit. The ridge rises to this summit in three distinct steps. Climb the first direct (IV) on excellent rock, or turn it on the S side using a snowy couloir to regain the crest. The second step can be turned on the L but it is better to climb the cracked slab (III+) to reach the final and biggest step. This is best climbed by keeping close to the crest although it may be ascended on the L via a broken chimney. An easy snow ridge leads to the top (c2½hr). The rest is fairly easy. Continue easily along the ridge at first and then make a steep descent to the snow saddle at 4,076m (the ridge could be abandoned here). Beyond this gentle snow slopes lead to the main summit (and the crowds) (1hr). Allow **6-7hr** from the bivouac

Schwarztor 3,731m

First traversed by J Ball with M Zumtaugwald, 18 Aug 1845

A glacier pass between Roccia Nera and Pollux that links the Monte Rosa hut on the Swiss side of the border with the Valle d'Ayas guides' and Mezzalama huts on the Italian side, although rarely used for that purpose these days. Its main function from a mountaineering point of view is that it provides a means of access to climbs on the N side of the Breithorn.

24a SOUTH-WEST FLANK
F Valley base: Champoluc

27

From the Valle d'Ayas guides' hut get on to the Grande Verra glacier terrace N of the hut and climb the terrace to a point below the SW ridge of Pollux. Turn WNW and continue up crevassed slopes to reach the pass. **1½hr**

24b NORTH FLANK
PD Valley base: Zermatt

28

Although there are other possibilities as starting points, the route from the Monte Rosa hut is the most dependable and of greatest interest.
1,160m

From the Monte Rosa hut descend the path on to the mainly snow free Grenz glacier and cross this SW to reach the main glacier torrent which is followed Swards to a region of large crevasses at the junction with the Zwillings glacier. Turn WSW and work your way through or around crevasses and seracs, usually close to the rocks of Schalbetterflue, to the first glacier plateau. Climb a rock couloir to reach the snow saddle at 3,282m on the long N ridge of Pollux. Climb the ridge via a steep snow slope passing over Pt 3,660m to the next snow saddle (c3,630m). Now climb a few more m along the ridge before contouring SW to reach the pass. **4-5hr**

Pollux 4,092m

J Jacot with J-M Perren and P Taugwalder, 1 Aug 1864

Pollux and Castor are together know as The Twins (Zwillinge), named from Greek mythology. Although overshadowed by higher neighbours they are frequently climbed together, usually by a southern or western approach.

25a WEST FLANK
PD First ascent party
27 Valley base: Champoluc/Zermatt

In good condition this route is entirely on snow but this generally turns to ice, at least on the steeper sections, quite early in the season and this augments the grade. Frequently used in descent when snow conditions are good. ***290m***

Reach the foot of the W flank, between the rocks of the SW ridge and those of the frontier (WNW) ridge, as for Route 24a from the Valle d'Ayas guides' hut or from the Kl Matterhorn/Theodulpass/Testa Grigia by following Route H15 towards the Rossi and Volante bivouac hut. Following this latter route, once below the central summit of the Breithorn, descend Rwards on to a glacier terrace below a band of seracs then continue traversing the plateau to pass below the rognon on which the bivouac hut stands.

Climb straight up the slope which steepens to a maximum of c50° at about mid-height and continue direct to the summit or slant L or R on to one of the ridges. **1½hr** from the Schwarztor

An alternative route starting at the Schwarztor is to traverse NNE on to the N ridge of the mountain and climb the steep upper part of this to the summit. **1½-2hr**

25b SOUTH-WEST RIDGE

AD Valley base: Champoluc/Zermatt

27

A fairly short but interesting climb with fixed ropes on the hard bits. Usually used for descent. **290m**

The approach routes are the same as for Route 25a. Climb easily up the crest to the first rope or start just on the N side of the ridge up snow leading into a narrow couloir. Up this to the first of the ropes. Use it to make a traverse L to a chimney/couloir and the second rope. Climb the couloir and then a steep step on the ridge with the aid of the third rope. A fine snow crest leads to the summit. **c1½hr** from the foot of the ridge

25c NORTH RIDGE

AD J Farrar and R Lloyd with J Pollinger, 18 Aug 1910

28 G Finch and M Liniger, 28 July 1919, climbed the entire ridge from Schwärze.

Valley base: Zermatt

The ridge, almost 4km long, provides the most obvious route to the summit of the mountain from the Monte Rosa hut. The route described is almost entirely on snow and in a fine and seemingly remote setting throughout. **1,420m**

From the Monte Rosa hut follow Route 24b to the second snow saddle. Continue S up the rounded snow ridge to reach a third snow saddle just S of Pt 3,817m and below the summit slope. Climb straight up this steep slope, avoiding a bergschrund near the top on the R, and reach the NNW ridge close to the summit. **5-6hr**

25d SOUTH-EAST RIDGE

PD Valley base: Champoluc/Gressoney/Zermatt

The SSE flank of the mountain has no special interest and can be climbed almost anywhere. The route described here gives as good a line as any and can be used as an alternative to the SW ridge as a route of ascent or descent when climbing Pollux in conjunction with Castor. **250m**

From the Zwillingsjoch one can climb directly up the crest of the ridge on loose rock or start a little further W starting up snow slopes. Climb these, at first straight up and then slanting R towards the ridge crest, and reach a short couloir. Up this and easy broken rock above to a final snow crest. **c1hr**

Zwillingsjoch 3,845m

First traversed N-S by S Winkworth with J Bennen and J Croz, 31 July 1863

A glacier pass between the complex Zwillings glacier to the N and the much easier Verra glacier to the S, it forms the low point between Castor and Pollux. Rarely crossed!

26a SOUTH-WEST FLANK
F

Valley base: Champoluc

From the Valle d'Ayas guides' hut get on to the terrace of the Grande Verra glacier, which slants up W-E, and climb this at a steady angle, passing below the SSE flank of Pollux before reaching the pass. **1½hr** and **425m**

26b NORTH FLANK
AD Valley base: Zermatt

28

The route climbs the complicated Zwillings glacier which can be seen almost in its entirety from the Monte Rosa hut. Examine it well beforehand. **1,180m**

Follow Route 24b from the Monte Rosa hut to the first glacier plateau. Now head S at first then up SW avoiding a zone of crevasses and seracs just N of the rocks in the middle of the glacier. When you are above the crevasses turn W into the glacier combe below the Schalbetterflue and climb up it until below the pass. Climb directly up the steep slope (very steep at the top). The rocks on the R can be climbed as an alternative to the steep snow slope. **4-6hr** depending on conditions

BREITHORN - LISKAMM CHAIN

Castor 4,228m

F Jacomb and W Mathews with M Croz, 23 Aug 1861

The dominant twin, most frequently climbed from the Italian side as the direct approach from the N involves a long ascent of the complex Zwillings glacier. It is only in winter that frequent ascents are made (on skis) from the Swiss side and then via the Felikjoch.

The base of the SW ridge of the mountain is formed by a massive rock buttress (below Pt 3,992m) which separates the Piccolo Verra glacier and the Castor glacier (not named on map). A cairn marks the top of the buttress and a little NE of this is a snow shoulder, known as the Colle del Castore, c3,980m (not named on map and not a true col). This 'col' provides a passage between the Theodulpass and the Quintino Sella hut section of the Italian Haute Route that avoids the traverse of Castor. This passage should not be attempted in the afternoon and the slopes on either side can be icy at any time. The buttress itself has a W and a S flank and it is the latter which provides two worthwhile climbs.

27a SOUTH-EAST RIDGE
F First ascent party
28 Valley base: Gressoney

The Normal Route and a pleasant climb from the Quintino Sella hut. The climb starts at the Felikjoch, which can also be reached from the Monte Rosa hut or from Liskamm, which is the usual approach when traversing the 4,000m peaks in the region. **640m from the Sella hut**

From the Quintino Sella hut follow Route 28a towards the Felikjoch. Just below the col slant up L to the crest of the ridge and reach a rocky shoulder (Pt 4,174m). Scramble over this and continue along the snow crest to the summit. **c3hr**

When approaching from the Monte Rosa hut it is not essential to reach the Felikjoch. From the glacier plateau below the col climb straight up to the rocky shoulder (PD). **c7hr**

27b SOUTH-WEST BUTTRESS - GUIDES ROUTE

D+

27

E Cavalieri with O Frachey and L Colli with A Favre, 5 Aug 1970
FWA: A Jaccod and R Nicco, 6 Jan 1984
Valley base: Champoluc

The route climbs the centre of the wall, mostly on good rock and with the original belay pitons left in place. The approach to the face is up the tortuous Castor glacier. ***450m*** *on rock*

From the Mezzalama hut get on to the Piccolo Verra glacier and work up this Ewards to the junction with the Castor glacier (not named on map) which passes under the S face of the buttress. Climb the complicated serac zone on the S side of the rock island. This is probably safer than climbing on the N side of the island since this is exposed to stonefall. Once above the seracs move into the centre of the glacier and climb up it until more or less at the height of a small amphitheatre at the foot of the buttress which is directly below Pt 3,992m (c2hr).

Start in the middle of the amphitheatre and climb four pitches up slabs (III with bits of IV) until below some overhanging rock. Now slant up L for another rope length before two more pitches lead up dièdres/chimneys (IV and bits of V) to a band of greyish rock. Below this slant up R for c20m on a ramp and then use pitons (in place) for aid to overcome a small overhang. Above this keep moving gradually R for several pitches of superb climbing up dièdres, chimneys and a rib (III and IV) to reach the cairn at the top of the buttress (4-5hr).

To continue to the summit of Castor, scramble across to the Colle del Castore (see above) then up the snow rib beyond to an easy angled rock rib. Scramble along this and reach a snow saddle below a rock step (descent is possible on either side). Climb the step (mostly II) and a nice snow crest to the summit. **c8hr** in all

27c SOUTH-WEST BUTTRESS - CLASSIC ROUTE

D+
27

C Fortina with A Welf, 4 Aug 1911. The exact line of their ascent is not known.
By the route described: E Marchesini with E Frachey, 1938
FWA: G Gualco with E and O Frachey, 20 Mar 1955
Valley base: Champoluc

Said to be one of the most interesting routes in the area but somewhat spoiled by the risk of stonefall in the lower part. It was one of the 'trade routes' of the Frachey family of guides. The route follows the line of the ridge separating the W and S facets of the SW buttress. **550m** *on rock*

Reach the foot of the face as for Route 27b and start c100m R of the ridge. Climb an obvious stony ramp Lwards to the crest of the ridge. Follow the ridge for c200m (some III and IV) to the base of a yellow gendarme. Turn it on either side (IV) to reach a gap above then continue quite easily to an obvious red dièdre. Climb this (III and IV) and make an awkward exit L (IV+). Now traverse R along a ramp before easy ground leads in c50m to some big slabs which are climbed to the crest of the ridge (IV).

The route continues up a couloir until it narrows and is abandoned on the R. Another small couloir leads back L to a reddish wall which in turn is climbed (III) to a ledge on the ridge crest. Next move Rwards to a reddish slab which provides some delicate climbing (IV and IV+), slanting L, to easy terrain. Above is a short but overhanging wall. Strenuous climbing up this (V-, beware of old pitons) leads to more easy climbing Rwards to another short, steep wall. Climb this (IV+) and then, a little higher, reach a barrier to further direct progress. Pass this step by traversing delicately L (IV) on to a sloping ledge. Climb the wall above starting c5m along this ledge (V). The difficulties ease in a few m and then easy climbing leads finally to the cairn at the top of the buttress (c6hr from the foot of the buttress). Continue to the summit as for Route 27b. Allow **10hr** from the hut

27d WEST-NORTH-WEST FLANK
PD
Valley base: Champoluc/Cervinia/Zermatt
27

Effectively the Normal Route on the W side of the mountain. A straightforward but fairly steep snow slope starting S of the Zwillingsjoch and leading to the foresummit of the mountain on the NW ridge. Snow conditions can be quite variable and there is considerable danger of avalanche after fresh snow. Icy conditions make the climb a more serious undertaking. It is used in descent when traversing the peak. The face can be reached from the W (Rossi and Volante bivouac hut) by skirting round the S side of Pollux: from the N, rarely, via the Zwillingsjoch or, most commonly from the Valle d'Ayas guides' hut via Route 24a. **320m**

Start more or less halfway across the face and follow a line slanting L towards the foresummit on the NW ridge. Gain the crest at this point or a little further R. Enjoy the snow crest leading to the summit. It is also possible to reach the upper part of the SW ridge rather than the NW ridge. **c1½hr** from the foot of the face

An alternative to this route, and possibly more interesting, from the Valle d'Ayas guides' hut is to get on to the Piccolo Verra glacier and follow its upper edge to the Colle del Castore (see introduction above). A steep slope leads to the 'col' from where you follow Route 27c to the summit. **3-4hr**

27e NORTH-WEST RIDGE
PD
F Schuster with P Baumann and P Mosser, 9 Aug 1878
Valley base: Champoluc/Cervinia/Zermatt
27

An alternative to the WNW flank route when that is icy or avalanche prone. It can be used in descent when traversing the peak. **c370m**

Start at the Zwillingsjoch and climb the rounded snow crest towards a rock rib. The route takes a line between this and some seracs on the L and there is one steep section that might be icy. Above this the ridge narrows into a pleasant snow crest over the foresummit and on to the main summit. **c1½hr**

27f NORTH FLANK

AD+ In descent: Miss K Richardson with J Bich and E Rey, 10 Aug
28 1890
G Finch and H Mantel, 16 Aug 1909
Descended on skis: C Cugnetto and F Ghisafi, 20 July 1987
Valley base: Zermatt

A very fine glacier excursion. **1,560m**

From the Monte Rosa hut follow Route 26b to the final steepening below the col. From here head SE and work through a zone of crevasses to reach the base of the snow rib descending NNE from the foresummit. Climb to the foresummit, at first slanting R to turn the bergschrund and then directly. Continue along the fine snow crest to the summit. **c8hr**

From the bottom of the NNE snow rib, it is possible to climb this directly (G Finch, G Forster, R Peto and G Travers-Jackson, 12 Aug 1924: D)

Felikjoch c4,066m

First traverse: F Jacomb and W Mathews with J and M Croz, 23 Aug 1861

Not the lowest point on the frontier ridge, there is a slightly lower col a little way to the NE (4,063m), but it provides the easiest crossing. It is situated at the foot of the SE ridge of Castor where the frontier ridge turns a right-angle before rising NE towards Liskamm. On its N side lies the chaotic Zwillinge glacier whilst on its S side is the much more benign Felik glacier.

28a SOUTH SIDE

F Valley base: Gressoney

From the Quintino Sella hut get on to the Felik glacier and head NNE, keeping R of Punta Perazzi (3,906m) and the col NE of this. Turn NE, slanting up the slope from L to R, to gain the snow ridge which is orientated SSE and descends from a small snow peak on the frontier ridge (the Felikhorn, 4,093m). Climb the ridge towards this peak but before reaching the top slant L to reach the saddle on its W side. A short descent leads to the Felikjoch. **2hr** and **460m**

28b NORTH SIDE

AD

28

Valley base: Zermatt

If you are into complex glacier terrain, this is the route for you. Try to plan the route beforehand as most of it can be seen from the hut. It is much easier in winter or spring. c1,400m

From the Monte Rosa hut follow Route 24b to the first glacier plateau. Above, a long rock band divides the glacier into two parts. Climb the glacier combe on the E side of this band, passing, at about 3,400 to 3,500m, through a zone of crevasses at right-angles to the line of progress. It may be necessary to do this close to the rock band mentioned above or on the E extremity of the glacier. Once past these crevasses keep in the middle of the glacier, slanting up R at c3,680m to gain the combe below the col at c3,800m. Climb the combe, avoiding more big crevasses before easier slopes give access to the col. **5-6hr**

Liskamm 4,527m

W Hall, J Hardy, C Pilkington, A Ramsay, T Rennison,
F Sibson and R Stephenson with J Cachet, F Lochmatter,
K Herr, J and P Perren and S Zumtaugwald, 19 Aug 1861

Formerly known as 'Silberbast', its outline being thought to resemble a 'silver saddle'. It is a big mountain with two distinct summits, although the W summit is significantly higher than the E summit (4,479m). The most stunning feature of the mountain is the massive, steep snow and ice covered face extending along the whole of the Swiss flank. Linking the two summits is a superb snow crest, sometimes referred to as the Grenzgrat. This crest extends beyond the E summit to the Lisjoch and from the W summit almost to the Felikjoch, a total distance of c4.5km, and provides a wonderful traverse route of the mountain. On the S side the mountain is far less impressive, the two summits appearing mainly rocky from this aspect with a hanging glacier, bordered by a rock rib on each side, separating them.

    An important feature of the S flank is the ridge extending S, starting c100m SE of the main summit, known as the Cresta Sella. Between this ridge and the E (frontier) ridge is the big rock wall of the SE face. Continuing down the S ridge, where it turns to snow, there is a snow saddle (difficult to cross) followed by a snow dome. Below this is fairly easy angled snow slope, known as the Passo del Naso, which allows a relatively easy passage to be made across the S flank of the mountain; a part of the Italian Haute Route. The rocks of Il Naso continue the ridge further S.

29a SOUTH-WEST RIDGE TO WEST SUMMIT
PD
27
31

E-N Buxton and L Stephen with J Anderegg and F Biner,
16 Aug 1864

FWA: M Piacenza with A Curta and E Lazier, 17 Jan 1907

Valley base: Gressoney/Champoluc

*The ordinary route to the lower of the two summits and climbed in its
own right from the Quintino Sella hut but more important as a
descent route from the W summit for alpinists who have made an
ascent of one of the N face routes or who are traversing the mountain.*
420m

From the Felikjoch (reached via Route 28a) contour round the
Felikhorn on its W side to the col at 4,063m and continue up
easy snow slopes to a snow hump at 4,201m. The ridge narrows
quite markedly beyond this point, becoming quite exposed,
particularly so on the L. Climb the narrow snow crest to reach a
foresummit (4,447m). The final approach to this point can be
climbed directly up the steep snow slope, or you can slant L to
the snow rib descending WNW, or you can move R on to rocks
and climb these (II) to just below the foresummit. Descend
slightly then continue to the W summit, usually keeping just on
the L side of the crest. **2hr**

29b NORTH-NORTH-WEST FLANK TO WEST SUMMIT
D
29 Mrs R Thomson with C Klucker and C Zippert, 19 July 1902
Valley base: Zermatt

*In good conditions this is a wonderful way up the mountain,
unfortunately only to the lower of the two summits. The line of the
route is roughly that which joins Pt 3,079m, at the confluence of the
Zwillings and Grenz glaciers, with the foresummit just W of the W
summit of the mountain. The lower part of the route is exposed to
danger from seracs and there are crevasse problems on the Zwillings
glacier. Sometimes the bergschrunds are more or less impossible to
cross so try to make an inspection beforehand.* **1,400m**

From the Monte Rosa hut follow Route 24b to the first glacier
terrace. Cross the glacier Ewards, in the line of crevasses, to
reach its R bank some way above Pt 3,079m. Keeping on the W
side of the long rock band, climb straight up to reach a small
glacier terrace above some seracs and about level with top of the
rock band. Quickly cross the terrace to the E and, after

overcoming a bergschrund, reach another glacier terrace NW of the triangular rock buttress below Pt 4,058m. Pass yet another bergschrund and climb up to the NW rib of the buttress. Follow this to the top of the buttress and continue up the snow ridge to the top. **6-8hr**

29c EAST RIDGE
AD
30 First ascent party
FWA: A, C and V Sella with P Gugliermina and J Maquignaz, 21/22 March 1885
Valley base: Alagna/Gressoney/Zermatt

The classic and very fine route to the summit along a long, narrow ridge which is usually encumbered with cornices. In the past these were often double sided and claimed many lives over the years but these days they form mostly on the S side. The starting point of the climb is the Lisjoch (4,151m) which can be reached from either the Gnifetti hut, the Monte Rosa hut or the Margherita hut. **c375m**

Reach the Lisjoch by Route 30a, 30b or by reversing 37a(i). Pass to the S of some rocks and climb up the E ridge to the top of the first snow dome. The ridge levels out here but can be very corniced. Continue along it, usually well down on the N side, to the snowy Pt 4,335m. The ridge remains horizontal and then steepens to the point where it forms a junction with the S ridge (Cresta Sella). Climb to this point, again mostly on the R side and below the cornice break line, and then scramble over some rocks to the summit in about another 100m. **c2½hr** from the Lisjoch

If the cornices are particularly bad on the lower part of the E ridge, it is possible to contour from the Lisjoch on the S side of the ridge to below Pt 4,335m and then climb the steep snow slope above to reach the ridge just R of this point. The bergschrund might prove difficult.

29d CRESTA SELLA

AD P Thomas with J Imboden and J Langen, 1 Sept 1878
31 By the route described: A and C Sella and G Rey with D and J Maquignaz
Valley base: Algna/Gressoney

This is the S ridge of the mountain. A useful descent route from the summit in the event of bad weather but can equally well be used for ascent. **c930m**

From the Gnifetti hut follow Route 30b towards the Lisjoch as far as the large crevasses SW of the Balmenhorn. Now circle round the glacier combe, descending gradually, to reach the SE foot of the snow dome mentioned in the preamble to the mountain. Cross a bergschrund and, if snow conditions are good, climb straight up to the top of the snow dome. Alternatively slant up more to the L to gain a glacier terrace contouring the S side of the dome (this is the Passo del Naso) and climb up to the top where the angle of the slope is easier.

    From the snow dome descend to the col on its N side and climb the nice snow crest beyond to the rocks of the ridge. Go up this (II), avoiding difficulties on the L, to reach the frontier ridge after a short, possibly icy section. The summit is c100m SE of this point. **c5hr**

The route can also be climbed from the Quintino Sella hut. Head N for a little way and then turn NE across the Felik glacier to pass above Pt 3,744. Now on the Lis glacier, climb its R bank and then turn E well above some large crevasses before contouring round to the W side of the snow dome, mentioned in the preamble to the mountain, and above some seracs. It should now be possible to climb directly to the snow dome, avoiding some rocks on their L. Alternatively climb direct for a little way then contour R on a glacier terrace (Passo del Naso). Continue as above. **c5hr** to the summit and **c960m**

29e TRAVERSE EAST-WEST

AD

29
30 31

J Kitson with C Almer, 1866 in this direction

Valley base: Zermatt/Gressoney/Alagna

A classic expedition and one of the finest ridge traverses in the Alps. It is almost entirely on snow with little in the way of technical difficulties, the grade reflects more the situation and the delicate nature of the E ridge. The ridge between the summits, the Grenzgrat, like the E ridge to the main summit, can have large cornices on both sides which present serious objective danger. The ridge is also quite long (c1km between the two summits) and if poor weather intervenes it may be difficult to escape quickly from the ridge (see Routes 29d and 29m). The traverse can equally well be done from W-E (see W summit first ascent party). The climb is not infrequently linked with a traverse of Castor and Pollux and even with the Breithorn to give an outstanding high level expedition. **c350m** *between the Lisjoch and the E summit*

Reach the Lisjoch from the Margherita hut, the Gnifetti hut or the Monte Rosa hut and then follow Route 29c to the E summit (2½hr). From this summit make a gradual descent of the ridge linking the two summits, usually keeping well down on the Swiss side, to where it becomes broader and easier and reach a snow saddle at 4,417m. Continue along a narrower section of the ridge over a hump before a section of rock and the W summit (1½-2hr). Reverse Route 29a to the Felikjoch (1-1½hr). Allow **5-6hr** from the Lisjoch

Liskamm West Summit: North-North-East Flank

Sweeping down from the W summit on to the Grenz glacier is a massive and magnificent face of seracs and snow and ice slopes interspersed with rock outcrops. Its average height is c1,000m and its mean angle is 53°. This face extends, at its base, between the rock rib at 3,663m and the foot of the NNW flank at 3,079m. Its complex nature is in sharp contrast to that of the NE flank which dominates the upper part of the Grenz glacier.

A multitude of routes have been climbed on the face but it is strictly a place only for the experienced alpinist since this is one of the most serious faces in the Alps. Most of the lines are seriously threatened, at least in part, by the seracs. Access to the face is quite easy from the Italian side via the Lisjoch, from the Monte Rosa hut one has to cross the highly crevassed Grenz glacier.

29f ANDREANI-NESSI ROUTE
ED1/2 G Andreani and P Nessi, 4/5 Aug 1961
29 FWA: A Georges, 19/21 Feb 1982
30 Valley base: Zermatt/Gressoney/Alagna

A serious undertaking, with rock difficulties of V/A2, but probably safer than most routes on the face since it follows a line of rock ribs and is thus less exposed to the objective dangers of seracs. It follows a similar, but safer line than that climbed by T Hiebeler and H Pokorski, 30/31 Aug 1961. Their route (ED1) climbed R of the rib. The main difficulties are an 80m section of rock and a 250m section of mixed climbing. The first ascent party engaged in some artificial climbing to overcome difficulties but apparently this can be avoided. ***c1,100m***

From the Monte Rosa hut reach the foot of the climb by following Route 30a. At a height of c3,350m cross the Grenz glacier to the foot of the face. Start below the central rock rib and climb up to it to the rocks on its L. Get on to the rocks by a 5m traverse R then climb a steep, loose rock dièdre/chimney for c20m (IV). Use aid to climb a 4m dièdre then traverse 2m L and gain a terrace and then use more aid (long pitons) to climb a Lward slanting crack. Now move easily up Rwards until you are forced back L on to slabs from where a chimney is climbed with more aid (V). Stepped rock leads up R to another terrace from where snow covered slabs lead L to a vertical dièdre c7m long. Climb this and then head straight up until a traverse R (15m) is possible to the other side of the rib.

Reach the central snow slopes above via a couloir (V, delicate) and climb straight up for 200m to the next rocks. Start on the R near the bounding rock rib, and climb several pitches (all mixed terrain) to below some reddish slabs. The first ascent party bivouaced here. Move 10m L then climb straight up for a further 7m (pitons in place) before slanting R to gain the crest of the rib. Follow this for 150m to reach the upper snow slopes. Climb these as far as a serac band then traverse R to pass this barrier via a few rocks and a short, steep ice wall. Another 150m of snow leads to the W summit. **12-15hr** from the foot of the face

29g DIRECT ROUTE

TD+/ED1 P Gabarrou, G Grassi and C Stratta, 10 Sept 1982
29 FWA: S Albasini and C Portmann, winter 1992/3 in particularly difficult conditions
Solo: A Jaccod, 29 July 1985
Valley base: Zermatt/Gressoney/Alagna

Although this route has not had many repeat ascents it is considered to be a superb outing which is only threatened by seracs at the start.
1,050m

Reach the start as for previous route. Start to the L of the central rib and almost directly below the W summit. Cross a difficult bergschrund a few m R of the avalanche runnel and then climb ice slopes to a goulotte in the centre of the rock band above. Follow the line of the goulotte which leads to a vertical step of ice covered rock. Above this move up the snow/ice slope in the centre of the face to another rock barrier. Climb round this on the L in three 45m pitches, the last of which involves 15-20m of very steep ice to reach a secondary rib and then c20m of easier mixed climbing. All that remains is the upper snowfield, a small serac band being passed on the L. **8hr** from the bergschrund

29h DIEMBERGER-STEFAN ROUTE

TD K Diemberger and W Stefan, 23 July 1956
29 FWA: C Raiteri and T Vidoni, 1/2 March 1980
First solo: J Taylor, 1972 (in 5hr)
Valley base: Zermatt/Gressoney/Alagna

About the safest route on the face, being exposed to seracs only in its lower part. The route climbs mainly on snow/ice (up to 55°) except for the crux section which is rock (IV). c1,000m

From the Monte Rosa hut reach the foot of the climb by following Route 29f to a point S of the rocks below Pt 3,554m. Cross the glacier to reach the L bank at a height of c3,450m (2½hr). Cross a bergschrund then climb steepening slopes on the R side of a rock outcrop to reach the main rock barrier (frequently verglassed) above the outcrop. On the R is a steep crack, itself inclined to the R. Climb this then belay on the R after a short traverse. Slabs and cracks lead gradually back L for two more pitches to regain the snow. Keep L of another rock outcrop before easier angled slopes lead to the top. **7-8hr** climbing

V Furlan, 22/23 July 1990, climbing solo through the night, avoided the main rock buttress by moving c60m L and so maximised the amount of ice climbing. This variation increases the grade to TD+ and also increases the exposure to serac fall. W Gross and T Hiebeler, 7/8 Aug 1960, climbed a variation start to the Diemberger/Stefan route, joining it a little above half-height. They started on the L side of the initial rock outcrop. This line is more exposed to the danger from seracs.

29i NORTH-NORTH-EAST AND NORTH-EAST FLANKS
D+
29 P Gabarrou and P-A Steiner, 4/5 Oct 1980
30 Valley base: Zermatt/Gressoney/Alagna

One of Gabarrou's four routes on the face, it follows a line to the R of the rock band separating the two flanks of the mountain and then crosses this band to finish on its L side. It gives a fine and varied climb in some impressive surroundings. The rock is quite good but there is some danger from seracs, especially the one on the R. The first ascent party climbed most of the route at night. c900m

Approach the face as for Route 29f. Cross the bergschrund close to the rock band then slant up Rwards to the next bergschrund, keeping out of the line of serac fall. Negotiate the bergschrund and then climb an ice slope to reach the rock barrier just below and L of a threatening serac band. Climb the rock band, trying to keep all the time to a line which avoids danger from the seracs. When close to the lower edge of the seracs slant Lwards to exit from the rock band more or less level with some more seracs on the L. Easy snow slopes lead to the top. Up to **12hr** climbing

Gabarrou, with P Girault, 14 Aug 1986, also climbed a line L of this route.

Liskamm East Summit: North-East Flank

This flank is much more amenable than the neighbouring NNE flank. It extends, at its base, between the Lisjoch and Pt 3,663m and, at its top, roughly between the E and W summits. Although the face is much more snowy than its neighbour, most routes on it are exposed to serac fall. The face, which has a mean height of c750m and mean angle of 50°, can easily be reached from the Italian side via the Lisjoch.

29j BLANCHET ROUTE
D+ E-R Blanchet with J Aufdenblatten and K Mooser, 5 Aug 1927
30 First solo: R Nicco, 28 Aug 1986
Valley base: Zermatt/Gressoney/Alagna

The route, entirely on snow, takes a line slanting R above the rock band separating this flank and the NNE flank. The climb finishes on the W summit and is somewhat exposed to the band of seracs which extends across the upper part of the face between the two summits. It is sometimes impossible to pass this serac barrier so it is important to examine the route before crossing the Grenz glacier. c680m

From the Monte Rosa hut follow Route 30a as far as Pt 3,699m before crossing the Grenz glacier to reach its L bank at c3,800m (3-4hr). Cross the bergschrund (often a double one) and then slant up gradually Rwards towards the upper seracs close to the rock band on the R. Pass through the serac barrier by whatever route is dictated by their condition and reach the summit ridge a few hundred m from the W summit. **c5hr**

29k NORMAN-NERUDA ROUTE
D+
30 L Norman-Neruda with C Klucker and J Reinstalder, 9 Aug 1890

FWA: G Fossion and O Franchey, 11 March 1956
FW solo: R Nicco, 4 March 1979
Valley base: Zermatt/Gressoney/Alagna

A classic route which is more or less completely safe from objective dangers and leads directly to the summit. Directly below the E summit the snow slope is split by a rock rib which extends down the face to a little below half-height (Pt 4,086m). The route climbs this rib. In good snow conditions, or if the rocks are verglassed or snow covered, it is easier to keep on the snow on the L side of the rib (W Welzenbach with R Walter, 8 Aug 1925). The snow slope on the R side of the rib also offers an alternative line of ascent. **730m**

From the Monte Rosa hut follow Route 29j to the foot of the face (3-4hr). Cross the bergschrund where possible and climb up to the foot of the rib. Climb the rib (which, contrary to a description in an earlier edition, can be well protected) as directly as possible to its top. A fairly straightforward snow slope leads to the E summit. **4-5hr** from the foot of the face although half this time is quite feasible

Liskamm East Summit: South-East Face
F Curta, G David and A Lazier, 26 Sept 1902

This rock face rises c400m from its base in the upper reaches of the E branch of the Lis glacier to the E summit of the mountain and is seamed with ribs and couloirs. The rock is a bit loose in places and so a good deal of stonefall can be experienced as the face catches the early morning sun. Avalanches also tumble down the couloirs in snowy conditions so routes are best

291 CENTRAL RIB
D- E Cavalieri with A Viotti, 6 Aug 1959
Valley base: Alagna/Gressoney

The most obvious line on the face since the rib rises directly to the summit. It makes an interesting and relatively safe climb. **c400m**

From the Gnifetti hut follow Route 30b towards the Lisjoch. When level with the Balmenhorn outcrop (the bivouac hut here is a possible starting point) turn W and reach the foot of the face. Climb a steep slope to the bergschrund and cross this close to the avalanche cone formed at the foot of the second couloir, counting from the L. Above this the slope steepens to c50°. Climb this slope to the foot of the rib and follow its crest as closely as possible. The climbing becomes more enjoyable as height is gained with some pleasant slabs and grooves (mostly II and III with bits of IV). Higher still the climbing becomes more mixed in nature with short rock steps interspersed with fine snow ribs. Reach the summit via the final part of the E ridge. **7-8hr**

Sella del Liskamm 4,417m
H Speyer and C Jossi, end Aug 1891

This snow saddle between the E and W summits of Liskamm is not named on the map. The name is used only by the Italians. Its main value is as a point at which the ridge can be abandoned during the traverse of the mountain, in fact it was descended about one week before the first ascent: J Kugy with L Bonetti and a porter.

North Ridge of the Weisshorn
(Route 12d) Martin Moran

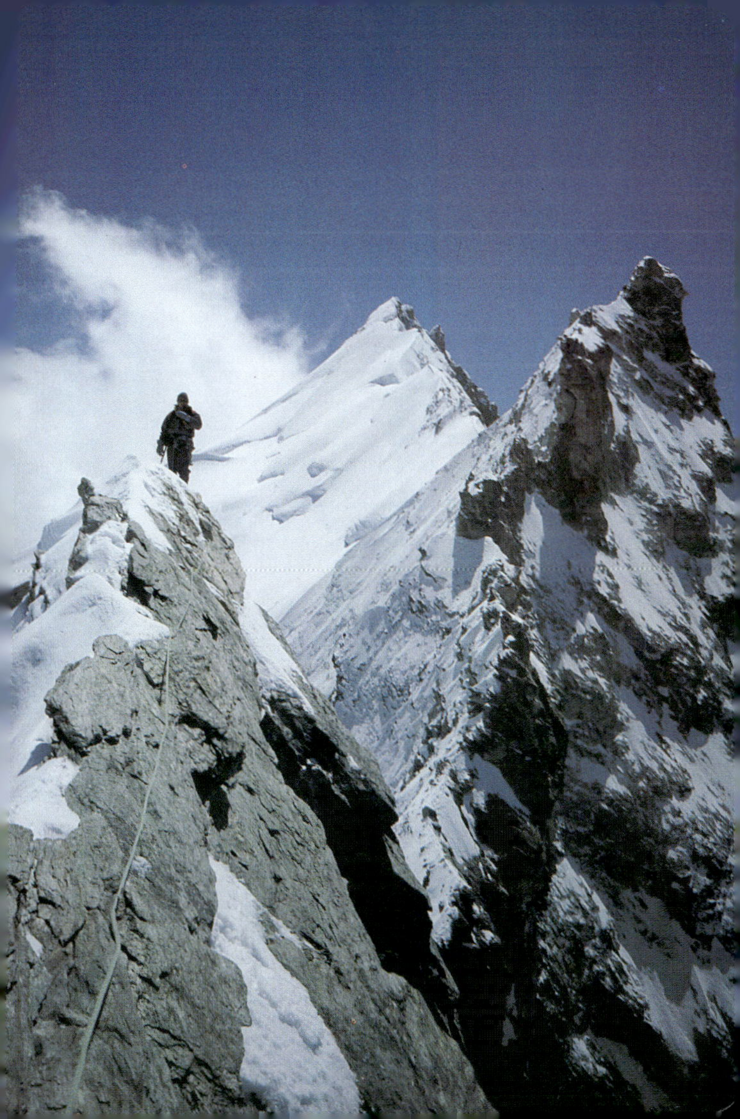

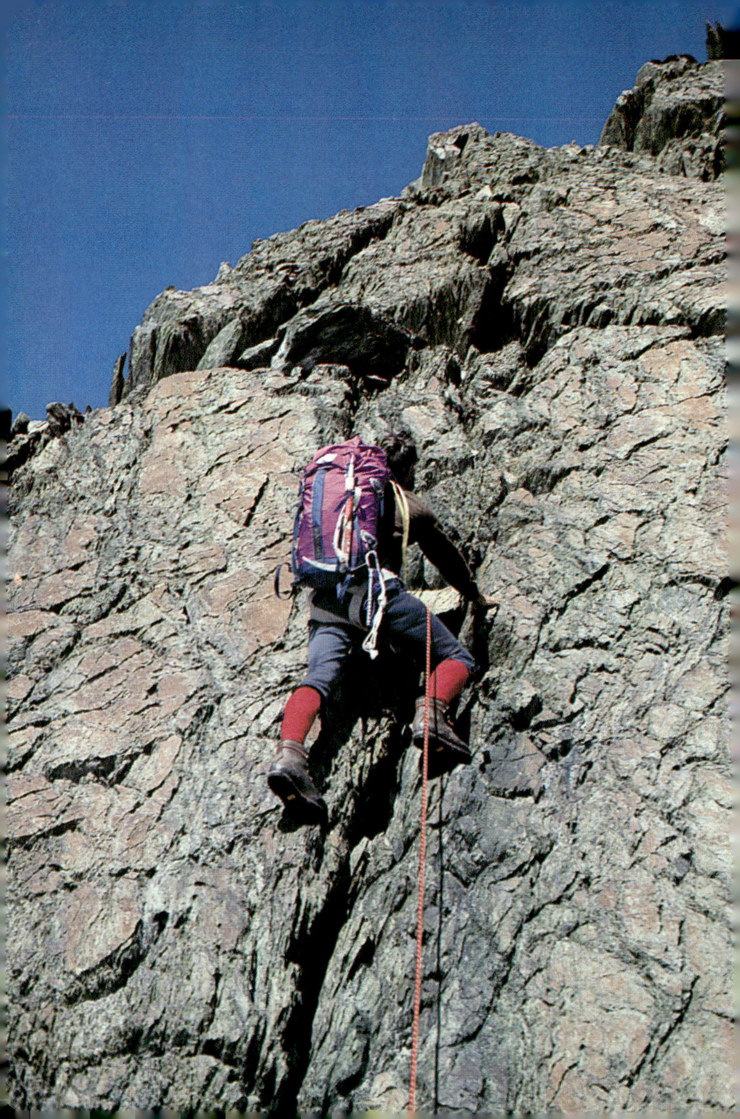

29m SOUTH-WEST FLANK
PD First ascent party
31 Valley base: Gressoney/Alagna

Provided snow conditions are favourable this route provides a safe means of descent from the ridge or even a possible route of ascent to it. The SW flank takes the form of a small hanging glacier at the foot of which is an ice cliff. This can be bypassed by rocks on the E side. The route is described in descent.

From the saddle slant down Lwards past some projecting rocks and descend the fairly steep snow slope into the glacier bowl below. Once across the bergschrund slant further L to the bounding rocks which form the WSW ridge rising to the E summit (Cresta Perazzi: PD+). Scramble down the rocks on to the upper part of the Lis glacier and descend to the Quintino Sella hut or the Gnifetti hut by Route 29d. **1-1½hr** (2½hr in ascent and c200m) to the Lis glacier

Lisjoch 4,151m and 4,246m

First recorded crossing from Gressoney la Trinité to Zermatt: G and W Mathews with M Charlet and J Croz, 23 Aug 1859

Situated on the frontier ridge between the Liskamm to the W and the Ludwigshöhe to the E, it is probably the most important pass from a mountaineering point of view on the whole of the Swiss/Italian border. The lowest point, and named on the map as the pass, does not form the crossing point. This is on account of the fact that on the N side, on the slope below the pass, there is a band of seracs. Moving E and then SE from the low point a broad, rounded snow slope leads to the snow shoulder of Pt 4,252m. Just below this shoulder, almost S of it, is the usual crossing point (track shown on map but no spot height) which, in the season, usually has a trench for a track with a marker post at the crossing point. On the S side, below both depressions, the

Torrione Maggiore on the Breithorn Traverse
(Route 23w) Barbara Swindin

30a SWISS SIDE

PD Valley base: Zermatt

36

The normal route from the Monte Rosa hut leads to the higher, W col from where the E col can be very easily reached. The route ascends the Grenz glacier which in places is very crevassed, and quite dangerously so in that many of the crevasses are hidden and are parallel to the line of travel. During the climbing season the route is normally well beaten but even so it is advisable to be on one's guard. Pay great attention to rope technique! Apart from the objective dangers the route enjoys some magnificent scenery as it progresses towards the pass and is worth doing from that point of view alone. **1,460m**

From the Monte Rosa hut, either follow a track up the hollow on the E side of the moraine flanking the R bank of the Grenz glacier or take the track along the moraine itself. Reach the glacier itself just SE of Pt 3,109m. From this point the route to the Dufourspitze goes off L.

Climb the R bank of the glacier but moving well out on to the glacier, crossing or turning several crevasses as necessary, to pass the point at which a branch glacier joins from the SE. Pass close to the foot of the rocky shoulder, Pt 3,472m. The next part of the route depends on the prevailing condition of the glacier. Provided the crevasses are passable it is easier to move well away from the rock to pass R of the rocky outcrop below Pt 3,699m. Otherwise climb the steep snow slope close to the rocks. Either way reach a glacier plateau at c3,720m. Now head ESE into a glacier combe leading up between seracs to another, much smaller glacier plateau at c3,950m. Cross this one SSE into the middle of the glacier and climb up it until it is possible to turn R to the col. **c5hr**

30b **ITALIAN SIDE**
F   Valley base: Gressoney/Alagna

33

Almost all climbs starting from the Gnifetti hut follow this route, at least in part. The most popular of these climbs are those heading for the higher tops of the Monte Rosa group and these all involve a crossing of the Lisjoch, hence the trench that develops through the passage of many feet during the climbing season. **640m**

From the Gnifetti hut climb the rocks above the hut to get on to the Lis glacier. Climb the glacier up gently inclined slopes towards the NE and then N to pass the W flank of Piramide Vincent. Somewhat steeper, crevassed slopes are now climbed whilst still heading N. The angle eases considerably as you pass the rock outcrop of the Balmenhorn (Pt 4,167m) on your R. On the rocks there is a statue of Christ which is visible from the trail and there is also a bivouac hut (Giordano) which cannot be seen. Straight ahead now is the W col of the Lisjoch, to reach the E col slant up NE. The summit of the Dufourspitze is visible through the gap. **c2½hr**

Monte Rosa group and the Weissgrat Lisjoch to Monte Moropass

The massif consists of no less than ten peaks of over 4,000m, forming the largest mountain mass in western Europe. Only Mont Blanc exceeds it in terms of height.

The Dufourspitze (4,634m), formerly known as the Höchste Spitze, was first climbed on 1st Aug 1855 and named in 1863 in honour of General Dufour, the Swiss cartographer who published the first accurate Swiss maps.

The Dufourspitze stands 140m W of the Italian frontier. It is the second highest mountain in the Alps and the highest point in Switzerland.

Nordend (4,609m) lies 700m N of the Dufourspitze at the end of a sharp snowy ridge beginning at the Silbersattel. This saddle is 100m below the very steep crest of the Dufourspitze. The normal and long approach to Nordend is therefore from the Monte Rosa hut on the Swiss side.

The Zumsteinspitze (4,563m) lies to the SE midway between the Dufourspitze and the Signalkuppe. It is easily incorporated with the others in a traverse. The Zumsteinspitze was the first major summit in the Monte Rosa massif to be climbed in 1820, 35 years to the day before the Dufourspitze had its first ascent. Its summit stands in the central position at the top of the huge Macugnaga Face (Monte Rosa E face) when viewed from the E. This is the largest and most continuous face in the Alps, offering long and serious routes of the highest standard.

The Signalkuppe (4,556m), is known to the Italians as Punta Gnifetti, named after a local clergyman from Alagna who was with the first ascensionists on 9th Aug 1842. This peak is distinguished by the hut on its summit, the Capanna Margherita, which is the highest building in Europe. Construction began in 1890 and in 1893 it was opened personally by Queen Margherita. The original building has since been replaced by a three storey structure sheathed in copper. The name Signal

MONTE ROSA GROUP AND THE WEISSGRAT

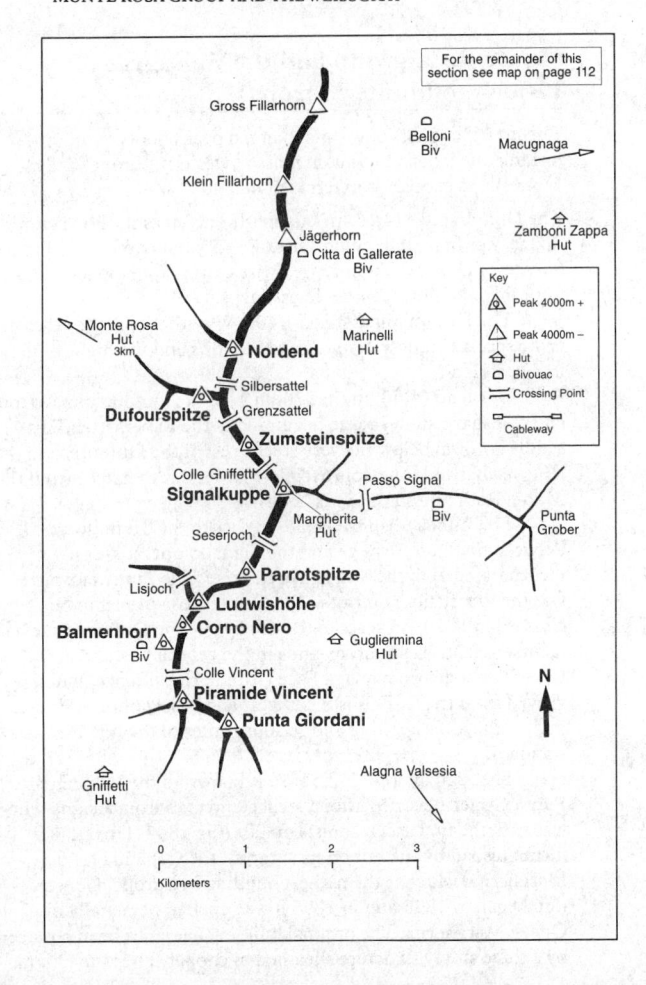

comes from the cairn-like gendarme NE of the summit.

The frontier continues S, first over the Parrotspitze (4,432m), named after a German doctor, and then over the Ludwigshöhe (4,341m) before crossing the Lisjoch. S of the frontier, entirely in Italy, are the small summits of Corno Nero (Schwarzhorn: 4,321m) and the Balmenhorn (4,167m), hardly worthy of separate 4,000m status. S again is Piramide Vincent (4,215m), a prominent summit first climbed in 1819 by Johann Vincent, the owner of gold mines in the Valle della Sesia, which the mountain overlooks.

The tenth and final 4,000er is the Punta Giordani (4,046m), which is merely a spur on the SE ridge of Piramide Vincent and may be regarded as an impostor.

The frontier to the N of the Monte Rosa's ten 4,000m summits continues along the 6km Weissgrat. The Swiss flanks to the W consist of extensive snowfields which feed the Gorner and Findel glaciers. These glaciers are divided by a rock ridge, the highest point being the Stockhorn (3,532m). A cable car from the Gornergrat station brings tourists to a point 1km from the summit. A pleasant mixed route to the Stockhorn can be made via the NW ridge starting at Berghaus Flue.

To the W of the Gornergrat, within easy reach of Zermatt, stands the fine little rock peak of the Riffelhorn. Here are found several worthwhile rock routes, those on the S face overlooking the Gorner glacier being up to 400m long. The Riffelhorn is traditionally used by local guides as a training ground for clients prior to an ascent of the Matterhorn. It is easily reached from Rotenboden station on the Gornergrat railway.

The E face of the Weissgrat overlooking Macugnaga is a vast and steep rocky face, seamed with snow-filled couloirs, frequently swept by stonefall. To reach the ridge crest from this side presents a more serious challenge. However there are relatively safe lines. The Italians are fond of bivouac huts and several will be found high on this side of the ridge. These enable ascents of the high points to be undertaken with greater ease, such as the Jägerhorn (3,970m), the Torre di Castelfranco (3,623m) and Cima di Jazzi (3,802m).

The final minor peak to the S is the Schwarzberghorn (3,609m). This marks the point where the frontier turns sharply E. Though not as impressive as the Weissgrat it has similar characteristics. Stretching for 5km it ends at Monte Moro (2,984m), where several routes of interest to the rock climber may be found. They are within easy reach of the cable car station on Monte Moropass or from the Swiss side approaching from Mattmark Dam.

Included in this group is the Pizzo Bianco which faces the E face of Monte Rosa from above the Zamboni and Zappa hut. Although quite modest in altitude it makes a worthy little objective.

Punta Giordani 4,046m

Named after P Giordano, a local doctor who appears to have climbed the peak in 1801. Although the peak exceeds the 'magic' 4,000m level it can hardly be considered to be a separate mountain, it is more a 'top' on Piramide Vincent although well detached from that summit. Its N and E flanks are predominantly rocky whilst its other flanks are mainly glaciated.

The name Gugliermina appears frequently in the first ascent details of this mountain. In particular the brothers Giuseppe Francesco and Giovanni Battista Gugliermina were very active in the Monte Rosa region and especially so on the Valsesia flank. The old Valsesia bivouac hut was renamed the Gugliermina hut in their honour. To confuse matters there were two, older guides also named Giuseppe and Giovanni Gugliermina as well as a Bortolo Gugliermina active in the same region who were also involved in first ascents and whose names should not be confused with the brothers. Both initials are used below where the brothers were involved in first ascents.

31a SOUTH-SOUTH-WEST FLANK

F G Calderini and V Zoppetti with Giuseppe Gugliermina, 10 Aug 1877

32
33 Valley base: Alagna/Gressoney

A straightforward climb up a glacier slope which has ski installations on its lower part. It can be used as a means of traversing Piramide Vincent (see Route 32g). c800m

Start from the Puntra Indren lift station and follow the Routes H19/20 towards the Città di Mantova and Gnifetti huts. When you meet the ski-lift coming from the Indren glacier, follow the line of the lift to its top. Continue up the glacier, moving Lwards where it steepens and is crevassed. The angle of the slope eases and leads to the snow crest of the summit ridge, which is almost level. **2½-3hr**

31b NORTH-EAST RIDGE

AD+ G B and G F Gugliermina and L Ravelli, 28 July 1908
Valley base: Alagna

The NE flank of the mountain is far more impressive than any other aspect of it, rising as it does for c700m from the steep Piode glacier and merging into the NE face of Piramide Vincent. The route follows the very L edge of this flank where it meets the R edge of the E face. The ridge itself can be climbed for a large part on snow but it is primarily a mixed route. c750m

From the Gugliermina hut follow tracks leading directly above the hut to a steep step in the ridge. Climb the step starting on the L then direct (III+, piton). Now slant L to reach the Piode glacier at c3,650m. Climb c50m up the glacier then contour round (slight descent) to below the couloir leading to Colle Vincent (Pt 4,087m: c2½hr). Beware of ice falling down this couloir. Continue SE to the foot of the ridge (2½-3hr).

Cross the bergschrund and slant up snow/ice slopes to the crest of the ridge. Keep on or close to the crest to a steep step of whitish rock. Turn this on the N side, regain the crest above it

31c SOUTH-EAST RIDGE

PD G Farinetti with Giovanni and Giuseppe Gugliermina, 13 Sept 1872
32 Valley base: Alagna/Gressoney

A pleasant route to the summit with one very nice pitch and some excellent views of the Alagna Valsesia cirque. **c800m**

From the Puntra Indren lift station get on to the R branch of the Bors glacier and then cross the glacier, moving in a R curving arc to reach the col NW of Punta Vittoria. Now climb the ridge up broken but easy rocks, passing short snowy sections on the L. Towards the top climb directly up a nice slab (III-) and so reach the summit. **c3½hr**

31d SOUTH-SOUTH-EAST FLANK

AD G B Gugliermina, F and M Ravelli, 23 Aug 1953
32 Valley base: Alagna/Gressoney

This flank of the mountain forms a triangular facet above the Bors glacier c300m in height on which a number of climbs have been recorded. The first ascent party included G B Gugliermina who had 45 years earlier been involved in the first ascent of the NE ridge. The route described here probably gives the best of the climbing and is also best sheltered from stonefall. It was first climbed on 18 April 1966 by V Piccolo and M Gabbio. **c800m**

From the Punta Indren lift station climb the Bors glacier to the rock barrier at its top to a point where a steep couloir cuts through the barrier more or less in line with the summit. Climb the couloir and a 15m rock step to reach the snowy terrace above. Cross this and climb the centre of a small, triangular rock wall (III, piton). Now slant up R until you are directly in the summit fall-line and then climb more or less directly to the summit. **3-4hr**

Piramide Vincent 4,215m

J-N Vincent with two youths and J Castel, a chamois hunter,
5 Aug 1819

This is the most southerly of the Monte Rosa 4,000ers that can be classified as a separate mountain. Its NW flank is entirely snow and gives an easy means of ascent in summer and for springtime skiers. Dramatically more impressive is its NE flank (merging into that of the Punta Giordani) which takes the form of a steep rock wall, c550m high which overlooks the W branch of the Piode glacier.

32a NORTH-NORTH-WEST FLANK
F   A and H Schlagintweit with P Beck, 15 Sept 1851
33 Valley base: Gressoney/Alagna

The normal means of ascent and very easy. **600m**

From the Gnifetti hut follow Route 30b towards the Lisjoch. At a height of c3,960m turn R towards the col at Pt 4,087m (Colle Vincent). Don't climb to the col but instead curve round further R to climb the easy snow slopes SE to the summit. **c2hr**

32b SOUTH-SOUTH-WEST RIDGE
PD   C Perazzi with P Maquignaz and A Welf, 22 July 1882
33 Valley base: Gressoney/Alagna
32

A very pleasant, yet straightforward climb that can be started from the Gnifetti hut or from the Puntra Indren lift station. **600m** *from the hut*

From the Gnifetti hut cross the glacier (Garstelet) on the E side of the hut to reach the crest of the ridge. Follow this to the top crossing snow and rock bands as they appear. **c2½hr**

Starting from Punta Indren (M Conway party, 14 Aug 1884) follow Route H19/20 towards the Città di Mantova and Gnifetti huts as far as the R bank of the Indren glacier. Climb this to the N most couloir cutting through the rock wall on the L. Scramble up the rocks N of this couloir to the crest of the ridge then proceed as above. **c3½hr** and **975m**

South-West Face

This is c400m high and largely rock, although early in the season, when there is reasonable snow cover, it provides several lines of good, mixed climbing all at about AD+ standard. The climbs are easily accessed from the Gnifetti hut, which probably accounts for the profusion of climbs on the face. Allow c1hr to reach the foot of the climbs. The route times given are from the base of the climb.

32c RIGHT-HAND ROUTE
AD+ E Andreis and A Rostagni, 30 Aug 1929
33 FWA: E Barbero, A Bonomi, A Caroni and L Ratto, 29 Jan 1967
Valley base: Gressoney/Alagna

This route climbs the rocky rib to the R of the central couloir. ***c400m: c3hr***

32d CENTRAL COULOIR
AD+ P Argentero, R Spanna and B Welf, 7 March 1963
33 First ski descent: C Schranz, 1977
Valley base: Gressoney/Alagna

The climb should only be undertaken in well snowed-up conditions otherwise stonefall dangers are high. ***c400m: c3hr***

32e LEFT-HAND COULOIR
AD+ A Jaccod and R Nicco, 23 Dec 1979
33 Valley base: Gressoney/Alagna

First climbed as a winter route it has had further ascents in summer, although, like other routes on the face, it should only be attempted in good snowy conditions. The route follows a twisting couloir line which branches off L from the central couloir after c100m climbing. ***c400m: c3hr***

32f RIGHT-HAND RIB OF NORTH-EAST FACE
D   V Sanguinetti with G Cerini and G Guglielminetti, 3 Sept 1902
35 FWA: C Raiteri and T Vidoni, 7/8 Jan 1978
34   Valley base: Alagna

The original route on the face and probably the least exposed to stonefall although the rock is not particularly good. An alternative means of ascent is the snow slope on the R of the rib (D+). c550m

From the Gugliermina hut follow Route 31b to below Colle Vincent. The route itself starts at the lowest rock rib beyond this same couloir and just L of a steep snow slope, the rib being continuous to the summit.

Cross the bergschrund and climb up to the lowest rocks. Continue on the crest of the gradually narrowing rib. Towards the top the rib splits into two branches. Follow the L branch to reach the ESE ridge and climb this to the summit. Alternatively, instead of taking the L branch at the split, continue on the R branch. On quite sound, smooth rock (IV) continue on the crest to the summit snow slope. **4hr** from the foot of the rib

32g EAST-SOUTH-EAST RIDGE

PD G Calderini and V Zoppetti with B and Giuseppe Gugliermina, 1877

Valley base: Gressoney/Alagna

A fine but quite short ridge linking the summit of Punta Giordani with that of Piramide Vincent. Some exposed climbing in a wonderful position. The final part of the ridge was climbed by the J-N Vincent party on the first ascent of the mountain. c160m

Reach the ridge via Route 31a or from the summit of the Punta Giordani then follow its snow crest to the first steep rock step. Turn the step on the R along ledges leading to broken rocks which allow the ridge to be regained. Another snow crest then leads to a longer section of rock which is climbed pleasurably, on the crest, to the summit snow slope. **1hr** for the ridge

Colle Vincent 4,087m

A and H Schlagintweit with P Beck, 15 Sept 1851

A fairly insignificant col between Piramide Vincent and Corno Nero and not named on the map. Its W flank is easily climbed in contrast to its E flank which takes the form of a very steep snow/ice couloir know as Canale Vincent. This couloir was first climbed by C Cametti with F Enzio, 4 Oct 1980 and is graded ED1. It has vertical or even overhanging ice pitches.

Sperone Vincent

F Pastore, G Rasario and T Zanetta, 16 Aug 1940

Unnamed on the map, this is a rock pillar (also known as the Pilastro Vincent) situated on the N side of the Canale Vincent (see above). The pillar is c350m high and is of excellent quality rock, certainly the best rock in the Alagna Valsesia cirque, and has plenty of good nut placements. Consequently it has attracted the attention of some leading alpinists.

33a ANTONIETTI-ENZIO ROUTE
TD O Antonietti and F Enzio, 1982
34 Valley base: Alagna
35

Reportedly an excellent route with a particularly fine chimney. 350m

Approach the foot of the pillar by Route 31b (2½hr). Cross the bergschrund and then climb a ramp and ledge (both snowy) Lwards to an obvious small couloir which slants Lwards towards the Colle Vincent. From a niche on the R at the bottom of this couloir there is a dièdre leading R into the centre of the pillar. Climb it for two pitches (80m in all, IV+ and two steps of V) to a rubble covered ledge. Follow the ledge R for 40m to the bottom of a magnificent chimney which appears to split the pillar in two. Climb the chimney, which may be icy in its upper part (4 pitches, 150m of IV and V with two moves of VI-, 1 piton in place). From the top of the chimney reach a gap between a smaller pillar on the R and the summit of the Sperone Vincent on the L. From the gap follow the airy ridge crest W (one step of IV at the start) to a steep section. Turn it on the L or climb it directly via smooth slabs, an overlap on the R and a dièdre (30m, III- and IV+). Finally a 40m snow slope (50°) leads to a cornice, which may prove difficult, and Colle Vincent. **7hr** for the pillar

33b SOUTH-EAST RIB

TD G Grassi and I Meneghin, 13 July 1983

Valley base: Alagna

Another reportedly good climb on the pillar which takes a line up its L edge. **350m**

Start as for Route 33a to the bottom of the small couloir. Climb the rib on the L for two pitches (III with a step of IV). At the top of the rib climb the long dièdre on the R for 15m (IV), avoiding a narrow and overhanging section on the R, to a good ledge. Continue via slabs on the R side of the crack in the bed of the dièdre (IV+) which lead to a ledge cutting across the pillar. Slightly overhanging rock (IV+) leads straight up and then the bed of the dièdre is followed to a good belay. Go straight up for another 15m to a short wall which is climbed (IV) via cracks towards the L side of the pillar where a big, snow and rubble covered ramp extends R into the centre of the pillar.

The route continues by a crack on the crest of the rib (IV+) to some jumbled blocks. Above these climb the R side of a dièdre (IV) and at its top climb another short, opposing dièdre (IV+) to a belay. Move R and climb a short, protruding wall (IV+) and then easier ground to a terrace. Above the terrace is a vertical wall split by two cracks. Climb the R-hand crack (V with a move of V+) and then easier rock to the next belay. Another 50m of climbing lead to the top of the pillar.

Climb down the crest of the ridge on the L to reach a gap then follow Route 33a to Colle Vincent. **c6hr** for the rib

Corno Nero 4,321m

M Maglioni and A de Rotschild with N and P Knubel and
E Cupelin, 18 Aug 1873

Situated on the ridge between Piramide Vincent and the
Ludwigshöhe, it is difficult to justify this summit as a separate
4,000er as the height gain in climbing it from the col on its NE
side (Colle Zurbriggen, not named on map), which separates it
from Ludwigshöhe, is only 50m. Its W flank, with the
Balmenhorn outcrop at its foot, along with the W flank of
Ludwigshöhe merge into the Lis glacier and form the E
bounding edge of it. Its SE flank is a steep rock wall which is
c600m high, split towards the top by a steep band of névé. The
rocks below this band are generally of good quality, smooth but
well endowed with cracks, whilst higher up the rock becomes
more broken. At least three routes have been climbed on the
wall.

34a SOUTH RIDGE
PD A Ferrari with A Pellissier and B Pession, 31 Aug 1894
33 Valley base: Gressoney/Alagna
34

The obvious route from the Gnifetti hut and in a very fine situation.
***c240m** for the ridge*

Reach Colle Vincent via Route 32a. From the col climb straight
up the snow slope, which gradually becomes more rounded and
ridge-like, to reach the summit rocks. Climb these over the W top
and on to the main summit. **2½-3hr** from the hut

34b NORTH-EAST RIDGE
PD First ascent party
Valley base: Gressoney/Alagna/Zermatt

A very short route. ***50m***

Reach the col on the NE side of the peak (Colle Zurbriggen)
from the Lisjoch by contouring round or traversing the

Ludwigshöhe. Climb straight up to the summit, overcoming two steps on the way (II and III+). ½**hr** from the Lisjoch

It is just as easy to climb the NW side of the peak when approaching from the Lisjoch.

Ludwigshöhe 4,341m

F von Welden and helpers, 25 Aug 1822

von Welden's second name was Ludwig and the day he climbed the peak was St Louis' (Ludwig) day, hence the name of the peak. Another 4,000m peak that is difficult to justify as a separate mountain. The height interval between the summit and the col on its NE side is only 58m. Like the Corno Nero, its W flank merges into the Lis glacier whilst its N flank forms the S limit of the Grenz glacier. The SE flank is less dramatic than that of its neighbours and has only one route of any note. The peak is rarely climbed other than in combination with the Parrotspitze.

35a SOUTH-WEST RIDGE
F   Valley base: Gressoney/Alagna/Zermatt

From the Lisjoch contour round the W flank of the peak to the col on its SW side (Colle Zurbriggen) and climb the snow slope to the top. ½**hr** and **95m**

35b NORTH SIDE OR NORTH-EAST RIDGE
F   Valley base: Gressoney/Alagna/Zermatt

A direct ascent to the summit can be made from the Lisjoch on the N side whilst climbers descending from the Parrotspitze will arrive at the foot of the NE ridge at the Piodejoch (not named on map). Only 58m climb from the Piodejoch

In either case climb easy snow slopes to the summit. ¼**hr** from the Piodejoch

Parrotspitze 4,432m

E Hall, F Grove, R Macdonald and M Woodmass with
M Anderegg and P Perren, 16 Aug 1863

A significant mountain in the Monte Rosa group but somewhat dominated by the neighbouring Signalkuppe from which it is separated, on its NE side, by the Seserjoch. On its SW side is the Piodejoch (not named on map), which separates it in turn from the Ludwigshöhe. From this col the frontier ridge extends NE to reach the W ridge of the mountain, which is entirely of snow and rises gently to the summit. Its N flank is a jumble of snow and ice cliffs overlooking the upper basin of the Grenz glacier.

The Italian flank of the mountain is quite complex. Its N limit is the couloir descending E from the Seserjoch (Canale Sesia, AD) and the principal feature is the long rocky promontory which extends ESE from a point some way E of the summit. The promontory splits into two branches, the Nmost terminating quite quickly in the Sesia glacier whilst the other branch (on which the Gugliermina hut stands) turns SE and separates the Sesia and Piode glaciers. The tiny (and unnamed on the map) Parrot glacier is sandwiched between the two branches. Extending from the Canale Sesia to the point where the N branch of the promontory terminates is a 400m high rock wall, split by two névé slopes. This is the ENE face and the site of several routes, although only one is described here.

On the S side of the promontory, before it splits, is a rock wall 200-300m high which is capped by snow/ice slopes. At least three routes have been recorded on this face.

36a WEST RIDGE
PD First ascent party
Valley base: Gressoney/Alagna/Zermatt

A fine snow crest which is quite narrow and can be corniced. When approaching from the Monte Rosa hut it is not necessary to go all the way to the Lisjoch. **c180m**

From the Lisjoch walk E to the foot of the ridge, or from the Piodejoch climb NE up steepening slopes on to the ridge. Either way climb the crest to the summit. **1hr**

36b NORTH-NORTH-WEST FLANK
AD Valley base: Gressoney/Alagna/Zermatt

In good snow conditions this short face gives an entertaining little climb starting from the trail to the Signalkuppe, the slope rising to c50°. **200m: 1hr**

36c NORTH-EAST RIDGE
F Valley base: Gressoney/Alagna/Zermatt

Reach the Seserjoch from the piste to/from the Margherita hut/Signalkuppe (Route37a) and gain the ridge on the L side of some rocks. Climb the ridge to the summit. **½hr and 146m**

36d EAST-NORTH-EAST FACE SNOW SLOPE
D A Cavanna with M Gabbio, 26 Aug 1972
35 Solo: G Cenerini, Aug 1982
Valley base: Alagna

A snow/ice climb in a remote setting and in good conditions is almost completely free of any objective danger. At one time this route was impossible because of a band of seracs blocking the way but these have now disappeared. **700m**

From the Resegotti bivouac hut follow the ridge W to the Passo Signal. Continue along the ridge for another 200m and then slant down L over rock and snow patches on to the Vigne glacier. Descend this to the glacier plateau (known as the Pianoro Ellermann) on the N side of Roccia Sesia. Now contour round to the foot of the Canale Sesia (2½hr). This is the steep couloir on the R side of a rock wall, the route climbs the snow/ice slope which bounds the L side of this wall.

Climb straight up the centre of the gradually steepening slope to the saddle at its top (55° max). Turn NW and climb the steep snow rib to where it joins the NE ridge and follow this to the summit (4-5hr). Allow **8hr**

36e SOUTH-EAST RIDGE

AD E Canzio and G Lampugnani with Giuseppe Gugliermina,
35 18 July 1906
FWA: E Cavalieri and C Sabbadini with A Viotti, 29 Dec 1956
Valley base: Alagna

A good mixed climb in a fine setting and with little in the way of objective danger. Rock difficulties of II and III. **1,220m**

From the Gugliermina hut follow Route 31b on to the Piode glacier. Cross this Nwards and cross the bergschrund before climbing easy rocks towards the obvious narrow ridge which is visible from below. The rock on the ridge is a bit loose but quite easy and leads to a steeper section of mixed climbing. Above this section climb the steep snow rib to join the NE ridge close to the summit. **c7hr**

36f SOUTH FACE LEFT-HAND PILLAR

TD D Deiana and M Moretti
35 Valley base: Alagna

To the W of the SE ridge, overlooking the N most part of the Piode glacier is a steep rock wall c700m high. The lower part of the wall is of good, smooth, compact rock and the scene of some hardish and remote rock climbs. The upper part of the wall leans back and becomes more broken and snow covered. The route described here, which follows the line of a reddish pillar for c400m, is quite well sheltered from stonefall. **c700m**

Reach the Piode glacier from the Gugliermina hut via Route 31b. Climb the glacier to the foot of the wall L of the central slabs. Start L of a couloir with a 15m high overhanging wall at its base. Climb the wall L of the overhang (IV) and then traverse R to the base of the pillar (20m). Start up a dièdre leading R and then a slab on the L followed by easier ground to a stance (50m: V+). Two considerably easier pitches (III and III+) lead to a chimney/crack line. Climb this in three pitches (IV and IV+) to a terrace below some overhangs. Avoid these by 15m of exposed climbing, slanting up R and another 25m straight up (V+ and V). Reach the top of the pillar by climbing two pitches on the crest (steps of IV and V). A further 300m of mixed climbing (40°) leads to the summit. **8-10hr**

Signalkuppe 4,454m

G Farinetti, C Ferrari, G and G Giordani, G Gnifetti and C Grober with two porters, 9 Aug 1842

Known to the Italians as Punta Gnifetti, its probably best known feature is the presence on its summit of the Margherita hut. Second in importance to the Dufourspitze in mountaineering terms, but at least as important geographically. It has three distinct ridges and consequently, three faces. The NNW and SSW ridges are quite short and are of little significance other than that they form part of the Swiss-Italian frontier. The E ridge is a classic route of ascent (Cresta Signal) and forms an important watershed.

The W face has a very benign nature compared to those of the NE and SE faces, being almost entirely of snow and the means of approach of most parties to the summit in both summer and in spring. The other two faces, among the highest in Europe, are wild and wonderful places of rock, snow and ice. The NE wall being a continuation of the massive E face of Monte Rosa whilst the SE face forms the dominant part of the Alagna Valsesia cirque.

37a WEST FLANK
F First ascent party
FWA: C and G Sella with J Maquingnaz, P Gugliermina and two porters, 18 Jan 1886
Valley base: Gressoney/Alagna/Zermatt

The route to the Margherita hut and climbed by vast numbers, on skis in spring and on foot in summer. Both approaches are very well tracked, especially in summer. **c300m** *from the Lisjoch*

(i) From the Gnifetti hut follow Route 30b to the E col of the Lisjoch. Now cross, almost horizontally, the upper slopes of the Grenz glacier below the N flank of the Parrotspitze and reach the slopes below the Seserjoch. Here turn N towards the Zumsteinspitze and climb steepening snow slopes towards that summit. At about the 4,000m contour, swing round to climb ESE up the steepening slope to the hut/summit. **c4hr**

(ii) From the Monte Rosa hut follow Route 30a to reach the upper part of the Grenz glacier. At c4,150m, and some way S of a crevassed part of the glacier below the Zumsteinspitze, swing L into the glacier combe below the Colle Gnifetti and join the route coming from the Lisjoch. **c6hr**

Signalkuppe: North-East Face
L Devies and J Lagarde, 17 July 1931

The setting for some superb but at the same time very serious routes. On this face of the mountain there are three prominent rock ribs plunging down to the Monte Rosa glacier. The L-hand rib starts on the E ridge (Cresta Signal) and ends at Pt 3,286m, the central rib, which is the longest and most well defined, starts more or less at the summit and terminates at c3,360m, whilst the R-hand rib starts close to Colle Gnifetti and descends to c3,900m before losing itself in the ice. Each of the ribs are bounded on both sides by snow/ice slopes and the inevitable seracs. All routes on the face are exposed to considerable objective dangers and should only be attempted in cold conditions. Approach to routes on the face is usually from the Zamboni and Zappa hut but, since this hut is so low, an intermediate bivouac is usually necessary. Sites are described in the route descriptions.

37b RIGHT-HAND RIB

TD W Romen and G Tagliaferri, 8/9 March 1977 by the route
38 described
Valley base: Macugnaga

Part of the ridge had been climbed earlier but the first ascent party noted here climbed the entire ridge and at the same time made the first winter ascent. ***c2,300m** from the foot of the face*

From the Zamboni and Zappa hut follow the moraine crest, or a path on the R (W) side of the W most stream, in order to pass the R (W) side of the moraine enclosing the Lago delle Locce. Make a short descent on to the glacier and then climb a massive cone of rubble formed by the glacier descending from the Punta Tre Amici. From its top head for a large, grassy sided rock hump which is best climbed from its N foot starting at c2,500m. It is about 3 pitches to the top of the hump (II and III). A little higher (c2,750m) is an isolated rock protuberance which can serve as a bivouac site (bivouac Intra: somewhat exposed to seracs: 2½-3hr).

From the bivouac site climb up the middle of the Monte Rosa glacier, avoiding crevasses (often large) as necessary, before slanting R to the foot of the L-hand rib at Pt 3,286m and a possible bivouac site (2-3hr). Keep slanting R and cross two bergschrunds near the bottom of the central rib before climbing a rocky gully which leads to the foot of the vast snow slope on the R side of this rib. Above is a threatening band of seracs. Cross the snow slope Rwards to the foot of the R-hand rib and follow this to the level of the threatening seracs (2hr).

Continue fairly easily up the L side of the rib until it steepens. There follows c40m of difficult climbing up steep rock which is interspersed with little icy runnels (V+, 4hr). Easier mixed climbing now leads to the foot of the glacier dome. Climb this and exit directly or, if necessary, traverse L to find a point to break through. Allow **10-12hr** from the lower bivouac

37c CENTRAL RIB

TD First ascent party
38 FWA: A Chiò and D Vanini, 26/27 Feb 1965
First solo: A Gogna, 17 June 1969 and FW solo: M Fanchini, 16/17 March 1987
Valley base: Macugnaga

A classic, mainly snow/ice route that was first climbed without the use of rock or ice pitons and at a time when step cutting was the norm. The route does not in fact climb the central rib itself but takes the line of the snow/ice slope to its R. It is seriously threatened by a serac band at about mid-height. The infrequently attempted Devies/Lagarde route climbs the R side of the rib immediately L of this route.

The route had its first ski descent on 24 June 1969 by S de Benedetti. He had climbed the route overnight from the Zamboni and Zappa hut in 11hr accompanied by G Comino. Comino descended the route alone on foot. On 17 June 1990, D Neuenschwander made a ski descent of the route having first climbed it unaided. He then traversed to the foot of Nordend and climbed solo up the Shroud Direct (TD: Route 42e) before ending the day with a ski descent of that route.
c2,300m *from the foot of the face*

Follow Route 37b to the foot of the snow slope and below the serac band. Climb the L side of slope keeping close to the rocks of the rib and passing to the L of the serac band. At c4,050m, reach the top of the rock rib and climb the continuation snow rib to the rocks defending the summit. Slant Rwards up these to a couloir which is then climbed direct (both rock and ice) to a snow/ice slope with some scattered rocks. A final steep ice slope leads to the ridge just N of the summit. **8-12hr** from the lower bivouac

37d CENTENARY ROUTE

ED1/2 P Borghi and A Cremonesi, 5/6 Aug 1972
38 FWA: N Cavallotti with A Squinobal, 18/20 Jan 1976
Valley base: Macugnaga

The route follows a fairly direct line up the L side of the central rib giving some difficult free climbing. In fact the route was climbed

entirely free and has pitches of VI. It appears to be relatively safe. The centenary was of the first ascent of the E face of Monte Rosa.
c2,300m *from the foot of the face*

Reach the foot of the L-hand rib via Route 37b. Start at the lowest point on the R and make a 35m slanting traverse L to a short rib and climb this to the main rib. Move up this (III and IV) until it merges into the slope (good bivouac site just above). Above is a snow rib which leads to the next rocks which form the L side of the central rib.

Climb straight up on broken rock for two pitches to just below some smooth slabs and then traverse R for 5m to a shallow dièdre. Climb a crack in the dièdre (V, 1 piton) to a good belay a few m offset to the L. Next move diagonally L c15m to a dièdre-chimney which is climbed to a ledge on the L, this is easy at first but then has moves of V. Now traverse 4m across a smooth slab (exposed) to a short, vertical crack which is climbed (V+, 1 piton) to its top. Step L and climb another slab (VI) to reach a small stance. Another steep (overhanging) crack is climbed for c8m (V+) before one can move L round a rib to a dièdre. Climb this over small overlaps in its bed and then on the L side (plenty of good holds) until it steepens. Surmount a wet and dirty overhang (V, VI, 5 pitons) to a good belay. Difficulties continue as you climb the dièdre (V, VI and pitons) via cracks and flakes to a big roof and good belay.

Avoid the roof by moving 2m L across an almost holdless smooth slab to its sharp edge. Climb the edge which is near vertical and very exposed (VI, 1 piton) and then straight up another 15m. A few easier pitches lead to the snow crest at the top of the central rib. Follow this to the rocks above and then traverse L for two pitches to the bottom of an icy couloir. Climb the couloir via the rocks on the R (5 pitches, III) to the summit ridge just N of the summit. Allow at least **12hr** from the lower bivouac

37e GRINGO
ED1 V Furlan and B Pockar, 14/15 July 1990
38 Valley base: Macugnaga

The route climbs the extreme L side of the face, almost parallel to the Cresta Signal for some way. The first ascent was made unroped except for two pitches and was climbed mostly during the night. Escape on to the Cresta Signal should be possible in places. **c2,300m** *from the foot of the face*

From the bivouac Intra (see Route 37b) ascend the Monte Rosa glacier as for the previous route but instead of heading for the foot of the L-hand rib continue up the steepening slopes of the Signal glacier towards the highest glacier bay on the L side of the L-hand rib. At the top of the bay a couloir slant up L towards the Cresta Signal whilst to the R of this another, steeper couloir curves up Lwards. Climb this couloir (60° with steeper steps up to 80°). At the top of this couloir continue up a series of smaller couloirs in a fairly natural line of ascent (60°-75°). From c4,000m mixed climbing leads straight up to the upper snow slopes on the R side of the summit edifice. **c12hr** from the first couloir

Pockar appears to have had a liking for this face: in 1986, with J Stritih he had already climbed the original route of Devies and Lagarde (TD+). After his ascent of Gringo he returned again, this time with M Jamnik, and on 7/8 March 1992 added another route in the same vicinity as Gringo (No Pasaran: ED2). From a bivouac at the foot of the prominent spur on the L side of the face they climbed 200m up 60°-80° slopes then 7 difficult pitches to overcome the rock barrier above the spur (1 pitch, A0: 2 pitches, VI+ and the others VI-/VI). There were also icy runnels up to 85°. From here, because of worsening weather, they joined the Devies/Lagarde route. The same pair were active again on the face in June 1993, climbing another line L of the central rib with pitches of up to VII- and A2 and 65° ice. To minimise objective dangers they reached the foot of the rib at 6pm after the sun had left the face and made a bivouac at about half-height on the

37f EAST RIDGE - CRESTA SIGNAL
D   H Topham with A Supersaxo and a porter, 28 July 1887
35 FWA: O Festa and A Vecchietti, 20 March 1948
38 Valley base: Alagna

A classic route although the rock is not particularly good and there is some delicate mixed climbing. The ridge rises fairly regularly from the Passo Signal although there are two distinct steps in it. The route stays fairly close to the crest so avoid any tempting terrain which takes you too far from it. **c900m**

Start at the Resegotti bivouac hut and follow the crest of the ridge or the rocks on the L side to the Passo Signal. Continue along the ridge with alternate sections of rock and snow, passing any difficulties on the L side, to reach the first step. This can be turned on either side but the S side is probably better. Climb a small couloir (icy) and then a short chimney to reach a little snowy shoulder back on the crest in c40m. Above this poor and steepening rock leads to a short step. Climb this by slanting up R in a couloir which is rather loose and has some snow and ice. This leads to another steep section on the crest. Climb this on good rock via a crack (IV with 1 piton), and then another 30m up more loose rock.

Some gendarmes now block the way along the crest. Keep to the R and skirt round the gendarmes, climb a mixed rock and ice slope and reach the foot of the second big step recognisable by an S-shaped vein of rock (c70m to here). Pass to the L of the step, keeping as close as possible to the steep rocks on the R. Descend gradually for c30m across slabs (a bit of a hand-traverse) to the foot of a small dièdre. Climb this and then some blocks, all quite nice climbing (IV, 1 piton), and gain the crest on the L. An alternative to climbing the dièdre is to continue traversing until a direct ascent to the crest can be made. Continue up the crest for another 40m and then move L and climb on this side for several pitches over mixed terrain until the crest is regained once more at a level section. Keep on the crest now to the summit (bits of III). **c6hr**

37g SOUTH-EAST FACE - AFRICA NOSTRA
TD+ F Loss, S Mondinelli and P Valentina, 9 Sept 1987
35 Valley base: Alagna

The SE face rises c800m above the glacier at its base (Pianoro Ellermann, not named on map). The most obvious feature of the face is a long line of weakness slanting up from R to L with its origin close to the Cresta Signal and which gives the line of the original route (D) on the face (A Orio and F de Zinis with G Chiara and G Guglielminetti, 31 Aug 1906) and which is exposed to stonefall. The route described here climbs the L side of the face and is on very steep and good rock in its upper half. **c800m**

From the Resegotti bivouac hut follow Route 36d to the Pianoro Ellermann. Contour along this to the start on the L side of the face at the lowest point of the rocks. Climb more or less straight up by way of shattered rock and smooth, overlapping slabs (D+: some stonefall danger) for c400m to a triangular snow patch at about mid-height on the face. The angle now steepens considerably.

On the R climb dièdres and cracked slabs for two pitches to a debris covered terrace (IV). Next avoid a big slabby section by climbing up L, via more dièdres and short slabs, for two pitches (V) to reach a massive Africa-shaped block. Climb to the top of this via an icy chimney (V). Two excellent pitches up compact slabs (possibly some melt-water streaks) lead up to a roof (VI then IV). Traverse R for 30m and then climb past the roof via a chimney (loose rock) to a belay 30m higher. Move L a little and climb steep rock and, via a dièdre and over a small roof (V), reach a big, open chimney (50m). Climb this using cracks and flakes (IV, beware of loose rock) to the summit snow crest. **c12hr**

Colle Gnifetti 4,452m

A big snowy saddle between the Signalkuppe and the Zumsteinspitze, which is easily reached on the Swiss (SW) side by Route 37a but is very dangerous on the Italian side where a large cornice often forms. It has been approached from the Italian side by parties escaping from the E face of Monte Rosa who traverse snow slopes below the Grenzsattel and the Zumsteinspitze. A relatively safe route climbs the rock rib on the L side of the NE face, the approach being made from the Marinelli hut (G Tagliaferri and W Romen, 24 Aug 1976, ED1). Routes to the Margherita hut pass close to the col on its SW side.

Zumsteinspitze 4,563m

J Niklaus, J Vincent, J Zumstein and Molinatti with the hunters J Beck, M Zumstein and other guides and porters, 1 Aug 1820

A relatively insignificant summit rising just 111m above both the Colle Gnifetti and the Grenzsattel. It is entirely snow covered on the S flank and on the NE (Italian) flank but there is a rocky SW ridge and a few rocks are apparent below the summit on the W side. The NE flank, although snowy, is very steep and merges into the rest of the E face of Monte Rosa, although the very top part of the face is less steep and does offer a means of passage between the Colle Gnifetti and the Grenzsattel. However, this passage is rarely undertaken and is not recommended. The NW face overlooks the upper basin of the Grenz glacier and is c250m high. This rarely climbed face offers the opportunity for some mixed climbing. A new route was created here on 19 Aug 1993 by C Schranz and M Perini and given the name 'Maria': TD- with some grade V rock.

38a SOUTH-EAST RIDGE
F First ascent party
Valley base: Gressoney/Alagna/Zermatt

Parties attempting to climb the Dufourspitze from the Italian side invariably traverse the Zumsteinspitze in the process. This is the route of ascent. **111m** *from the Colle Gnifetti*

From the Colle Gnifetti climb the snow ridge to the summit rocks. **½hr**

38b SOUTH-WEST RIDGE
PD   Valley base: Gressoney/Alagna/Zermatt

37

A slightly more interesting way of reaching the summit of the peak than the much more frequented SE ridge. **400m** *from the Lisjoch*

From Route 37a to the Signalkuppe get on to the ridge, which is on the L as that route turns towards the Colle Gnifetti. Climb the ridge which is mostly easy rock. **1½hr** from the Lisjoch

38c NORTH RIDGE
PD+ K Blodig with C Ranggetiner (in descent), 28 July 1882
W Coolidge and W Conway with C and R Almer, 22 July 1886
Valley base: Gressoney/Alagna/Zermatt

Of no great intrinsic value in its own right but climbed and descended frequently by parties going to or from the Dufourspitze. **111m** *from the Grenzsattel*

From the Grenzsattel climb the narrow snow ridge, with a short section of rock at about half-height, to the summit. **½hr**

Grenzsattel 4,452m

Situated between the Zumsteinspitze and the Grenzgipfel (not named on map), which is the foresummit of the Dufourspitze on its E side. There are in fact two distinguishable saddles separated by a rocky knoll. The W (Swiss) flank is a straightforward snow slope whilst the E flank forms a part of the formidable E face of Monte Rosa.

39a WEST FLANK
PD Valley base: Zermatt

36
37

Parties may wish to climb to the Dufourspitze from the Monte Rosa hut by an alternative to Route 40a. This route offers that possibility, but it is best done reasonably early in the season and is not recommended as a descent route. The summit of the Dufourspitze is attained from the Grenzsattel by following Route 40f. ***1,660m***

Follow Route 30a as far as the first glacier plateau. It should now be possible to climb a narrow couloir between the rocks below Pt 4,026m and the seracs on the glacier. Continue E under the S flank of the Dufourspitze to the steeper slope leading to the saddle. Climb straight up this. **c5hr**

If the couloir is impassable, continue on Route 30a to the second glacier plateau and then turn NE to the steep slope below the saddle.

39b EAST FACE DIRECT
TD A and A Bich, B and C Maquignaz and G Pession, 15/16 Aug 1925

38

Valley base: Macugnaga

A serious route on account of the exposure to icefall and avalanche. The first ascent party were guides looking for the body of a colleague (C Bich) who had been blown from the Colle Gnifetti. In the process they found a relatively safe means of approach to the upper part of the Monte Rosa E face by the Crestone Zapparoli. ***c2,400m***

Follow a track SSW from the Zamboni and Zappa hut across a flat, grassy area. Cross the R lateral moraine of the Monte Rosa glacier and then climb up the middle of the glacier to the foot of the Crestone Zapparoli (c2,950m) by a waterfall. Smooth but easy rock leads up to a sort of small valley, pass through this and reach the crest of the rib. Climb this (II with steps of III and IV) to its top at c3,600m. It is possible to bivouac here in relative safety.

The route continues on a snow/ice crest which then merges into the face. Keep in as direct a line as possible towards the saddle, turning large crevasses as necessary. If conditions are suitable climb direct to the L-hand depression, otherwise take to the rocks separating the two depressions. **14hr** from the hut

Dufourspitze 4,633.9m

J Birbeck, C Hudson, C and J Smyth and E Stevenson with U Lauener and J and M Zumtaugwald, 1 Aug 1855

The culminating point of the Monte Rosa group, situated entirely in Switzerland on a ridge branching W from the frontier ridge and main chain of mountains. The frontier ridge rises NW from the Grenzsattel to a point at the E end of the summit ridge, which has a spot height of 4,618m (not marked on map), before turning N and descending to the Silbersattel. 40m along the ridge E of Pt 4,618m is a rocky shoulder c4,596m. Both these points have, at various times, been referred to as the Grenzgipfel, today the higher point is the one given this name. From the rocky shoulder the ridge continues Ewards, but it now descends steeply and quickly loses itself in the snow and ice of the E face.

Moving W along the ridge from the Grenzgipfel for 140m you reach the summit of the mountain. A little way before this point is reached there is another high point (c4,632m), sometimes referred to as the Ostspitze. Moving further W the ridge descends steadily before turning SSW and reaching, in 650m, a snowy saddle at Pt 4,359m (referred to as Sattel). The N side of this entire ridge is a mixture of rock and ice and is not easily climbed. Its S side is similar but with a very prominent, subsidiary rock ridge running S from the summit - Cresta Rey. Beyond Sattel the ridge turns SW before terminating in the Grenz glacier at c3,880m.

Undoubtedly the easiest way (physically) of climbing the Dufourspitze is from the Margherita hut via a traverse of Zumsteinspitze, there is only c180m of height gain compared

40a NORMAL ROUTE FROM THE MONTE ROSA HUT
PD

36 First ascent party
37 40 Valley base: Zermatt

A rather tedious plod up the Monte Rosa glacier as far as Pt 4,359m (Sattel) on the W ridge with the possibility of some loose shale, depending on the degree of snow cover, in the early part of the route. Where there is snow, the route becomes a piste in summer. The best time of year is Spring when one can use skis. ***1,850m***

From the Monte Rosa hut follow Route 30a to Pt 3,109m and then turn NE up a steep snow or shale slope with a few rocks to reach the Monte Rosa glacier SW of Pt 3,303m (1½hr). Climb the glacier ESE, working through a complex of crevasses, and then turn ENE into a little glacier combe. At c3,520m turn ESE again up steeper slopes until S of the rock outcrop at Pt 3,827m in a little combe. Climb SE out of the combe but then turn E to reach, at c4,000m, a broad, rounded snow spur leading R (SSE: 2hr). Most of this will have been done in the dark.

Follow the steeper slopes of the spur and pass some massive crevasses before the Sattel is seen. Now head direct to this point. There is a bergschrund to cross and a steep snow/ice slope to climb. Reach the saddle a bit to the L of the lowest point. Continue along the W ridge on snow, or the rocks on the R, then over a rock hump to a small snow saddle. More snow then leads to the narrow crest of the final rock section. Pass a step on the L side via a couloir then, after a gap, climb to the summit via a chimney (2½-3hr). Allow **6-7hr**

A less tedious approach to the slopes below Sattel can be made from the Grenz glacier (W Conway with F Imseng, 17 Aug 1878). This involves following Route 30a to the rock shoulder of Pt 3,472m and then climbing the glacier bay on the N side of

40b CRESTA REY

AD+
37
E Hutton with J Moser and P Rubi, 20 Aug 1874
FWA: V Sella with D and J Maquignaz, 26 Jan 1884
Valley base: Gressoney/Alagna/Zermatt

A classic route on excellent rock, steep but not difficult. The ridge is quite prominent as it descends S from the summit to a height of c4,400m, it then turns SSW becoming a decreasingly narrow rib before petering out in the glacier slope at c4,200m. It can be climbed from any one of four huts; Monte Rosa, Gnifetti, Margherita or the Balmenhorn bivouac. **c400m**

Reach the foot of the route via Route 39a from the Monte Rosa hut, or from the Lisjoch (E) by reversing Route 30a to a point where a traverse into the glacier combe can be made on the E side of the Zumsteinspitze. Start below the rib and climb a steep snow slope to the lowest rocks, crossing a bergschrund c50m below these. It is also possible to traverse on to the rib from the R, arriving at a point c50m above the lowest rocks after turning seracs on the R. Climb the ridge all the way to the summit with rock moves of II, occassionally III and some snow and with the possibility of verglas. At about half-height there is a 5-6m wall which can be climbed direct (IV, 1 piton) or turned on the L - there used to be a ladder. **3-4hr** from the base

A couloir just to the L of the Cresta Rey is a good mixed climb when in condition (A Cavanna, V Perini and M Gabbio, 21 Aug 1973: D). To the L again is another rib, much less well-defined than the Cresta Rey. It was climbed by E and M Cavalieri and L Pession, 25 Aug 1992 and was considered as good as the Cresta Rey although a little more difficult. There is plenty of III and IV and odd bits of V all on sound rock.

40c SOUTH-WEST RIDGE TO SATTEL

D   M Piacenza with J Carrel and J Pellisier, 20 July 1907
By route described: G Rham and A Tissières, 8 Aug 1944
Valley base: Zermatt

A good climb that you will almost certainly have to yourself, at least as far as the Sattel. ***c450m***

Reach the foot of the ridge via Route 30a. Start up slabs on the L of an inverted V shaped snow slope and reach an icy couloir. Climb this to a wall on the R below the first gap in the ridge (just N Pt 4,026m). Climb the difficult wall to the gap. The rest of the climb follows the crest of the ridge to Sattel and involves climbing; a chimney with some loose blocks (IV); a big gendarme and a steep wall. The gendarme is climbed by slanting slightly R up slabs to an overhang (niche), then through the overhang (IV+) before moving back L. A few more difficult moves lead to its top and a rappel descent to a gap. From the saddle continue as for Route 40a to the summit. **10hr** from the Monte Rosa hut

40d NORTH FLANK FROM THE SILBERSATTEL

AD   Probably J Madutz and M Zumtaugwald, 12 Aug 1848 but they did not visit the summit
Valley base: Zermatt

Parties traversing all the Monte Rosa summits in a single expedition will need to climb to the Dufourspitze after visiting the summit of Nordend. Most of the early attempts to climb the Dufourspitze were made from this side and all were repulsed by the difficulties. This approach to the summit remains quite difficult today unless you are fortunate enough to have perfect snow conditions. Various possibilities are available and are described below. (i) is the least inviting since it is longer and involves considerable height loss, but it is the easiest technically. (ii) is rarely climbed, (iii) and (iv) depend very much on the state of the snow. (v) is probably the surest way if not quite so direct as (ii), (iii) and (iv). ***120m***

Starting at the Silbersattel:

(i) Reverse Route 41a to below Sattel then follow Route 40a. **c3hr**

(ii) Contour under the N face until directly below the summit and climb the rock rib above by zigzagging up ramps to the crest of the W ridge just W of the summit. **1½hr**

(iii) Contour as for (ii) to reach the foot of a narrow couloir slanting steeply up L to R, reaching the crest of the summit ridge to the E of the summit. Climb the couloir, which can be mostly ice, and then follow Route 40f to the summit. **1½hr**

(iv) This route is most frequently used if the slope is not too icy or the snow is not too soft and deep. Slant R up the snow/ice slope in the direction of the first gap on the summit ridge on the W side of Grenzgipfel (see the introduction). Below the gap, climb rocks to reach the crest and join Route 40f to the summit. **1½hr**

(v) Follow the ridge S and pass the first rocks on the R. Climb the snow/ice slope and some steep rocks to the rocky shoulder at 4,596m (see the introduction). This gives a height gain of only 81m. If the slope is too icy it is possible to climb further L on the NE flank but this involves the ascent of a short but tricky slab. From the shoulder follow Route 40f to the summit. **c2hr**

40e EAST FACE - MARINELLI COULOIR

D
38
41

R and W Pendlebury and C Taylor with F Imseng, G Oberto and G Spechtenhauser, 22 July 1872
FWA: L Bettineschi, F Jacchini, M Pala and L Pironi, 5/6 Feb 1965
Valley base: Macugnaga

The E face of the Dufourspitze is just a part of the E face of Monte Rosa, which is the collective name applied to this truly magnificent sight which is of Himalayan proportions. It is the highest face in the Alps, rising c2,400m and extending from the Signalkuppe to Nordend as a massive sheet of snow and ice sweeping down to the Belvedere glacier at its base. The face is made even more impressive as it extends Ewards from the Signalkuppe to the Punta Tre Amici and NNW towards the Jägerhorn. Three long rock ribs interrupt the smoothness of the slope, reaching up to heights of between c3,800m and c3,500m. The most prominent and important of these is the Emost, Crestone Marinelli upon which stands the Marinelli hut. This rib borders the couloir known as Canalone Marinelli down which sweep frequent avalanches originating from the slopes of Nordend, the Silbersattel and the Dufourspitze. These avalanches start early in the day since the upper part of the face catches the sun from dawn. This couloir provides the line of the classic route of ascent although possibly the most dangerous. All routes on the face are exposed to a high degree of objective danger and should only be tackled during very cold weather, when a cold N wind is blowing, and should be started at about midnight.

This particular route should only be attempted by fast and fit parties so as to minimise the time one is exposed to objective danger. It is probably best climbed in early summer after a snowy Spring. Not recommended other than to parties interested in repeating historical ascents. Prospect the start beforehand. **c1,600m**

Take a rising track from the Marinelli hut to the L bank of the Marinelli couloir which is c50m wide. Cross it (deep icy runnels) above a rock outcrop in its middle, or via the outcrop. If snow conditions are good climb the R bank to the top of the Crestone Imseng, otherwise climb this rib overcoming steps of II and III. The four steps can give some shelter from avalanches.

Above the rib one enters the most dangerous part of the climb. Continue straight up the slope on the L side of the couloir which becomes less well defined, passing some seracs on their R side or finding a route through them, to reach the highest seracs. Start moving L where the slope is slightly less inclined and head towards the lowest rocks of the rib descending from the rocky shoulder at 4,596m referred to in the introduction. Pass two or three bergschrunds on the way. Just below the rocks the angle of the usually icy slope is c55° and it is exposed to stonefall.

In favourable snow conditions or if the rocks are wet, climb up to the L of the rib as high as possible on snow and then up rock to the ridge below the shoulder. Otherwise climb steep and difficult rocks to the crest of the rib. Follow the rib to the shoulder and then Route 40f to the summit. It is also possible to climb to the Silbersattel, given good snow conditions. **6-10hr**

40f SOUTH-EAST RIDGE

AD **37**

F Barlow and G Prothero with A Carrel and P Taugwalder, 31 Aug 1874
FWA: M Piacenza with A Curta and A and O Lazier, 18 Jan 1907
Valley base: Gressoney/Alagna

*This is the ordinary route from Italian huts and the route of descent for parties undertaking the traverse of the Monte Rosa summits and en route to the Margherita hut. It requires a certain amount of care as some of the rock is loose and there may be some ice. The summit ridge from the Grenzgipfel can be quite delicate if snow covered. **280m** from the Margherita hut*

From the Margherita hut traverse the Zumsteinspitze by Routes 38a and 38c to reach the Grenzsattel. Coming from the Gnifetti hut go straight up to the Colle Gnifetti instead of to the Margherita hut. Follow the ridge towards the Grenzgipfel (see the introduction), crossing some rocks to where it steepens and becomes almost entirely rock. Pass L round a gendarme then keep as close to the crest as possible, reaching the summit crest close to the Grenzgipfel. Follow the ridge W over a foresummit (Ostspitze) then almost horizontally, with a couple of gaps and, after passing a gendarme on the S side (a short chimney leads back to the crest), reach the summit. **3hr** from the Margherita hut: **7hr** from the Gnifetti hut

Silbersattel 4.515m

E Ordinaire and V Puiseux with J Brantschen, J Moser, J Taugwalder and M Zumtaugwald, 12 Aug 1847

Situated on the frontier ridge immediately S of Nordend, its W flank is formed by the easy angled upper part of the Swiss Monte Rosa glacier whilst its E flank forms a part of the E face of Monte Rosa. Most parties climbing Nordend by its ordinary route climb first to this col (see Route 42a).

41a WEST FLANK
PD First ascent party
40 Valley base: Zermatt

A rather boring glacier plod. ***1,720m***

From the Monte Rosa hut follow Route 40a to the rounded snow spur at c4,000m. Climb the spur towards Sattel to gain another 100m in height then turn L towards the foot of the WNW ridge of Nordend at Pt 4,200m. c200m short of this point turn SE up the steepening glacier to the saddle. Below the saddle there are often some large crevasses. Unless you are unlucky, these are usually easily circumnavigated. **5-6hr**

Nordend 4,609m

E and T Buxton and J Cowell with M Payot and Binder, 26 Aug 1861

The Nmost summit in the Monte Rosa group and a stunning peak when viewed from the N or NW. On this side is a broad ridge projecting out between the Monte Rosa glacier and the upper part of the Gorner glacier which terminates at Pt 3,197m on the Gorner glacier. It takes the form of a gently angled glacier slope supported on three sides by steep walls of compact rock. A number of routes have been climbed on these walls. Part of this wall forms the NW ridge, the line of one route described below. The E bounding edge of the wall on the N side of the ridge, falling ENE from Pt 4,355m to the Jägerjoch, gives the line of the classic Cresta di Santa Caterina, also described below. The S ridge, falling to the Silbersattel is almost entirely of snow and is the line taken by the ordinary route. The E flank merges with the rest of the E face of Monte Rosa although the character of the face changes here, becoming much more rocky.

42a SOUTH RIDGE

PD First ascent party
40 Valley base: Zermatt

The normal route and quite straightforward except when it is icy. A cornice forms on the Italian side. ***c1,800m** from the Monte Rosa hut*

From the Monte Rosa hut follow Route 41a to the Silbersattel and then follow the ridge keeping on the W side if there are any cornices. It may be possible to climb more directly to the ridge from the Monte Rosa glacier but this will depend on the size of the bergschrund. **6-7hr**

42b MORSHEAD RIB

D F Morshead and M Anderegg, 13 Aug 1877
36 Valley base: Zermatt

An interesting route to the summit, especially if you are climbing the peak for its own sake and not intending to continue over the Dufourspitze. Good rock. ***400m** from the foot of the rib*

As for Route 41a to the Silbersattel but go to the foot of the rib at 4,200m (4hr). Cross the bergschrund, usually on the R, and reach the R side of the rib and climb up to its crest. Continue on the crest to the point where it steepens abruptly, fairly close to the top of the rib. Slant up L to the shortest part of a steep wall (rappel piton) and climb it (IV). Use an iceaxe in a crack for aid if necessary. Step on to the snow slope and follow this easily to the summit. **c7hr**

It is also possible to stick to the rib at the steepening. This is a little more difficult (IV+).

42c NORTH-WEST RIDGE

AD+/D- Miss G Scott with H Lehner, 22 Aug 1933 although an approach
40 from the SW to the upper part had been climbed earlier.
36 39 Valley base: Zermatt

If the crest of the ridge, which is characterised by a distinctive red tower, is climbed integral from its base it gives a route of TD standard with rock pitches up to V and A1 (M Bena, G Lamka and K Zivny, 15/16 Aug 1976). The route described here avoids the difficulties on the lower part of the ridge by a line L of the crest and it avoids the red tower on the R. All the difficulties are concentrated in the first part of the climb, below c3,900m. **c1,400m**

Reach the foot of the ridge from the Monte Rosa hut by following Route 43a (2hr). Start well to the E of the ridge crest. Cross the bergschrund and a few rocks leading up to a slightly concave snow/ice slope. At the top of this slope slant up L to reach a narrow couloir leading to the crest of the ridge. Follow the crest, good climbing on fine gneiss, to the base of the red tower mentioned above. Turn the tower on the R and then keep on the crest over several teeth to where it merges into the snow (c3hr). The rest is a snow plod to the summit (2hr). **7-8hr**

Further E, below Pt 3,985 is a steep rib which bifurcates at half-height. Both branches have been climbed and each branch is graded TD+. The most direct line via the R-hand branch gives the most technically difficult climb on Nordend: H Furmanik, A Tarnawski and A Zysak, 21/23 Aug 1969: V+ and A1

42d CRESTA DI SANTA CATERINA
TD V Ryan with F and J Lochmatter, July 1906 but descended three
40 times (mostly by rappel) before this.
41 FWA: L Bettineschi, C and F Jacchini, M Pala and L Pironi, 10/11 Feb 1967
Valley base: Zermatt/Macugnaga

A superb, sustained route on good rock and worthy of the great partnership of its authors. The ridge rises from the Jägerjoch and has four distinct steps, two of which are close to vertical. Each step is overcome by a flanking movement, generally on the R side. Much of the climbing is of a slabby nature but cracks and chimneys are also encountered and there are quite difficult sections between the various steps. The route is not overlong, there being a height gain on the ridge of c450m, and the technical difficulties are not excessive. Belay pitons and some pitons that can be used for aid (although aid is not strictly needed and was not used on the first ascent) are in place. **450m**

From the Citta di Gallarate bivouac hut, descend to the Jägerjoch then follow the ridge along to the first of the difficulties. Start just R of the crest at a steep couloir system. Climb this (IV), gradually trending R (somewhat loose), to a ledge below the first steep step. Move R to a chimney and climb this by slabs on the R and then turn the overhang at the top on the R. Continue Rwards up a large, sloping terrace and then climb gradually Rwards for c30m up a series of slabs and cracks (V) to a small terrace. Next climb a wide crack (25m, V) before traversing delicately across a slab on the R (V) and then continuing on the slab (IV) to a good belay at the top of the largest step.

Cross mixed snow, rock and ice Rwards to a couloir. Climb this for c50m (some loose rock, IV) and then move L (IV: more loose rock). Ahead lies a zone of overlapping slabs leading to the second step. Climb these more or less directly (IV: delicate). The whole of this section is devoid of good belays and is very difficult if verglassed, although it has been climbed when banked out with snow.

The third step is reached by slanting L up light coloured rock, with cracks, to the crest of the ridge (IV). Exposed climbing up the crest for c20m (IV) leads to foot of the step. Find a crack on the R and climb this (III) to bypass the step and reach a snow ridge leading to the fourth step. Turn this on the R (III). A fairly even angled snow slope now leads to the summit. **6-8hr**

42e EAST FACE - SHROUD DIRECT
TD P Gabarrou and C Viard, 18/19 June 1984
41 FWA: and probably second overall ascent, S Albasini and C Portmann winter 1992/3
Descended on skis by D Neuenschwander, 17 June 1990 (see Route 37e)
Valley base: Macugnaga

The E face is principally of rock in the form of long ribs interspersed with snow or ice filled couloirs. The main features on the face are well indicated on the map. Of particular interest are: (i) the long couloir whose base is marked by the 3,400m contour line and which curves up Lwards towards the summit (the couloir provides the line of this route, the upper part of the couloir being the 'shroud') and (ii) the rock rib S of this couloir and with the broadest base whose lowest point is c3,550m, which gives the line of Route 42f.

The obvious starting point is the Marinelli hut but the first ascent party climbed up the Nordend glacier (bivouac on the L lateral moraine) with some steep pitches through a zone of seracs. The climb on the face proper is mostly snow or ice but there is some mixed climbing and rock at about half-height and some more rock at the top. The grade might vary somewhat from that given, in good conditions it might be only D+ but in mean conditions it could be as much as ED1. **c1,200m**

From the Marinelli hut climb up the crest of the rib on rock and then snow to reach a glacier terrace at c3,500m. Above is the start of the Brioschi route. Traverse R below a snowy bay and a rock buttress to a L slanting, steep icy couloir. Climb this (c70m, 60°/65°) and then the snow slope above to its upper L edge. A broad snow couloir is then followed to the point were it narrows significantly. Leave the couloir here by moving R below a steep rock wall. Turn the wall on its R via a narrow, delicate section, at first ice then rock (c15m) to reach a section of steep ice. Climb this direct (vertical) at the start then on the L and continue up enjoyable mixed ground with a few rock steps to reach the ice slope of the 'shroud' itself. Climb up the middle of it (stone and icefall danger) and at the top, on the L, climb a steep rock (and possibly ice) couloir. Beyond this a steepish ice slope leads to the summit. **8-10hr**

42f EAST FACE - BRIOSCHI ROUTE

D+ L Brioschi with A and F Imseng, July 1876

41 FWA: T Micotti, G Rognoni, P Sartor and P Signini, 11/13 Feb 1967

Valley base: Macugnaga

A classic route in a wonderful situation and which is said to follow the most natural line on the E face of Monte Rosa. The rock is steep with moves of III and IV, but quite straightforward, whilst the snow and ice sections can be a bit tricky and up to 60°. Like all the routes on the E face it should only be undertaken in cold, settled weather. However, the danger of avalanche is much lower than on most of the face and in fact the route is considered the least exposed to objective danger on the face, although the threat of stonefall is always present. All in all a fairly serious mixed climb. For the location of the rib see the introduction to Route 42e. **c1,050m**

Follow Route 42e to the foot of the rib at c3,550m. Cross the bergschrund below and R of the rib then slant up L to get on the rock. Crossing the bergschrund and setting foot on rock may be difficult. Climb up the rib L of the crest then on it for c500m without much difficulty, turning obstacles on one side or the other rather than scrambling over them, to reach a short, narrow crest leading L to R. Cross this close to the crest on the L side (exposed). The next obstacle is a short wall. Climb this quite easily on the extreme R before continuing fairly easily to the L edge of the 'shroud'.

Climb the snow/ice slope close to the L edge (it is less threatened by stone and icefall) for three pitches. At the top of the slope climb a steep, icy goulotte onto an icy ramp with some projecting rocks. Climb the ramp, using the rocks for placing protection, towards the bottom of a steep, rocky couloir (possibly some ice). Climb the couloir and a little chimney at the top without too much difficulty and reach the summit in a few more minutes climbing up steepish ice slopes. **8-10hr**

Jägerjoch 3,913m

C Mathews and F Morshead with C Almer and A Maurer,
17 July 1867

Parties intent on climbing the Cresta di Santa Caterina will visit this col en route to or from the Gallarate bivouac hut, otherwise it is of little practical value and is certainly not a crossing point of the frontier ridge.

43a NORTH-NORTH-WEST FLANK
PD Valley base: Zermatt

Approach on this side can be made from the Monte Rosa hut or, more easily (F), from the Stockhornpass. The latter route is facilitated by the availability of a lift almost to the summit of the Stockhorn as well as the glacier being much less crevassed. **c500m** *from the Stockhornpass*

(i) From the Monte Rosa hut follow a path E and then ENE up the huge rocky hump overlooking the hut to reach the L lateral moraine of the Monte Rosa glacier. Climb the moraine to a height of c2,900m and then get on to the glacier at the most convenient point. Head across the glacier towards Pt 3,074m which is the top end of the R lateral moraine. Turn N and look for a cairn showing the easiest crossing point of the ridge ahead, this is c400m WNW of Pt 3,263.9m. There are fixed belay/rappel rings on the rocks at the top. Once across the ridge descend on to the Gorner glacier. Head up the L bank of the glacier, passing under the NW buttress of Nordend to reach the glacier combe below the col. Climb the combe to the col. The bivouac hut is 150m N from the col. **c5hr**

(ii) From the Stockhorn lift station cross the summit of the mountain and then descend the E ridge, mostly on névé on the N side to reach the Stockhornpass. Head SE up the broad snow ridge descending from Pt 3,632m. At a height of c3,540m start contouring SSE and pass below the Gr and Kl Fillarhorn to reach the glacier combe below the col. Continue as for (i) above. **c4hr**

43b EAST SIDE - JÄGERRÜCKEN
AD Valley base: Macugnaga

41

The Jägerrücken is the name given to the ridge descending ENE from the summit of the Jägerhorn. It provides a relatively easy means of ascent from the Italian side although the climbing is of no great interest, in contrast to the views. **c1,400m**

From the Belloni bivouac hut follow a cairned route R over boulders to reach a stony/snow basin. Go up this and continue up the E ridge of the Gr Fillarhorn until c200m above the hut. Here a wall, split on the R by a deep crack and having an ill-defined couloir on the L, is encountered. Climb the couloir (II and III) for c100m to the ridge and a view of the Piccolo Fillar glacier. Continue up the ridge to a height of c2,900m then slant down L along a succession of ramps on to the glacier.

Cross the glacier, circling round above the crevassed area and gain the Jägerrücken at c3,100m where the snow slopes lead on to the crest. Continue directly up the ridge without any real difficulty as far as the steep rocks c100m below the summit. Now slant up L along ramps and ledges to reach the S ridge of the Jägerhorn above the col. **6-7hr**

The final 100m to the summit of Jägerhorn, if climbed, is considerably more difficult than anything else encountered on the route and is D/D+

Jägerhorn 3,970m

C Mathews and F Morshead with C Almer and A Maurer, 17 July 1867

Sited elsewhere this peak might be more imposing, but placed alongside Nordend it is of little significance. It has twin summits, the Nmost being c2m higher than the S and much more difficult to reach. Most parties visit only the S summit against which stands the Gallarate bivouac hut.

Altes Weisstor 3,560m: 3,584m: c3620m: 3,581m

The name Weisstor comes from Weissgrat which is the name given to the long ridge extending N and then NE from Monte Rosa to the Schwarzberg Weisstor. The lowest point, 3,560m, can be considered to be the actual pass but there are three other potential crossing points of the frontier ridge in the same vicinity. Each one is easy of access on the Swiss side but the Italian side is more arduous and potentially more dangerous. On the E side of the lowest point is a couloir, seriously threatened by stonefall, called Canalone Ellerman (AD). The next depression, the central one is not marked as such on the map although the couloir (Canalone Tyndall, AD-) on its E side is clearly indicated. It rises to the saddle between Pt 3,642m (Cima Brioschi) and Pt 3,632m (Torre di Castelfranco) and is the safest of the three couloirs. The N depression, which has the third of the couloirs on its E side, is a few m NE of the summit of Torre di Castelfranco. The couloir is known as Canalone Tuckett (AD+) and should only be attempted in well snowed up conditions. The fourth crossing point is the NE depression, the spot height being shown on the map between Torre di Castelfranco and Cima di Jazzi. This is entirely on rock and is also subjected to stonefall (AD).

For parties wishing to cross the frontier ridge hereabouts, undoubtedly the best way from the Italian side is via the ESE ridge of Torre di Castelfranco (Route 44a). This is the ridge splitting the tiny Castelfranco glacier and is quite easily reached from the Belloni bivouac hut. On the Swiss side follow Route 43a.

44a EAST-SOUTH-EAST RIDGE OF TORRE DI CASTELFRANCO
PD+

42 Valley base: Macugnaga

From the Belloni bivouac hut head N across grass and stony slopes to pass below Pt 2,394m and get on to the tiny Castelfranco glacier. Climb this, passing L of the long rock island (Castelfranco), to the foot of the ridge proper. Avoid the lower part of the ridge by climbing the couloir on the L side until it is easy to move on to the crest c200m above the foot of the ridge. Follow the easy ridge, turning any obstacles on the N side, to the summit. At the top of the rocks is a cairn, the summit is 120m NW from here. Any of the four depressions of the Altes Weisstor can be easily reached from the summit. **1,070m**: allow **5hr**

Cima di Jazzi 3,803m

First tourist ascent: G Sykes probably with M Zumtaugwald, Aug 1851

One of the principal points on the Weissgrat, the long ridge extending N and then NE from Monte Rosa to the Schwarzberg Weisstor. Viewed from the Swiss side it is entirely snow covered and appears no more significant than other peaks along this ridge. Descending NW from the summit is a broad, even-angled, snow covered promontory which merges into the upper regions of the Findel glacier. The upper edge of the promontory forms the NE ridge of the peak which descends to the Neues Weisstor, interrupted by some seracs at c3,650m. There is a short S ridge, partly of rock, which terminates at the top of a massive, triangular rock wall which effectively forms the mountains SSW face. Unfortunately the face offers little in the way of good routes. The face is bounded on its W side by the WSW ridge, which forms a continuation of the S ridge, and on its E side by a long ridge projecting SE from the foot of the S ridge. This ridge extends almost as far as the Belvedere glacier. This SE ridge forms the S edge of the mountain's E flank, a complex of rock and ice whose most notable feature is a long couloir (over 1,000m in height, D+, E Cavellini and R Pe, 1 Feb 1989) which rises to meet the S ridge. The gully immediately L of the one climbed by Cavellini and Pe also came into condition after heavy snowfalls in autumn 1993 and was climbed on 5 Dec that year by T Bresciani and O Trentin. It gave a 700m climb with steps of 70°-75° and a little tricky mixed climbing. It was given an overall grade of D.

45a WEST-SOUTH-WEST AND SOUTH RIDGE
PD Valley base: Zermatt/Macugnaga

The ridge forms a part of the Weissgrat and starts at the NE depression of the Altes Weisstor (3,581m). **220m**

Reach Pt 3,581m from the Stockhornpass via Route 43a or from the Belloni bivouac via Route 44a. Follow the line of the ridge WNW over a snow hump to a higher saddle and then on to the foot of the S ridge. Climb the crest of this ridge on rock and then snow to the summit. **1hr** from Pt 3,581m

45b NORTH-WEST FLANK
F   Valley base: Zermatt

39
45

A straightforward glacier plod, access being provided by the Stockhorn lift system. It is also possible to climb from Berghaus Flue utilising Route H30(iv). **410m**

From the upper lift station on the Stockhorn follow Route 43a(ii) up the ridge towards Pt 3,632m. As crevasses permit, contour round the glacier bowl on the E side of the ridge to gain the NW flank of Cima di Jazzi at c3,650m before climbing to the summit. **3hr**

45c SOUTH-EAST RIDGE INTEGRAL
D   G Buscaini, 16/17 May 1952
42 Second ascent: E Boschi and T Micotti, 6/7 Sept 1959
FWA: L Bettineschi and C di Pietro, 17/19 Jan 1967
Valley base: Macugnaga

A reliable route to the summit from the Italian side probably best attempted from a bivouac at Alpe Fillar. On the first ascent Buscaini avoided the more difficult sections encountering pitches no harder than IV, whilst the second ascent party kept more to the crest and found some more difficult climbing. **c1,600m**

Reach Alpe Fillar by Route H28. Climb steep grassy slopes to the first steepening of the ridge. Climb this on the crest and then reach a second and higher step. Climb up a little way before traversing R into a dièdre with a crack. Climb this before exiting L by a traverse (pitons) on to the ridge crest. The next steep section is c250m higher. Start this by climbing up slabs to the bottom of another dièdre with a crack in its bed. 10m up the dièdre traverse L to a good ledge (pitons) and then climb a slab to a ramp. Another slab and crack (piton) lead to easier ground and the top of the step. A further step is reached c100m higher. Climb this at first up white granite slabs before moving up a dièdre and then traversing R to a terrace and the end of the difficulties (6-8hr). Continue up the ridge to the junction with the WSW ridge and from there climb the S ridge to the summit (2hr). **8-10hr**

Neues Weisstor 3,499m and Passo Jacchini c3,520m

First tourist crossing of Neues Weisstor: Blomfield and Walters with J and S Zumtaugwald, 29 Aug 1856

Passo Jacchini: S Biner and M Zumtaugwald, 8 Aug 1848

This is the lowest of all the depressions along the Weissgrat and is in fact the lowest point in the long mountain chain extending from the Gobba di Rollin, SE of the Theodulpass, and the Balfrin, N of the Mischabel group. The lowest depression is of no value as a crossing point in the present day, its Italian side being a steep, narrow couloir, usually capped by a cornice. The usual crossing point is another depression a little further E, usually referred to as the Passo Jacchini (not marked or named on the map). The lower depression is very easily reached from Passo Jacchini.

46a NORTH-WEST FLANK

F Valley base: Zermatt

39

An easy glacier plod from the Stockhornpass but more interesting from Berghaus Flue. See Route H30(iv). **c200m**

From the Stockhorn lift system, follow Route 43a(ii) on to the NW flank of the Cima di Jazzi, aiming to reach this at c3,600m. Turn ENE and slant down to pass just N of a band of seracs then turn E to reach the lowest depression. 200m further on reach the Passo Jacchini. **c3hr** from the lift station

46b EAST SIDE

PD Valley base: Macugnaga

42

The means of approach starts at the Euginio Sella hut. **500m**

From the hut follow Route H30(i) to the Passo Jacchini. **2hr**

Schwarzberghorn 3,609m

The summit is not named on the map, only the spot height is given. However this is an important geographical point on the frontier ridge where it makes a sharp turn the E and where another ridge joins from the NNW. Adjacent to the peak along its NNW ridge is the Schwarzberg Weisstor. One might expect this to be a crossing point on the ridge but this is quite impractical: the E side is a steep rock wall over 100m high. As a consequence all crossings are made over the summit of the mountain. A little over 100m from the summit, along the E ridge, is the Citta di Luino bivouac hut. The summit can be reached from the NE (Mattmark), from the E (Monte Moropass), from the W (Zermatt) and from the S (E Sella hut), see Routes H30(i), (ii), (iii) and (iv).

MONTE ROSA GROUP AND THE WEISSGRAT

Monte Moro 2,984m

A well-known name but a quite insignificant mountain. Its S side has some short but steep walls which can provide some entertainment for rock climbers.

47a NORTH-WEST FLANK
F Valley base: Saas

A little more interesting than the walk to the Monte Moropass and it gets one away from the crowds. **c700m**

From the Mattmark dam car park follow Route 48a to Pt 2,327m which is a stream crossing. Now head directly S to reach the tiny glacier on the NW side of the peak. Climb straight up to the summit from here. **c3hr**

47b EAST-SOUTH-EAST RIDGE
F Valley base: Saas/Macugnaga

The obvious route from the Monte Moropass. Often enshrouded in mist. **125m** *from the lift station*

From the statue above the pass itself (all the signposts lead to this point) follow the ridge easily to a high point. Descend c25m to a gap (the lowest point of the frontier ridge in this vicinity, Pt 2,846m) and then climb the steeper ridge ahead to the summit. **1hr**

Monte Moropass 2,868m

On the frontier ridge between Monte Moro and the Joderhorn, it forms an easy crossing point between Mattmark in the Saas valley and Macugnaga. However the crossing point is not the lowest point in the ridge, this is c400m further ESE. Just above the crossing point is a large statue of the Madonna. Approach from the S is facilitated by a lift from Staffa so you can expect to see hordes of people who rather detract from the magnificent views of the E face of Monte Rosa. If you go for the views it is advisable to be there early. Even in fine weather mist wells up from the Italian side quite early in the day, ruining the views and making navigation quite difficult.

48a SOUTH SIDE
W1 Valley base: Macugnaga

c500m walk from the téléphérique top station and from the Gaspare Oberto hut. On foot from Staffa follow the road towards Chiesa Vecchia. The path starts just before the bridge. **4-5hr** and **c1,550m** from Staffa on foot

48b NORTH SIDE
W2 Valley base: Saas

Signposted from the Mattmark dam car park. Follow the roadway on the W side of the reservoir to its S end then continue on a good path to Tälliboden. The path continues up the hillside on the R. Starting from a 4m high boulder it slants SE up slabby ramps with steps in places and a cable in one spot and is marked with paint flashes all the way. A signpost and more paint flashes lead to the statue and crossing point. Snow patches can persist until late in the season. **2-2½hr** and **c650m**

Pizzo Bianco 3,215m

H-B de Saussure with T and G Jachetti, 31 July 1789

A fine, fairly isolated peak situated at the head of the Valle Anzasca, SE of the Zamboni and Zappa hut and having a commanding view of the E face of Monte Rosa. It is a rocky peak presenting four faces. There are routes on the remote S face and on the NW flank. However, the peak is only described here as a viewpoint for the Monte Rosa and two climbs are described which can be combined to provide a worthwhile traverse.

49a WEST AND NORTH FLANK
F Valley base: Alagna

43

The usual means of ascent in summer and on skis in Spring. **1,150m**

From the Zamboni and Zappa hut follow a path heading roughly S across the meadows towards the hollow between two high moraines. Take a small path which branches off L and soon steepens. Climb the stony slope, which is often snow covered, below the S flank of Pt Battisti. Towards the top of the slope follow a sort of ramp leading Lwards on to the broad ridge above a shallow col (Colletto del Pizzo Bianco: not marked or named on the map) at c2,900m (2½-3hr). The ridge NW of the col leads to Pt Battisti.

Continue along the broad ridge towards a rocky pinnacle. Don't climb this but instead traverse round on the E side across steepish stony, or possibly snowy slopes to the col on its S side. Ahead is the broad crest of the N foresummit. Here slant down a snowfield on the E flank before reascending it to reach the saddle separating the main summit and the foresummit. The short N ridge over easy rocks leads to the top (1½hr). **c5hr**

49b SOUTH-WEST RIDGE
AD S Esquenazi with A Burgener, Z Lagger and L Ruppen, 1924

43 FWA: G Bertone, E Braggini, A Silvola (or Servola) and G Tessitore with F Jacchini, and C and M Pala, 13 March 1961
Valley base: Alagna

Some good climbing with sections of III and IV. The start of the climb, which is fairly short, is reached via the slopes on the flank of the rib NW of Pt 2,927m which give access to the Colletto di Salti (c2,970m: not marked nor named on the map) at the foot of the ridge. **c250m** *on the ridge*

Start as for Route 49a but continue to the base of the L-hand moraine. Here turn L and climb scree and snow to the base of the rib at c2,400m. Start on the N side of the spur up a ribbon of snow then move up Lwards across slabs and loose stone on to a broad, low profile rib. Climb up this on to snow covered slopes on the N side of Pt 2,927m and follow these to the col (c3hr).

On the ridge, turn a gendarme on the R and reach a 'window'. A ledge leads R here to the S Buttress (TD). Above this follow some slabs with one pitch of III to reach a grassy area. The ridge steepens. Climb a 20m pitch of IV (pitons) on the R and a few m higher a slabby pitch of IV (30m: pitons). Above this negotiate some blocks and then follow the easy crest to the summit (1½-2hr). **5-6hr**

Riffelhorn 2,927.5m

First known tourist ascent: J Barwell, Lushington, V and W Smith and guides, 8 Aug 1842. However, in 1872 an ancient spearhead was found on the summit by an American party which suggests that an ascent could have been made in prehistoric times.

Situated above the N bank of the Gorner glacier and close to the Rotenboden station on the Zermatt-Gornergrat railway, this rocky peak has long been an important training ground for rock climbing. There is some fixed protection but this has not been overdone so it is necessary to carry a standard rack. Routes on the N side are fairly short but longer routes are possible on the S side, up to 400m, although only the upper parts are steep and worth climbing.

50a ORDINARY ROUTE
F Valley base: Zermatt

44

The route follows the line of the E ridge but most of the time keep below the crest on its N side. A convenient descent route. ***c100m***

From Rotenboden station follow a path to the foot of the E ridge. Contour on the N side to reach an easy angled, slabby dièdre which leads to the crest. Climb it to the crest then follow the ridge to a steep step. Descend on the N side to a terrace and follow this to turn the step. At the end of the terrace climb a crack and a couple of short steps to another terrace. Keep on this debris covered terrace below the crest to pass below the next steep step in the ridge. Just past the step climb up easy, stepped rocks and then a L slanting dièdre to reach the top of the step and the E summit. Continue along the ridge to the W summit. **½-1hr**

50b SKYLINE
AD+ Valley base: Zermatt

44

This route follows the E ridge along the crest. It is the skyline seen from Rotenboden station. ***c100m***

Reach the foot of the ridge by path from the station. Climb the first steep section of the ridge direct then reach a 4m high slab. Climb this (IV) and gain the second step which is climbed slanting L (II). Continue along the ridge, climbing each step direct to the final steep section. This takes the form of a slab which has a dièdre on its L (the top of Route 50f) and is split by a crack. Climb the slab (III+) or the crack (III) and so reach the E summit. **1hr**

In descent, down climb the dièdre and rappel the second step. You can avoid the 4m slab.

50c GLETSCHER COULOIR
AD Valley base: Zermatt

Between the E and W summits on the S side are two steep couloirs separated by a steep rib. This route climbs the L (W) one of these couloirs. ***c70m***

To reach the foot of the routes, climb to the W summit then rappel (or down climb) 40m down slabs slanting slightly E on to a terrace. A short dièdre leads down to another terrace and yet another dièdre leads down 20m to a flattish grassy patch and a niche. Rappel or climb down to this niche. A slab leads down another 3m to where the dièdre becomes easy. Descend another 25m to a third terrace. Traverse into the couloir from the terrace.

Climb two pitches up the couloir (III) with some smooth rock in places and then the final 10m chimney. **1½hr**

50d KANTE
D Valley base: Zermatt

One of the best climbs on the mountain. **60m**

Approach the route as for Route 50c to the couloir and then descend the couloir for 10m.

Climb the R side of the rib to a detached block at c10m and belay here. Continue on the R side of the rib for a further 8m then traverse on to the crest of the rib (ring peg). Climb the crest for a further 30m (IV) to a small ledge and belay point. Keep on the crest to a short dièdre which leads to a terrace and belay. Finally, the last 10m is climbed on the crest (III). **1½hr**

50e BINER COULOIR
ED1 Valley base: Zermatt

Climbed in error by K Biner and two ladies who thought they were in the Gletscher Couloir. Serious in that the overhang at the top is both difficult and not protectable. **70m**

Approach as for Route 50c to the third terrace then continue down to a second grassy patch. Traverse R (E) into the couloir and climb it for three pitches (III) to a terrace below the big overhang. Climb this (VI). **1½hr**

50f THERMOMETER COULOIR
D Valley base: Zermatt

The first ascent party found a clinical thermometer that had, presumably, been dropped from Skyline. **70m**

Approach from the foot of the E ridge by an almost horizontal traverse on the S side.

The couloir starts as a dièdre with a narrow crack. Climb it for c25m (III+, pitons) to a niche. Climb another 25m on the R side of the dièdre (III+) to reach a second niche and belay point. A steep chimney c10m higher (IV) leads to the easy dièdre on the L side of the last step of Route 50b. Climb this or the crack or slab on the R. **1hr**

50g CENTRAL DIEDRE
AD+ Valley base: Zermatt

44

This route is on the N side overlooking the Riffelsee and very easy of access. The dièdre itself is quite obvious although the climb starts in a shorter dièdre on the L. A worthwhile and popular climb. ***c150m***

Start at the foot of the dièdre c10m L of the line of the central dièdre, reached by easy scrambling. A pleasant 10m slab (III+) leads to easier climbing and a terrace. Descend Rwards to reach the bottom of the central dièdre. The first 8m are (III+) there then follows two pitches up slabby terrain on the R of the dièdre (III) to reach its top and a ledge. Now slant up gradually R for a further 20m to where the ground steepens again. Two pitches of fairly easy climbing lead to a ledge below an overhang. Avoid this on the L and climb a crack (III) leading to its top. Just above is an isolated block and belay. Very easy climbing leads to the summit. **2½hr**

Stockhorn 3,532m

A good viewpoint and a worthwhile training peak if you avoid the use of the lift system.

51a WEST RIDGE
W2 Valley base: Zermatt

45

A very easy climb that can be undertaken from Gornergrat but is spoiled somewhat by the téléphérique overhead. ***440m***

From the Gornergrat station follow the ridge path up the Hohtälligrat, over its summit (Pt 3,286.3m) and then down the ESE ridge to a col at 3,245m (not marked as such on map).

Keep on the ridge to the top station of a ski-lift on the N side. From here follow a path on the S side of the ridge following a pipeline. Regain the ridge shortly before the upper téléphérique station. Beyond this keep on the ridge or the névé on the N side of the ridge to the summit rocks. Climb these easily. **2-2½hr**

51b NORTH-WEST RIDGE
PD Valley base: Zermatt

The best climb on the mountain, partly rock and partly snow.
c1,000m

From Berghaus Flue take a path descending to Tällinen and from there follow the path leading on to the R lateral moraine of the Findel glacier. A less pronounced path leads down on to the tongue of the glacier. Head SE across the glacier, cross the L lateral moraine and reach grassy fields of Triftji close to Pt 2,577m. Grassy slopes lead SE to Pt 2,704m and then more stony ground leads in roughly the same direction to the pond at Pt 2,783m. Pass to the W of the pond and climb up more pleasantly to the Triftji glacier which is reached E of Pt 3,030m. Climb a short way up the glacier then slant up L on to the ridge itself. Climb this on rock at first then snow (possible crevasses) to reach the summit rocks. Climb these on the W side. **4hr**

Stockhornpass 3,394m

Crossed frequently on skis by parties travelling between the Monte Rosa and Britannia huts by way of the Adlerpass. In summer it provides the simplest means of access to the Weissgrat and the Citta di Gallarate bivouac.

The Saas peaks and the Mischabel
Strahlhorn to the Gross Bigerhorn

The highest mountains in the chain dividing the Mattertal from the Saastal are collectively known as the Mischabel. The highest peak is the Dom (4,545m) which is the highest mountain entirely in Switzerland. The ascent via the normal route is fairly easy but tedious. Nevertheless after fresh snowfall the route is prone to avalanche. Connected to the Dom via a high ridge to the S is the Täschhorn (4,490m). Three major ridges meet to form its sharp summit. It is one of the most difficult peaks in the Zermatt area. Since the erection of the bivouac hut on the Mischabeljoch in 1966 and a larger one in 1997, ascent by the SSE ridge (the Mischabelgrat) has become a more attainable proposition. Many parties now combine the Täschhorn and Dom in one continuous traverse, but each year several are benighted having underestimated the length and difficulties of the route.

The WSW ridge of the Täschhorn has two subsidiary summits, the Kinhorn and the Leiterspitzen. The summit ridge of the Leiterspitzen is of good rock with two gendarmes and it provides a very sporting and enjoyable traverse when the big peaks are out of condition. The end of the road at Täschalpen is the obvious starting point.

NE of the Dom the Lenzspitze (4,294m) rises, offering interesting ridge routes, and the classic NNE face. Most ascents are made from the Saas side. The mountain is often combined in a traverse with the Nadelhorn (4,327m) via the excellent gneiss ridges.

The ridge to the NW is generally known as the Nadelgrat, and includes the Stecknadelhorn, the Hobärghorn and the Dirruhorn. All of these exceed the 4,000m altitude. They are frequently linked in a continuous traverse using the Bordier hut, the Dom hut or the Mischabel hut, and if the Nadelhorn and the Lenzspitze are included it becomes one of the finest expeditions of its kind in the Alps.

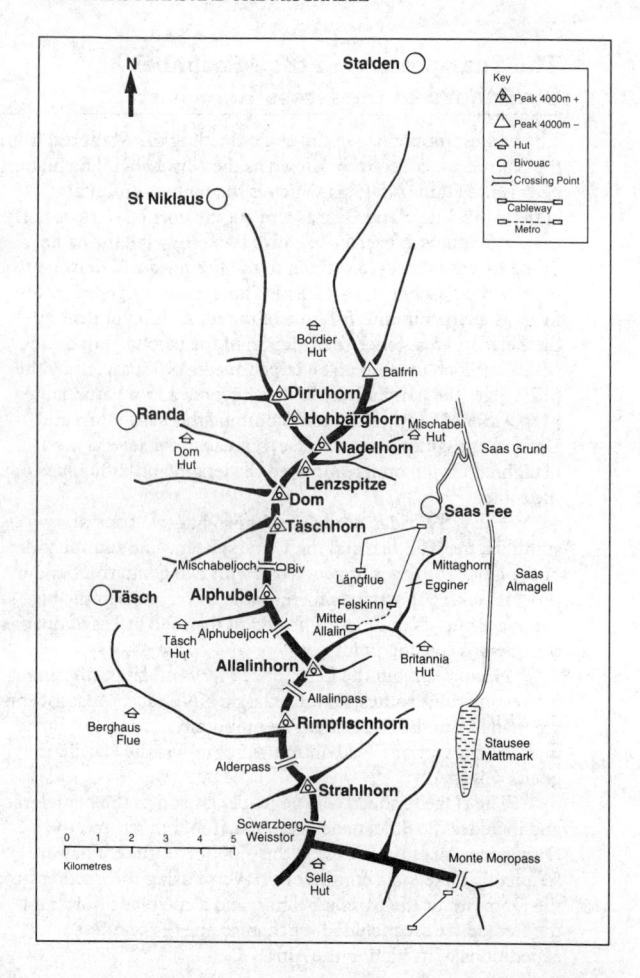

THE SAAS PEAKS AND THE MISCHABEL

From the Nadelhorn a ridge spur runs off to the NE crossing the Windjoch (3,850m), an important crossing point in the Mischabel chain. Beyond it is the snow summit of the Ulrichshorn which is frequently ascended. Further to the N rises the Balfrin (3,795m) and the Gross Bigerhorn (3,626m) where several worthwhile routes are to be found starting mainly from the Bordier hut via the Ried glacier.

For splendid but limited rock climbing in this area the Gabelhorn (3,136m), above the village of Grächen, is recommended. The climbing is confined to a large, conspicuous detached tower on the skyline high above the village, which claims to have the lowest rainfall in Switzerland. Access to it is via a cable car to the Seetalhorn then a walk of 1½hr reaches the base of the tower which, when viewed from the N, can resemble a giant sphinx. Local guides have been climbing here since the 1920's.

Returning to the Mischabeljoch, the main ridge continues S over the distinctive flat topped Alphubel (4,206m), a popular training peak with many ascents made from both the Saas side and the Zermatt valley. Probably the most rewarding ascent can be made via the W ridge, the Rotgrat.

SE of the Alphubel, beyond the minor summit of the Feechopf rises the Allalinhorn (4,027m). Since the construction of the Alpine Metro this has become a much frequented mountain, requiring less than 600m of ascent from the station. The view from the summit is renowned. The Allalinpass is the easiest crossing point on the ridge between Saas Fee and Zermatt. It lies between the Allalinhorn and, to the S, the Rimpfischhorn (4,198m). This peak is notable for its crenellated N ridge and prominent gendarme. The E face is very rocky and precipitous and is the location of certain rare minerals and crystals. The mountain stands isolated, surrounded by an extensive glacier system. It is most frequently approached from the Zermatt side. At the time of writing there is a proposal to link the ski-ing areas of Sass Fee and Zermatt by a tunnel under the Allalinhorn as far as the Allalinpass. Let us hope that those opposed to this scheme are successful in their opposition.

The final peak in this chain is the Strahlhorn (4,190m) often approached from the Zermatt side via the Adlerhorn (3,988m). It is also climbed from the Macugnaga (Italian) side using the Sella hut.

Schwarzberg Weisstor 3,535m

The lowest point on the ridge between the Schwarzberghorn and the Strahlhorn and separating the Findel and Schwarzberg glaciers. Actual crossings are made via the summit of the Schwarzberghorn as there is a 100m high rock wall on the E side of the low point. See Routes H30(i), (ii), (iii) and (iv).

Strahlhorn 4,190m

C, E and G Smyth with F Andenmatten and U Lauener,
15 Aug 1854

A fairly complex mountain whose summit lies on an E-W orientated ridge. Its N side is predominantly snow and ice with a prominent snow ridge extending NW then N and which terminates in the Allalin glacier at the rock buttress marked Pt 3,658m. The E face is a steep, broad rock wall, c750m high, which terminates at a rock shoulder at the E end of the summit ridge. This face is separated into two parts by a snowy terrace below which the rock is quite sound. In contrast, the upper part of the face is fairly loose. From a foresummit at the W end of the summit ridge a snow crest leads SW to a saddle before rising slightly to the summit of the Adlerhorn (3,988m), in effect a subsidiary summit of the Strahlhorn. On the S side of the peak there are two rock walls separated by a big glacier terrace bounded on the E by the S ridge and on the W by S face of the Adlerhorn. From the foresummit mentioned above, snow slopes lead WNW to the Adlerpass and provide the line of ascent of the ordinary route.

Fixed rope on the South West Ridge of Pollux
(Route 25b) Wil Hurford

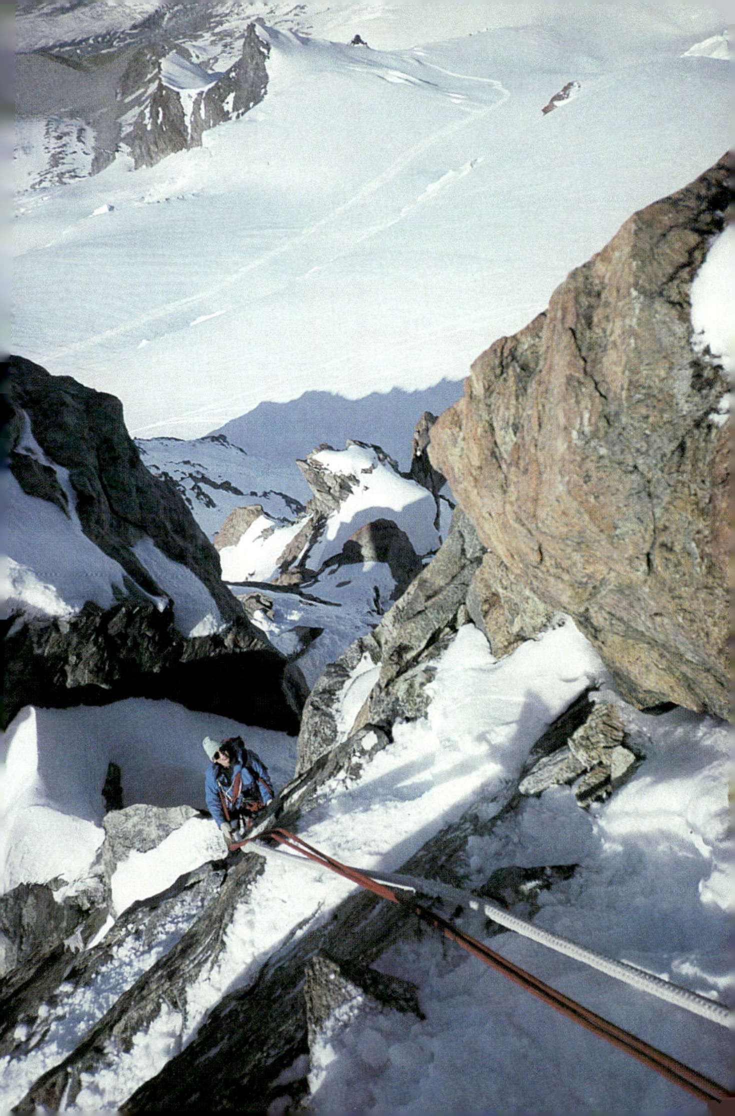

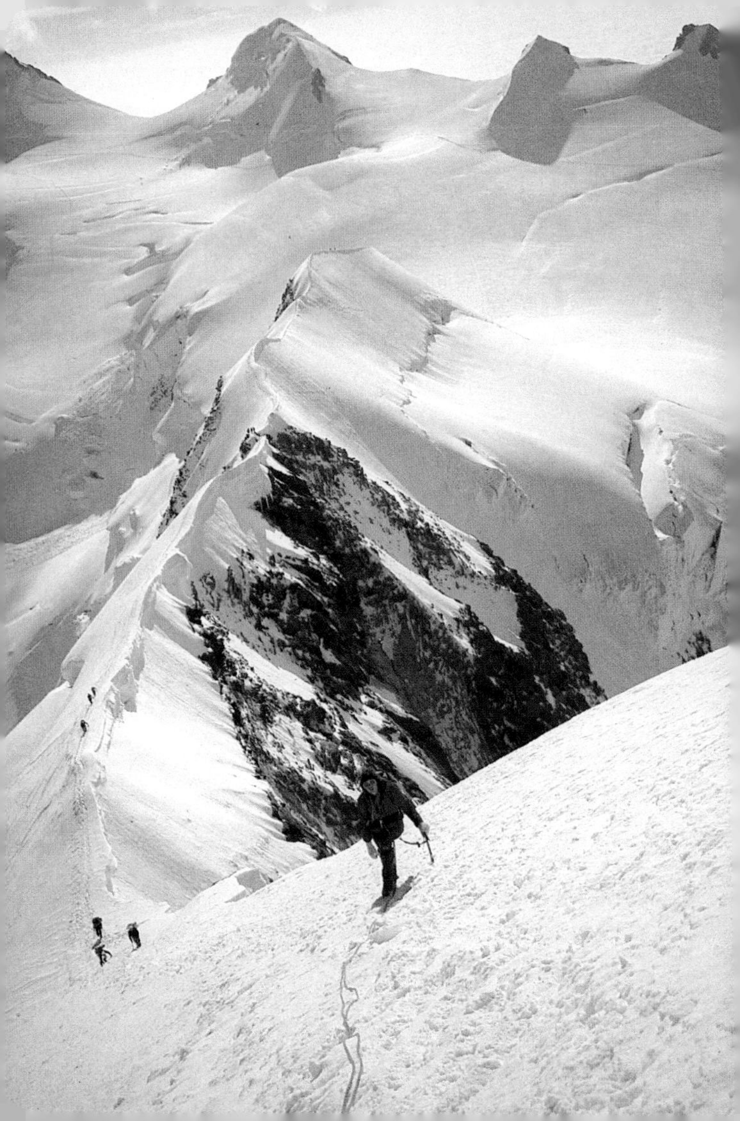

52a WEST-NORTH-WEST FLANK

PD First ascent party
46 Valley base: Saas/Zermatt
45 48

A very popular climb on foot and on ski. It starts at the Adlerpass which is generally reached from the Britannia hut although it can also be approached from Berghaus Flue or even the Monte Rosa hut. Most of the difficulties are experienced on the route to the Adlerpass, the climb to the summit is only F from this point. **400m** *from the Adlerpass*

Reach the Adlerpass via Route 53a or 53b and then climb the rounded snow ridge SSE to Pt 3,954m before continuing on more open slopes ESE to the E-W orientated summit ridge. A few rocks lead easily to the top. **4-5hr** from the Britannia hut, **5-6hr** from Berghaus Flue

52b SOUTH RIDGE

AD+ Probably A Crespi with a guide, 1907
45 Valley base: Zermatt/Saas/Macugnaga
47 48

A fine route, much neglected because of its remoteness. Climbed most frequently by Italians starting from the Sella hut, however the Citta di Luino bivouac makes an admirable starting point. The S ridge is not a true ridge but is the line at which the S face and E face meet. It presents a mixed climb to the alpinist which has been compared to the Triftjigrat on the Breithorn although it is much less serious than that route. **655m**

From the Eugenio Sella hut reach the W side of the Schwarzberg Weisstor from the Jacchini Pass on Routes H30(i) or from the Citta di Luino bivouac hut by reversing the upper part of the same route. From the low point climb snow slopes N to the first rocks. Overcome these by a narrow snow gully and then climb a steep snow slope to the broad glacier terrace. Head up the terrace towards the summit but before reaching the rocks turn to the E to reach Pt 3,883m at the start of the terrace crossing the E face. Above is an obvious rib which gives good climbing to the

*Ascending the East Ridge of the Liskamm
(Route 29c) Wil Hurford*

shoulder at the E end of the summit ridge. Follow the summit ridge W along a snow crest before easy rocks lead to the summit. **3½hr** (add 2½hr if starting from Eugenio Sella hut)

52c WEST-SOUTH-WEST RIDGE OVER THE ADLERHORN
AD
48
45
Valley base: Zermatt

Probably the best way of climbing the Strahlhorn from the Zermatt side. **c1,560m**

From Berghaus Flue follow Route H30(iv) towards the Citta di Luino bivouac hut. Instead of passing under the S face of the Adlerhorn, from a height of c3,160m turn the rock shoulder of Pt 3,421m on its W side via some loose stony slopes, keeping fairly close to the rocks to avoid any remaining seracs. Pass N of this spot height and climb the snow slope beyond and then the continuation rock ridge (easy but rather loose) to more snow at c3,800m. Climb snow slopes ENE at first and then ESE to the top of the Adlerhorn. Descend the snow crest ENE to a saddle and then, in more or less the same line, climb a steep snow rib to the foresummit of the Strahlhorn. Turn W to reach the summit by snow and a few rocks. **c6hr**

An alternative approach to the summit of the Adlerhorn is to follow Route 53a to a height of c3,450m on the Adler glacier and then turn ESE and climb the steep snow spur leading directly to the summit (PD+: 4-5hr)

52d NORTH-NORTH-WEST RIDGE
PD E Francis with A and H Supersaxo, 26 Aug 1913
46 Valley base: Saas

A fine snow ridge leading directly to the summit and, whilst not often done, it gives a much nicer climb than the WNW Flank Route. **1,230m**

From the Britannia hut follow Route 53b towards the Adlerpass and reach the foot of the ridge at the rocks below Pt 3,658m.

Climb these on the W side and then continue up the snow ridge to the summit. **5hr**

52e NORTH-EAST RIDGE
AD G Foster with H Baumann, 10 Aug 1872
46 Valley base: Saas

An infrequently climbed route but no worse for that. In combination with the WNW Flank Route it makes a pleasant traverse of the mountain from the Britannia hut. ***1,230m***

From the Britannia hut follow Route 53b towards the Adlerpass. From a height of c3,400m cross the Allalin glacier to the S side of Pt 3,451m. Now either climb to the summit of the Fluchthorn up its N flank or pass it heading SSE into the glacier combe which leads to the saddle at Pt 3,721m (Fluchtpass) on its WSW side.

From the saddle climb the steep, rounded snow ridge to a snow dome and then more easily to the snow shoulder at Pt 3,898m. Very easy slopes lead to the final steepening. Climb this slope directly (crevasses) to the snow shoulder at the E end of the summit ridge. Turn W and reach the summit via the snow crest and a few rocks (II-). **c5hr**

52f EAST FACE ORIGINAL ROUTE
TD L George, Miss G Goddard and V Russenberger, 3 and 6 Aug
47 1951
Valley base: Saas/Macugnaga

The first ascent party climbed the route in two stages, Miss Goddard accompanying the other two for the upper part. This is a fine rock climb in a very remote situation which follows very roughly the line of light coloured rock descending from the summit. The lower wall, which is climbed via a series of steep slabs separated by small ledges, is topped by a snowy terrace where the first ascent party split the route. Above this the rock deteriorates. There is no suitable hut so the preferred starting point is a bivouac at the foot of the face. ***c770m***

Start a little way L of the light coloured rock at a series of short slabs interspersed with terraces. Climb these for several pitches (III and IV) moving L wards at first and then R wards to reach a ledge at the foot of a steep, icy chimney. Make an easy but airy traverse L then climb up to an obvious, c50m chimney. Climb a steep slab on the R (V: delicate: 1 piton) to a very small belay. Traverse L into the smooth chimney and climb it with difficulty (V with a move of V+). There may be some ice at the exit.

Above is a very steep wall. Continue below this wall by slanting R across steep slabs interspersed with open grooves (IV: sustained). Overcome the wall by way of a 40m chimney slanting up L to R which cuts through it (IV and V: 2 pitons). An interesting finish gains the snowy terrace. Cross the terrace to a vertical chimney and climb this (III and IV) to reach broken rocks and snow. Climb this mixed ground directly to the apex of the wall. To reach the summit follow the snow crest W. **c10hr**

On the L side of the face is a route climbed solo by J Straub, 21 Aug 1984. It is on good rock, at least below the terrace, and climbs a series of chimneys, dièdres and slabs which can all be well protected. Difficulties range from IV to VI- and A0 and there is one 10m section of A1.

A Cremonesi and C Vedani followed by M Marinello and E Palermo, 22 July 1984, climbed a 32 pitch route on the R side of the face (called Rita). It was graded TD

Adlerpass 3,789m

First tourist crossing: G Lauterburg, G Studer and M Ulrich with F Andenmatten, F Anthamatten and J Madutz, 9 Aug 1849

An important pass connecting the Allalin and Findel glaciers and situated between the Strahlhorn and Rimpfischhorn. It is one of the most frequented passes in the Alps, most notably crossed by skiers but visited by all parties ascending the ordinary route on the Strahlhorn.

53a SOUTH-WEST SIDE
PD Valley base: Zermatt

Regularly ascended and descended during the ski-touring season but much less frequently visited in summer. The upper part is quite steep but not difficult. **1,180m**

From Berghaus Flue follow Route H30(iv) to the point where the Findel and Adler glaciers once met. Pass S of Pt 3,001m and climb on to the N side of the Adler glacier via rubble slopes. Keeping on the R (N) bank of the glacier take a direct line to the col, climbing the steep final slopes by an ascending line from L to R (possibly ice). **4-5hr**

53b NORTH-EAST SIDE
PD Valley base: Saas

A fairly straightforward glacier expedition with some crevasses. These can become difficult to negotiate, especially late in the season. **830m**

From the Britannia hut a marked track leads diagonally down a rubble strewn slope on to the Hohlaub glacier. Cross the glacier SW until directly below the snow saddle marked Pt 3,105m and climb up to this point. Make a slight descent on the other side on to the L bank of the Allalin glacier and climb this side of the glacier under the walls of the Hohlaubgrat. At c3,240m, where this wall turns W, reach a glacier plateau. The col should now be in sight.

Cross the plateau SSW, keeping L of a zone of seracs below the first rocks of the Rimpfischhorn. Once past these seracs turn SW then follow the L bank again close to the rocks of the Rimpfischhorn. From c3,600m take a direct line to the col. **3-3½hr**

Rimpfischhorn 4,198.9m

R Liveing and L Stephen with M Anderegg and J Zumtaugwald,
9 Sept 1859

As with his route on the N ridge of the Zinal Rothorn, Stephen's
party climbed to the summit from the valley in the day, in this
case from Zermatt. Viewed from the E and S the Rimpfischhorn
appears predominantly rocky with steep walls overlooking the
Allalin and Adler glaciers respectively. Unfortunately these walls
are composed of loose rock and, although routes have been
climbed on them there is nothing worth recommending. From
the W it appears predominantly snowy with rocky ribs descending from the crenellated rock ridge leading N from the summit.
Viewed from the N one sees a tapering snow slope capped by the
rocky spire of the Grand Gendarme, the last and largest of the
crenellations on the N ridge. This point is significant in that it
exceeds 4,000m.

54a WEST-SOUTH-WEST RIDGE - RIMPFISCHWANG

PD/PD+ First ascent party
49 Valley base: Zermatt/Saas
48 50

*The ordinary route to the mountain starting from Berghaus Flue or
the Täsch hut for Zermatt based climbers and from the Britannia hut
for those based in Saas. The actual ridge is quite short, starting at the
Rimpfischsattel which is situated between the summit and the snow
dome marked as Pt 4,009m. All three routes to this point are without
any great difficulty but beyond this the last 200m is quite steep and
can be quite trying, especially if conditions are not favourable.*
*c1,600m from Berghaus Flue and the Täsch hut: 1,240m from the
Britannia hut*

(i) From Berghaus Flue follow the path on the N side of the
moraine before taking a L fork just beyond the tarn at Pt 2,683m.
Continue across grassy slopes and then scree (cairns and paint
flashes) to the col (Pfulwe) at Pt 3,155m (1½hr).

Now either traverse Pt 3,314m (Pfulwe: same name as the

col) and descend to the col beyond (Pt 3,270m) or contour round to this col on the N side of the peak (stony ground and snow slopes). Continue up the long, broad snow ridge to a height of c3,820m where you encounter easy rocks. Climb these more or less direct and then cross the snow dome (Pt 4,009m) to the Rimpfischsattel below the interesting bit (2½-3hr).

(ii) From the Täsch hut or the Britannia hut reach the Allalinpass via Routes 55a or 55c (coming from the Täsch hut it is not necessary to climb up to the pass). From the pass head almost horizontally SW across the upper slopes of the Mellich glacier and cross the snow and rock rib below the lowest rocks or at a height of c3,650m between the rocks. Either way, continue more to the S to pass below Pt 3,662m at the foot of the rib descending from the Grand Gendarme. Here enter the glacier combe leading to the Rimpfischsattel. Climb the combe to the saddle by heading SE, to where the slope starts to steepen abruptly, and then S. There is a crevassed area at c3,900m (1½-2hr).

From the Rimpfischsattel climb the snow slope ahead and reach the rocks of the R-hand of two rock ribs. Climb to a terrace at about one third height which slants up to the L. Follow this to a notch (difficult if icy) then climb the more amenable rock pleasantly (II+/III-) to the foresummit. Decend into the gap and scramble up easy rocks to the true summit (1-1½hr). **c5hr** from Berghaus Flue, **6-7hr** from Täsch hut or Britannia hut

54b NORTH-WEST FLANK
D
50 E-R Blanchet with H Imseng, 13 July 1923
FWA: R Arnold 11 Jan 1976
Valley base: Zermatt/Saas

Best climbed early in the season before the slope turns to ice. Steep (55°) but quite straightforward if it is not icy. ***c300m***

Reach the foot of the face via Route 54a(ii). Climb the slope leading to the saddle between the summit and the first gendarme on the N ridge. In icy conditions make use of the rocks on the L, these are difficult at the start and the rock is not too good but it does improve with height. **c3hr** from the bergschrund

54c NORTH RIDGE
AD G Passingham with F Imseng and L Zurbriggen, Summer 1878
50 Valley base: Zermatt/Saas
49 51

A fine rock ridge with a series of gendarmes, the final one at the N end of the ridge being the most pronounced. This is the Grand Gendarme and is marked as Pt 4,108m on the map. Certainly the best climb on the mountain. Many parties use the route for descent having climbed to the summit via the SSW ridge but this is less interesting than the ascent. The Grand Gendarme is usually traversed but it is possible to avoid it fairly easily on the E side although this does not look too inviting from the approach. **c700m** *from the Allalinpass*

From the Täsch hut or the Britannia hut, reach the Allalinpass via Routes 55a or 55c respectively (3hr). From the pass climb the steepening snow slope to the base of the Grand Gendarme. To avoid the gendarme: before reaching the foot of the gendarme descend on the E side on to snowed-up or possibly stony ledges and follow these more or less horizontally until you are below the gap on the S side of the gendarme. Climb up to the gap. To traverse the gendarme, simply follow the crest to the summit (easy but exposed climbing). From the top make two rappels (a short one then a longer one) or, much better, one long one (c45m) into the gap on the S side. Ignore any beckoning fixed ropes on the W and SW sides.

From the col the climb continues over the series of gendarmes (steps of III) which are linked by snow crests. The most difficult climbing is left to last. To reach the summit climb a steep narrow chimney on the E side of the ridge (good holds but possibly icy) direct to the summit (4hr). **c7hr**

In descent turn the Grand Gendarme on the E side or climb over it by a direct ascent of its S ridge. This is very steep and exposed at the start but the rock and holds are good (IV): the difficulties diminish after the first few m. Alternatively climb a chimney (III) to gain the easier ground.

54d SOUTH-EAST RIDGE

AD+ A and A-C Slee with two guides, before 1878
49 Valley base: Saas/Zermatt
48 51

Parties visiting the Adlerpass may be tempted to climb the Rimpfischhorn which towers above the pass. This route is the obvious means of satisfying that temptation but it has no great merit and is not particularly recommended as the rock is poor. **410m**

From the pass follow the snow crest and then broken rocks to reach a snow covered terrace which skirts the S flank of the mountain. From the top of the terrace slant up R for c20m on to the E flank of the now less well-defined ridge. Climb this flank as direct as possible to a well-defined shoulder: avoid wandering to the R. Difficulties increase towards the top. From the shoulder follow the crest to the foresummit, turning a pinnacle before you reach this point. It is easy now to the summit. **c3hr**

Allalinpass 3,564m

First tourist crossing: E-H Michaelis with guides, 11 Sept 1828

A broad snow saddle between the Rimpfischhorn and Allalinhorn which links the Mellich and Allalin glaciers. It provides an easy passage between the Britannia and Täsch huts. The pass can also be reached from the Mittel Allalin station by crossing the Feejoch.

55a WEST-NORTH-WEST FLANK

F Valley base: Zermatt
54

From the Täsch hut follow the gradually rising path into the Chummiboden combe and then climb up the combe keeping the stream on your R to reach the Alphubel glacier at c3,200m. The exact line of the path can be difficult to follow in the dark. Climb the glacier heading SE and, ignoring tracks leading off L to the Alphubeljoch, reach the rounded glacier rib descending ENE to Pt 3,421m. Contour round at c3,500m on to some stony ground then descend diagonally, losing as little height as possible, on to the R bank of the Mellich glacier. Now climb easy slopes SE to the pass. **3hr** and **c870m**

55b FROM THE FEEJOCH
PD Valley base: Saas

Reach the Feejoch via Route 56a(i) from the Mittel Allalin station. A little to the W of the lowest point, descend loose rocks and then steep snow (bergschrund) on to the Mellich glacier. Cross this heading SSW then S to the pass. **2-2½hr** and **c590m**

55c EAST FLANK
PD Valley base: Saas

From the Britannia hut follow Route 53b towards the Adlerpass as far as the glacier plateau where the wall of the Hohlaubgrat turns W. Now, heading WSW, take as direct a line as possible to the pass. **3hr** and **c600m**

Allalinhorn 4,027.4m

E Ames and J Imboden with F Andenmatten and an Imseng, 28 July 1856

A highly frequented summit in both summer and winter, the more so since the advent of the Alpine Metro to Mittel Allalin. The N flank of the mountain is predominantly of snow and ice, rising above the Fee and Hohlaub glaciers which are separated by the peak's NE ridge. The long ENE ridge or Hohlaubgrat bounds the S side of the glacier of that name and presents one of the finer ascent routes of the mountain. The rocky S side of the mountain is of little interest, the rock being of poor quality, but this is terminated on the W side by the SW ridge which provides an easy means of access to the summit from the Allalinpass. A further short ridge rises from the Feejoch to the summit and forms the final section of the ordinary route.

56a WEST-NORTH-WEST RIDGE

F   C Fischer, F Jacomb, W Short and L Stephen with
52 F Andenmatten, J Kronig and P Taugwalder, 1 Aug 1860
51 54 Valley base: Saas/Zermatt

The ordinary route and frequently climbed in a day from Saas Fee by taking advantage of the Alpine Metro. Other starting points are the Britannia hut, Längfluh hotel or even the Täsch hut. The advantage of the latter starting point is that you avoid the skiers on the Fee glacier who form the greatest objective danger on the approach route from the other starting points as well as ruining the aesthetics of the ascent. **c590m** *from Mittel Allalin*

(i) From Mittel Allalin follow the pisted track SW on to the Fee glacier. Head out into the middle of the glacier before taking a fairly direct line to the Feejoch (1hr). If the crevasses are bad, as in the summer of 1998, it is better to keep close to the NW flank of the mountain to reach the Feejoch.

(ii) From the Britannia hut descend the path on to the Hohlaub glacier. Climb the L bank of the glacier, passing below Pt 3,249m (Hinter Allalinpass). Continue SW, passing below Mittel Allalin, until you see a small snow saddle on the R. Climb to this saddle (Pt 3,597m) via a narrow couloir (2½hr). From the saddle traverse on to the Fee glacier and join the track from Mittel Allalin to the Feejoch (1hr)

(iii) From the Längfluh hotel climb S up the Fee glacier (piste machine tracks and ski pistes) keeping well E of Pt 3,179m. Eventually join the track from Mittel Allalin to reach the Feejoch (3hr).

(iv) From the Täsch hut follow Route 59a to the Alphubeljoch and then climb easy snow slopes SE to the summit of the Feechopf (3,888m), passing on the N side of the snow dome of Pt 3,846m. From the summit climb down the ESE ridge over rock (PD: II) and snow to the Feejoch (4hr).

From the Feejoch climb ESE up easy snow slopes to a point just S of the summit. Reach the summit itself by passing beyond it on the S side and approaching it from the E up a short snow/ice rib (45min). **2-5hr** depending on starting point

56b SOUTH-WEST RIDGE

PD First ascent party

54 Valley base: Zermatt/Saas

Probably a better approach to the summit than the traverse of the Feechopf described above (which can then be used for descent) when starting from the Täsch hut. The ridge can equally well be climbed from the Britannia hut. Although the climbing can hardly be described as good (poor quality rock) the route has the advantage that it is unlikely to be crowded and skiers are not a problem. c460m from the Allalinpass

From the Täsch or Britannia hut follow Route 55a or 55c respectively to the Allalinpass. From the pass turn the foot of the ridge on the W side, passing below the rock rib descending from Pt 3,752m to reach a snow slope leading to a snow saddle (3,734m) on the ridge just beyond the point mentioned. Coming from the Täsch hut the snow slope is reached without going to the Allalinpass. Climb the snow slope to the saddle. Sometimes the slope turns to ice, in which case it is probably better to climb the ridge from the pass crossing over Pt 3,752m.

From the snow saddle climb the ridge on poor rock before moving on to the E flank to follow shale ramps to gain the upper part of the ridge. On account of the poor rock it is better to keep on the E side of the ridge even in its upper part where the ramps are likely to be snow covered. At the top of the ridge a rounded snow slope is climbed before reaching the summit by a short snow/ice rib from the E. **c6hr** from either hut

56c NORTH-EAST RIDGE

AD+/D- H Dübi with A and P Supersaxo, 27 July 1882

52 Valley base: Saas
51

A very direct route to the summit, short but steep with the possibility of some serac danger although under the conditions prevailing at the

time of writing the seracs have all but disappeared. A good introduction to steeper snow/ice slopes (50°). ***430m** for the ridge*

Reach the snow saddle at Pt 3,597m as for Route 56a(ii) from the Britannia hut. Continue up the steepening ridge on snow to the bergschrund defending the upper face. The bergschrund is often wide and impossible to cross directly but in the summer of 1998 it was relatively easy. To overcome it make a traverse R (W) across steep and exposed snow slopes to where it peters out. Now take a direct line to the summit, crossing a second bergschrund in the process, via steep and sometimes icy slopes. **c5hr** from the hut

The face bordering the E side of the ridge (NE face) was climbed direct by G and H Bumann, 26 Feb 1976 in 8hr. The climb involved some 4hr of effort overcoming the serac barrier by aid climbing on ice screws.

56d EAST-NORTH-EAST RIDGE - HOHLAUBGRAT

AD G Rendall and H Topham with A Supersaxo, 12 July 1882
51 although previously descended.
52 Valley base: Saas

An excellent route to the summit from the Britannia hut, almost entirely on snow. The one section of rock just below the summit accounts for the grade. The route is much more popular since the installation of iron spikes to protect the 30m rock step, even so the step usually takes time to climb and can see queues developing below it.
1,060m

From the Britannia hut descend the path on to the Hohlaub glacier. Climb the L bank of the glacier to a height of c3,050m then cross it, heading SW to gain the broad, lower part of the ridge. Climb this, crossing a few crevasses to a snow dome at c3,530m. Make a short descent to a snow saddle then continue up the ridge to pass N of Pt 3,837m. The ridge levels off for a while then steepens to the rock barrier barring access to the summit slopes. Climb the broken (loose) rocks by a line slanting up R to reach the final easy snow slope leading to the summit.
4-5hr

Egginer 3,366.6m

A rocky peak, like its near neighbour the Mittaghorn, which provides a number of reasonably pleasant training routes that are made easily accessible by the lifts to Felskinn and to Plattjen. A traverse of the two summits is a particularly fine outing (Route 57e).

57a SOUTH-SOUTH-WEST RIDGE
AD Valley base: Saas

53

From the Egginerjoch (reached easily from Felskinn or the Britannia hut) climb the ridge to the first steep step. Turn this on the R and regain the almost level ridge crest. The next step is climbed on the L side and leads to a large rubble strewn niche. Cross this and leave it by climbing up to the L to a saddle. Keep on the ridge to the shoulder at Pt 3,242m and so reach the next steep section of the ridge after crossing a snow saddle. Ideally climb this direct, at first on the R side of the ridge and then up a narrowing chimney on the L side. From the top of the step there are no further difficulties to the summit. **3hr** and **c380m**

57b SOUTH-WEST FACE OF POINT 3,242m
TD H and G Bumann, 12 Nov 1973

53 Valley base: Saas

A good climb on sound rock, some aid is used and the route is fully equipped. **220m**

The start of the climb is marked by a red 'E'. Climb the smooth wall and a slab to a belay (20m). Traverse L for 10m then climb to a belay in a small niche (IV, 30m). Continue straight up to a belay on a small ledge (III+, 20m) then climb a dièdre and a slab to a belay on a small platform (V, 20m). Follow a line of weakness L then climb 10m higher to the next belay (V, 25m). Climb directly to an overhang and pass it on the R before reaching a slanting roof. Climb this then make a delicate traverse to a small belay (A2, 35m). Now climb gradually Lwards to a big overhang and traverse R below it to reach the next belay

(IV,40m). Straight up now and over a small roof before slanting Rwards to a belay (A2,30m). Climb up to a ramp from which a final short wall leads to the top. **7-9hr**

57c NORTH-NORTH-WEST FLANK OF POINT 3,242m
PD

53 Valley base: Saas

Useful as a means of descent and described in that sense. **c450m**

From the snow saddle of Route 57a descend the small Egginer glacier (not named on map) NW to reach moraine slopes below it. Descend these towards the W to pass N of Pt 2,794m. A path leads N towards Saas Fee and another climbs SW to the Egginerjoch. **½hr**, but longer from the summit

57d NORTH-WEST FLANK OF NORTH-NORTH-EAST RIDGE
F

53 Valley base: Saas

Probably the best descent route for parties returning to Saas Fee and described for that purpose. **c700m**

From the summit locate the top of a big chimney on the E side and make a rappel descent down the chimney on to a terrace. Follow the terrace N to reach the crest of the NNE ridge and continue along this over the gendarme of Pt 3,189m. A little way beyond this slant down L on to the upper edge of the Ritz glacier (not named on map). Slant down this, descending moraine slopes lower down, all the time heading towards Pt 2,687m on the NW ridge of the Mittaghorn. Shortly before reaching this point join a track zigzagging down grassy slopes to Pt 2,332m. The path leads back to Saas Fee. **2-2½hr**

THE SAAS PEAKS AND THE MISCHABEL

57e NORTH-NORTH-EAST RIDGE
AD H King with A Supersaxo, Summer 1883
53 Valley base: Saas
51

A good climb on sound rock with short sections of III+. There are a number of gendarmes which can be traversed or turned according to preference but it is always better to stay on the crest. **c250m**

From the summit of the Mittaghorn follow the crest SSW crossing, in a little under 200m, a gendarme which is c20m higher than the Mittaghorn itself. Beyond this gendarme descend to the lowest point on the ridge. Continue easily along the ridge to a prominent gendarme (Pt 3,189m) just beyond the highest point of the glacier (Ritz glacier) on the NW flank. After a few more short steps the ridge rises steeply towards the summit of the Egginer. Climb as high as possible up the ridge before traversing on the E side across a terrace to a big and often damp chimney. Climb this to the summit. **c4hr**

Mittaghorn 3,143m

Another popular training peak readily accessible from Saas Fee.

58a EAST FLANK
W2 Valley base: Saas

The easiest route to the summit and probably the best approach for parties intent on the traverse from the Mittaghorn to Egginer since quick access is possible using the Plattjen lift. It is also the quickest means of descent. **575m**

From the top lift station follow the path leading round the E side of the Mittaghorn. Just after the path makes a short descent and where its direction changes from SSE to SSW look for a small, steep path leading up R. Follow this path more or less directly to the summit. **1½-2hr**

58b NORTH-WEST RIDGE

AD
Valley base: Saas

53

The most entertaining route to the summit with some interesting climbing in the upper part. **c450m**

From Chalbermatten on the S edge of Saas Fee follow the Plattjen path to Pt 2,054m. From here take the path leading towards Felskinn as far as Pt 2,332m. Now turn up into the combe, zigzagging up grassy slopes to reach the ridge at Pt 2,687m (marker post). Continue on the track up more grassy slopes, the ridge gradually narrowing as height is gained. Eventually reach the predominantly rocky section of the ridge. Keep on the crest up the slabby rock to the foot of the final steep section below the summit (II with bits of III). Climb this section in two pitches keeping to the crest (III+ and III) before easier ground leads to the summit. **c5hr**

Alphubeljoch 3,782m

C Fischer, F Jacomb, W Short and L Stephen with F and M Andenmatten, J Kronig and P Taugwalder, 1 Aug 1860

First crossing: C Fox and F Tuckett with J Bennen and V Tairraz, 13 June 1861

Situated at the foot of the SE ridge of the Alphubel, it connects the Alphubel and Fee glaciers and was at one time a much frequented passage between Zermatt and Saas Fee.

59a WEST SIDE

F
Valley base: Zermatt

54

A much frequented route for parties climbing the easier routes on the Alphubel from the Täsch hut. The climb to the pass is quite easy but there are crevasses and these pose the main danger. **1,080m**

From the Täsch hut follow Route 55a to the S branch of the Alphubel glacier at c3,200m. Climb SE up the glacier then, at a height of c3,400m, turn E to pass Pt 3,510m on your L and reach the pass via easy angled slopes. **c3hr**

59b NORTH-EAST SIDE
PD Valley base: Saas

55

There are a number of possible starting points but the most obvious is the Längfluh hotel. Starting from Felskinn or the Britannia hut one joins the route from the Längfluh hotel whilst a start from Mittel Allalin involves climbing to the Feejoch and traversing the Feechopf (see Route 56a(iv)). 910m from Längfluh

(i) From the Längfluh hotel walk on to the Fee glacier and head SW up this towards the rocks of Pt 2,989m. Before reaching these rocks turn SSW and climb parallel to the band of rock up steeper slopes, passing a badly crevassed section which can involve lengthy detours, to a height of c3,600m. Here the slope eases considerably and leads to the pass. **3-3½hr**

(ii) From Felskinn, walk down through the tunnel on to the Fee glacier then cross the glacier bowl to pass N of the rocks below Pt 3,083m. Now climb a steeper slope SW until just W of the point. Keep heading W to pass between Pt 3,352m and Pt 3,179m and close to the latter. Continue W to join the route from the Längfluh hotel. Adds 1½hr

Alphubel 4,206m

T Hinchliff and L Stephen with M Anderegg and P Perren, 9 Aug 1860

The E aspect of the peak is of a vast glaciated hump with a long flat summit plateau, this is in contrast to the W side which presents a sombre rock wall to the viewer with two significant ridges projecting towards the W, one from each end of the summit plateau. Unlike most Alpine peaks the mountain has what amounts to two ordinary routes, one readily accessible from the Täsch hut and the other from the Längfluh hotel although each route is not infrequently climbed from the 'wrong' hut.

60a SOUTH-EAST RIDGE

PD First ascent party
55 Valley base: Zermatt/Saas
56

This is undoubtedly the better of the two ordinary routes although in descent it can be a bit intimidating if the steepest part of the ridge (40°) is icy. In such circumstances parties returning to the Täsch hut may prefer to descend the E flank route and contour back to the Alphubeljoch from c3,800m. **525m from the Alphubeljoch**

From the Täsch hut reach the Alphubeljoch by Route 59a. Climb the ridge, keeping to the crest, over Pt 3,904 to reach the point where it steepens by a band of rock. The amount of rock exposed will depend on the degree of snow cover. In good conditions this section is quite easy but if the snow cover is thin there can be a good deal of ice. Either keep to the crest which is delicate, alternatively climb some rocks on the L (this is more difficult) or climb the rock band. Above this the going is much easier and you soon reach the summit plateau. The true summit is not that easy to distinguish, especially if there is any mist. **4-5hr**

60b EAST FLANK

PD Probably H Dübi and K Munzinger with A Supersaxo, 29 July 1882
55 Valley base: Saas/Zermatt

The route requires less effort than any other on the mountain since a lift can be used to reach the starting point at the Längfluh hotel. Otherwise the route has little to recommend it, being a rather monotonous snow plod. It is frequently climbed on skis during Spring. As for the Alphubeljoch, a start can also be made from Felskinn but this only prolongs the monotony. **1,335m from Längfluh**

From the Längfluh hotel follow Route 59b to a height of c3,600m where the angle of the slope eases. Now slant up R, keeping roughly parallel with the rocks to the N, and reach at c4,000m a steep glacier combe. Cross the bergschrund and

60c WEST RIDGE - ROTGRAT

AD+ G Broke with A and X Andenmatten, Summer 1889
56   Valley base: Zermatt
55

The ridge descends from the S end of the summit plateau, at first as an easy angled snow slope then steep rocks for c160m before the angle again eases as the ridge narrows to Pt 3,637m where it splits into two. The route of ascent from the Täsch hut takes the valley between the two branches of the ridge, then follows the crest of the N most branch (the Wissgrat) to reach the main part of the ridge. A popular route and generally quite safe if the correct line is taken. All the difficulties are on rock with moves of III+/IV. Much harder after fresh snow or if verglassed. **c1,500m**

From the Täsch hut follow Route 61a to the saddle on the Wissgrat. Now climb the Wissgrat, which is usually scree and easy rock, to the junction with the Rotgrat itself. The junction takes the form of a rock knoll which can be turned on the L or R (delicate slabs) to reach a rock wall above. Climb this direct for c20m then traverse R (III+). Continue along the easy snow ridge to the point where it merges with the steep upper rocks of the ridge (3-3½hr).

   Make a traverse to the R and climb up to a good ledge below the steeper rocks. Do not enter the couloir on the R however inviting it might appear as this is extremely loose and dangerous. Instead climb the improbable looking terrain above for c20m to a ledge which enables a traverse R on to the edge of the ridge. A little higher there is a blocky belay. Steep climbing on good holds leads up slightly Lwards to a piton belay. Keep on in the same line over a bulge to the point where the angle relents. All this is more or less continuous III with the odd move of IV and on sound rock. Several easier pitches lead finally to easy snow slopes on the edge of the summit plateau. Turn L to reach the summit (2½-3½hr). **5½-7hr**

60d WEST RIB

D
56
E Wyss-Dunant with A Lerjens and P Mooser, 27 July 1945
FWA: F Bircher and H Müller, 23 Feb 1964
Valley base: Zermatt

Descending W from the N summit (Pt 4,116m) is a rock ridge of fairly constant inclination, which terminates on the Weingarten glacier at a height of 3,242m and provides the line of a fine climb on sound rock. The climbing is mostly grade III but there are bits of IV and IV+. **c1,500m**

From the Täsch hut follow Route 61a to the foot of the ridge at Pt 3,242m (1½-2hr). Reach the crest of the ridge by climbing the first couloir on its N side then continue along it to the first gendarme at c3,600m (III with bits of IV). Climb over the gendarme (IV) and continue to the next one at c3,800m. Climb this on the R side by somewhat exposed moves (IV+) and then continue along the ridge to the next major difficulties at c4,000m. These take the form of steep slabs on the N side which are climbed for c30m (IV+, delicate). Complete the climb by making a traverse R (III) into a couloir between the ridge and an adjacent rib which is then followed to the summit snowfield. Turn R to reach the main summit (c6hr). Allow **7-9hr**

60e NORTH RIDGE

PD W Coolidge with C and C Almer also M Courtenay, F Gardiner and F Wethered with H and P Knubel, 27 July 1876
Valley base: Zermatt

Probably more frequently descended (by parties heading for the Mischabel bivouac hut after climbing one of the other routes on the mountain) than it is ascended in its own right. The ridge is fairly short, being mainly rock in its lower part and then becoming mixed in nature, but is worth climbing despite the less than perfect rock and can be incorporated into a pleasant traverse of the mountain. **c350m**

From the Mischabeljoch (reached in 4-5hr from the Täsch hut: see Route 61a) follow the ridge to the N summit (Pt 4,188m) then walk across the summit plateau to the main summit. **c1½hr**

Mischabeljoch 3,851m

Sandwiched between the Alphubel and Täschhorn, it links the Weingarten glacier on its W side with the Fee glacier on its E side. The col is rarely if ever used as a crossing point and is very infrequently reached from the E side because of the state of the glacier. Its importance to this guide book is that it is the site of the Mischabeljoch bivouac hut. It is most often reached by parties decending the N ridge of the Alphubel (see Route 60e) after climbing this peak by one of its other routes. It is accessed quite frequently by Saas based climbers from the Mittel Allalin station of the Alpine Metro. They climb to the Feejoch and then traverse the Feechopf to the Alphubeljoch (see Route 56a(iv)) before climbing the SE ridge of the Alphubel.

61a WEST SIDE
PD Valley base: Zermatt

57
56

The usual starting point is the Täsch hut but it is possible to make a more direct approach from Täschalpen. The route from the latter is frequently used in descent by parties wishing to avoid a return to the Täsch hut. **c1,200m** *from the Täsch hut*

From the Täsch hut follow a good path leading NE round the end of the Rotgrat into the Tälli valley. Keep on this path to the point where it crosses the Wissgrat at a saddle between Pt 3,103m and Pt 3,195m. Descend a path on the N side of the saddle and continue along it until you are just E of the small lake at 3,060m (1½hr). Keep off the glacier to the R but climb on to the moraine (the route is marked) then head NE towards the rocks between Pts 3,223m and 3,481m (the latter Pt is not well delineated but the notch on its E side is).

A number of possibilities now exist but the most reliable way is to climb the rocks starting at a point about one third distance between the two points mentioned above. The start is marked by a cairn and there is another cairn at the point where the rib linking the two points is joined. The rock is solid and the

climbing is no more than II. Once on the rib work E along it to the point where a short descent can be made on to the central branch of the Weingarten glacier. Head NE into the centre of the glacier and then turn E to reach the col. Beware of crevasses!
4-5hr

Coming from Täschalpen, follow the roadway towards the Täsch hut to the point where it splits with one branch leading N. Follow this to the Rotbach then gain the path leading up the moraine crest between the two branches of the stream. At c3,000m the path turns R to reach the small lake at 3,060m. Join the route from the Täsch hut just E of the lake. Adds an extra 2½hr to the ascent

Täschhorn 4,490.7m

J Llewellyn-Davies and J Hayward with P-J Summermatter and J and S Zumtaugwald, 30 July 1862

One of the more formidable of the 4,000m peaks and certainly a much more difficult summit to attain compared with that of its close neighbour, the Dom. It is a most impressive sight when viewed from almost any direction. Its E flank merges with those of the Dom and the Lenzspitze into an impressive wall of rock and ice. Unfortunately objective dangers make the numerous routes on the face unattractive propositions, especially in summer. Its NW flank is far more interesting and no less impressive, the dominant feature here being the Kin glacier, the upper part of which leads almost to the summit and provides the line of one of the most elegant routes on the mountain. The SW flank is primarily rock but somewhat loose, thus making the routes on the face as unattractive as those on the E flank. This was the scene of an epic ascent by F and J Lochmatter and V Ryan along with G Young and J Knubel, 11 Aug 1906.

It is the three principal ridges for which the mountain is best known. The SSE ridge provides the line of the most frequented route, the NNE ridge is the one taken, usually in

THE SAAS PEAKS AND THE MISCHABEL

descent, by parties traversing the Täschhorn and Dom, whilst the WSW ridge is the best known and longest, although most infrequently climbed. This is the dramatic Teufelsgrat, at one time a classic means of ascent.

62a SOUTH-SOUTH-EAST RIDGE

AD J Jackson with C and U Almer, 15 Aug 1876

57 Valley base: Zermatt

55

The ordinary route but much more difficult than most routes of this classification. The ascent is facilitated by the existence of the bivouac hut at the Mischabeljoch. The ridge itself descends steeply from the summit at first mainly rock and then snow but less steep. Beyond this it again becomes rocky to a point where it bifurcates. The main ridge turns SE and is again mainly snow before a final section of rock leads to the Mischabeljoch. The subsidiary ridge from the bifurcation leads SSW on to the Weingarten glacier. In good conditions there are no great problems but in less than perfect conditions, which are not too much nor too little snow, the climb becomes a more serious undertaking than the grade suggests. There are moves of III on rock. Descent is not that easy and the climb should only be attempted if the weather conditions are settled. **c640m**

From the site of the old Mischabeljoch bivouac hut traverse horizontally E at first then follow traces of path and cairns up to the crest of the ridge. The ridge from here is quite easy with both snow and rock sections. Continue along it, scrambling over a number of pinnacles, to reach Pt 4,175m (2hr). This point can be reached more directly by parties starting from the Täsch hut (see below). A further easy section, mostly rock, leads on to the predominantly snowy part of the ridge. This section can be complicated by the formation of cornices on the E side. Continue along the crest, moving on to the steep and possibly icy W side as dictated by cornices. The section of snow terminates at a horizontal snow shoulder below the steep and final rock buttress. Start this up rather loose rock by moving up Rwards on to the poorly defined crest. From here sound rock leads directly to the summit. **c5hr**

Starting from the Täsch hut follow Route 61a on to the central branch of the Weingarten glacier. Cross the glacier towards the foot of a snowy couloir which leads on to the subsidiary ridge described above (descending from Pt 4,175m) where it steepens. The foot of the couloir is at c3,670m. Climb it, possibly starting via rocks on the E side, on to the crest of the ridge which is then followed quite easily to the junction with the SSE ridge. 4hr

This alternative route can also be used in descent as a quicker way of returning to the valley. From the small lake at 3,060m a direct descent to Täschalpen can be made (see Route 61a).

62b WEST-SOUTH-WEST RIDGE - TEUFELSGRAT

D
57
59

A and Mrs Mummery with J Andenmatten and A Burgener, 16 July 1887
FWA: G Gnos and A Herger with G Bumann, 20 March 1973
Valley base: Zermatt

At one time this ridge was relatively popular and something of a classic. It is not far short of 2km in length and there is a height gain of c850m from the start of the ridge at the Kinlücke (not marked on map) which is just E of the Kinhorn; this makes for a long climb in terms of time as well as distance. The main features of this predominantly rock ridge are two towers and some steep rock steps, otherwise there are few obstacles. Unfortunately the quality of the rock is not the best that might be hoped for and, although it is better on the crest than on the flanks, it requires constant care in handling. The hardest pitches are grade IV. Probably the best starting point is a bivouac in the vicinity of the Kinlücke. A climb for the fit connoisseur! ***c850m from the bivouac site***

From Täschalpen (Ottavan) reach Pt 2,539m on the Rotbach and then follow the moraine on the NW side of the Weingarten glacier to reach the foot of a wide, snowy couloir rising to the W side of the Kinhorn. Climb the scree slopes then the couloir to about one third of its height where stone covered ramps lead off diagonally R below steep rocks on the SE face of the Kinhorn.

Just past these rocks and in sight of another couloir (descending from the Kinlücke), climb up Lwards to reach further ramps leading R again to join the E ridge of the Kinhorn just above the Kinlücke. Descend to the col and a bivouac site, but no water (5hr). It is also possible to climb to the Kinlücke on the E side of the couloir descending from it on to the Weingarten glacier.

From the col keep on the crest to the first tower at 3,790m which is climbed on the crest (III). Above this the ridge narrows, dramatically in places, with flakes of rock forming the crest and good hand holds. It leads to a steep step which turns out to be easier than it at first appears. An easy section of ridge leads to another step which is turned on the R side. The crest is rejoined at a snowy saddle just before the second tower at 4,088m. Climb this by the crest (IV). The ridge again eases for a while to another step which this time is turned on the L. Ledges lead to a chimney which is climbed for 25m (IV) and is usually verglassed or snowy and never easy. Back on the crest reach a narrow gap c10m deep. Descend into the gap then climb out by a series of short steps. Beyond this the ridge turns to snow for a while and leads more easily to the summit. **c5hr** from the Kinlücke

62c NORTH-WEST FACE - KIN FACE
AD+ First ascent party
59 Valley base: Zermatt
60

The NW flank of the Täschhorn is formed by a magnificent, tumbling glacier, the highest extension of the Kin glacier. It provides the line of ascent of what, in good conditions, is the most rewarding route on the mountain. There is a great feeling of remoteness and commitment amongst some stunning scenery. Equally well the route can be used as a means of descent by parties climbing the SSE ridge although such parties would need to know that the route is passable before venturing forth. Conditions on the glacier change considerably from year to year. There are always seracs and crevasses which, in good conditions can be turned or crossed without difficulty. When the glacier is in a less favourable state an ascent may require some steep ice climbing and probably difficult crevasse crossings. The guardian at the Dom hut is usually able to give information on the conditions.

For parties wishing to complete the Täschhorn-Dom traverse, this route makes an ideal way of ascending the Täschhorn. Since the route starts and finishes at the Dom hut it avoids the possibility of becoming weather-bound at the Mischabeljoch as well as the need to carry gear used at the hut. It also gives a great contrast in climbing styles between the snow/ice of the face and the rock of the summit to summit traverse. Very highly recommended. **c830m** *for the face*

From the Dom hut follow Route 64a to a height of c3,400m where the Festi glacier levels out beyond a crevassed region. Now cross the glacier heading roughly SE into the glacier combe NE of Pt 3,768m. The saddle on the E side of this point is the Festi-Kinlücke (not named on map) and is the first objective. Cross the bergschrund (which can be difficult) and climb the steep slope to the saddle. Sometimes it is necessary to traverse L below the rocks towards the top of the slope and reach the ridge some way above the low point (3hr). In descent, easy slabs lead down to a rappel piton c15m lower.

Once on the ridge there is the opportunity to examine the face itself and to work out the best line of ascent through the seracs and crevasses. Continue E along the ridge for c100m to where a line of ramps slant down (vague track across some very loose terrain) on the S side on to the N branch of the Kin glacier. Cross this branch of the glacier Swards to reach the foot of the face which starts steeply then eases as it broadens. Climb the face as directly as possible towards the very upper part of the WSW ridge (on the uppermost part of the face you may encounter some mixed climbing - Scottish II). Join the WSW ridge a little way from the summit via a little rock couloir and follow it to the summit. **c6hr**

Sandwiched between the N edge of the Kin glacier and the NNE ridge is a 600m high face of mixed rock and ice. This was the scene of a P Gabarrou/F Marsigny/G de Thé route, 26/27 June 1991. The climb, which was done overnight, involved negotiation of thin ice smears and verglassed rock which were the result of a storm (TD+).

62d NORTH-NORTH-EAST RIDGE

AD+/D- F Cullinam and G Fitzgerald with P Knubel and J Mooser,
59 2 Sept 1878
Valley base: Zermatt

Invariably climbed or descended by parties traversing the interconnecting ridge between the Dom and Täschhorn. It descends to the Domjoch, the low point between the two summits. (There are routes to this col from both the Saas and Randa sides but these are rarely if ever climbed these days). The route between the two summits is one of the finest high level ridge traverses in the Alps. It is usually done S-N although occasionally parties do it in the reverse direction, that taken by the first traverse party. From the summit the ridge at first is almost entirely rock. It is narrow, can be quite difficult if verglassed or snowy and leads to a tower. Beyond this it gradually becomes more snow covered with a few short sections of rock. It is described here in descent. **210m**

From the summit descend the ridge to where it narrows at a foresummit. This narrow section, which necessitates the use of hands on the crest and feet on the flanks (usually the W flank), leads to a tower. Climb this (III) more or less on the crest then continue down the ridge on easier terrain and with more snow to the Domjoch. **1-2hr**

Leiterspitzen 3,409m

The long rocky WSW ridge of the Täschhorn has two subsidiary peaks, the Kinhorn and the Leiterspitzen. The latter has a fine jagged crest rising to its twin summits from a col just to the E of the culminating point of the ridge at 3,214m.

63a TRAVERSE WEST - EAST

AD First ascent party is not known
58 FWA: L Imesch and G Willisch, 10 Jan 1976
Valley base: Zermatt

LEITERSPITZEN

A pleasant climb but with a long approach and descent. It is a particularly suitable climb when higher peaks are out of condition but is not really suitable as a training climb. If overtaken by bad weather on the route there are some possible escape points to the N, although none of them will be particularly inviting. **c1,200m,** *most of it on the approach*

Start from Täschalpen (Ottavan). Walk down the road to where it crosses the Rotbach and then ascend the R bank of the stream until further progress is halted by steep rocks. Here pick up a small path which traverses L before cutting back R to turn a band of cliffs. Zigzag steeply upwards to a broad grass terrace (Fad) above the cliffs and follow the path L across this until it peters out at c2,500m. Keep traversing L round a shoulder making for the junction of two stream beds. Just above the junction, cross the E branch of the stream and continue up the steep grass and scree slope overlooking the W branch of the stream which here forms a deep ravine. Higher up awkward slabs push one into the loose scree of the stream bed before being forced out R again by a vertical step. More scree leads to the col just E of Pt 3,214m (3½hr).

From the col easy slabs lead to a steepening which is climbed by an obvious crack (IV). Continue along the ridge until a steep, exposed descent leads to a brèche (the Portje). The next obstacle is a steep gendarme, climbed with the aid of several metal spikes (IV). Continue by traversing or turning several small gendarmes until further progress is barred by a vertical wall. Climb it by a broad crack (III+, piton in place at the top). Next descend 10m (easier than it looks) before proceeding along the knife-edged crest to where the ridge peters out into scree. Rejoin the crest by way of some loose rocks and an awkward step (III+) and continue to the W summit (3-4hr).

Descend by going along the ridge for a few m from the small metal cross on the W summit to reach a brèche between the two summits. From here descend the R (S) side of the ridge for c15m to a metal stanchion (a possible rappel point) and then traverse L (looking out) and slightly down for 20m to a rappel point. Rappel 20m to ledges and then, a few m lower, gain a descending traverse line leading easily to scree. Below is a nasty looking combe filled with slabs and loose scree with traces of path in places. Descend the combe which is not as bad to negotiate as it looks. At c3,100m there is a major step which is avoided by traversing R to a grassy shoulder. Keep traversing across and slightly up a scree slope for c200m to the crest of the SSW ridge and then descend this to the saddle (Pt 3,051m). Now head W down interminable boulder fields, scree and steep grass to rejoin the ascent path.

From the grassy shoulder an alternative way is to continue steeply downwards, following a faint path before eventually picking up a good path where it crosses the Rotbach stream.
10-12hrs for the round trip

Dom 4,545m

J Llewellyn-Davies with H Brantschen, J Krönig and J Zumtaugwald, 11 Sept 1858

Considered to be the highest mountain entirely in Switzerland. The only contender to this title is the Dufourspitze which is higher but whose summit is only 140m from the Italian border. Viewed from the N or NW it appears as an attractive snow/ice peak and it is on this side of the mountain that the principle routes of ascent are located. Its E flank is similar to that of the Täschhorn and has been described earlier. To the SW a steep rock wall plunges down to the Kin glacier, this is the setting for two routes, one by G Young and the other by O Eckenstein neither of which can be recommended. The faces are separated by three ridges. The NE ridge leads to the Lenzjoch and links the mountain with the Lenzspitze, unfortunately it does not offer an attractive means of ascent. The S ridge is quite frequently climbed by parties traversing the Täschhorn and Dom but it is hardly a route one would choose to climb in its own right. The W ridge is more interesting. Less than 200m from the summit a subsidiary ridge runs NW (Festigrat) and provides a fairly direct means of ascent from the Festijoch. The W ridge itself runs down to the Festi-Kinlucke (not named or marked on the map) which lies just E of Pt 3,365m. It is infrequently climbed but is worthy of consideration (AD+). Between the Festigrat and the W ridge is the interesting NW and WNW flank on which a number of routes have been established.

64a NORTH FLANK
PD
First ascent party
63
Valley base: Zermatt
60

The ordinary route and that followed by the majority of parties climbing the mountain, it is however a fairly tedious snow plod with another unattractive feature. That is running the gauntlet below the seracs in the section beyond the Festijoch. Crossing the Festijoch itself accounts for the most difficult part of the ascent. **c1,600m**

From the Dom hut follow a path ESE to reach the moraine on the N side of the Festi glacier. Continue along the crest of the moraine to reach the glacier itself which is then followed on its R bank past Pt 3,303m. At about this point the glacier becomes quite tortuous and crevassed for a while. Keep fairly close to the rocks in this section before easier slopes lead on to the foot of the Festijoch (3,723m). The route climbs to the ridge a little way before the lowest point. Slant up towards the ridge (cairns and tracks) and then climb the rock wall to the crest (c2½hr). In descent it is usual to rappel.

Scramble E along the ridge then slant down on the N side on snow on to the Hohbärg glacier. Cross this towards the NNE, as quickly as possible, into the middle of the glacier (crevasses) keeping a respectful distance from the serac band on the R. Once beyond the threat from seracs, gradually turn towards the SE and climb towards the Lenzjoch. Where the slope eases at c3,940m turn R and climb the slope ahead as direct as possible to the snow saddle between the summit itself and the gendarme of Pt 4,479m. From the saddle follow the snow ridge to the summit (3-4hr). **c6hr**

THE SAAS PEAKS AND THE MISCHABEL

64b SOUTH RIDGE

AD   W Conway and W Penhall with F Imseng and P-J Truffer,
57 19 Aug 1878
59 60 Valley base: Zermatt

A fine looking ridge which is disappointing on close inspection. The quality of the rock is in sharp contrast to that of the NNW ridge of the Täschhorn to which it connects. It is only towards the summit that it achieves an acceptable quality. Handle it with care! **265m**

From the Domjoch, reached by descending Route 62d, follow the snowy ridge to the first gendarme which can be climbed (II+) or turned on the E side. Above this the ridge is quite jagged but the rocky spikes can be turned on the E side but never too far from the crest. This section is quite delicate if there is a lot of snow. It leads to a level shoulder which in turn leads to the foot of the final buttress. Here the rock improves and is climbed direct (II). Finally snow and easy rocks lead to the summit cross. **2-3hr**

64c NORTH-WEST AND WEST-NORTH-WEST
D   FLANKS
60 Valley base: Zermatt

Sandwiched between the W ridge and the Festigrat is a predominantly snow/ice face which is more or less free of objective dangers and on which three routes have been climbed, each one taking a fairly direct line to the summit. **c750m** *for each route*

(i) Climbed by G Simonetta and M Ziegenhagen on 31 July 1978, this route (D) takes a line roughly parallel to the W ridge starting below the Festi-Kinlucke (see Route 62c). The lower part of the slope is not very steep but there are a number of icy steps and the possiblity of a difficult bergschrund to cross. This leads to a terrace below the steeper section. Climb this (45°) and then a couloir interspersed with rock ribs (45°-50°) to the foot of the final capping rocks. An icy couloir leads on to the W ridge which is followed to the summit. **c8hr**

SSE Ridge of the Täschhorn
(Route 62a) Peter Fleming

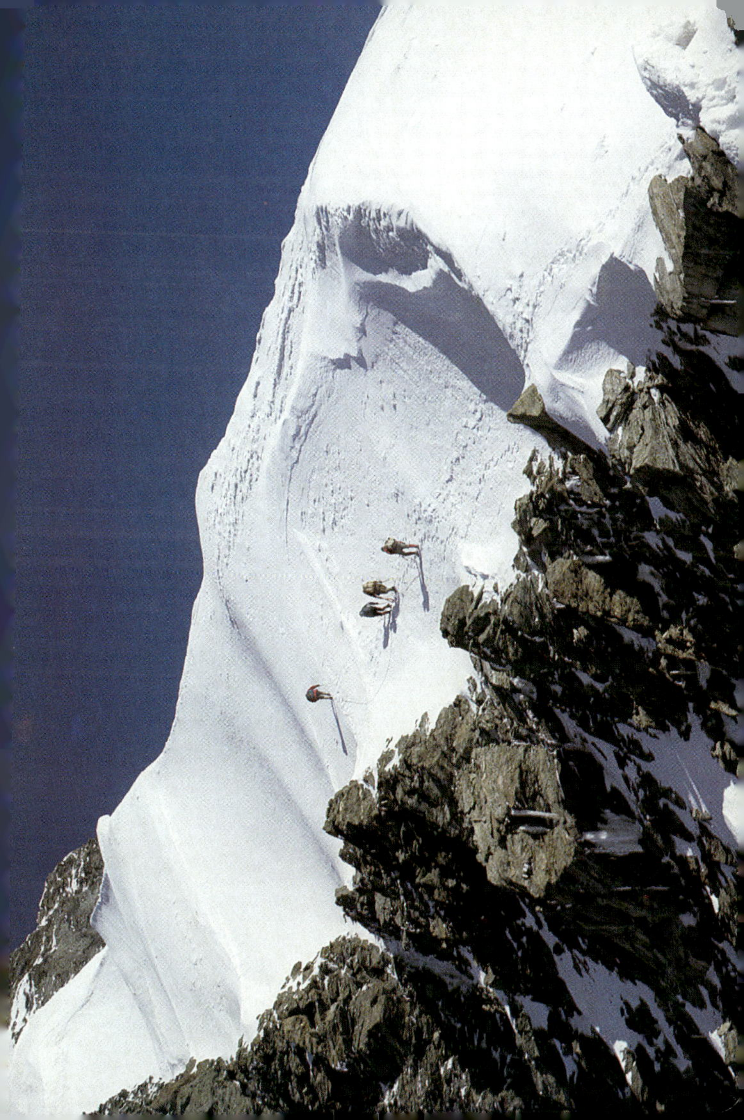

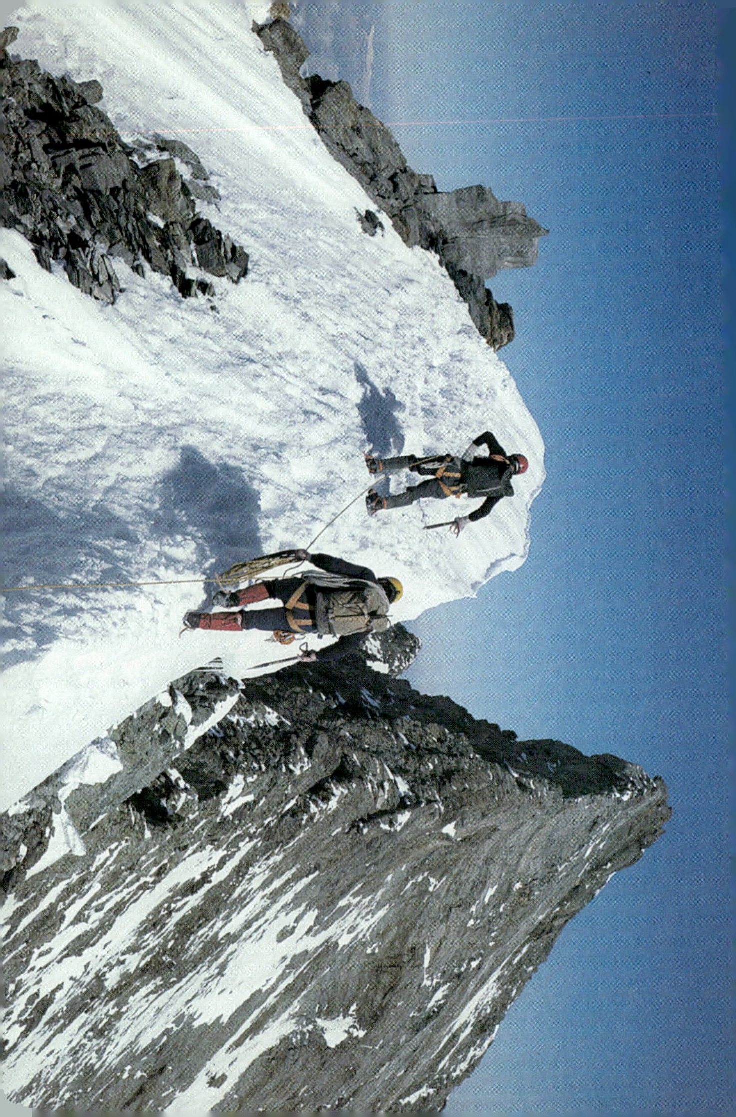

(ii) Climbed solo by P Gabarrou on 16 June 1984 in 2½hr from the Dom hut, this route (D) starts in the glacier combe just S of the Festijoch. Climb the face on the R side with a serac band on the R. Climb past the serac band on its L edge and so reach the upper slopes. Climb these moving gradually Rwards to reach an ice couloir on the R side of the rocks forming the gendarme at Pt 4,479m. 10m of rock (III and IV) lead to the top of the gendarme from where the summit is easily attained. Allow **8hr**

(iii) Climbed by F Driessen and P van Lookeren-Campaque on 20 July 1962, this route (D) lies roughly parallel to the Gabarrou route. Climb the L side of the face (45°-50°), the line rising between two long rock ribs, to gain the Festigrat at a height of c4,400m. Follow Route 64d to the summit. **c8hr**

64d NORTH-WEST RIDGE - FESTIGRAT
PD+ First ascent party
60 Valley base: Zermatt

A much better route for ascent than that of the N flank (Route 64a), much more direct and avoiding the seracs of that route. However, the N flank route is better in descent. The one drawback is that ice can develop on the ridge above the Festijoch. ***c1,600m***

From the Dom hut follow Route 64a to the Festijoch (c2½hr). Climb the ridge along the easy rock crest or on snow on its L (N) side (better, if the snow is consolidated) to where it narrows and merges into snow/ice. Pass the next rocks on the L, between the rocks and some seracs, and continue above on snow on the L side of the ridge. Towards the top turn the gendarme of Pt 4,479m on the L and then link up with the N flank route to reach the summit. **5-6hr**

Traverse between the Nadelhorn and the Lenzspitze
(Routes 65c and 66b) Les Swindin

Lenzspitze 4,294m

C Dent with A and F Burgener, Aug 1870

The central peak of the Mischabel chain and sometimes considered part of the Nadelgrat although this title should strictly only be used for the section of the Mischabel chain extending N from the Nadelhorn to the Galenjoch. From many directions the peak appears quite unremarkable but when seen from the NE one has an entirely different impression. The obvious feature is the sweeping snow/ice face on this flank of the mountain which plunges down 500m on to the Hohbalm glacier and is an obvious target for any alpinist. Its two other faces are of little if any interest but the faces themselves are separated by three fine ridges. There is no simple 'ordinary' route to the summit and once on the summit one is faced with the problem of descent. The simplest way is to traverse the ridge linking this mountain with the Nadelhorn and then to descend its NE ridge. Once committed to this ridge there is no quick exit so it is advisable to watch the weather carefully and avoid being caught in stormy conditions on it.

65a EAST-NORTH-EAST RIDGE
AD W Graham with T Andenmatten and A Supersaxo, 3 Aug 1882
61 Valley base: Saas

*An excellent route but much easier in ascent than in descent. The ridge is mostly of rock with the crux pitch at the Grand Gendarme and although the climbing is nowhere difficult in good conditions any snow or ice on the rock pushes up the grade at least one notch. Be prepared to turn back if the weather shows signs of deteriorating as there is no quick way off. Combined with a traverse of the Nadelhorn it makes for one of the finer outings in the Valais. **c970m***

From the Mischabel hut follow a track up the rocks above the hut to the point where tracks to the Windjoch lead down on to the Hohbalm glacier (c45min). Continue along the ridge, turning any obstacles easily on the L side whilst taking care with the loose rock, to reach Pt 3,815m. From here a level snowy section leads to a considerable steepening. Climb the steep rocks as close to the crest as is possible and reach a shallow gap. Beyond this lies the Grand Gendarme. Climb this direct to its summit (III+) and then make a short rappel on to the crest of the horizontal ridge beyond (2hr). The rappel can be avoided by down climbing a crack on the S side which is exposed but not technically difficult. At the next rise climb the crest itself (III) or more easily its L side (take care again with loose rock) as far as a final section of snow. This takes the form of a fine crest and leads directly to the summit. **c5hr**

65b SOUTH RIDGE

PD+ R Ball with A Supersaxo and L Zurbriggen, 28 July 1888
61 Valley base: Zermatt
63

The obvious route from the Dom hut for parties based in the Zermatt valley but quite a lengthy outing. It is used as a means of ascent or descent by parties traversing the Nadelgrat from this side (not recommended). The ridge itself starts at the Lenzjoch and can be climbed from this point although it is possible to take a short cut, at least in ascent, if snow conditions are suitable. The short cut involves climbing the snow slope leading to the obvious pointed gendarme on the ridge. Provided there is plenty of snow and that this has not turned to ice, this is the preferred line. **c1,400m** *from the hut*

From the Dom hut follow Route 64a to the point where it turns R. Continue on to the upper slopes of the Hohbärg glacier and reach the bergschrund below the lowest point on the ridge. Cross it and climb a short but quite steep snow/ice slope and a few rocks to the crest (3-4hr). It is also possible to reach this point by moving further SW where the snow slope merges with the crest and then scramble back along the crest (one short and steep descent).

From the col follow the ridge to the foot of the pointed gendarme. The rock is not very good but nowhere is it difficult. Turn the gendarme on the E side. The gendarme can be reached by taking the shortcut. Instead of heading up the Hohbärg glacier to the low point on the ridge, bear L to reach the bergschrund below the gendarme. Cross it and then climb the snow slope above. This leads to easy but loose stony slopes which are followed to the ridge which can be gained on either side of the gendarme.

Above the gendarme, after a short step of down climbing, climb a twisting couloir on the L (W) side of the ridge. At the top of the couloir climb out Rwards to gain the crest of the ridge ahead a short distance from the summit. **6-7hr**

65c NORTH-WEST RIDGE

PD First ascent party
61 Valley base: Saas
63

A short ridge descending to the Nadeljoch (not named on map) which is the lowest point on the ridge linking the Lenzspitze and Nadelhorn and mainly used in descent by parties traversing the two peaks from the Mischabel hut. It is a mixture of snow and rock (except in very dry years) and is quite narrow. **80m**

From the summit of the Lenzspitze follow the crest of the ridge turning or scrambling over rock outcrops as appropriate to the Nadeljoch. **½-1hr**

65d NORTH-NORTH-EAST FACE -
D+ **DREIESELWAND**
61 D von Bethmann-Hollweg with O and O Supersaxo, 7 July 1911
FWA: P Etter and H Wenin, 1/2 March 1968
Valley base: Saas

The 'piece de resistance' of the mountain. A popular route that has been soloed as well as descended on foot and on ski, in fact it is/can be used as a means of descent in good snow conditions and can prove easier than the ridges if they are snow covered. A snow/ice face with a mean angle of 50°, steeper in its upper half. When the face is covered in good névé it is quite straightforward and parties can move together, at least on the lower half, but it becomes a much more demanding proposition when it is icy. It is often compared with the N face of the Ober Gabelhorn but with an easier approach. Avoid it after fresh snow. One effect of the dry winters of recent years is a decrease in the depth of snow on the face. This is resulting in the emergence of a rock barrier which is beginning to extend across the face from the L side above the bergschrund. So, don't leave it too long before attempting the route or alternatively pray for a return to wet winters. **c500m**

From the Mischabel hut follow Route 66a(i) to the tracks leading to the Windjoch. Follow these on to the Hohbalm glacier then work up the glacier to the foot of the face directly below the Nadeljoch. Cross the bergschrund where feasible and then take as direct a line as possible to the summit. Often parties exit on to the ridge a little way N of the summit. **4-7hr**

Nadelhorn 4,327m

F Andenmatten, B Epiney, A Supersaxo and J Zimmermann, 16 Sept 1858

Like its close neighbour, the Lenzspitze, it has three ridges and three faces although only the ridges are of much interest. The NE ridge is quite easy and is the line taken by the ordinary route. It can be approached from either the Mischabel hut or the Bordier hut. The SE ridge links the mountain to the Lenzspitze and, although short, gives the best climbing on the mountain whilst the NW ridge forms part of the Nadelgrat (see notes later). This ridge leads to the Hohbärgjoch, Pt 4,142m (not named on map - see introduction to Route 66c), at the foot of the Hohbärghorn. Before reaching this point it rises to an important subsidiary summit, the Stecknadelhorn (4,241m). Whilst some lists consider this to be a separate 4,000er it should more correctly be listed as a 'top'. Of the faces, only the N face sees any traffic and even then not very much. This face is essentially a snow/ice climb (D), relatively short and quite straightforward although the approach can be complex depending on the state of the Ried glacier in its upper part. The N face of the Stecknadelhorn provides a short but worthwhile snow/ice route of 350m. It has an angle of 50° with some mixed climbing below the summit. The short NNE rib is also worth looking at (D).

66a NORTH-EAST RIDGE

PD First ascent party
61 Valley base: Saas
62 65

The ridge terminates at the Windjoch just below the attractive little summit of the Ulrichshorn which is frequently climbed at the same time. From the Windjoch the ridge is mostly snow at first but as it narrows it has interspersed sections of both rock and snow before finally becoming almost entirely rock close to the summit. The rock in the upper part is fairly sound. **1,000m** *from the Mischabel hut*

(i) From the Mischabel hut climb the path up rocks behind the hut to the point where a descent can be made on to the Hohbalm glacier from a height of c3,600m. Cross the glacier, curving round the glacier bowl with little height gain to below the Windjoch. Climb the steep snow slope, at first towards the summit of the Ulrichshorn and then back L to the col (1½-2hr). In lean snow years or late in the season the snow slope leading to the Windjoch can be interrupted by a band of rock.

(ii) From the Bordier hut walk along the hut approach path for c100m before taking a track leading off L towards the moraine on the R bank of the Ried glacier. Scramble down some large boulders just before reaching the moraine. Follow the crest of the moraine (ignoring a descent path to the glacier a few m beyond a prominent boulder) to its upper end and so reach the glacier without any loss of height. Climb the glacier, curving R to pass below Pt 3,376m at the foot of the SW ridge of the Balfrin N summit. In unfavourable conditions the glacier close to this point will be very crevassed and it will be necessary to take to the rocks (loose and some danger of stonefall especially later in the day). Now head towards the Ulrichshorn before turning SW and curving round so as to approach the foot of the Windjoch from the NW. Cross the bergschrund and climb the sometimes icy slope to the col (c4hr). It is possible to climb to the Riedpass from this route by slanting L at the point where it turns SW.

From the Windjoch climb the ridge close to the crest but mostly on the N side to the summit (2hr). **c4hr** from the Mischabel hut and **c6hr** from the Bordier hut

66b SOUTH-EAST RIDGE

AD H Topham with X Imseng and A Supersaxo, 29 Aug 1886
61 Valley base: Saas
63

A fine, high level ridge formed of excellent rock (gneiss) and with several gendarmes to negotiate. Usually used on the route of descent to the Mischabel hut by parties having ascended the Lenzspitze. **114m**

From the Nadeljoch (the low point on the ridge between the Lenzspitze and Nadelhorn) climb the ridge by traversing (best) or turning the gendarmes as you prefer. The most difficult pitch is III+. **1½-2hr**

66c NORTH-WEST RIDGE

PD+ O Eckenstein with M Zurbriggen, 8 Aug 1887
62 Valley base: Zermatt/Saas
63 65

A mixed ridge of rock and snow forming a part of the Nadelgrat whose appearance is more intimidating than the reality. As mentioned above, a prominent top on this ridge is the Stecknadelhorn. This summit gives its name to an adjacent snow saddle but there appears to be some confusion as to which snow saddle since there are two. One of these lies between the Stecknadelhorn and the Nadelhorn itself and is the one referred to in this guide book as the Stecknadeljoch. The second snow saddle, marked on the map as Pt 4,142m, on the E side of the Hohbärghorn is/has been referred to by the same name. For the purposes of this guide book this saddle is known as the Hohbärgjoch, a name which has also been used to identify the col separating the Hohbärghorn and Dirruhorn. This latter col is described here and on the map as the Dirrujoch. **c200m**

From the Hohbärgjoch (Pt 4,142m) on the E side of the Hohbärghorn, which can be reached by Route 67a, follow the narrow rock crest across or round the various teeth to reach the summit of the Stecknadelhorn (bits of II and III). Descend easy rocks to the Stecknadeljoch and the start of a fairly level snow crest. Continue along the crest to the final section which is mainly rocky. Climb over the first gendarme (III), or turn it on the L if snow conditions permit, descending steeply to a snow saddle on the other side. Now either climb direct to the summit via a 40m crack line (III) or move L across snow slopes to gain the NE ridge below the summit rocks and finish by that route. **1½-2hr**

Hohbärghorn 4,219m

R Heathcote with F Biner, P Perren P Taugwalder jnr, Aug 1869

The spelling used in the name is that used on the latest issues of the Swiss CN (LK) maps, the peak was previously known as the Hohberghorn. It is a relatively insignificant peak for a 4,000er but quite appealing, at least when viewed from the E from where its elegant NE face is well seen. From most other aspects it is somewhat less attractive. It is rarely climbed other than by combining it with the ascent of one or more of the adjacent peaks by parties traversing part or all of the Nadelgrat.

67a EAST-SOUTH-EAST RIDGE

PD First ascent party

62 Valley base: Zermatt

63 64

A very short ridge but it has a lengthy approach. 77m: c1,300m from the Dom hut

From the Dom hut follow Route 64a on to the Hohbärg glacier. Pass as quickly as possible below the seracs then cross the glacier more or less horizontally to the bottom of the couloir descending from Pt 4,142m (Hohbärgjoch). If the couloir is snow-filled climb it tediously direct to the col, otherwise climb the scree-like slopes on its R bank (4-5hr). The couloir can equally well be used as a means of descent. From the col follow the easy snow ridge to the summit (¼hr). **c5hr**

67b NORTH-NORTH-WEST RIDGE

AD F Oliver with A Burgener and A Supersaxo, 20 Sept 1894
64 Valley base: Zermatt
62 63

Used in ascent or descent on the extended version of the Nadelgrat or by parties approaching the mountain from the Bordier hut. The ridge itself is PD, the main difficulties associated with the route are those of the approach to the Dirrujoch (Pt 3,916m) which marks the foot of the ridge. The Dirrujoch can also be approached from the Dom hut, a longer route but it can be easier than the Bordier hut alternative.
***300m: c1,350m** from the Bordier hut*

(i) From the Bordier hut follow Route 66a(ii) until you are past Pt 3,376m then head S up the glacier and then SW, keeping some distance below the rock outcrop, to reach the foot of the couloir below the Dirrujoch. In good snow conditions climb the steep couloir direct to the col (c4hr), otherwise, when the couloir is icy or avalanche prone, climb the broken rocks on the L bank of the couloir after the first three rope lengths in the couloir (much slower: some danger of stonefall: stakes in place at 30m intervals with some bolts between them) or traverse the Dirruhorn via Routes 68b and 68a. The foot of the couloir can be reached from the Mischabel hut by crossing the Windjoch (c3hr).

(ii) From the Dom hut follow Route 64a on to the Hohbärg glacier. Descend the glacier NW, before turning R at c3,520m to reach the base of the massive W buttress of the mountain. On the N side of the lowest rocks a couloir, usually snow filled, leads up the buttress. Climb this for c100m to the point where a ramp line (at least partly snow covered) slants off L. Follow the ramp quite easily on to the little, unnamed glacier on the N side of the W buttress. Traverse L across the initial steep glacier slope then climb up the glacier to the col. There are a few rocks to finish (4-5hr). This route is not recommended for descent.

From the Dirrujoch climb the ridge on the crest or on the R side, on rock at first and then snow, to reach the base of a rock step.

Turn this on the L if snow conditions are favourable, otherwise climb the rocks on the crest (II+). Above the step easy slopes lead to the summit (c1hr). **4½-5hr** in good conditions from the Bordier hut

67c NORTH-EAST FACE

D O Williamson with H Fuchs and J Maître and H Symons with
64 F Lochmatter, 29 July 1910
62 Valley base: Zermatt

A plain, fairly short snow/ice slope with a fairly constant angle of 50°. The face was descended on skis in May 1986. ***c320m***

Approach the face as for Route 67b(i): a fairly direct route can be taken from the Windjoch. Cross the bergschrund and climb direct to the summit. **5-6hr** from the Bordier hut

Dirruhorn 4,035m

A Mummery and W Penhall with A Burgener and F Imseng, 7 Sept 1879 although probably climbed by chamois hunters before this date

In earlier editions of this guide book and in many other compilations the name used was/is Dürrenhorn. Here we use the name in current use on the Swiss CN (LK) maps. It is the final 4,000m summit at the N end of the Mischabel chain and thus of the Nadelgrat. It is a fairly uninteresting peak and the only reasons for climbing it appears to be that it exceeds the 'magic' 4,000m height or that it is part of the Nadelgrat. Most parties will approach from the Bordier hut but an approach from the Dom hut is quite feasible (see Route 67b(ii)).

68a SOUTH-SOUTH-EAST RIDGE

AD O Eckenstein with M Zurbriggen, 30 July 1887
64 Valley base: Zermatt
63

Of very little interest other than as a way of reaching the summit. The ridge itself is F+, the difficulty lies in the approach to its foot. **120m**

From the Dirrujoch, reached by traversing the Hohbärghorn from the Hohbärgjoch or via Route 67b(i) or (ii), follow the easy rock ridge to the summit. **½hr**

68b NORTH RIDGE

AD+ First ascent party
64 Valley base: Zermatt
63

The ridge itself is somewhat easier than the overall grade might suggest. The main difficulty lies in the approach to the snowy col at the foot of the ridge. **c1,200m** *from the Bordier hut*

From the Bordier hut follow Route 67b(i) until below the rock island. Instead of climbing to the foot of the couloir leading to the Dirrujoch, contour round to the bottom of the snow-filled couloir leading to the snow saddle at Pt 3,860m. In good snow conditions climb the couloir direct to the col (some stonefall danger). If the couloir is icy it is better to climb the loose but easy rocks on its L bank, slanting across to the col at the top (c4hr).

From the snow saddle follow the crest of the rock ridge (II and III-) to the summit. About halfway traverse a pointed gendarme or turn it high on the R side by a slab with some cracks (III+). **c5hr**

Nadelgrat

Strictly speaking the Nadelgrat is the section of the Mischabel chain extending from the summit of the Nadelhorn at its S end to the Galenjoch in the N, thus it includes along its length three separate 4,000m summits plus a top. Beyond the Nmost of these, the Dirruhorn, is one further summit, that of the Chli-Dirruhorn, Pt 3,890m (not named on map). It is fairly common to traverse the ridge but it is rare for parties to continue beyond the summit of the Dirruhorn when traversing S-N. Parties traversing in the opposite direction may well join the ridge at the snow saddle between the Chli-Dirruhorn and the Dirruhorn itself. The natural extension of the Nadelgrat is to include the ridge extending S from the Nadelhorn to the Lenzspitze and even on further S to the Lenzjoch.

There are three huts from which the ridge can be approached, namely the Mischabel, Dom and Bordier huts although the guardian at the Dom hut might well laugh at you if you suggest doing it from there, especially if you intend to return to the hut. The extended version can be traversed N-S or S-N and it can be traversed in its entirety or in part. Indeed it can also by climbed in two days rather than one with the Mischabel hut used for the overnight stop. Consequently there are a number of decisions to be made when planning the expedition.

Starting at the Dom hut you can traverse S-N from the Lenzjoch. In this direction you can leave the ridge at the Nadelhorn (without setting foot on the true Nadelgrat) and descend to the Mischabel hut. Use Routes 65a, 65b, 66b and 66a. Alternatively you can continue to the Hohbärghorn then descend to the Dom hut via Route 67a, or continue to the Dirruhorn via Routes 67b and 68a descending Route 67b(i) from the Dirrujoch to the Bordier hut. The couloir below the Dirrujoch can prove to be the hardest part of the route in the late afternoon when the snow is soft and is inclined to slide. It might well be necessary to down climb the rocks on its L bank. If you are really adventurous you can descend Route 68b and then traverse the Chli-Dirruhorn to the Galenjoch and then reach the Bordier hut (see detail below). If you choose to take two days over the route you will need to reverse the descent from the Nadelhorn. In this case it is not necessary to return to the summit of the Nadelhorn. Instead, from high on the NE ridge you can contour across the upper slopes of the N face on to the snow ridge leading to the Stecknadelhorn. This saves c½hr.

Starting at the Mischabel hut on a S-N traverse you have the choice of including or excluding the Lenzspitze. If you include it then follow Route 65a to its summit, then the options are the same as for starting from the Dom hut. If you exclude it then follow Route 66a to the summit of the Nadelhorn then select from the same options. If you descend on to the Ried glacier it is possible to return to the Mischabel hut by crossing the Windjoch (see Route 66a(i) and (ii)).

A N-S traverse of the classic Nadelgrat is best done from the Bordier hut. Climb the Dirruhorn by Route 68a. If you wish to complete the whole ridge from the Galenjoch you must reach this by walking down the L bank of the Ried glacier below the E flank of the Chli-Dirruhorn. If the crevasses are impassable, look for a zone of yellowish rock on the E flank of the NNW ridge of the Chli-Dirruhorn and above this is a sort of ramp which slants up on to the ridge. Follow this line easily on to the ridge. The traverse of the Chli-Dirruhorn from the Galenjoch to the snow saddle at the foot of the N ridge of the Dirruhorn is quite straightforward (mostly II with bits of II+) and takes c2½hr. On the ascent of the NNW ridge you can turn Pt 3,816 on the W side. From the snow saddle follow Routes 68b, 68a, 67b, 67a and 66c to the Nadelhorn. Descend its NE ridge to the Windjoch then return to the Bordier hut via Route 66a or traverse the Ulrichshorn to the Riedpass and join the same route from there.

A N-S traverse could be made from the Dom hut by following Route 67b(ii) to the Dirrujoch. From here the Dirruhorn is easily climbed (Route 68a) up and down and then the reverse of the options above are open to you. It makes for a very long day if you choose to return to the Dom hut since the only sensible descent routes are from the Hohbärgjoch (Route 67a) and via the S ridge of the Lenzspitze (Route 65b). A two day expedition might well be the best option, traversing the Nadelhorn and Lenzspitze on day two.

Whatever option you take, make sure that the weather is fine and settled. Being caught on any part of the ridge in a storm is no fun at all.

Ulrichshorn 3,925m

J-J Imseng and M Ulrich with F Andenmatten, S Biner,
J Madutz and M Zumtaugwald, 10 Aug 1848

A fine little peak tucked on to the end of the NE ridge of the
Nadelhorn and frequently ascended in conjunction with that
peak: a fine viewpoint. A traverse of the summit can be made by
parties climbing to or descending from the Windjoch when poor
conditions on the N slopes of this pass make direct access from/
to the Ried glacier unfavourable.

69a SOUTH-WEST RIDGE
PD Valley base: Saas/Zermatt
65

A fairly narrow crest that can be quite icy.

From the Windjoch, reached by Route 66a(i) or (ii), follow the
ridge to the summit. **c½hr** and **75m**

69b NORTH FLANK
F First ascent party
65 Valley base: Zermatt

*The easiest way to the summit and often preferred as a means of
descent to the Ried glacier rather than the N slopes of the Windjoch.*

Reach the Riedpass from the Bordier hut by deviating from
Route 66a(ii) just below the pass (2½-3hr) and then climb the
easy snow slopes and a rounded ridge to the summit (½-1hr).
3-4hr and **c1,150m**

Balfrin 3,795.7m

Mr and Mrs R Watson with F Andenmatten, J-M Claret and
J Imseng (the priest of Saas), 6 July 1863

At the Nadelhorn the long ridge of the Mischabel chain
bifurcates with one ridge running NE and the other NW and

enclosing between them the Ried glacier. The first summit along the NW branch is the Ulrichshorn (see above). Beyond this summit the ridge swings N to the Riedpass from which rises the Balfrin by a rocky ridge. At the summit of the Balfrin there is another bifurcation. One ridge runs NE and is of little interest whilst the main ridge leads NW towards the Gr Bigerhorn and eventually the Färichhorn. On this ridge, at c600m from the Balfrin summit, is a second top that appears possibly to be higher than the Balfrin. It is in fact lower at 3,783m and is referred to as the Balfrin N summit and differs from the main summit in that it is a snow peak.

70a SOUTH RIDGE

PD First ascent party
Valley base: Zermatt/Saas

The obvious route from the Mischabel hut but necessitating a traverse of the Ulrichshorn. It is equally accessible from the Bordier hut. The ridge itself leads NNW at first from the Riedpass, then turns NE before finally, after a slight descent, turning N to the summit. **230m** *from the Riedpass*

Reach the Riedpass from the Mischabel hut via Routes 66a(i), 69a and 69b or from the Bordier hut by Route 66a(ii). From the pass climb the ridge on snow at first and then on rock, crossing or turning on the L any obstacles, past Pt 3,644m and so reach the foot of the true S ridge. Climb the crest to the summit. **c1hr** from the Riedpass

70b SOUTH-WEST RIDGE OF NORTH SUMMIT

PD First tourist ascent: probably C Beck and M Besson. 17 July 1935
Valley base: Zermatt

From the snowy Balfrin N summit a prominent rock ridge descends SW reaching the Ried glacier at Pt 3,376m. The route follows the crest of the ridge on quite good rock. **c900m**

From the Bordier hut follow Route 66a(ii) until just past

Pt 3,376m and gain the S side of the ridge. Climb up to the crest of the ridge via a scree slope and then follow the ridge itself to the summit. Towards the top the ridge narrows and can be climbed on the S side. **3-3½hr**

70c NORTH-WEST RIDGE VIA THE GROSS BIGERHORN
PD

First tourist ascent: W Conway with A Pollinger and P Truffer, 13 July 1878
Valley base: Zermatt

The ridge links the mountain with the Gr Bigerhorn (and is only F), a traverse of the two peaks making for a reasonably interesting outing from the Bordier hut. **c1,150m**

Reach the summit of the Gr Bigerhorn by Route 71a. Descend the mainly snowy SW ridge to the saddle at Pt 3,594m (Balfrinjoch) and then climb easily up snow slopes to the Balfrin N summit. Another descent on snow and stony ground leads to a further col from where the main summit is easily reached (1-1½hr). **3½-4hr**

Gross Bigerhorn 3,626m

First tourist ascent: W Gröbli with A Pollinger snr, 5 Oct 1891

A fine viewpoint above all else and worthy of an ascent for that reason, especially if combined with an ascent of the Balfrin (see previous route).

71a WEST-SOUTH-WEST RIDGE
PD First ascent party
66 Valley base: Zermatt

Of very little interest as a climb but it gives access to a fine viewpoint and can be climbed in poor weather. **740m**

From the Bordier hut follow Route 66a(ii) to the upper end of the moraine. Now move L to reach the slope of jumbled boulders. Climb the slope direct to reach a flat part of the ridge or follow a slanting line L towards to the col separating the Kl and Gr Bigerhorn (some cairns). From the col follow a cairned route back R to the flatter part of the ridge. Reach the summit by scrambling up more broken rocks. **c2hr**

71b NORTH-NORTH-WEST RIDGE

AD C Fleck and M Besson, 16 July 1925 although the ridge had previously been descended
66
Valley base: Zermatt

A fine ridge bristling with strangely shaped gendarmes of good quality rock. **c600m**

From the Bordier hut follow traces of track NE (cairns) to cross the lower part of the NW ridge of the Kl Bigerhorn. Turn E and reach the foot of the scree slope below the col of Gässi (Pt 3,044m). Climb the slope (scree and boulders) to the col (1hr).

Now climb the ridge heading ESE over large boulders, turning difficulties on the R side, to reach the first large gendarme. Traverse R then climb straight up to regain the ridge crest beyond the gendarme. Continue along the crest, over two smaller gendarmes, to reach the base of a slim, tapering gendarme (2hr). Contour round this on the R side then follow the crest (excellent climbing) to Pt 3,345m (1½-2hr). The ridge now turns SSE and leads to an overhanging gendarme. Contour round this and the next two gendarmes keeping on the L (E) side on ramps and grassy slopes and then regain the ridge crest beyond another gendarme which is c25m high. Next reach a vertical step which is also turned on the L, the ridge being regained by a difficult chimney and some slabs. More good climbing along the crest leads to easy boulders and the summit (2-2½hr). **7-8hr** from the hut

East side of the Saas Valley
Monte Moropass to the Simplonpass

The Monte Moropass is a popular and easy crossing point on the frontier ridge and marks the southern limit of the chain of peaks on the eastern side of the Saas valley. The pass is served with a cable car and skiing facilities from the village of Pecetto in Macugnaga. From the cable car station there remains a thirty minute walk over very stony terrain to reach the crossing point on the ridge near to a very large statue of the Madonna. The view of the E face of Monte Rosa from here is one of the best in the district. The pass is reached from the road head at Mattmark dam on the Swiss side after a 2½hr walk.

Just E of the pass rises the small peak of the Joderhorn (3,037m) where there are several routes of interest to the rock climber. The frontier ridge turns to the NE from here and includes several minor peaks spaced at approximately 2km intervals. They are seldom climbed. The Saas flanks are composed of high scree-covered slopes and small glacier fields whilst the eastern flanks on the Italian side offer more scope for the climber but are remotely situated. Several bivouac huts are strategically placed for this purpose. The names given to many of the features on this section of the ridge vary depending on whether you use a Swiss or an Italian map so be wary of confusion.

The Sonnighorn (3,487m) is an important summit and offers good mixed climbing on sound rock. 2km N beyond the Mittelrück, is the start of the Portjengrat, the best known and most popular rock ridge in the Saas district. It clears quickly after snow and the rock is good. The highest point is the Pizzo d'Andolla (3,653m), where the frontier swings to the E, with the main chain of mountains continuing N. An important pass, the Zwischbergenpass cuts the ridge between the Portjenhorn and the Weissmies. Just W of the pass is a subsidiary ridge, the Dri Horlini, overlooking the Almageller hut. The traverse of this fine granite ridge is very popular as are many of the more recent rock climbs on its SE face.

276

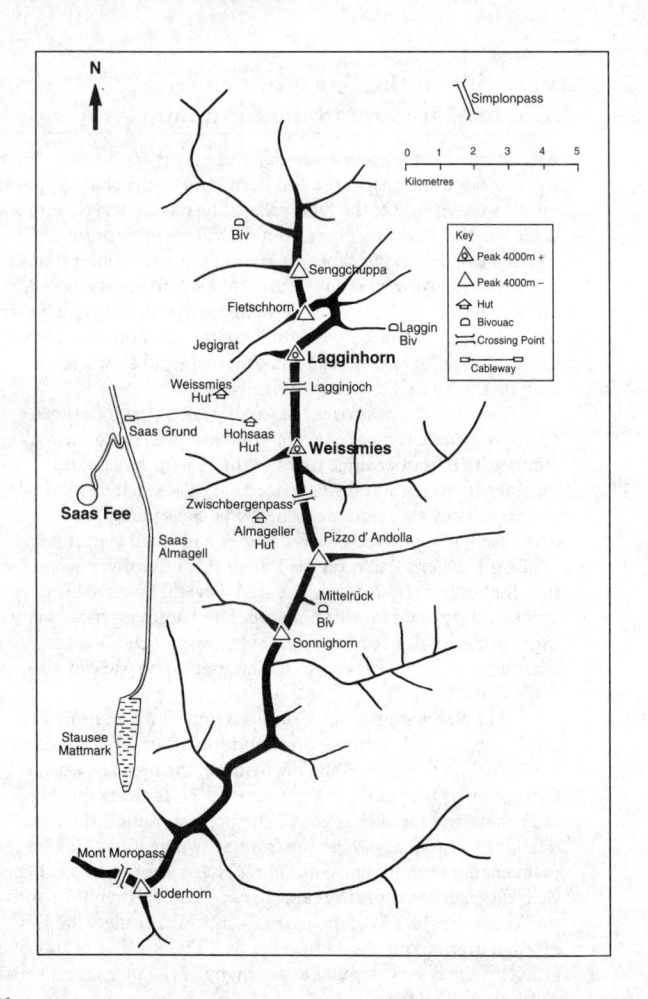

The next peak to the N is the Weissmies (4,023m), the major peak in the chain. It is one of the easiest 4,000m peaks in the Alps and is therefore very popular particularly since the cable way to Hohsaas (3,098m) was constructed. The ridges are often linked to give a good traverse of the mountain. The W face is largely covered by the Trift glacier and provides the first section of the ascent via the ordinary route.

The N ridge provides the most rewarding route on the mountain, being a classic route of the district. Beginning at the Lagginjoch (3,499m) it is, like the Rothorngrat of the Zinal Rothorn, 2½km long and mostly on rock. The Lagginjoch can also provide the starting point for the ascent of the Lagginhorn (4,010m) via its S ridge. This peak is the only other 4,000er in the chain and is the most northerly one in this range. Like the Weissmies and the Portjengrat the rock is gneiss. A traverse of this mountain combined with the Fletschhorn (3,993m) to its N makes a worthwhile expedition due to the ease with which one can avoid the crevassed glaciers on these peaks by using rocky ridges which present few problems. They are frequently climbed solo.

The eastern aspect of the peaks just briefly described, presents a much more serious choice of routes because of the steep angle of mixed terrain and glacier systems which are more complex. The Fletschhorn in particular has several ridges running towards the Simplon and Laggintal areas offering such routes to climbers based at the Laggin bivouac hut.

Within easy reach of the Weissmies hut on the Saas side is the Jegihorn and the Jegigrat, where splendid rock routes of the middle grades are to be found, including two fine gendarmes.

Finally, east of the summit of the Simplonpass, in full view, is a rocky peak, the Hübschhorn (3,192m), the NW ridge of which provides a fine climb.

EAST SIDE OF THE SAAS VALLEY

Joderhorn 3,035.7m

A quite insignificant peak situated just to the E of the Monte Moropass and easily climbed from there. It is worth climbing for the views, mist permitting, of the E face of Monte Rosa. On the E face of the mountain there is some good quality rock on which several routes c200m in length have been developed. There are other routes on the S face but the lines of ascent here are fairly indistinct. Between these two faces is the SE ridge, which also has excellent quality rock and which presents a very good but fairly short route.

72a WEST-NORTH-WEST RIDGE
F Valley base: Saas/Macugnaga
67

The peak can be easily climbed in a day from the valley, starting from Mattmark or Staffa. Approaching from the former it is not necessary to climb to the Monte Moropass, instead turn off L from the path to reach the foot of the broad ridge (take note of any features in case of mist on the descent). **170m** *from the Monte Moropass*

From the Monte Moropass walk across to the foot of the ridge on the Swiss side of the frontier (snow patches) and follow the boulder-strewn ridge, mostly on its N side, to the summit. **½-1hr**

In descent go down the NE ridge for c50m from where a faint track leads back L and can be followed to its termination in a boulderfield. Scramble down the boulders to the plateau at the foot of the ridge.

72b NORTH-EAST RIDGE
PD Valley base: Saas
68

Useful for making a traverse of the peak by parties starting from Mattmark. **c400m** *from the Tälliboden glacier*

From the Mattmark dam follow Route 48b as far as Tälliboden then follow the valley SE on to the tiny Tälliboden glacier. Climb the R bank of the glacier or the stony ground further L to reach the S Mondellipass (there are two cols, the S col is 7m higher than the N col which is distinguished by it having a small chapel and table).

From the col climb scree slopes towards Pt 2,915m, turning this point on the N side via broken rocks. Beyond this reach a small saddle and then follow the crest of the ridge pleasantly (II) to reach a second protuberance. Cross this then descend slightly before climbing slabs (II) and scrambling over boulders to reach the summit. **1hr** for the ridge: **c4hr** in total

East Face

The lower part of the E face is very steep and compact gneiss in the form of walls cut by cracks and dièdres and provides some excellent rock climbing possibilities. Several routes have been and are being developed on the face, all by Italian climbers. The route starting in the middle of the wall (Via Gildo Burgener) is marked with a red dot in a circle. The starts of other routes are best identified from here. The approach to the face is included in the description of that route.

72c VIA DIRETTA 17 NOVEMBER
TD D Bossone and M Pellizzon, 17 Nov 1988
68 Valley base: Saas/Macugnaga

This climb starts 20m R of Via Gildo Burgener. ***200m***

Start by climbing the obvious crack splitting the pillar and continue in the L slanting groove above for a few m before moving R to another crack which is followed to a belay (40m; VII-). Follow the next crack line to a bolt then traverse L to another system of cracks leading to a ledge (45m;V). Move R and climb slabs to reach a curving crack which is followed for a few m before taking a direct line to a belay below a triangular block (45m;VI+). Reach the NE ridge 100m from the summit in two more 50m pitches up the obvious rib (III+ and IV+). **c3hr**

72d VIA GILDO BURGENER
TD+ R Morandi and C Schranz, 18 Aug 1980
68 Valley base: Saas/Macugnaga

Named after a Macugnaga guide who died on the same date in 1958 on the Dufourspitze. 7 pitches of sustained climbing of V and VI with a crux section of VI+. The route is fully equipped and climbs steep slabs with the crux section in an overhanging, wide chimney/crack. **200m**

Reach the face by following Route 72h to the obvious saddle and then descend the couloir on the E side and reach the foot of the climb, marked with a red dot in a circle, on the R side of the wall. Follow the line of gear to the summit. **3-4hr**: add c3½hr for the approach from Mattmark or 1hr from the Monte Moropass

72e MARLENE
ED R Sala and C Schranz, 21 Sept 1987
68 Valley base: Saas/Macugnaga

The route, which is the most difficult on the wall, has quite varied climbing up slabs, cracks and grooves with difficulties up to VII free otherwise A2. The route is equipped but some belay pitons have been removed. **200m**

Start L of Gildo Burgener up slabs (V+) leading to a large 'plaque'. Slant up to the L of this to a belay (VI+/VII-). Continue straight up for a few m (V) before making a pendulum move L to a flake crack and then climbing up to the next belay (VI and VI+). Now climb over small overlaps to reach a roof (VI+). Cross this athletically on the L (crux: VII) and reach the belay almost immediately. Above is a groove which is followed (VI+) before an exit on to easy ground can be made. Two further pitches (III and IV) lead to the summit. **3-4hr**

72f VIA LUINO 78
TD A Giacobbe, P Merlo, A Rinaldin and E Volonté, 18/19 Aug 1978
68 Valley base: Saas/Macugnaga

An attractive looking line but probably the least inviting route on the face. The original party used a large number of wooden wedges all of which were left in place. There is now some modern gear. Difficulties don't exceed V except at a roof on pitch 3 on which aid is used (A1). ***200m***

The start of the route L of Marlene is marked. The line is easily followed: look for the gear. Take care on the first slab after c15m where there are minimum holds and the rock is a bit lichenous and again on pitch 4 where there are some large and very suspect blocks just above and L of the third belay. The climb finishes towards the top of the SE ridge which is followed to the summit. **2-3hr**

72g EAST FACE - CLASSIC ROUTE
AD/D M Bisaccia, D Macchi, F Malnati and P Polonelli, 19 June 1965
Valley base: Saas/Macugnaga

A pleasant climb on good rock but not sustained. ***200m***

Reach the foot of the face as for Route 72d and locate the start of the climb 30m R of a small cascade. Climb a dièdre for 30m (IV-) then follow ledges L on to the crest of a rib (III+). Climb the rib for a rope length and then either a couloir or another rib to an area of grass and stones. Above this reach a flattish section which may be snow covered. Next climb some slabs, slanting up L towards and crossing some blocks (III) to reach a fore-summit. From here the summit is easily reached by an easy ridge leading R. **2hr**

72h SOUTH-EAST RIDGE
D Valley base: Saas/Macugnaga

67
68

A very enjoyable route on solid rock which can be easily undertaken in a day starting from Mattmark in the Saas valley. The route is entirely rock and so no snow/ice gear is necessary on the climb nor on the approach, although you are likely to have to cross some snowfields on the approach.

Approaching from Mattmark it is not necessary to go to the actual crossing point of the Monte Moropass (2-2½hr from the dam) but bear L to the top of the ski-lift rising from the Italian side. Walk through the col by the lift then descend into the stony/boulder- strewn combe on the other side (traces of track). Pass below the slabby foot of the S face of the mountain and climb up to the obvious saddle in the ridge (30-45mins from the Monte Moropass). **c240m**

Start at a ledge on the L and climb a slightly overhung corner (III+) to another ledge (piton belay). Move along the ledge and climb up R to reach a steep dièdre crack. Climb it (crux: IV+ and A0: pitons) to a niche with piton belays. Continue in the same line, but more easily, to the crest of the ridge. The steep step above is turned on the L by a terrace and a slanting line back Rwards to its top. 10m higher, up an easy step, is a fine wall split by a crack. Climb this (IV: excellent) to the top of the step and the end of the major difficulties. Three more rope-lengths lead, first almost horizontally, with a pull up a corner, then up the slabby ridge to a fine wall with a zigzag crack. Climb this and the continuation dièdre (III+: piton) to reach the R side of a square gendarme. The summit cross and book are a few m higher (just below the actual summit). **c2½hr** climbing

Sonnighorn 3,487.2m

A Mummery with A Burgener and A Gentinetta, Aug 1879

The mountain (also known as Pizzo Bottarello) marks the S boundary of the Almagellertal at the head of the Rotblatt glacier. It has three ridges, two of which form part of the frontier ridge. The quality of the rock is particularly good and the summit makes a fine viewpoint.

73a **NORTH-EAST RIDGE**
PD First ascent party
69 Valley base: Saas

The ridge, which is c1km long, rises from the Sonnigpass (Pt 3,147m) as a mixed snow and rock crest. About halfway along the ridge there is

*an impressive rock tooth which presents the main difficulty of the climb in ascent and descent. A good combination is to traverse the peak by an ascent of the NW ridge and a descent of this one. **340m on the ridge***

From the Almageller hut follow a waymarked path signposted to Port from just beyond the helipad and then marked with yellow paint flashes every 10m or so. This leads SE at first and then more SSE to a little way above the small lake at Pt 2,922m. Leave the waymarked path and, keeping roughly at the same height, head S across stony slopes and some rock bands towards the S branch of the Rotblatt glacier. When level with the Mittelrück turn SE to reach the glacier. Climb it to the Sonnigpass (2hr).

From the col climb snow slopes or the pleasant rock crest to a large cairn at Pt 3,332m. Continue along the ridge on either the snow crest or the rock crest to reach the rock tooth. Climb this easily to its top. The other side is steep but is well supplied with holds. Descend it (II) to the ridge crest beyond. Follow this, knife edged in part, to a section of more broken rock. Cross this and then keep on the E side of the ridge, for a while moving along fine ramps and ledges, before returning to the crest. Keep on the crest now, or on the W side, to reach a shoulder just below the summit. A fine slab leads to the top (1½-2hr). **c4hr**

73b NORTH-WEST RIDGE - SONNIGGRAT

AD J James with E Imseng and A Supersaxo, 26 July 1889
69 Valley base: Saas

*The NW ridge descends as a gendarmed ridge to a prominent snow saddle then rises to a rocky subsidiary peak (Pt 3,339m) before terminating at the Steintällisattel (Pt 3,189m: not named on map). The rock is good and the ridge gives some enjoyable and varied climbing although the approach to the Steintällisattel is a bit tedious especially if you start from Almagelleralp. **c700m***

From the Almageller Hut follow Route 73a until level with the Mittelrück. Now descend on to the Rotblatt glacier and cross it

to the bottom of a sort of ramp, part snow and part rock which
lies to the N of the Steintällisattel and E of the rib descending
from Pt 3,224m. Enter the combe at the foot of the ramp then
climb up on to the rib on its E side. Follow this to the main ridge
(2-2½hr: c1hr longer from Almagelleralp).

From the col traverse the subsidiary peak, which is quite
exposed in places but otherwise pleasant and straightforward
apart from the necessity of a short rappel, and reach the snow
saddle at the foot of the main part of the ridge. The first step on
the ridge can be climbed direct (IV) or turned more easily on the
R side. Return to the ridge, which is quite narrow, as soon as
possible then follow it to the summit (most parties tend to keep
on the R side of the crest). Allow **5hr** from the hut

It is possible to reach the Steintällisattel from the SW in c3½hr
from Zer Meiggern (F).

Mittelrück 3,363m

First known tourist ascent: G Broke, W Conway and G Rendall
with X Andenmatten, 25 July 1887

A very modest peak when viewed from the Swiss side but much
more impressive on the rocky Italian side especially when viewed
from the S and E. It is known to the Italians as Pizzo di Loranco.

74a SOUTH RIDGE
PD Valley base: Saas

70

A short but enjoyable climb on good rock from the Sonnigpass. **c220m**

From the Almageller hut follow Route 73a to the Sonnigpass.
Follow the ridge to the summit over large boulders and slabs
with a steep finish (II). **c1hr** from the pass

74b EAST RIDGE
D O, Q and R Zurbriggen, 22 Sept 1947

70 Valley base: Saas/Simplon

MITTELRUCK

The mountain has two steep slabby faces orientated SE and NE on which a number of climbs have been recorded. The E ridge separates the two and gives what is considered one of the best climbs in the region, with the harder climbing reserved for the final c200m where the ridge steepens and begins to merge into the face. It can be approached by climbers based in Switzerland by a crossing of the Sonnigpass. There is a bivouac hut (Città di Varese) at the foot of the ridge.
c700m

(i) From the Almageller hut follow Route 73a to the Sonnigpass. 20m E of the block marking the pass is a rappel point. Rappel to a terrace and follow this N to a pig's tail belay piton. Climb down to a second rappel point and descend to a grassy terrace. Follow this N to its end and make a third rappel on to a stony ledge. Cross this Nwards to a rock rib and make another rappel, or climb down, to reach scree or snow. Contour NNE towards the ridge and reach its crest at c2,700m at the first step by climbing a grassy slab which has two big vertical and some smaller horizontal cracks (c3hr).

(ii) From the Italian side reach the Varese bivouac hut by Route H40 (4hr). From the hut follow the ridge keeping close to the crest with no special difficulty to the first step.

The first step is climbed by a crack and dièdre (IV) then move R. The second step is started on the R then climb a short chimney (III+). After a level section make a 25m rappel on the L from a block and regain the crest via ramps. At the next rise move 10m L on a fine terrace then climb a 40m slab (1 piton high on the slab) to another fine terrace. Keep on the crest now until just below the overhang of the final shoulder. Traverse R and climb a dièdre/chimney (IV+: 1 piton), exiting R on to yet another terrace. Move R for 20m to the end of a ramp then climb straight up to an earthy ramp slanting up L. This ramp is quite delicate but leads quickly to more secure ground. Some short steps over solid blocks lead to a short chimney and the upper part of the S ridge. Follow this to the summit. **5-6hr** from the bivouac hut

EAST SIDE OF THE SAAS VALLEY

Portjengrat 3,653.6m

C Dent with A and F Burgener, 7 Sept 1871

The name Portjengrat is not that of a peak but is given to the section of ridge extending N from the unnamed col at Pt 3,228m, N of the Mittelrück, to the Zwischbergenpass. The highest point of the ridge is the summit of Pizzo d'Andolla. Here the frontier ridge makes a sharp turn E whilst the main mountain chain continues NNW. Further along the main chain is the minor summit of the Portjenhorn. Between the S and E ridges there is an impressive steep wall which is almost 700m high on which there is one worthwhile route. Branching SE from Pt 3,492m on the S ridge is a subsidiary ridge which also provides the scene for a recommended climb.

The quality of the rock on the ridges is excellent and similar to that found on the Sonnighorn and Mittelrück.

75a TRAVERSE

AD+ Valley base: Saas

71
70

This is a very popular and worthwhile outing with a fairly easy approach from the Almageller hut. In fact it is considered to be one of if not the best climbs of its type in the Saas valley. There can be delays caused by other parties, especially when the route is busy. The vast majority of parties traverse only part of the ridge and it is this part which is described here. The route starts below the gap in the ridge called Port (3,295m), climbs to the summit of the Pizzo d'Andolla and then, a little way beyond this summit, descends the NW flank to return to the hut. The best of the climbing is found in the first section of the ridge above the Port and so any temptation to avoid this part of it should be dismissed from the mind.

You may well see parties climbing to the ridge by the rib ascending E above Pt 3,007m. This rib is quite straightforward and makes an excellent escape route should you be overtaken by bad weather. However, care must be exercised in locating the start of the descent if visibility is poor. **c400m**

From the Almageller hut follow Route 73a until just above the small lake at 2,922m. The way now turns uphill to Pt 3,007m and continues SE to reach the N edge of the central part of the Rotblatt glacier. Climb straight up this towards Port (2hr).

The start of the climb is very clearly marked at the foot of the rocks on the L below the gap. A groove and slabs (III+) lead to the crest of the ridge in two pitches. Continue on the crest via some very enjoyable climbing to reach a steep step and piton belay. Climb this on the very edge (using the aid provided if necessary). Above this the climbing eases considerably. Scramble up the rocky shoulder at Pt 3,492m and on to the next shoulder (reached from the W side of the ridge) where the ridge becomes horizontal and snow covered. The escape rib descends from hereabouts. The best way is to start on the snow itself c30m along the horizontal section, heading straight down to reach rocks. Keep on the crest of the narrowing ridge at first and then, lower down, choose one side or the other to avoid any steps.

Walk along the ridge to a small gap at the start of the final, rather jagged part of the ridge leading to the summit of the Pizzo d'Andolla. The ridge rears up now and can be climbed direct (IV with a piton for aid), or it can be turned more easily on the L (III+) by making a slanting descent L to reach the foot of a chimney/crack (hidden from view) which leads back to the crest at the top of the step. The remaining teeth on the ridge, which are less difficult, are either traversed or avoided on the L side (3-4hr).

From the summit the route follows the NW ridge towards the Portjenhorn for c150m to gain access to a snow covered ramp which leads down the W side of the ridge. Start with a 10m rappel then scramble down to the gap before the first gendarme. Turn this by an exposed ramp on the E side, descending a little (III), before regaining the crest at the next gap. Climb over the next obstruction (a 'tooth') to reach a ledge leading to the gap between the second and third gendarmes. Turn the latter on the E side (one move of III) and then traverse another gendarme with ease. Descend the ridge until it becomes snow covered

EAST SIDE OF THE SAAS VALLEY

(usually). A little further along slip off the ridge by slanting down L (W) on to the ramp mentioned above which slopes downwards, towards the SW ridge of the Portjenhorn, and outwards. Follow the ramp down to cross this ridge at c3,300m and then continue over stony ground in roughly the same direction to the hut (2½hr). Allow **9-10hr**

The snow covered ramp is gradually receding leaving more of the descent on loose rock. The same snow slope can also be dangerous after fresh snow when it is liable to avalanche. It may well be a better proposition to continue further along the ridge and descend via a low profile rib to reach the snow.

75b SOUTH-EAST FLANK DIRECT
AD+ A Bonacossa and G Vitali, 6 Aug 1947
70 Valley base: Saas/Simplon

A nice climb on pretty good rock up the face which is split by three, almost parallel couloirs, and with, towards the top, a conspicuous near vertical band of grey rock. Mostly III with a few sections of IV. **680m**

From the Città di Varese bivouac hut descend from the ridge into the combe on its N side and on to the S branch of the tiny Andolla glacier. Cross the combe to gain the tiny glacier below the SE flank of Pizzo d'Andolla. Climb to the upper edge of the glacier and cross the bergschrund, possibly with difficulty, to reach a 30m dièdre which slants up L on the rocks between the L and central couloirs. Climb the dièdre and then continue up for another 150m. Now cross the couloir on the L and climb up another 100m before making another traverse L into a small couloir with an overhang. Climb the couloir (and the overhang) before traversing R across the L-hand couloir on to the rocks separating it from the central couloir. Climb the rocks for 150m, gradually moving L. A slightly overhanging wall and a dièdre lead now to some large, grey slabs. Climb these for c80m before moving R to the summit. **7-8hr**

75c SOUTH-EAST RIB OF POINT 3,492m

AD+ A Bonacossa and A Malinverno, 24 July 1941
70 Valley base: Saas/Simplon

The rib separates the N and S sections of the tiny Andolla glacier (not named on the map), splitting into two near its foot. The line of the climb is up the S branch. The route is equipped for descent with pitons for rappels. **750m**

From the Città di Varese bivouac hut descend N on to the S part of the Andolla glacier and then climb the glacier to the foot of the S fork of the SE rib. Climb on to the crest of the rib from its L side and follow it to a height of c3,300m where it steepens dramatically. Move down L slightly past some blocks and then, ignoring a tempting line back to the crest, continue up L on to a small shoulder. Now cross smooth rock Rwards to the start of an easy terrace which leads back to the crest above the step. Very nice, steep climbing then leads to a 7m high step. Climb this (IV+: one piton) possibly with aid, before easy climbing up less solid rock leads on to the S ridge of Pizzo d'Andolla. **5hr**

Portjenhorn 3,567m

A relatively minor summit, in fact more of a protuberance on the NW ridge of the Pizzo d'Andolla. Nevertheless its NW ridge provides a pleasant climb that is worth considering as a training route.

76a NORTH-NORTH-WEST RIDGE

PD+ O Liebling with K Kain and F Pospischil, 27 July 1906
71 Valley base: Saas
70 76

Almost entirely rock, there are pitches of II and III and an enjoyable gendarme that is equipped for ascent and descent on each side. The ridge starts at the Zwischbergenpass but can be reached easily by either of the two low profile ridges on the W side between the pass and the Wysstal or via the W flank of the saddle at Pt 3,411m.

An easy descent (F) can be made down the SW ridge. Descend the top part of the ridge then the snow slope on N or S side. **c300m**

From the Almageller hut follow Route 77a to reach the lower depression of the Zwischbergenpass. From here follow the ridge crest in its entirety. It starts as a broad ridge but then narrows and becomes jagged. After a crossing a very minor top, a cockscomb ridge leads to a short descent to the saddle of Pt 3,411m. The best of the climbing is found between this point and the summit. **c5hr**

Zwischbergenpass 3,268m

A long-frequented passage between the Almagellertal on the W side and the Zwischbergental on the E. It forms the start of climbs to the Weissmies to the N and the Portjenhorn to the SE. The actual crossing point is c250m NE of and somewhat higher than the lowest point which is at c3,242m and has a steep rock wall on its E side.

77a WEST SIDE
W2 Valley base: Saas

76 The route is signposted 20m from the Almageller hut. Follow black/red/white paint flashes heading NE into the stony combe below the col (cairns). The final slope climbing to the higher, N depression is quite unpleasant with loose stones, earth and sand. **1-1½hr** and **370m**

Dri Horlini 3,096m and 3,209m

This is a very fine, compact granite ridge just N of the Almageller hut which has a steep SE face ranging in height from c150-200m. The face has been developed for rock climbing with numerous worthwhile routes some of which have been recently re-equipped with in situ protection by the guardian of the hut (who is also a mountain guide). A traverse of the ridge is a well recommended excursion.

78a TRAVERSE SW-NE
AD G Kruseman with A Bumann and O Supersaxo, 5 July 1929
73 Valley base: Saas
74 76

With an approach time from the Almageller hut of only ½hr or less you can wait for the sun to be high in the sky before you start this splendid outing. In places the ridge is knife-edged and it has several gendarmes, each of which must be climbed. Although it is a fairly short outing the climbing is reasonably sustained in some sections. The difficulties are mostly III with a couple of moves of IV. **c200m**

From the Almageller hut walk past the wooden hut then follow yellow paint flashes over the boulderfield to reach the foot of SW wall at the start of the ridge. Reach the start by scrambling up an earthy ramp on the L. At the top move up R to start the climbing proper at a well-trodden ledge by a large block. This same ledge can be reached by an equipped line starting a few m R of the ramp.

Turn the block on either side and then zigzag up slabs (III) to a belay. A few moves up Rwards give access to a groove which is followed to the crest (IV- and III) which is then followed (IV and IV-) to the top of the first summit (Pt 3,096m). The next section of ridge is quite easy (II and III) and leads to a second summit. Beyond this the ridge is almost level but there are three steps to down-climb before it rises again in the form of a smooth slab. Climb to the top of the next gendarme (IV-) and make a 12m rappel from an in situ piton. Continue to the third summit (Pt 3,209m) and subseqently to the final summit over stony ground with a sharp drop on the R. Leave the ridge c300m further along by descending to the R down scree slopes with some scattered rocks. Allow **3-4hr**

South-East Face

Something like two dozen routes have been developed on this superb wall although only those on the main parts of the crag, the SW and Central sectors, closest to the hut are detailed here.

EAST SIDE OF THE SAAS VALLEY

All the routes are equipped with in situ protection but it is worthwhile carrying a few Friends and wedges. Some of the routes are equipped for descent (40m rappels) or you can descend via the traverse route. All the routes are numbered at the base and these are the numbers used on the photographs. There are some single pitch routes (see hut topo) and there are also some new routes that are not included here. A topo guide is available at the hut (3SFr) of the routes that have been re-equipped. There are plans to re-equip more routes during autumn 1998. More detail is available in *Swiss Plaisir West* and *Kletterführer Oberwallis*.

73

1. Take it Easy (re-equipped: IV, with a groove of V that can be passed on the R at III). Rappel Memory
1a. After Eight (one short section of V-). Rappel Memory
2. Memory (re-equipped: 2 short sections of V+). Equipped for rappel
2a. FM (sections of sustained V+). Rappel Memory
2b. Living in America (VII). One pitch up a steep wall
3. Double D (re-equipped: mostly IV with one section of V). Equipped for rappel
4. Edelweiss (re-equipped: mostly III to IV+ with one section of V-). Descend via the traverse
5. Heimweh (re-equipped: IV+ with a slab of VI+). Can be finished at a terrace: rappel descent
6. Platte (avoidable first pitch of VI- then V+ and VI). Equipped for rappel

74

7. Indianertanz (mostly V and V+ with a chimney of VI-)
8. 1st August Pfeiler (IV and V with a short section of V+). A superb climb
9. Chämireiu (IV- to V)
10. Müry (Sustained at IV to V on the rib)
10a. Hittuliecht (re-equipped: III to IV+). Considered to be a classic climb
11. Spiezer Weg (IV and V with a short section of V+)
12. Verschneidung (III to IV+)

Weissmies 4,023m

J Häusser and P Zurbriggen, end-Aug 1855

The most easterly 4,000er (just) described in this guide book and an attractive mountain, especially when viewed from the W. It has three principal ridges, two of which, the N ridge and the SW ridge, are quite long. The first of these provides the best climb on the mountain. Unlike most high mountains, the Weissmies has two ordinary routes which are frequently combined to produce a very fine traverse. Unfortunately the development of ski-ing facilities has made access to the mountain on the W side very easy, there being a gondola lift to Hohsaas at 3,098m. This has resulted in relatively large numbers climbing the mountain from the valley in a day (first lift: 7am) even though there is accommodation available at Hohsaas. Probably the best combination to make in order to traverse the peak is to start at the Almageller hut and climb the SSE ridge before descending the NW flank to Hohsaas.

On the E side the mountain is of mixed character with both rock and snow but, although quite a few routes have been climbed on this side, there is little of any real note although possibilities probably exist for winter climbing. For anyone interested in this side of the mountain, probably the most desirable route is the NE rib leading to the foresummit at Pt 3,965m. This is AD and is started from the Laggin bivouac hut.

79a NORTH-WEST FLANK AND SOUTH-WEST RIDGE (UPPER PART)
PD
75 Valley base: Saas

The most frequented route on the mountain, it climbs interesting glacier terrain to gain access to the easy upper section of the SW ridge. There is usually a trench to follow in the height of the climbing season but there is still danger from hidden crevasses. Don't underestimate the risk! **c900m**

From the Weissmies hut reverse Route H42(ii) to Hohsaas. From here follow a broad track on to the E side of the Trift glacier. Climb the glacier a little way on this side then work out into the centre as crevasses permit. Head SE for a while and then swing S up steepening slopes to reach the broad snow ridge decending NW from the snowy knoll of Pt 3,820m. Climb to the snow saddle just NE of the knoll or, if the crevasses are bad, traverse it from the SW side. Now follow the easy SW ridge to the summit. **c3½hr** from Hohsaas, **c1hr** extra from the Weissmies hut

79b SOUTH-SOUTH-EAST RIDGE

PD The first ascent party is not known but FWA: A and R Calegari
76 and G Scotti, 12 Feb 1912
Valley base: Saas

This means of ascent has increased considerably in popularity since the construction of the Almageller hut. Before this it was used mainly as a means of descent. The ridge commences at the Zwischbergenpass and is mostly rock as far as the foresummit (Pt 3,965m). Although it is possible to follow the ridge in its entirety, the route avoids most of it and instead follows the steep snow slope on its E side to a height of c3,800m. From the foresummit a fine snow crest leads to the true summit. ***1,130m***

From the Almageller hut follow Route 77a to the higher depression of the Zwischbergenpass. Keep on the E side of the ridge and cross stony ground and patches of snow to reach a continuous, triangular snow slope ahead. Climb this as high as possible before taking to the easy rocks leading on to the ridge itself (traces of track). Follow the ridge to the foresummit. If the snow is soft or the slope is icy it may be preferable to take to the rocks lower down by traversing L off the snow slope and on to the crest of the ridge. This is followed easily to the foresummit. The final snow crest rises gently to the summit. **4½-5hr**

79c SOUTH-WEST RIDGE - TRIFTGRAT

PD Valley base: Saas

75

This long ridge is infrequently climbed but for those who wish to get away from the crowds it offers a pleasant enough means of ascent.
1,425m

From Chrizbode (the mid-station on the Saas Grund to Hohsaas lift system) follow the path towards Mälliga. Where convenient, close to Pt 2,478m head SE up grassy slopes before slanting S to the foot of the Schwarzmies ridge. Follow the slopes on the S side of the ridge, keeping close to the base of the ridge to ease progress, before patches of névé allow easy access to the ridge itself at a saddle just SW of Pt 3,517m (c3hr: this is the Triftjoch, c3,360m).

Now follow the ridge crest, which has some pleasant slabs before it turns to snow (possible cornices), to reach the snow knoll at Pt 3,820m. Here Route 79a is joined and the summit easily reached. Allow **6hr**

North-West Flank

NW of the summit a relatively gentle snow slope leads down for c200m to an abrupt steepening. The steep section is c400m high and formerly took the form of a snow and ice slope (50°-55°) above which was a band of mixed snow/ice/rock and with the whole of this topped by a broad band of seracs which slant down on the S side of the face. In the mid and late 1990s almost all the snow and ice has disappeared, at least in summer leaving a slabby wall of rock topped by the band of seracs. At least seven routes have been climbed on the face in its former condition, all subject to some extent or other to icefall. It may still be possible to climb these routes in winter or very early in the season in conditions similar to those experienced on the first ascents

The original and easiest route in terms of technical difficulty is on the R (S) side and climbs through seracs to the R of the last rocks. It is best climbed early in the season

(AD: 1926). Four further routes (all TD) take a fairly direct line towards the summit. The Steinmann/Vanis route (1971) is on the R and avoids the worst of the serac barrier by slanting R to overcome it. It is however thought to be the most hazardous of the routes and has rock difficulties of III. L of this is the Rothwangl/Straub route (1986) which has rock difficulties of IV leading to the serac barrier. The serac band was climbed by slanting steeply L with climbing up to 90° and continuing at 60°. It is considered much less dangerous than the previous route. The Guillon/Louvel route (1977) climbs up to the rock barrier then crosses this by slanting L. On the snow/ice slope below the serac barrier it continues slanting L to reach the barrier which was climbed with one 10m section of 75°. Patrick Gabarrou paid a visit in 1988 with Pascal Girault and climbed a very direct and relatively safe line with hardly any deviation. It climbed the lower slope just R of the lower rock band to reach a narrow, icy couloir in the main rock band. The couloir was 55° with a few m of 65°-70°. The serac barrier was climbed via three steep steps of 75°-80° ice with snow slopes between them. The last route (Paleari and Vidoni: Jan 1987) climbed to the R of the lower rock barrier then slanted diagonally L to reach a chimney/couloir with its exit blocked by overhangs. They climbed a dièdre on the L with aid (A1 and 8 pitons). The serac band was climbed in two pitches of 70°-80° and 65° respectively.

79d NORTH RIDGE

D W and Miss Paine with T Andenmatten and one other, 25 Aug 1884
75
76 77 FWA: F Schnarf and R Willisch, 6 Jan 1964
Valley base: Saas

A very fine, long ridge rising fairly steeply at first from the Lagginjoch to Pt 3,722m. This section of the ridge is the most difficult with the 'Grande Dalle' at half-height accounting for the difficulty. Beyond this the narrow rock ridge continues, now leading SSE, over a number of gendarmes to the rock knoll of Pt 3,830m. Not far beyond this the ridge turns S and to snow to reach the summit. There is a variation start to the ridge which avoids the initial section and the 'Grande Dalle' and reduces the overall difficulty to AD. **525m**

From the Weissmies or Hohsaas follow Route 81a to the Lagginjoch. From the col follow the ridge on the E side over slabby terrain to reach the more serious difficulties of the 15m high 'Grande Dalle' (IV). The slab is smooth, especially at the start, with rounded holds and is climbed on the R (W) side. Higher there are two stakes which can be used for aid (or can even be lassoed). Above the slab progress eases to the top of Pt 3,722m (c2hr). Continue along the crest (III) traversing each of the gendarmes except one which overhangs and is turned on the L side. Eventually reach the top of Pt 3,830m (c1½hr).

The ridge now descends a little. Follow it to the last of the rocks. The snow ridge is easy but steepens severely close to the summit necessitating a detour on the W side (1hr). Allow **5-6hr** from Hohsaas and an extra **1hr** from the Weissmies hut

The alternative start (H Haworth, G Heywood and R Irving, 13 Aug 1925) follows Route 81a to the E side of the gendarme of Pt 3,330m. A little further E reach the foot of the rock spur dropping from Pt 3,722m. Climb the spur on loose but generally easy rocks and possibly some snow before slanting R to reach the low point on the N ridge S of Pt 3,722m (2-2½hr from Hohsaas).

Schwarzmies 3,194m

Probably R Hughes and W Utterson-Kelso with A Andenmatten and J-M Blumenthal, 6 Sept 1884

An E-W orientated spur attached to the SW ridge of the Weissmies. It is entirely rock and provides an entertaining training route which is readily accessible from Saas Grund.

80a TRAVERSE WEST-EAST
AD Valley base: Saas

Good climbing on sound rock as long as you keep to the crest of the ridge. Short steps up to III+. c400m

From Chrizbode follow Route 79c to the W foot of the ridge (1hr). Climb the crest over a series of slabs to reach the top of the first gendarme. Descend this by a 10m rappel. Continue along the ridge to a second gendarme and then, a few m beyond this, descend on the N side to a small gap, easily identified by the large block in it. More slabby rocks lead to a further small gendarme. The ridge now descends steeply to a gap from where a descent can be made on the N side. This necessitates making a 15m rappel.

The upper part of the ridge is now climbed easily to the summit block. Start up a chimney but leave this on the L before moving back R above an overhang. Continue round the final block to the S side and so reach the top (2-2½hr).

Descend on the S side then turn E to reach the crest of the E ridge. Descend a steep wall on the N side and gain a gap with a prominent pointed gendarme. From the gap make some exposed moves L, descending via a detached flake to a shoulder where a couloir descends to the NW (possible descent route: 15min to the Mälliga glacier). The ridge continues over a number of teeth, which maintain the climbing interest, before it effectively ends at a small col at c3,200m (1½hr). From the col descend on to the Mälliga glacier and walk down this to regain the path to Chrizbode. Allow **6-7hr**

Lagginjoch 3,499m

First tourist crossing: G Heathcote and J Robertson with F Andenmatten, P Venetz and P Zurbrücken, 1 Aug 1864

Of little interest other than a means of access to the N ridge of the Weissmies and the SSW ridge of the Lagginhorn.

81a WEST SIDE
F   Valley base: Saas

75
77

The traditional approach to the pass was from the Weissmies hut but these days it is more common to approach from Hohsaas. **400m**

From the Weissmies hut it is probably better to reverse Route H42(ii) to Hohsaas and follow the route described below from there. However it may be possible to shortcut this by taking a small path leading off L after c½km which climbs the stony ground below the Hohlaub glacier (this is the glacier on the W side of the pass) or follow the bulldozed roadway from the vicinity of the hut which leads to Hohsaas to reach the same spot. Continue up the glacier taking as direct a line as possible to the pass.

From Hohsaas head more or less due E (path with paint flashes and cairns) towards the gendarme at Pt 3,330m. Turn this on the S side and reach the broad snow rib on its E side. Climb this and then contour NE to reach the bergschrund below the pass. Cross this and climb some rocks and scree to the crest. **c1½hr** and **400m** from Hohsaas and an extra **1hr** from the Weissmies hut

Lagginhorn 4,010.1m

E Ames and three companions with J Imseng and F Andenmatten plus three other guides, 26 Aug 1856

In contrast to the Weissmies, the Lagginhorn is mainly rocky. On its W side it has two prominent ridges, one leading directly to the summit and forming the line of the ordinary route, the other descending from the S end of the fairly horizontal summit crest. The summit ridge runs N-S and beyond its relatively horizontal section, dips steeply down to the Lagginjoch. From the summit a shorter ridge dips steeply NNE to the Fletschjoch. All these ridges make worthwhile routes of ascent. The E side of the mountain has a remote and massive feel to it but the rocks here are none too stable and of the several lines that have been

82a WEST-SOUTH-WEST RIDGE
PD First ascent party
77 Valley base: Saas

Not especially interesting climbing but the most frequented route of ascent and almost invariably used as the route of descent. The route joins the ridge at about half-height (although it is hardly more difficult to climb the ridge all the way from its foot) and can be started from the Weissmies hut or from Hohsaas although there is no great advantage in the latter. Conditions can vary considerably but the climbing is always easier if the ridge is entirely free of snow. The upper part of the ridge can be quite delicate, especially in descent if it is snow covered or icy. c1,300m from the Weissmies hut

(i) From the Weissmies hut follow a path heading roughly E to where it joins a roadway. Follow this L almost to a stream crossing before turning R up the moraine via a cairned track. Follow this to gain access to the Lagginhorn glacier (not named on the map, this is the small glacier enclosed by the two ridges on the W side of the mountain) and then climb the glacier (possibly with some tricky crevasses) heading NNE into its Nmost bay. From the top L of the bay cross the bergschrund and then climb easy rocks to reach the crest of the ridge (2-2½hr).

(ii) Approaching from Hohsaas follow a path descending slightly and heading ENE to the combe on the L bank of the Hohlaub glacier (not named on map). Continue descending N to c3,050m before turning R towards the tongue of the glacier. Keep below this at a height of c3,100m and reach the start of a ramp slanting up to the L giving access to the Smost of the two ridges on the W side of the mountain. Follow the ramp (cairns) on to the ridge itself and so reach the Lagginhorn glacier mentioned above (c2hr).

Continue up the broad ridge quite easily with pleasant scrambling over blocks and short slabs and then over more scree-

82b SOUTH-SOUTH-WEST RIDGE

AD

77

72

W Utterson-Kelso and three ladies with J Blumenthal, P Knubel and J Zurbrücken, 11 Aug 1883
Valley base: Saas

Often referred to as the S ridge, this enjoyable climb, almost entirely on rock, deserves greater popularity than it currently has. The rock is quite sound on the crest where the best climbing is to be found. The difficulties nowhere exceed III. The route is possible after fresh snow but this will slow progress and augment the grade a little. **c500m** *from the col*

Start from Hohsaas or the Weissmies hut and reach the Lagginjoch via Route 81a. From the pass the ridge is easy at first apart from one step, involving a pull on to a slab, which should be climbed direct although it can be turned on the W side. Continue on or close to the crest to the point where a long ridge leads off to the WSW. A little further on reach the gendarme of Pt 3,906m. It is better to climb this although it can be turned on the W side. The ridge now becomes quite narrow. Follow it, generally keeping just below the crest on the W side, to reach the top of a rocky hump at Pt 3,971m (c3hr).

A little further along the ridge is a sharp gendarme. This can be turned by an easy but exposed movement on the E side but again it is better to climb it. Descend from the top by rappel or down climb a steep slab on the R for c12m (III, good holds) to a little terrace. Next reach a gap by descending a steep wall. This is the crux and whilst relatively easy for tall people, for those with short arms or legs judicious use of the rope may help (piton in place). Some pleasant scrambling now leads to the summit (1hr). **c5hr** from Hohsaas: **c6hr** from the Weissmies hut

EAST SIDE OF THE SAAS VALLEY

82c WEST-SOUTH-WEST SPUR
PD Valley base: Saas
77

This prominent rib meets the SSW ridge some 150m S of Pt 3,906m. It can be climbed as an alternative approach to the more horizontal section of the SSW ridge to make a traverse of the mountain at a fairly modest grade. **c1,300m** *from the Weismies hut*

From the Weissmies hut or from Hohsaas, approach the base of the spur as for Route 82a. Start up the spur over easy, broken rocks along the crest. The rock develops into inclined flakes which are followed and become more difficult as height is gained. As difficulties increase it is possible to move on to the S side of the spur and climb along easy ledges/ramps for a little way before returning to the crest of the ridge above the difficulties. Once back on the crest, climb along it to the point where the spur joins the SSW ridge c150m S of Pt 3,906m (c4hr). Continue via Route 82b to the summit (1½hr). Allow **c6hr**

82d NORTH-NORTH-EAST RIDGE
AD- W Coolidge with C and R Almer, also G Broke with A and
77 T Andenmatten, 27 July 1887
72 Valley base: Saas

This short ridge rises from the Fletschjoch, which itself is best approached by traversing the Fletschhorn, and is predominantly of quite sound rock interspersed with a few snowy sections. Short steps of II and III are encountered. A combination of this ridge with an ascent of the W flank and NW ridge of the Fletschhorn and descent of the WSW ridge makes for an excellent high alpine experience. **316m**

From the summit of the Fletschhorn head E towards the E summit and then, from the snow saddle at Pt 3,904m turn S and descend the glacier slope to the Fletschjoch. Now follow the ridge more or less directly to the summit. Take care with possible cornices that tend to form on the E side. **1½hr**

82e EAST RIB OF POINT 3,971m
AD
72 M von Kuffner with A Burgener and A Kalbermatten, 17 July 1885
FWA: A Paleari, 17/18 Feb 1980 solo up and down
Valley base: Simplon

The rib is the most prominent one on the E flank of the mountain, rising from Pt 2,776m between the Laggin and Holutrift glaciers. The route, which is in a very fine and remote situation, is the only one on this flank of the Lagginhorn that can be recommended for a summer ascent.

From the Laggin bivouac contour the moraine slopes heading SW, passing below some broken, low relief crags (vague track). Continue in roughly the same direction as far as the R lateral moraine of the Holutrift glacier. Climb this, passing Pt 2,449m, to a height of c2,620m and then slant L into the moraine combe. Climb this, possibly snow filled, to a fault line leading to a small col separating a rocky promontory from the wall of the mountain itself. Climb up to the col (3hr).
    From here follow the rib along its crest all the way to the summit ridge which is joined close to Pt 3,971m. Follow Route 82b to the summit (4-5hr). Allow **8hr**

Fletschhorn 3,993m

M Amherdt with J Zumkemmi and F Klausen, 28 Aug 1854

A large and complex mountain which fails by only a few m to exceed the 4,000m mark, although earlier maps did suggest that it did meet this 'magic' value. There have also been suggestions that some summit construction be added to raise its height to this figure. Its most striking feature is its N face which can be well seen from the vicinity of the Simplonpass and rises c2,000m from its base at Rossbode. Its broad E flank is mostly of rock with three prominent ridges rising to the E summit, which is some ½km E of the main summit. There is some potential for winter routes on the flanks of these ridges which each provide a reasonable route of ascent.

On the S side, descending SW from the saddle between the E and main summit, is a long narrow glacier enclosed on its SE side by the short SW ridge of the E summit and on its NW side by the mountains SW ridge. The glacier provides an easy means of approach from the summit to the Fletschjoch and the NNE ridge of the Lagginhorn. The W flank is mostly glaciated and forms the S branch of the Grüebu glacier. The upper edge of this glacier abuts the NW ridge which turns S before rising as the S ridge of the Senggchuppa. The NW ridge is climbed in part by the ordinary route.

83a WEST FLANK AND NORTH-WEST RIDGE

PD Possibly J-D James with A Supersaxo, July 1889
77 Valley base: Saas

A fairly straightforward if somewhat circuitous line of ascent passing through some fine and varied mountain terrain. Very popular although the approach to the saddle mentioned below by either approach is somewhat tedious. ***c1,300m***

From the Weissmies hut follow a path leading E to meet a roadway. Follow this L to a stream crossing and then climb to the crest of the moraine beyond this. Follow it until a descent path leads on to the rubble strewn glacier on the L (Tälli glacier). Cross the glacier to its N side and then climb its NW bank, heading for the N side of the base of the rib (the end of the SW ridge) protruding into its upper part. The remnants of the glacier steepens on the NW side of this rib. Climb it, over rubble and snow if you are lucky, before finally slanting steeply L up snow to reach the saddle just E of Pt 3,527.4m (c3hr). The steep snow slope can be intimidating, especially in descent, and it is probably better to use the alternative route to return to the hut.

Late in the season and in years of inadequate snow cover, or when the steep snow slope is icy, this same place can be reached by following Route 85a to the foot of the buttress and continuing along the moraine slopes to the foot of a broad couloir leading up to a saddle on the Jegigrat between Pt 3,451m and Pt 3,527.4m of the Inner Rothorn. Climb the couloir, which is difficult to enjoy, to the saddle. Now follow the ridge NE, turning the latter point to reach the snow slopes beyond (c3hr). This route provides probably the safest means of descent.

Continue along the snow crest before slanting off L across steepening snow slopes towards the NW ridge which is reached at a saddle at c3,810m below its steep upper part. There are one or two bergschrunds to cross on the steeper parts of the slope. Climb the ridge and easier snow slopes above to reach the summit (c1½hr). There is a cairn on a lower point some 120m to the SSW. **4-5hr**

83b SOUTH-WEST RIDGE
PD G Rendall and H Topham with A Supersaxo, 16 July 1887
77 Valley base: Saas

The upper part of the ridge is worth climbing and makes an interesting alternative to the ordinary route. ***c1,300m***

From the Weissmies hut follow Route 83a to the saddle E of Pt 3,527.4m. Continue up the ridge, turning any difficulties on the SE side, to reach the largest gendarme. Climb over this and the smaller protrusions above to reach the cairn some 120m SSW of the summit. Follow the easy snow crest to the summit itself. **c5hr**

North Face
E-R Blanchet with K Mooser and O Supersaxo, 25 July 1928
FWA: R Allenbach, H von Kanel and H Müller, 28/29 Dec 1971

Rising above the upper plateau of the Bodmer glacier is a broad, 800m high face of mixed rock and ice. On the extreme R of the face is a buttress that provides a mixed route (M Pellizon and R Pe, 3 Jan 1993: D) which avoids the main challenge. To the L of this is a continuous, steep snow/ice slope which is taken by

EAST SIDE OF THE SAAS VALLEY

one of the best and safest routes (Weiner). This slope is bounded on its E side by a snow slope above which is a slanting rock band capped by seracs. The original route (TD/TD+) climbed the rock band directly below the lowest seracs before exiting on their E side. It is not recommended at the present time. In late Oct 1993 T Heymann climbed solo and unroped up the R side of the slanting rock band, L of the Weiner route. Although seriously threatened by seracs at the top of the face, the route may be safer then it at first looks since it weaves its way round some very steep buttresses for much of its length and these provide some protection. The main difficulties after the lower slopes were 300m of IV+ rock interspersed with 75° ice and a further 150m of 65°-85° ice to overcome the seracs: graded TD+. Spanish climbers X Cullell and J Gordito in 1996 added a serious variation just L of the original route (entitled: Game) which climbs an 80° serac barrier. Further L still, descending from the upper part of the slanting rock band, is a long rock rib. This was used as an escape route (D) by one of the original route's second ascent party (M Rossi) after being overtaken by a storm. His partner was rescued by helicopter. Further L still is more steep, mixed ground on which at least three routes have been climbed.

The most convenient starting place is a bivouac close to Pt 3,014m on the rock rib on the NW side of the Bodmer glacier. This can be reached from Egga on the Simplonpass road by following a path to Rossbodenstafel (1,922m). Above the chalets head N at first but soon turn W to reach the Griesserna combe which is climbed to the glacier at its head. Climb snow slopes S to the ridge. Bivouac gear can be collected on the descent (see below).

83c WEINER ROUTE
TD E Eidher, G Godai, K Mach, P Pernitsch, H Regele, E Vanis and
78 W Wherle, 17 July 1960
FWA: A and L Montani and A Paleari, 4 Jan 1975
Descended on skis by S de Benedetti, 6 July 1983
Valley base: Simplon

A fine ice climb with sections up to 60° which is much less threatened by seracs than most of the face. At the time of writing the finish of this route is blocked by seracs so it will be almost certainly necessary to exit on to the NW ridge. **c800m**

From the bivouac at Pt 3,014m descend on to the W side of the Bodmer glacier and climb it S to its upper plateau and so reach the foot of the slope. Cross the bergschrund and climb to a rocky outcrop where the slope steepens. Climb up, slanting slightly L, to a small rock protrusion (belay) and then follow the line of a slight snow rib (50°) to reach some seracs high on the face. Climb through these as conditions permit via steep ramps and ice slopes before a further snow rib leads in three pitches to the NW ridge only a few minutes climb below the summit. **5-7hr**

To return to the bivouac, descend the NW ridge and traverse Pt 3,775m to the Senggjoch at the foot of the S ridge of the Senggchuppa and then climb to the summit of this peak, crossing a few gendarmes in the process (see Route 86a). Continue down snow slopes to the Rossbodenpass then via easy rocks (hints of track) reach the Griesserna glacier which is crossed to the bivouac. In good snow conditions a direct descent can be made from the summit of the Senggchuppa to the bivouac.

83d ASSELIN/GABARROU ROUTE
D+ J-M Asselin and P Gabarrou, 20 June 1982
78 Valley base: Simplon

Another Gabarrou route climbed during his blitz of the Alps in the early eighties. This particular route is probably the safest climb on the face as far as objective dangers are concerned. The route crosses a rock barrier on the L side of the face extending L from the foot of the rib described as Rossi's descent route in the introduction. It continues up an ice slope to a higher rock barrier, which presents the greatest difficulties, and then finishes up a fine rib on mixed terrain. **c800m**

Reach the foot of the face as for Route 83c to below the L side of the lower ice slope on the E side of the face. Cross the bergschrund and climb up to the lower rock barrier. Climb this where feasible (c45m) or turn it on the R. Continue straight up the central ice slope and then up some mixed terrain to the upper rock barrier. This is climbed direct at first and then by slanting gradually L in four delicate and exposed 45m pitches (III to IV+). Follow the less steep rib above to the top of Pt 3,919m. **c8hr** from the bergschrund

The FWA party climbed a line further R (D+) which passed the lower rock barrier by a steep (60°), L slanting couloir. They continued straight up the central icefield and climbed the upper rock barrier direct. Above this they climbed more ice to the bottom of a rocky gully leading up R to a band of seracs. They followed this (ice covered) and then exited L, up more ice, to the top. **8-10hr**

M Manoni and M Rossi, 27 Dec 1987, climbed a route (Puffi Magici) further L still in 5hr from the Simplonpass road (D+). They moved unroped all the way encountering mostly ice (some of it quite hard with sections up to 65/70°) but with some short sections of mixed climbing.

83e NORTH-EAST RIDGE INTEGRAL - BREITLOIBGRAT

PD

78

72

First ascent party

Valley base: Simplon

This long ridge descends from the E summit almost to Bodme at 1,836m, just above the village of Simplon. The first ascent party reached the upper part of the ridge from the N but it is probably better to climb the whole of the ridge. The going is quite straightforward and also quite lonely. ***c2,150m***

Start from Bodme, which can be reached by car from Simplon. Park on the last bend before a barrier at c1,800m. Follow the road and then a track leading up a crest through woods. Follow the crest for a while before turning S (at c2,020m: path is less well defined) to the first stream issuing from the glacier above. Cross this and reach the second stream. Here turn up the bilberry covered slopes to reach grassy moraine slopes. Above the source of the first stream cross to the foot of Pt 2,401m and then climb up steep grass slopes to a shoulder on the R. From here gain the crest of the ridge (1½-2hr).

Now follow the crest of the ridge without difficulty to reach Pt 3,331.9m (c2hr). Just beyond this is a snow shoulder. Cross this and continue along the ridge over broken but easy rocks before a snow section finally leads to the E summit. The summit is easily reached in a further 20min (c2½hr). Allow **6-8hr**

83f SOUTH-EAST RIDGE - HOSAASGRAT
AD T Cox and F Gardiner with J Dorsaz and P Knubel, 5 July 1876
72 Valley base: Simplon

The best and shortest of the three ridges on the E side of the mountain. It is entirely rock except for its upper part where it turns N to reach the E summit. It has some pleasant yet not too difficult pitches with plenty of route choice. ***1,565m***

From the Laggin bivouac hut follow the path leading up the moraine on the S side of the Sibilufluc glacier. You pass close to the site of the old bivouac hut and then on to the glacier. Climb its R bank, moving L where convenient on to the ridge which is usually reached at c3,100m. Follow the ridge over several humps (II and bits of III) to where it steepens considerably at c3,700m. It is possible to continue along the ridge but it is probably better now to cross the couloir on its W side and climb the face on the other side. This gives some good climbing (up to III+). In places the rock here is indifferent but it is sound where it matters. At the top you can walk on to the Fletschhorn glacier close to Pt 3,866m. Cross the glacier NW to the summit. **5-7hr**

Jegihorn 3,206.3m

Situated close to the Weissmies hut, this modest, rocky peak at the SW termination of the Jegigrat makes a fine viewpoint and can be easily reached in a day from the valley. On its SE face there is a worthwhile climb on generally sound rock with another one on the steep E face. A traverse of the peak was at one time recommended as a means of approaching the Jegigrat but a rockfall has made the descent of the NE ridge somewhat less than inviting than it once was.

84a ORDINARY ROUTE
W2 Valley base: Saas
79

A steep walk up stony ground with some scrambling over blocks: no gear required. **480m**

From the Weissmies hut follow the path heading roughly N towards Tälli. Ignore a low path leading off L and instead follow a dusty, zigzagging path (start is marked JH) upwards in the line of a broad couloir towards the L-hand skyline (paint flashes). After climbing a short gully, with a massive jammed block a few m away on the R, continue for c100m to reach a flatter area. Now bear R scrambling over boulders (more paint flashes) towards an obvious saddle on the W ridge. Reach the ridge in the vicinity of the saddle and then continue the scramble up the crest to the summit. **c1½**

84b EAST WALL
D B Burgener and D Zurbriggen, 24 Aug 1977
79 Valley base: Saas

The wall overlooks the steep couloir on the E side of the peak (Puiseux Couloir) which is very obvious when seen from the Weissmies hut. Quite sound rock. **250m**

From the Weissmies hut follow the path leading roughly N to Tälli and then climb up to the bottom of the couloir. Make your way up it to about half-height (c2,900m) where there is a sloping terrace leading on to the SE face. Climb three pitches slanting up R (II, III and then II) to reach a couloir. Climb this still slanting R for another pitch (III) to a cairn. Now traverse easily R along a ledge below a steep wall before climbing up, moving slightly L, to a broken rib (IV). Cross a smooth slab Rwards (IV) before climbing straight up over a little overhang (V, piton). Two more pitches (IV) lead pleasantly to the summit. **c3hr**

84c SOUTH-EAST FACE

AD E-R Blanchet with J Imseng, 4 or 5 Sept 1918
79 Valley base: Saas

A number of climbs have been made on the face of varying degrees of difficulty. This one is as good as any. It climbs to a prominent yellowish pillar in the middle of the face and follows a line of chimneys from there to the summit. **c300m**

From the Weissmies hut follow Route 84b to the foot of the Puiseux Couloir. Start L of the couloir and climb the buttress above or the chimney line on the L side of the buttress to a ramp which leads Lwards to the yellow pillar. From the bottom of the pillar follow the line of chimneys, sometimes climbing in the chimneys and sometimes climbing alongside them. **1½-2hr**

84d SOUTH RIB

AD E-R Blanchet, 19 Sept 1922
79 Valley base: Saas

The rib marks the L edge of the SE face and has a distinguishing pointed pillar at its base. The route avoids the pillar itself (V if climbed direct) and the overhanging gendarme above it. There are pitches of III/III+ with the option of some IV/IV+ to finish. **200m**

From the Weissmies hut follow Route 84a to the point where it reaches the flatter area above the short gully. Traverse R on to the rib above the initial pillar. This point can be reached by climbing slabs and chimneys in a sort of gully on the E side of the pillar. The gendarme above the tower overhangs on the L. Follow a chimney below the overhang (III+) to the crest of the rib. Follow this until c50m below the summit where the difficulties suddenly increase. Move R and follow a line of chimneys to the top. It is possible to continue on the crest of the rib by some exposed climbing on smooth slabs (IV and IV+). **c2hr**

Jegigrat

This fine rock ridge dominates the R bank of the Tälli glacier (not named on the map) and is a sort of extension of the SW ridge of the Fletschhorn. The highest point, the Inner Rothorn, 3,451m, is at the NE end of the ridge. Moving NE along the ridge from the Jegihorn at its SW end there is a saddle at 3,098m where the Puiseux Couloir meets the ridge. This saddle is the start of the ridge traverse described below. From here the ridge rises to a rounded top at c3,170m before a fairly long section which rises gently to a height of 3,263m before dipping to a col just below Pt 3,350m. This point is the beginning of the most interesting part of the ridge which continues over a series of gendarmes, the principal ones being the Jegiturm, 3,368m, and the Grand Gendarme neither of which is named or marked on the map. The traverse ends at the next col, c3,300m.

The SE face of the Jegigrat is steep and rocky and has seen the development of several worthwhile rock climbs. One of these is frequently used as a means of access to the ridge which avoids the slog up the Puiseux Couloir and is more in keeping with the rest of the traverse.

85a TRAVERSE SOUTH-WEST TO NORTH-EAST
AD W Bloch with T Bumann, 14 Aug 1917
80
79
Valley base: Saas

A very enjoyable climb, especially if the alternative start is used.
c300m

From the Weissmies hut follow Route 84b up the unappealing Puiseux Couloir, continuing to the top of the couloir (1½hr). Follow the crest of the broad ridge NE to the top of Pt 3,350m where the ridge narrows (½hr).

The alternative start (A and A Andenmatten and S Bumann, c1935) is to follow the same route to the second torrent. Once across the bridge climb to the crest of the R lateral moraine of the Tälli glacier and then follow it to its termination close to the foot of the buttress below Pt 3,350m. The buttress is pointed at its base and has rubble strewn slopes (possibly some snow) on each side, the slope being much larger on the R side than on the L. Climb up the slope on the L (SW) side of the buttress to the point where two parallel ramps lead up R. Climb the lower of these on to the crest of the buttress and then follow a line of fairly steep chimneys and slabs (all well marked) to reach a prominent, pointed yellow pillar high on the buttress. Pass this on the R and continue via a couloir with a fine crack leading to a gap between overhangs. A fork R leads to the ridge close to the top of Pt 3,350m (c3hr).

Continue on the narrow crest and at a steep drop into a gap either down-climb (III+) or make two rappels to reach it. The gap is at the foot of the Jegiturm which is climbed fairly easily (II) to its top (c1½hr). More down climbing (III) or a rappel leads to the gap below the Grand Gendarme which has a prominent lower tower. Climb the crest to the top of the lower tower fairly easily (II+) then make some exposed moves (III) to reach the higher point (1-1½hr). Descend steeply from the top to a rappel point from where a 15m rappel leads to an ample ledge. From here descend to the next gap in the ridge, which requires an 8m rappel to reach it.

This is the start of the final section of the traverse but it has the most difficult climbing. Continue along the ridge (III+) to where a perched block forms a barrier to progress. Climb over the block (a bit of IV+) or turn it on the S side and so reach the next saddle at c3,300m on the SW side of Pt 3,451m (c1½hr).

Descend from the saddle by an easy couloir on the SE side to reach the foot of the SE wall. Walk SW below the wall to reach the crest of the moraine on the R side of the Tälli glacier. Reverse the alternative start route to the Weissmies hut. Allow **7-9hr** from hut to hut

EAST SIDE OF THE SAAS VALLEY

85b CARMEN
TD M Benoit and R Sensfelder, 23 July 1988
80 Valley base: Saas

An equipped route (except for the last pitch) up the R side of the S face of the Jegiturm. Take a selection of pitons, wedges and Friends.
300m

Use the late season start to Route 83a. At the foot of the S face of the Jegiturm is a scree cone created by stonefall. Start on the R side of this by making a horizontal traverse R for 15m (III) to a ledge. Follow this to a belay further R. Climb compact rock to a crack slanting R and follow this (IV) to a niche. Keep moving up R (III) in a steep couloir. From the top of the couloir make a few exposed moves R to reach a rib and follow this (IV) to a stone covered terrace. Above the terrace a dièdre leans to the L. Climb it to the rib at its top (V+, A0 then IV). The next two pitches follow a crack line leading Lwards up a big slab (III and IV) and terminating at a large block. Turn the block on the L (V) and find a belay above it on the R. Climb c15m to a roof which is turned on the R: all fine slab climbing (V, V+ and VI). Now cross the ridge and climb Rwards more easily (V then III) before two much easier pitches lead to the top. **c6hr** from the base

To return to the start it is possible to head SW to the first gap and descend the couloir on the S side.

85c JEGITURM SOUTH-EAST FACE
D T Betschart and Miss E Münger, 28 Sept 1969
80 Valley base: Saas

A recommended climb on sound rock which requires aid on one pitch to surmount an overhang. ***250m***

From the Weissmies hut follow the late season start to Route 83a. The most distinctive feature is the narrow SE rib of the Grand Gendarme. The climb starts c40m to the L of and a little bit lower than this, where a ramp line slants L across the lower part of the face. Follow the ramp for c40m and then a steep crack straight up for a further 80m to a ledge. There is a small belay on smooth slabs on the R. Climb a slightly overhanging chimney (unpleasant) for 10m and then traverse L for 4m across a smooth slab. Continue directly up a small buttress and then follow a crack to an overhang. Climb this with aid (A1: ideally use an etrier: excellent belay above). A 15m dièdre leads to the top. **2½hr** from the base

Descend as for the previous route or as for the next route.

85d GRAND GENDARME SOUTH-EAST RIB
D O and R Zurbriggen, 6 Oct 1947
80 Valley base: Saas

A fine line and a worthwhile climb. There are a few old pitons in place.
c200m

Start as for the previous route. The rib is obvious at the top of a scree slope. Climb the rib for four pitches (the first 3 at III+ and the last at IV) and then a 10m dièdre and the overlap that caps it (IV). Continue upwards climbing a 6m wall (IV) and a 10m crack which slants slightly L (III). At the top of the crack move 6m R (IV) from where an exposed finish (III and IV+) can be made. **2½hr** from the base

Descend by following the Jegigrat traverse or from the gap reached by the 8m rappel descend the couloir on the S side following a series of easy ledges.

Senggchuppa 3,606m

First tourist ascent, in descent from the Fletschhorn: E and F Burckhardt with C Jossi and G Taugwalder, 26 July 1880

A modest summit worthy of an ascent for its view of the Fletschhorn's N face if for no other reason. A traverse of the mountain (AD-) followed by an ascent of the NW ridge of the Fletschhorn and on to the Lagginhorn makes an excellent alternative to the traverse of these two peaks from the Weissmies hut.

86a NORTH-WEST FLANK
F Valley base: Saas

77
78

A straightforward climb up a glacier which extends almost to the summit of the mountain. **550m**

From the Fletschhorn bivouac hut walk on to the Mattwald glacier and head towards the Gamserchopf. Swing R before reaching this summit and reach the watershed between the Saastal and Simplon. Climb the steepening snow slope to the summit avoiding a few crevasses that cross the slope. **1½-2hr**

To proceed to the Fletschhorn follow the broad S ridge to a group of gendarmes. Cross these (quite nice climbing on good rock) and continue to the snowy depression of the Senggjoch at 3,616m (not marked or named on the map). Follow the crest to the rocks below Pt 3,775m. Climb these, steep and broken but quite easy. Keep on the crest over any obstacles that follow (the first gendarme is started on the L) and so reach a snow shoulder. A little further along the ridge reach a snow saddle (c3,810m) where Route 83a is joined (2hr).

Hübschhorn 3,192m

This rocky peak dominates the Simplonpass on its SE side immediately above the hospice. Its W and SW faces are no more than massive stone covered slopes but its NW flank is quite different. Here there are massive slabby walls. The SWmost of these, known as the Ofeflue, has some routes. The centre of the face, above the tiny glacier, is stoneswept and no place to climb. The slabs on the L side of the face are bounded on the L by a distinct ridge. This, the NW ridge, drops steeply from the summit region in a series of steps before easing in angle towards its foot. It is the line of ascent of the route described below.

87a NORTH-WEST RIDGE - ALBERT 1st RIDGE
D   Albert 1st of Belgium with B Supersaxo, 1913
81 Valley base: Simplon

A fine climb on generally sound rock, although some care is needed towards the top, and with easy access from the Simplonpass. It is best climbed in dry conditions as there is some lichen on the rock. Carry an ice axe for the descent. **540m**

From the hospice or from Kulm reach the large detached block at Pt 2,363m. Keep on the stony ground on the SW side of the ridge to the edge of the tiny glacier. On the L a couloir, partly rock and partly grass, is climbed to the ridge (1½hr). Climb the ridge over blocks, passing more difficult ones on the L, to reach a short wall. Climb this (III) to reach the first shoulder.

The step above the shoulder is overcome by climbing a dièdre/chimney on the L side of the ridge. Regain the ridge as soon as possible above the chimney and then continue on some splendid slabs for several pitches before easier ground is reached. Pass some more blocks on the L to reach another steep section. Climb this on the L making use of some dubious looking rocks then move back R and follow a 30m crack (IV) to a terrace.

Move R up short steps to the next steepening. Turn the initial overhanging part on the L by climbing two pitches in a dièdre which has some loose rock. This leads to another shoulder below an overhanging wall. Avoid this by moving well to the R before climbing back to the crest. Keep on the crest past even more blocks to the final step. Climb this step direct, slanting up gradually R and so reach the last shoulder not far from the top. Beyond this a couple of short steps are all that remain to reach the summit (3-4hr). Allow **5-6hr**

To descend, follow the long summit ridge SW (possible cornice) to the cairn at Pt 3,187.2m. From here follow the W ridge until you reach, at c3,000m, the top of the stone strewn slopes bordering the W side of the Ofeflue slabs. Descend the slope picking as good a line as possible but avoid going too far to the R.

Enchaînements

The linking of the ascents of several routes in both winter and in summer has been practised for many years in the Alps although it is only in fairly recent times that media publicity has brought such feats to the attention of the public. This is especially so when the enchaînement involves serious routes climbed in the winter season. For the less ambitious climber easier routes can be linked in a similar way, particularly ridge routes. Many of the climbs described in this guide book can be combined to make fine traverses of individual mountains and many of these are at least hinted at in the text. However, the region described in this guide lends itself to extended traverses that can be completed over a number of days with overnights spent in conveniently sited mountain huts. There is in fact a long history of such traverses.

Mischabel Chain

One of the most frequented traverses is that of the Nadelgrat which is described elsewhere in the book but an obvious extension of this route is to link it with a traverse of the Täschhorn and Dom or even with the Allalinhorn and Alphubel as well. This combination might best be started at the Britannia hut with an ascent of the Allalinhorn and Alphubel and an overnight stop at the Mischabeljoch bivouac hut. Traverse the Täschhorn and Dom on day 2 with an overnight stay at the Dom hut before continuing over the Lenzsptize, Nadelhorn and maybe the Hohbärghorn and Dirruhorn (or leave these to day 4) and finish the traverse at the Mischabel hut or the Bordier hut. In fact this traverse, as far as the Nadelhorn and Mischabel hut, was completed in a day on 29 July 1921 by A Lötscher with E Anthamatten and A Zurbriggen.

Monte Rosa

One of the most popular multi-day traverses is that of the Monte Rosa summits. Very commonly this traverse is commenced at the

Monte Rosa hut with an ascent of Nordend, although a start could be made from the Citta di Gallarate bivouac hut with an ascent of the Cresta di Santa Caterina. Move on from the Nordend to the Dufourspitze, usually the most difficult part of the traverse, and then over the Zumsteinspitze to overnight in the Margherita hut on the summit of the Signalkuppe. Day 2 starts with a stroll downhill and ascents of the Parrotspitze, Ludwigshöhe, Corno Nero and Piramide Vincent. Return to the Monte Rosa hut via the Lisjoch. A better alternative is to continue over the Punta Giordani and spend a night at the Gnifetti hut. On day 3 traverse the Liskamm, Castor and Pollux and stop in the Rossi and Volante bivouac hut or the Valle d'Ayas guides' hut overnight. On day 4 traverse the Breithorn before returning to Zermatt.

Whilst making this extended traverse think of Geoffrey Winthrop Young and his guide, who, in about 1907, set off from Riffelberg about midnight and climbed all the Monte Rosa summits, including Nordend, as far as the Ludwigshöhe. They then climbed to the Lisjoch and continued over Liskamm and on to Castor. Young's original plan was to include Pollux and the traverse of the Breithorn in this one continuous effort but the guide refused to proceed any further (he was doing the step cutting). Somehow Young persuaded the guide to retrace their steps over the Liskamm rather than descend the Zwillings glacier. To Young's regret he was unable to cajole the guide into reversing their route over Monte Rosa so they were forced to descend the Grenz glacier in the late afternoon heat.

A fairly obvious extension to this traverse is to start at the Monte Moropass and join the traverse described above at Nordend. If you stick to the frontier you would need to climb the Cresta di Santa Caterina but there is an easier alternative way of reaching the summit of Nordend accessible from the Citta di Gallarate bivouac (Route 42c). The net result would be a traverse from the Monte Moropass to the Theodulpass, a distance of c34km.

Part of this traverse was achieved in winter by G Masciaga and R Pe, 24-26 Jan 1983. They started at the Monte Moropass and reached the Gallarate bivouac the same day. Next day they climbed the Cresta di Santa Caterina and reached the Margherita hut for their second night, completing their traverse by a return to Macugnaga, descending the Cresta Signal in the process.

The East Saas Peaks

The principle summits on the E side of the Saas valley make an obvious if relatively short traverse which could start at the Fletschhorn hut. It would traverse the Senggchuppa, Fletschhorn and Lagginhorn, descending the S ridge of this peak to overnight at Hohsaas. Next day traverse the Weismmies, ideally via its N ridge.

Weisshorn Group

The chain of peaks on the E side of the Zinal valley form a very attractive target for a reasonably sustained high-level traverse starting at the Schönbiel hut. This would involve crossing Mont Durand, Ober Gabelhorn and Wellenkuppe (a descent of its N ridge to the Triftjoch is AD) followed by a night at the Rothorn hut. Follow this by a traverse of the Trifthorn and Zinal Rothorn and spend the next night at the Mountet hut. To reach the Schalijoch bivouac from here, reverse the route towards the N ridge of the Zinal Rothorn as far as l'Epaule. From here contour the snow slopes to reach the Pt Sud de Moming. Traverse this summit and the Pt Nord de Moming (AD/AD+) followed by the Schalihorn. The final day you would traverse the Weisshorn, and the Bishorn if you descended the Weisshorn N ridge.

On 20 Aug 1943, H Berret and A Visoni with B Bournissen followed this ridge as far as the Mountet hut in 19hr. Most of the chain (including the Weisshorn and Bishorn) was traversed in under 24hr by the guides A Georges and A Salamin on 28 July 1986. Their traverse however started at the Dent Blanche hut and involved climbing the Dent Blanche and Pt de Zinal as well but apparently not the Ober Gabelhorn.

André Georges, who appears to have a liking for this sort of thing, was involved in a most formidable undertaking with Erhard Lorétan in 1986. They made a winter traverse starting at Grächen and finishing in Zinal which involved the traverse of 38 summits of which 30 were over 4,000m. Starting on Feb 14th, they were dropped by helicopter on to the Ried glacier before climbing to the summit of the Dirruhorn. They traversed the ridge as far as the Lenzjoch where they bivouacked. The next night saw them at the Mischabeljoch bivouac after the Dom-Täschhorn traverse and on the night of the 16th they bivouacked again, this time on the Findel glacier after crossing the Alphubel, Allalinhorn, Rimpfischhorn and Strahlhorn. From here they climbed to the Gallarate bivouac where bad weather delayed them until the 19th when they reached the Margherita hut. One day later they spent the night in the Rossi and Volante bivouac hut before traversing the Breithorn on the 21st. They had a day of rest at the Testa Grigia on the 22nd.

After a traverse of the Matterhorn, on the 26th, from the Carrel hut they climbed the E ridge of the Dent d'Herens, in the process making the first winter ascent of it, before spending a night at the Perelli bivouac hut at the Col des Grandes Murailles, and then on the 27th crossed the Tête de Valpelline to reach the Dent Blanche hut. Next day they climbed the Dent Blanche, Pt de Zinal, Mont Durand, Ober Gabelhorn and Wellenkuppe, ready for a night's rest at the Rothorn hut 19½hrs later. It took a further two days to reach the Schalijoch bivouac with an intermediate bivouac at l'Epaule after traversing the Zinal Rothorn. What a feeling of satisfaction they must have experienced the following day as they crossed the Weisshorn and Bishorn to complete their epic.

List of Climbs

The following table of routes in numerical sequence is designed to provide a quick reference to climbers who, from a particular valley base, want to know which routes are available to them in terms of grade, style of climbing and overall length. Routes in the table are usually listed by orientation and feature (ie NW Ridge) rather than specific name (e.g. Teufelsgrat). Where there is a choice of valley bases, two alternatives are listed; any others will be found in the main text. Style (such as Rock, Mixed etc) generally refers to the type of ground predominant on the route and more detailed description will again be found in the text. Length is termed either Short, Medium or Long, attempting to give an idea of the length of day one should expect when climbing the route from the usual starting point (hut, valley etc). On Short days the ascent times will normally be 4hr or less. Long days will generally have an ascent time of 8hr or more.

Some routes described in the text appear to be short according to the times quoted but are classified Medium or Long in this index. This implies that these routes can only be climbed in combination with another route.

Mountain	Route Number	Route	Valley base	Grade	Style	Route Length	Page
Col Durand	1a	S Side	Zermatt	F	path/glacier	short	74
	1b	N Side	Zinal	PD	glacier	short	75
Mont Durand	2a	SW Ridge	Zinal/Zermatt	PD	snow/rock	short/medium	75
	2b	NE Ridge	Zinal/Zermatt	PD	snow/rock	medium	75
Ober Gabelhorn	3a	ENE Ridge	Zermatt	AD	snow/rock	medium	76
	3b	S Face	Zermatt	D	rock	medium	77
	3c	WSW Ridge	Zermatt	AD	rock	medium	78
	3d	NNW Ridge	Zinal	AD	snow/rock	medium	79
	3e	N Face	Zinal	TD-	snow/ice	medium	80
	3f	SE Ridge	Zermatt	AD+	rock/snow	medium	80
Wellenkuppe	4a	E Flank and ENE Ridge	Zermatt	PD	rock	short	81
Trifthorn	5a	S Ridge	Zermatt	AD	rock	short	82
	5b	NE Ridge	Zinal	F	glacier/snow	short	82
Zinal Rothorn	6a	SE Ridge via the Gabel	Zermatt	AD-	snow/rock	medium	83
	6b	SW Ridge	Zermatt/Zinal	AD+	rock	medium	85
	6c	N Ridge	Zinal	AD	rock	medium	86
	6d	E Face direct	Zermatt	TD	rock	long	87
	6e	Kanzelgrat	Zermatt	D	rock	medium	88

323

Mountain	Route Number	Route	Valley base	Grade	Style	Route Length	Page
Mammouth	7a	Traverse	Zinal	AD-	rock	short/medium	90
Blanc de Moming	8a	SW Ridge (descent)	Zinal	PD	snow/rock	medium	91
	8b	NW Ridge	Zinal	AD	snow/rock	medium	91
Besso	9a	SW Ridge	Zinal	AD	rock	medium	92
	9b	Ladies Route	Zinal	PD	rock	short/medium	92
Schalihorn	10a	Traverse S-N	Zermatt	PD	snow/rock	long	93
Schalijoch	11a	W Side	Zinal	AD	snow/rock	medium	95
	11b	E Side	Zermatt	AD	snow/rock	medium	95
Weisshorn	12a	E Ridge	Zermatt	AD	glacier/rock	medium	97
	12b	SSW Ridge	Zinal/Zermatt	D	rock/snow	medium	98
	12c	W Face	Zinal	D-	rock	medium	98
	12d	N Ridge	Zinal	AD+	rock/snow	long	100
	12e	NE Buttress	Zermatt	TD-	snow/ice	long	101
	12f	E Face of NE Buttress	Zermatt	TD-	mixed/snow	long	102
	12g	NE Face direct	Zermatt	D+/TD-	snow/ice	long	103
Bishorn	13a	NW Flank	Zinal	F	glacier	short	104
	13b	NE Face	Turtmanntal	D	snow/ice	long	105
	13c	E Ridge	Zermatt/Turtmanntal	AD	rock/snow	medium	105
Col de Milon	14a	S Side	Zinal	F	moraine	short	106
	14b	N Side	Zinal	W2	grass	short	106
Bisjoch	15a	N Side	Zermatt/Turtmanntal	PD	glacier	short	107
Brunegghorn	16a	SW Ridge	Zermatt/Turtmanntal	F	snow	medium	108
	16b	NW Ridge	Zermatt/Turtmanntal	PD+	rock/snow	medium	108
	16c	NNE Face	Zermatt	TD	snow/ice	medium	108
	16d	NE Ridge	Zermatt	AD	snow	medium	109
Brunegggioch	17a	W Side	Turtmanntal	F	glacier	short	110
	17b	E Side	Zermatt	PD	glacier	short	110
Schöllijoch	18a	W Side	Turtmanntal	F	snow/rock	short	111
	18b	E Side	Zermatt	F	snow	short	111

Barrhörner	19a	Traverse N-S	Zermatt/Turtmanntal	PD	snow/rock	medium	111
Mettelhorn	20a	From the Trift Gorge	Zermatt	W2	path/snow	medium	112
Theodulpass	21a	Italian Side	Cervinia	F	path/snow	medium	115
	21b	Swiss Side	Zermatt	F	glacier	short	116
Klein Matterhorn	22a	NW Ridge	Zermatt	AD-	rock/snow	medium	117
	22b	NE Face	Zermatt	D	rock	medium/long	117
Breithorn:	23a	SSW Flank	Zermatt/Cervinia	F	glacier	short	118
	23b	NNW and SSW Flanks	Zermatt	AD	rock/glacier	medium	119
N and NNW face	23c	Bethmann-Hollweg	Zermatt	TD	rock/ice	long	120
of main summit:	23d	Bethermin-Gabarrou	Zermatt	TD-/TD	rock/ice	long	121
	23e	Triftigrat	Zermatt	D-	rock/snow	long	122
Central summit:	23f	SSW Spur	Cervinia/Zermatt	PD	snow	short	124
Central summit	23g	Original	Zermatt/Champoluc	D+	mixed	long	124
N face:	23h	Dessert Semi-Freddo	Zermatt/Champoluc	D+	ice/mixed	long	125
	23i	Viaggio di Ordinaria Follia	Zermatt/Champoluc	TD	ice	long	126
	23j	Gabarrou-Steiner	Zermatt/Champoluc	TD-	snow/ice	long	126
	23k	Goulotte Spettro Glauco	Zermatt/Champoluc	TD/TD+	mixed	long	127
SE face:	23l	Central Spur	Zermatt/Cervinia	AD	rock/snow	medium	128
East summit:	23m	Younggrat	Zermatt/Champoluc	D	rock/snow	long	129
N flank	23n	NE Couloir	Zermatt/Champoluc	TD-/TD	rock/snow	long	131
	23o	NE Spur	Zermatt/Champoluc	TD	mixed	long	132
Point 4,106m:	23p	NE Face	Zermatt/Champoluc	TD+	ice/mixed	long	133
	23q	ENE Wall	Zermatt/Champoluc	D+	rock/ice	medium/long	134
Roccia Nera:	23r	SW Flank	Zermatt/Champoluc	F	snow	short	135
	23s	Gran Diedro Ghiacciato	Zermatt/Champoluc	TD+	mixed	long	135
	23t	N Wall	Zermatt/Champoluc	TD-	mixed	long	136
	23u	NE Wall	Zermatt/Champoluc	TD	rock	long	136
	23v	SE Ridge	Zermatt/Champoluc	D+	rock	medium	138
	23w	Traverse of the Breithorn	Zermatt/Champoluc	AD	rock/snow	medium/long	138
Schwarztor	24a	SW Flank	Champoluc	F	glacier	short	140
	24b	N Flank	Zermatt	PD	glacier	medium	140

325

Mountain	Route Number	Route	Valley base	Grade	Style	Route Length	Page
Pollux	25a	W Flank	Champoluc/Zermatt	PD	snow	short/medium	141
	25b	SW Ridge	Champoluc/Zermatt	AD-	rock/snow	short/medium	142
	25c	N Ridge	Zermatt	AD-	glacier/snow	medium	142
	25d	SE Ridge	Champoluc/Zermatt	PD	rock/snow	short/medium	142
Zwillingsjoch	26a	SW Flank	Champoluc	F	glacier	short	143
	26b	N Flank	Zermatt	AD	glacier	medium	143
Castor	27a	SE Ridge	Gressoney	F	snow	short/medium	144
	27b	SW Buttress-Guides Route	Champoluc	D+	rock/glacier	long	145
	27c	SW Buttress-Classic Route	Champoluc	D+	rock/glacier	long	146
	27d	WNW Flank	Champoluc/Zermatt	PD	snow	short/medium	147
	27e	NW Flank	Champoluc/Zermatt	PD	snow/rock	short/medium	147
	27f	N Flank	Zermatt	AD+	snow/glacier	long	148
Felikjoch	28a	S Side	Gressoney	F	glacier	short	148
	28b	N Side	Zermatt	AD	glacier	medium	149
Liskamm	29a	SW Ridge	Gressoney/Champoluc	PD	snow	medium	150
W Summit:	29b	NNW Flank	Zermatt	D	snow/ice	medium/long	151
E Summit:	29c	E Ridge	Alagra/Gressoney	AD	snow/rock	medium	152
	29d	Cresta Sella	Alagra/Gressoney	AD-	rock/snow	medium	153
	29e	Traverse E-W	Alagra/Gressoney	AD	snow/rock	medium	154
W Summit:	29f	Andreani-Nessi	Zermatt/Gressoney	ED1/2	ice/rock	long	155
NNE flank	29g	Direct	Zermatt/Gressoney	TD+/ED1	ice/rock	long	156
	29h	Diemberger-Steffan	Zermatt/Gressoney	TD	ice/rock	long	156
	29i	NNE and NE Flanks	Zermatt/Gressoney	D+	ice/rock	long	157
E Summit:	29j	Blanchet	Zermatt/Gressoney	D+	snow/ice	medium/long	158
NE Flank	29k	Norman-Neruda	Zermatt/Gressoney	D+	snow/rock	medium/long	159
SE Face	29l	Central Rib	Alagra/Gressoney	D-	rock	medium/long	160
	29m	SW Flank descent	Zermatt	PD	snow	medium	161
Sella del Liskamm	30a	Swiss Side	Zermatt	PD	glacier	medium	162
Lisjoch	30b	Italian Side	Alagra/Gressoney	F	glacier	short	163

Punta Giordani	31a	SSW Flank	Alagna/Gressoney	F	snow	short	169
	31b	NE Ridge	Alagna	AD+	rock/snow	medium/long	169
	31c	SE Ridge	Alagna/Gressoney	PD	snow/rock	short	170
	31d	SSE Flank	Alagna/Gressoney	AD-	rock	short	170
Piramide Vincent	32a	NNW Flank	Alagna/Gressoney	F	glacier	short	171
	32b	SSW Ridge	Alagna/Gressoney	PD	snow/rock	short	171
SW Face:	32c	Right-hand Route	Alagna/Gressoney	AD+	mixed	short/medium	172
	32d	Central Couloir	Alagna/Gressoney	AD+	snow/mixed	short/medium	172
	32e	Left-hand Couloir	Alagna/Gressoney	AD+	snow/mixed	short/medium	172
NE Face:	32f	Right-hand Rib	Alagna	D	rock	medium/long	172
	32g	ESE Ridge	Alagna/Gressoney	PD	snow/rock	medium	173
Sperone Vincent	33a	Antonietti-Enzio	Alagna	TD	rock	medium/long	174
	33b	SE Rib	Alagna	TD-	rock	medium/long	175
Corno Nero	34a	S Ridge	Alagna/Gressoney	PD	snow/rock	short	176
	34b	NE Ridge	Alagna/Gressoney	PD	snow/rock	short	176
Ludwigshöhe	35a	SW Ridge	Alagna/Gressoney	F	snow/rock	short	177
	35b	N Side or NE Ridge	Alagna/Gressoney	PD	snow	short	177
Parrotspitze	36a	W Ridge	Alagna/Gressoney	AD	snow/ice	short	178
	36b	NNW Flank	Alagna/Gressoney	F	snow	short	179
	36c	NE Ridge	Alagna/Gressoney	D	snow	short	179
	36d	ENE Face Snow Slope	Alagna	AD	snow/rock	long	179
	36e	SE Ridge	Alagna	TD-	rock	medium/long	180
	36f	S Face Left-hand Pillar	Alagna	F	snow	long	180
Signalkuppe	37a	W Flank	Alagna/Zermatt	TD	rock/ice	short/medium	181
NE Face:	37b	Right-hand Rib	Macugnaga	TD	rock/ice	long	183
	37c	Central Rib	Macugnaga	ED1/2	rock/ice	long	184
	37d	Centenary Route	Macugnaga	ED1	rock/ice	long	184
	37e	Gringo	Alagna	D	rock/snow	long	186
	37f	E Ridge	Alagna	TD+	rock	medium/long	187
SE Face:	37g	Africa Nostra				long	188

327

Mountain	Route Number	Route	Valley base	Grade	Style	Route Length	Page
Zumsteinspitze	38a	SE Ridge	Alagna	PD	rock	short	189
	38b	SW Ridge	Alagna/Gressoney	PD	rock	short	190
	38c	N Ridge	Alagna/Zermatt	PD+	snow/rock	medium	190
Grenzsattel	39a	W Flank	Zermatt	PD	glacier	medium	191
	39b	E Face Direct	Macugnaga	TD	snow/rock	long	191
Dufourspitze	40a	Normal Route	Zermatt	PD	glacier/rock	medium	193
	40b	Cresta Rey	Alagna/Gressoney	AD+	rock	medium	194
	40c	SW Ridge to Sattel	Zermatt/Alagna	D	rock	long	195
	40d	N Flank from Silbersattel	Zermatt	AD	snow/ice	medium	195
E Face:	40e	Marinelli Couloir	Macugnaga	D	snow/ice	long	196
	40f	SE Ridge	Alagna/Gressoney	AD	rock	medium	198
Silbersattel	41a	W Flank	Zermatt	PD	glacier	medium	199
Nordend	42a	S Ridge	Zermatt	PD	snow/rock	medium	200
	42b	Morshead Rib	Zermatt	D-	rock/snow	medium	200
	42c	NW Ridge	Zermatt	AD+/D-	rock/snow	long	200
	42d	Cresta di Santa Caterina	Zermatt/Macugnaga	TD	rock	medium/long	201
E Face:	42e	Shroud Direct	Macugnaga	TD	rock/ice	long	202
	42f	Brioschi	Macugnaga	D+	rock/snow	long	204
Jägerjoch	43a	NNW Flank	Zermatt	PD	glacier	short/medium	205
	43b	E Side - Jägerrücken	Macugnaga	AD	snow/rock	medium	206
Altes Weisstor	44a	ESE Ridge	Macugnaga	PD+	rock	medium	207
Cima di Jazzi	45a	W/SW and S Ridge	Zermatt/Macugnaga	PD	snow/rock	medium	209
	45b	NW Flank	Zermatt	F	snow	short	209
	45c	SE Ridge integral	Macugnaga	D	rock	long	209
Neues Weisstor/	46a	NW Flank	Zermatt	F	glacier	short	211
Passo Jacchini	46b	E Side	Macugnaga	PD	snow/rock	short	211
Monte Moro	47a	NW Flank	Saas	F	glacier	short	212
	47b	ESE Ridge	Saas/Macugnaga	F	rock	short	212

Monte Moropass		48a	S Side	Macugnaga	W1	path	medium	213
		48b	N Side	Saas	W2	path	short	213
Pizzo Bianco		49a	W and N Flank	Macugnaga	F	snow/rock	medium	214
		49b	SW Ridge	Macugnaga	AD	rock	medium	214
Riffelhorn		50a	Ordinary Route	Zermatt	F	rock	short	215
		50b	Skyline	Zermatt	AD+	rock	short	216
		50c	Gletscher Couloir	Zermatt	AD	rock	short	216
		50d	Kante	Zermatt	D	rock	short	217
		50e	Biner Couloir	Zermatt	ED1	rock	short	217
		50f	Thermometer Couloir	Zermatt	D	rock	short	217
		50g	Central Dièdre	Zermatt	AD+	rock	short	218
Stockhorn		51a	W Ridge	Zermatt	W2	rock/snow	short	218
		51b	NW Ridge	Zermatt	PD	snow/rock	medium	219
Strahlhorn		52a	WNW Flank	Saas/Zermatt	PD	snow/rock	medium	225
		52b	S Ridge	Zermatt/Macugnaga	AD+	snow/rock	medium	225
		52c	WSW Ridge over Adlerhorn	Zermatt	AD-	snow/rock	medium	226
		52d	NNW Ridge	Saas	PD	rock/snow	medium	226
		52e	NE Ridge	Saas	AD	snow	medium	227
		52f	E Face	Saas/Macugnaga	TD	rock	long	227
Adlerpass		53a	SW Side	Zermatt	PD	snow	medium	229
		53b	NE Side	Saas	PD	glacier	short	229
Rimpfischhorn		54a	WSW Ridge	Zermatt/Saas	PD/PD+	snow/rock	medium	230
		54b	NW Flank	Zermatt/Saas	D	snow/ice	medium	231
		54c	N Ridge	Saas/Zermatt	AD	rock	medium	232
		54d	SE Ridge	Saas/Zermatt	AD+	rock	medium	233
Allalinpass		55a	WNW Flank	Zermatt	F	glacier	short	233
		55b	From the Feejoch	Saas	PD	snow	short	234
		55c	E Flank	Saas	PD	glacier	short	234
Allalinhorn		56a	WNW Ridge	Saas/Zermatt	F	snow	short/medium	235
		56b	SW Ridge	Zermatt/Saas	PD	snow/rock	medium	236
		56c	NE Ridge	Saas	AD+/D-	snow/ice	medium	236
		56d	ENE Ridge	Saas	AD	snow/rock	medium	237

Mountain	Route Number	Route	Valley base	Grade	Style	Route Length	Page
Egginer	57a	SSW Ridge	Saas	AD-	rock	short	238
	57b	SW Face of Pt 3,242m	Saas	TD	rock	medium/long	238
	57c	NNW Flank Pt 3,242m	Saas	PD	snow	short	239
	57d	NNW Flank NNE Ridge	Saas	F	rock	medium	239
	57e	NNE Ridge	Saas	W2	path	short	240
Mitaghorn	58a	E Flank	Saas	AD-	rock	medium	240
	58b	NW Ridge	Saas	F	rock	short	241
Alphubeljoch	59a	W Side	Zermatt	PD	glacier	short	241
	59b	NE Side	Saas	PD	glacier	medium	243
Alphubel	60a	SE Ridge	Zermatt/Saas	PD	snow	medium	243
	60b	E Flank	Saas/Zermatt	AD+	snow	medium	243
	60c	W Ridge	Zermatt	D	rock	medium	244
	60d	W Rib	Zermatt	PD	rock	medium/long	245
	60e	N Ridge	Zermatt	PD	snow/rock	medium	245
Mischabeljoch	61a	W Side	Zermatt	AD	glacier/rock	medium	246
Täschhorn	62a	SSE Ridge	Zermatt	D	snow/rock	medium	248
	62b	WSW Ridge	Zermatt	AD+	rock/snow	medium/long	249
	62c	NW Face	Zermatt	AD+/D-	glacier	medium	250
	62d	NNE Ridge (descent)	Zermatt	AD	rock	long	252
Leiterspitzen	63a	Traverse W-E	Zermatt	PD	rock	long	252
Dom	64a	N Flank	Zermatt	AD	snow	medium	255
	64b	S Ridge	Zermatt	D	rock	long	256
	64c	NW and WNW Flanks	Zermatt	PD+	snow/rock	medium/long	256
	64d	NW Ridge	Zermatt	AD	snow/rock/snow	medium	257
Lenzspitze	65a	ENE Ridge	Saas	PD+	rock/snow	medium	257
	65b	S Ridge	Zermatt	AD	rock	medium	258
	65c	NW Ridge	Saas	PD	snow/rock	medium	259
	65d	NNE Face	Saas	D+	snow/ice	medium	260

Nadelhorn	66a	NE Ridge	Saas	PD	snow/rock	medium	262
	66b	SE Ridge	Saas	AD-	rock	medium	263
	66c	NW Ridge	Zermatt/Saas	PD+	rock/snow	medium	263
Hohbärghorn	67a	ESE Ridge	Zermatt	PD	snow	medium	264
	67b	NNW Ridge	Zermatt	AD	snow/rock	medium	265
	67c	NE Face	Zermatt	D	snow/ice	medium	266
Dirruhorn	68a	SSE Ridge	Zermatt	AD	snow/rock	medium	267
	68b	N Ridge	Zermatt	AD+	snow/rock	medium	267
Ulrichshorn	69a	SW Ridge	Saas/Zermatt	PD	snow	short	270
	69b	N Flank	Zermatt	F	snow	short	270
Balfrin	70a	S Ridge	Zermatt/Saas	PD	rock/snow	short	271
	70b	SW Ridge of N Summit	Zermatt	PD	rock/snow	short	271
	70c	NW Ridge v G. Bigerhorn	Zermatt	PD	rock/snow	medium	272
Gross Bigerhorn	71a	WSW Ridge	Zermatt	PD	rock	short	272
	71b	NNW Ridge	Zermatt	AD	rock	medium	273
Joderhorn	72a	WNW Ridge	Saas/Macugnaga	F	rock	short	278
	72b	NE Ridge	Saas	F	rock	short/medium	278
East Face:	72c	Diretta 17 November	Saas/Macugnaga	TD	rock	medium	279
	72d	Gildo Burgener	Saas/Macugnaga	TD+	rock	medium	280
	72e	Marlene	Saas/Macugnaga	ED	rock	medium	280
	72f	Luino	Saas/Macugnaga	TD-	rock	medium	280
	72g	Classic	Saas/Macugnaga	AD/D	rock	medium	281
	72h	SE Ridge	Saas/Macugnaga	D	rock	medium	281
Sonnighorn	73a	NE Ridge	Saas	PD	snow/rock	medium	282
	73b	NW Ridge	Saas	AD	rock	medium	283
Mittelrück	74a	S Ridge	Saas	PD	rock	short	284
	74b	E Ridge	Saas/Simplon	D	rock	medium	284
Portjengrat	75a	Traverse	Saas	AD	rock	long	286
	75b	SE Flank direct	Saas/Simplon	AD+	rock	medium	288
	75c	SE Rib of Pt 3,492m	Saas/Simplon	AD+	rock	medium	289
Portjenhorn	76a	NNW Ridge	Saas	PD+	rock	medium	289

331

Mountain	Route Number	Route	Valley base	Grade	Style	Route Length	Page
Zwischbergenpass	77a	W Side	Saas	W2	path	short	290
Dri Horlini	78a	Traverse SW-NE	Saas	AD	rock	short	291
Weissmies	79a	NW Flank, Upper SW Ridge	Saas	PD-	snow	short/medium	293
	79b	SSE Ridge	Saas	PD-	rock	medium	294
	79c	SW Ridge	Saas	PD	rock/snow	medium	295
	79d	N Ridge	Saas	D	rock/snow	medium	296
Schwarzmies	80a	Traverse W-E	Saas	AD	rock	medium	298
Lagginjoch	81a	W Side	Saas	F	snow	short	299
Lagginhorn	82a	WSW Ridge	Saas	PD	snow/rock	medium	300
	82b	SSW Ridge	Saas	AD	rock/snow	medium	301
	82c	WSW Spur	Saas	PD	rock	medium	302
	82d	NNE Ridge	Saas	AD-	rock	medium	302
	82e	E Rib of Pt 3,971m	Simplon	AD	rock	medium/long	303
Fletschhorn	83a	W Flank and NW Ridge	Saas	PD	snow	medium	304
	83b	SW Ridge	Saas	PD	rock	medium	305
North Face:	83c	Weiner Route	Simplon	TD	snow/ice	medium	306
	83d	Asseling/Gabarrou Route	Simplon	D+	ice/rock	long	307
	83e	NE Ridge integral	Simplon	PD	rock/snow	medium	308
	83f	SE Ridge	Simplon	AD	rock	medium	309
Jeghorn	84a	Ordinary Route	Saas	W2	rock	short	310
	84b	E Wall	Saas	D	rock	short	310
	84c	SE Face	Saas	AD-	rock	short	311
	84d	S Rib	Saas	AD	rock	short	311
Jegigrat	85a	Traverse SW-NE	Saas	AD	rock	medium/long	312
	85b	Carmen	Saas	TD-	rock	medium	314
	85c	Jegiturm SE Face	Saas	D	rock	short	314
	85d	Grand Gendarme SE Rib	Saas	D	rock	short	315
Senggchuppa	86a	NW Flank	Saas	F	snow	short	316
Hübschhorn	87a	NW Ridge	Simplon	D	rock	medium	317

General Index

A
Adlerpass	228
Allalinpass	233
Allalinhorn	234
Alphubel	242
Alphubeljoch	241
Altes Weisstor	207

B
Balfrin	270
Balmenhorn	47
Barrhorn	111
Besso	91
Bishorn	103
Bisjoch	107
Bivouac huts	
Arben	38
Balmenhorn	47
Belloni	50
Città Di Gallerate	47
Città Di Luina	51
Città di Varese	56
Fletschhorn	58
Gugliermina	47
Laggin	58
Marinelli	49
Mischabeljoch	54
Ressegotti	48
Rossi and Volante	43
Schalijoch	41
Blanc de Moming	90
Breithorn	118
Brunegghorn	107
Bruneggjoch	109

C
Castor	144
Cima Di Jazzi	208
Col de Milon	106
Col de Tracuit	39
Col Durand	74
Colle del Castor	144
Colle Gnifetti	189
Colle Vincent	174
Corno Nero	176

D/E
Dirruhorn	266
Dom	254
Dri Horlini	290
Dufourspitze	192
Egginer	238

F
Felikjoch	148
Fletschhorn	303
Fillarhorn, Gross	205
Fillarhorn, Klein	205

G/H
Grenzsattel	190
Gross Bigerhorn	272
Hohbärghorn	264
Hübschhorn	316
Huts	
Almageller	57
Ar Pitetta	39
Berghaus Flue	52
Bordier	55
Britannia	53
Cervinia Guides	42
Città di Mantova	46
Dom	54
Euginio Sella	50
Gandegg	42
Gnifetti	46
Hohsaas	58
Längflue	54
Margherita	47
Mezzalama	43

GENERAL INDEX

Mischabel	55
Monte Rosa	45
Mountet	38
Oberto	56
Quintino Sella	44
Rothorn	39
Schönbiel	37
Täsch	53
Theodule	42
Topali	41
Tracuit	39
Turtmann	41
Valle d'Ayas Guides'	44
Weisshorn	40
Weissmies	57
Zamboni and Zappa	49

I/J/K

Il Naso	150
Jägerhorn	206
Jägerjoch	205
Jegigrat	312
Jegihorn	309
Joderhorn	278
Klein Matterhorn	117

L

Lagginhorn	299
Lagginjoch	298
Leiterspitzen	252
Lenzspitze	258
Lisjoch	161
Liskamm	150
Ludwigshöhe	177

M

Mammouth	89
Maps (sketch)	
Ober Gabelhorn, Weisshorn Chain	72
Breithorn, Liskamm, Weissgrat Chain	114
Monte Rosa Group	166
Strahlhorn, Mischabel Chain	222
Monte Moropass, Weissmies Chain	276
Mettelhorn	112
Mischabel	221
Mischabeljoch	246
Mittaghorn	240
Mittelrück	284
Mont Durand	74
Monte Moro	212
Monte Moropass	212
Monte Rosa	see Dufourspitze
Monte Rosa Group	165
Monte Rosa, Tour of	59

N

Nadelgrat	267
Nadelhorn	261
Neues Weisstor	210
Nordend	199

O/P

Ober Gabelhorn	76
Parrotspitze	178
Passo Jacchini	210
Passo Signal	179
Piodejoch	177
Piramide Vincent	171
Pizzo Bianco	213
Pizzo d'Andolla	286
Pollux	141
Portjenhorn	289
Portjengrat	286
Punta Giordani	168

R/S

Riffelhorn	215
Rimpfischhorn	230
Roccia Nera	135
Schalihorn	93
Schalijoch	94
Schöllijoch	110
Schwarzberghorn	211

Schwarzberg Weisstor	224
Schwarzmies	297
Schwarztor	140
Sella del Liskamm	160
Senggchuppa	315
Seserjoch	178
Signalkuppe	181
Silbersattel	198
Sonnighorn	282
Sperone Vincent	174
Stockhorn	218
Stockhornpass	219
Strahlhorn	224

T

Täschhorn	247
Tête de Milon	106
Theodulpass	115
Torre di Castelfranco	207
Torrione Maggiore	123
Trifthorn	82

U/W

Ulrichshorn	270
Weisshorn	96
Weissmies	293
Weisstor	207
Wellenkuppe	81

Z

Zinal Rothorn	83
Zumsteinspitze	189
Zwillingsjoch	143
Zwischbergenpass	290

Ober Gabelhorn and Mont Durand W Flanks

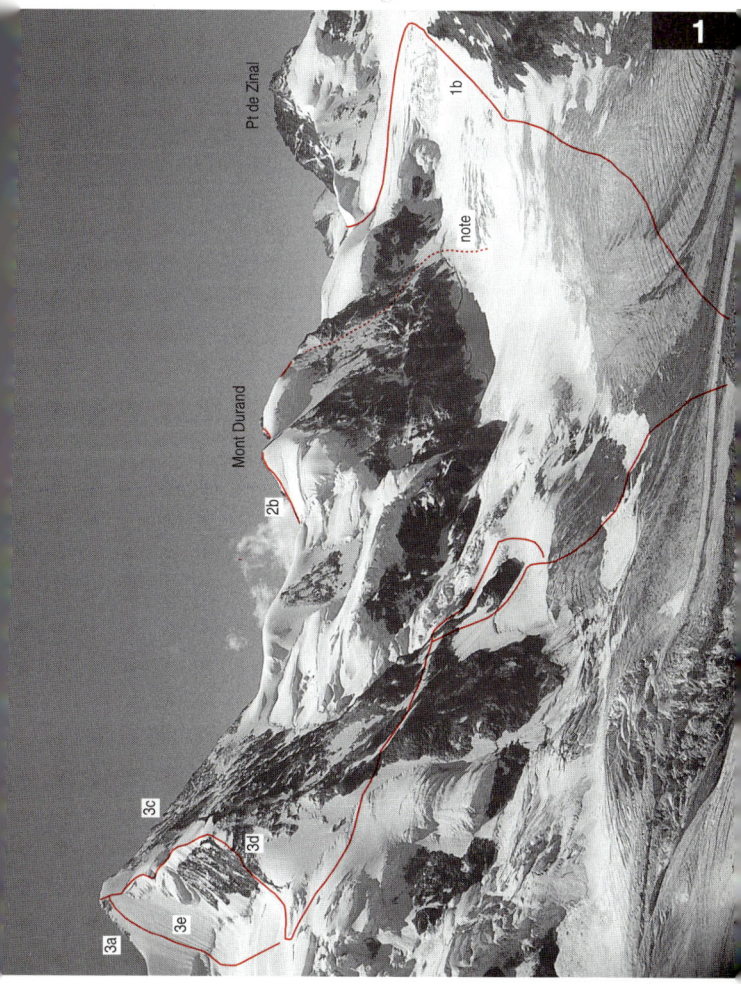

Ober Gabelhorn S Face

Ober Gabelhorn N Face

Wellenkuppe and Trifthorn E Flanks

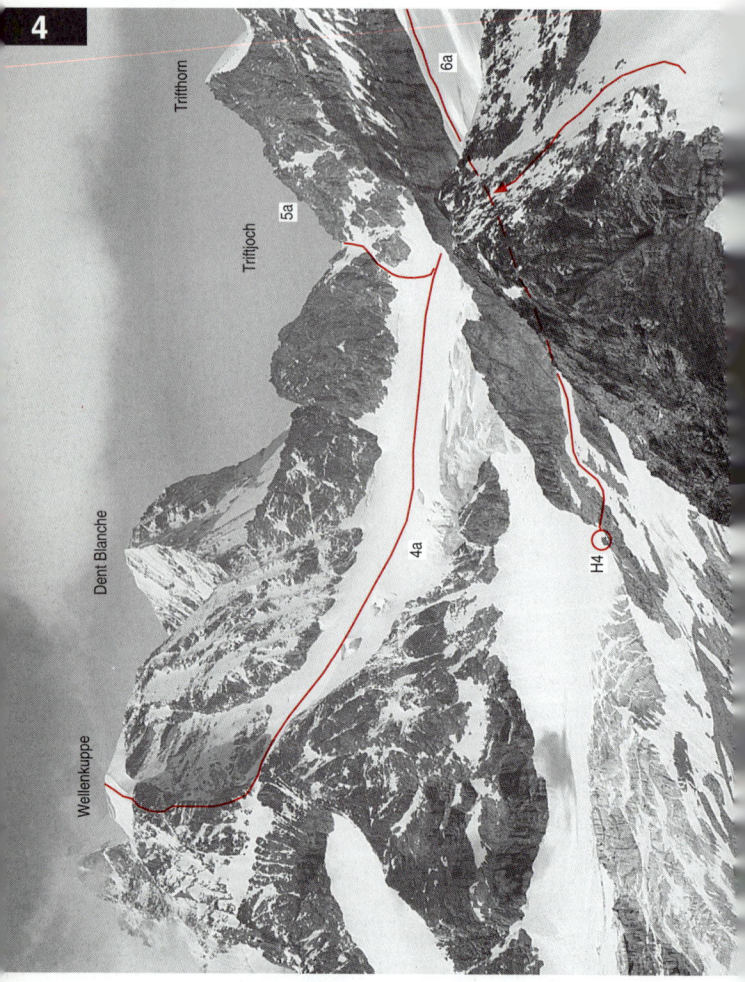

4

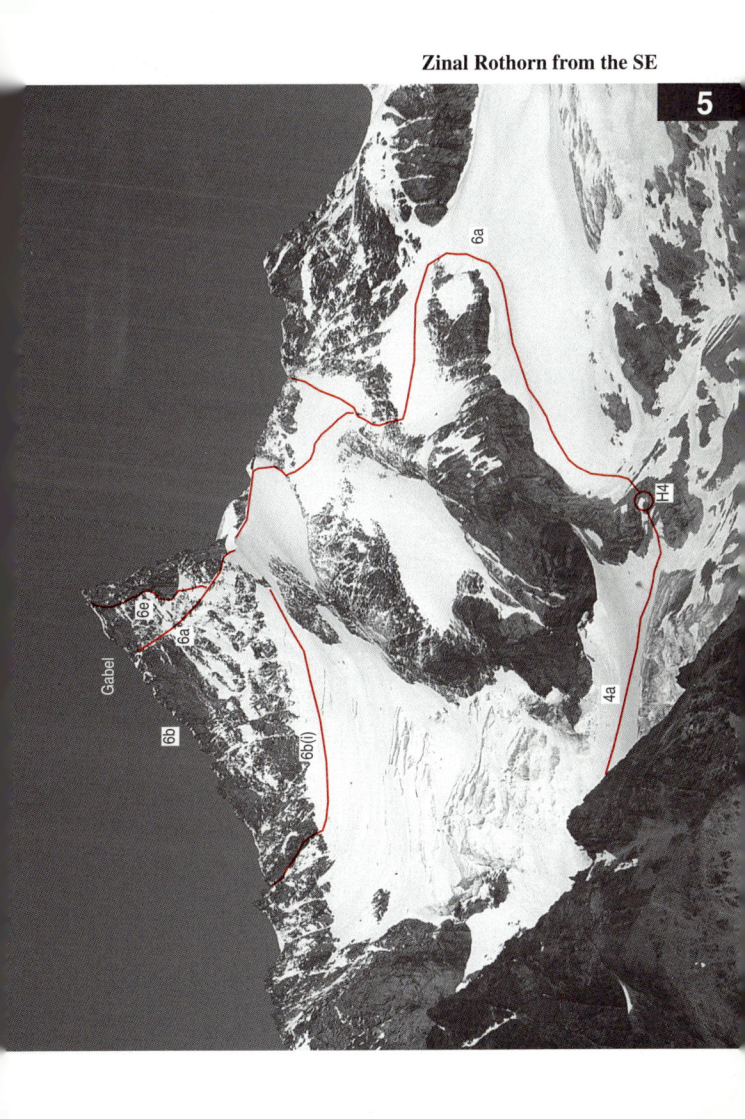

Zinal Rothorn from the SE

Zinal Rothorn W Flank

6

Trifthorn and Zinal Rothorn (part) W Flank

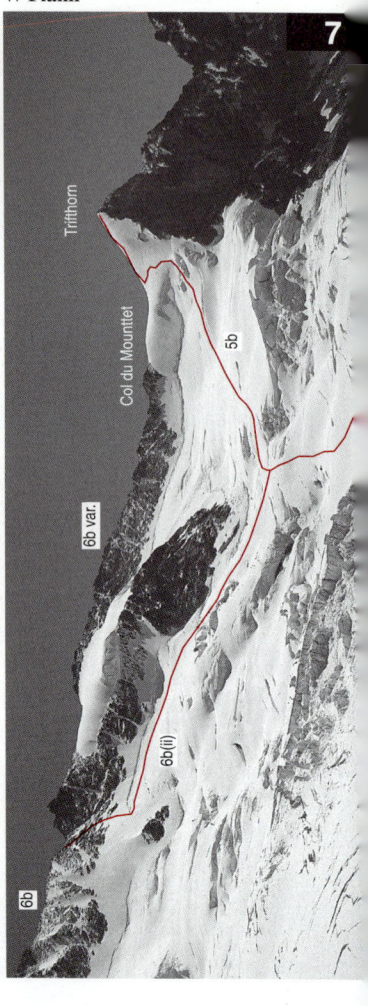

7

Zinal Rothorn E Face

8

Mammouth SW Sector

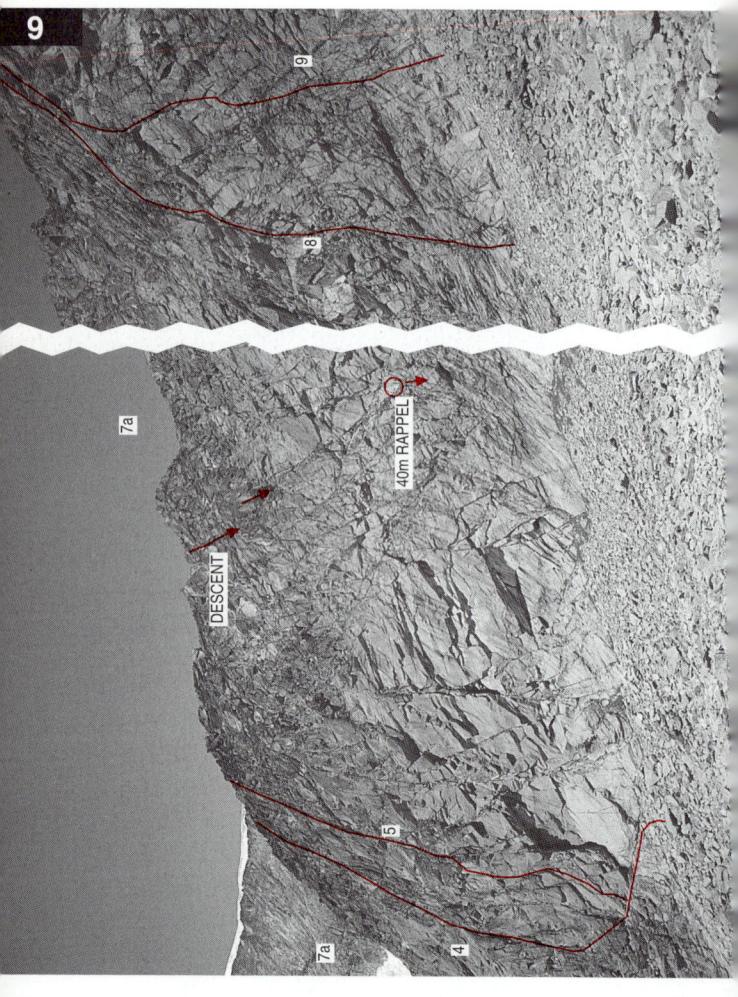

9

40m RAPPEL

DESCENT

7a

5

7a

4

8

9

Mammouth NE Sector

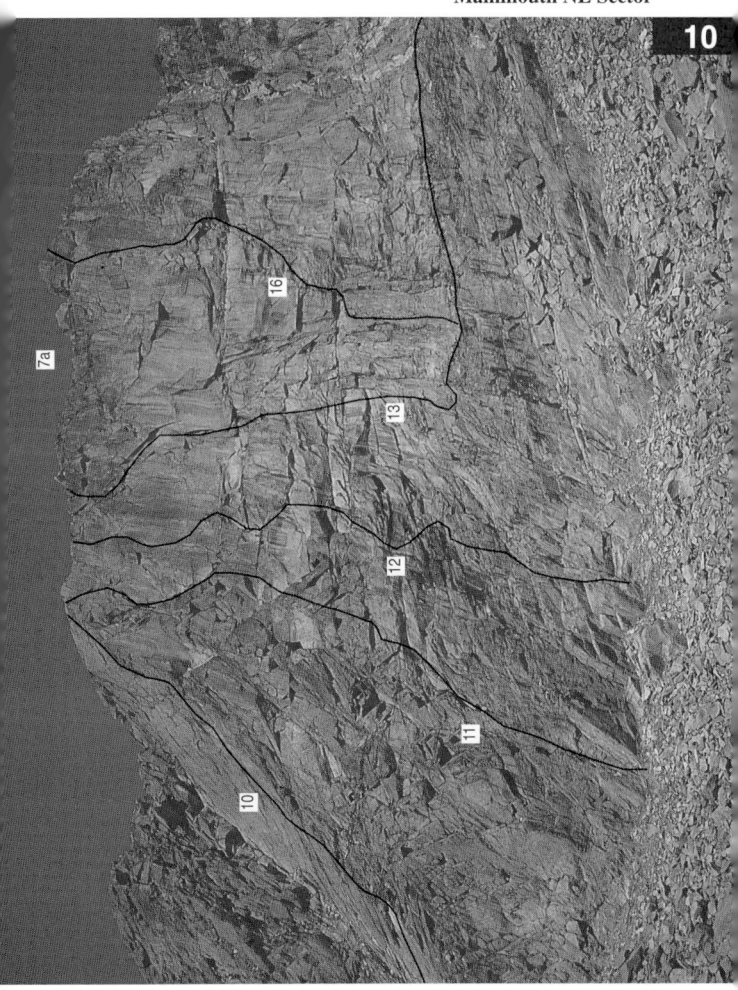

10

Besso and Blanc de Moming S Flanks

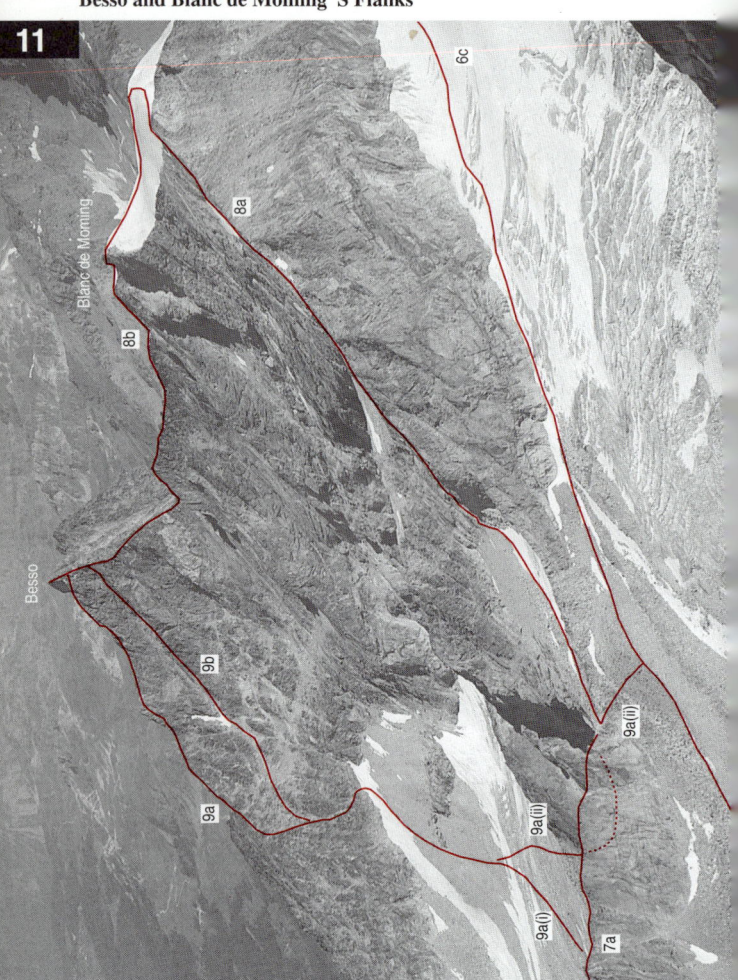

Zinal Rothorn and Schalihorn E Flanks

Weisshorn SE Flank

Weisshorn W Face

14

Weisshorn NE Face

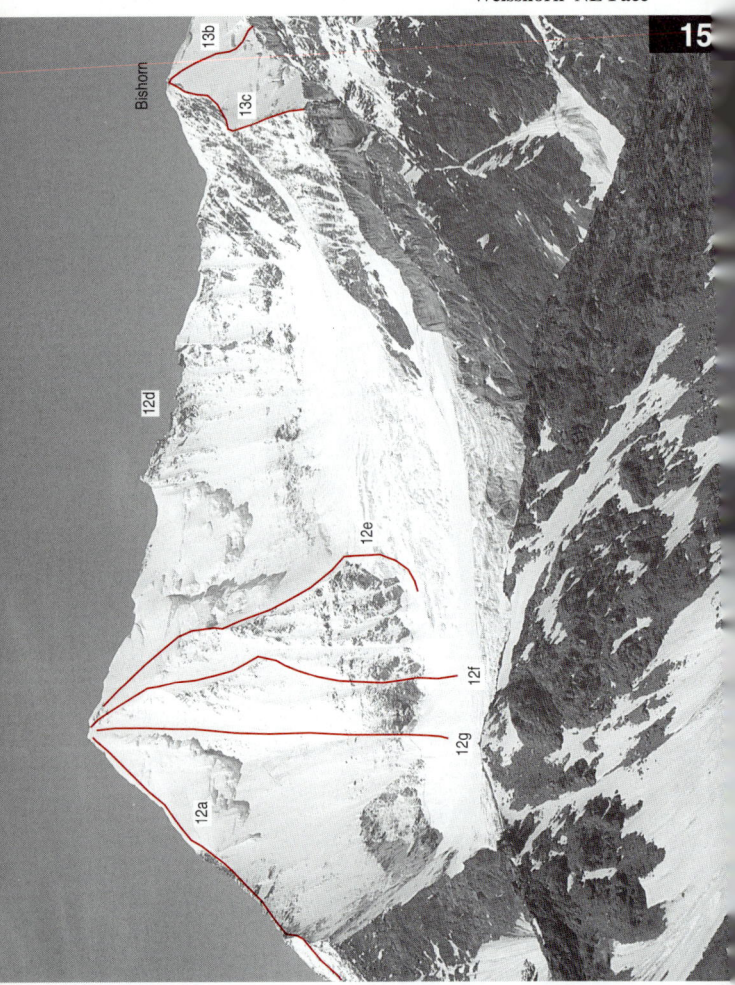

Bishorn and Weisshorn from the N

16

Brunegghorn and Bisjoch N Flanks

Schöllihorn and Barrhorn E Flank

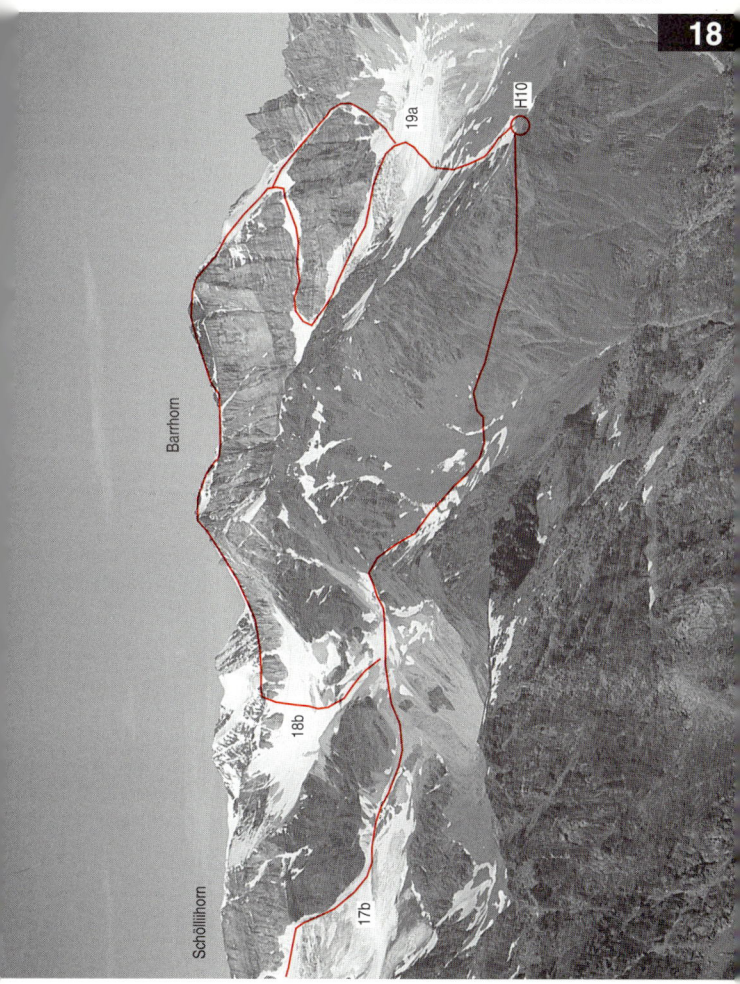

18

Klein Matterhorn N Flank

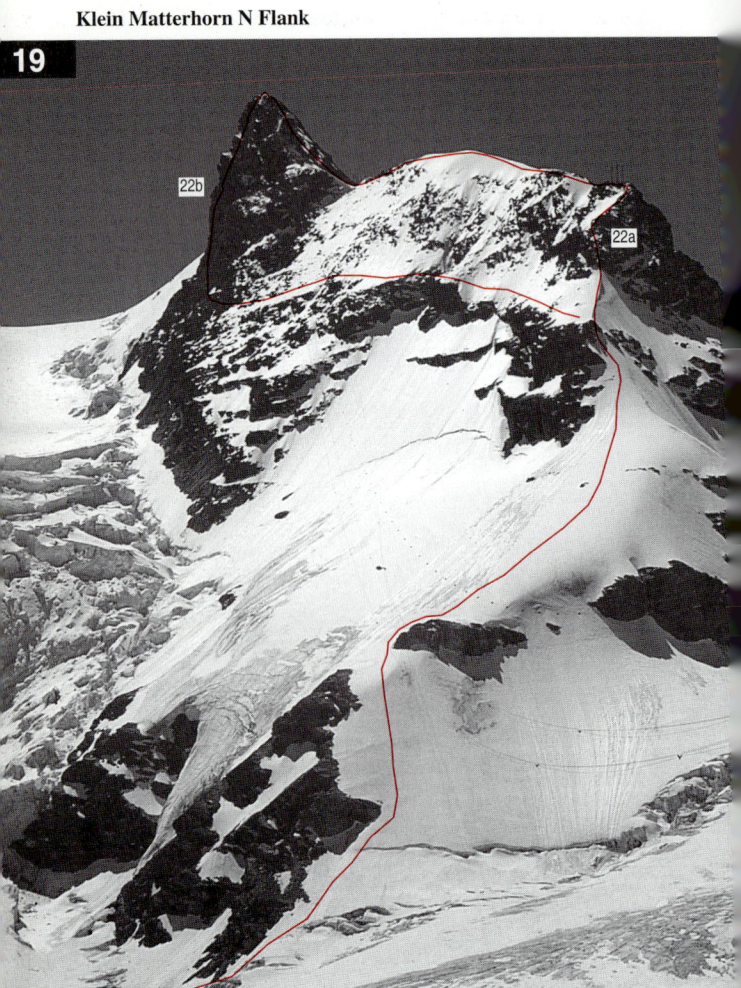

19

22b

22a

Breithorn S flank from the SW   Breithorn Central Summit from the SE

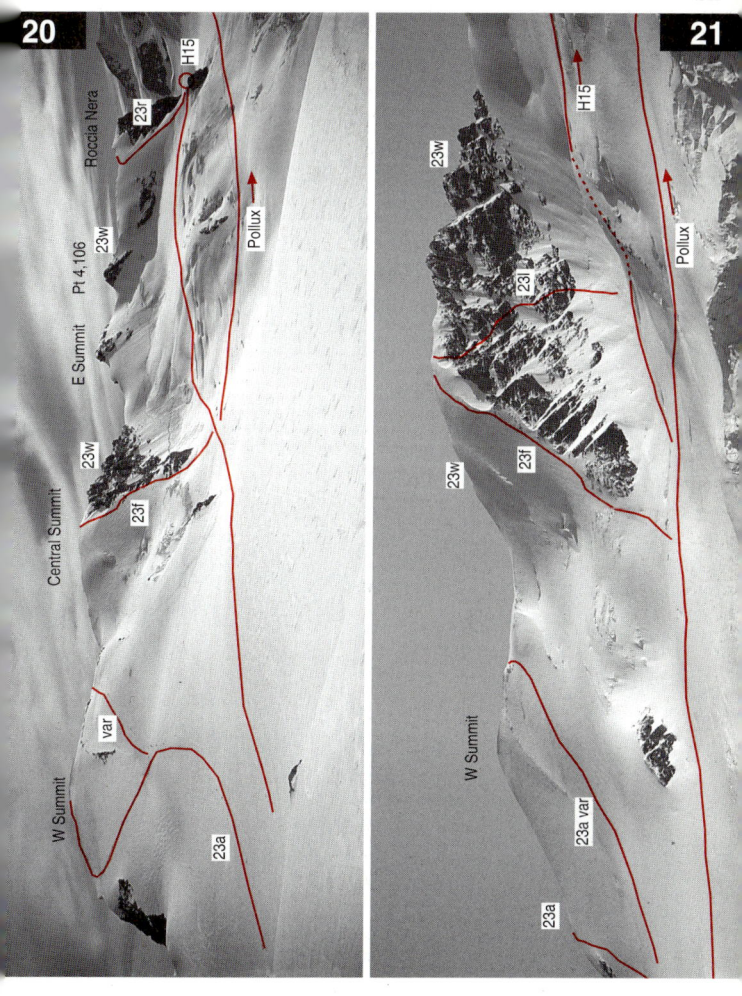

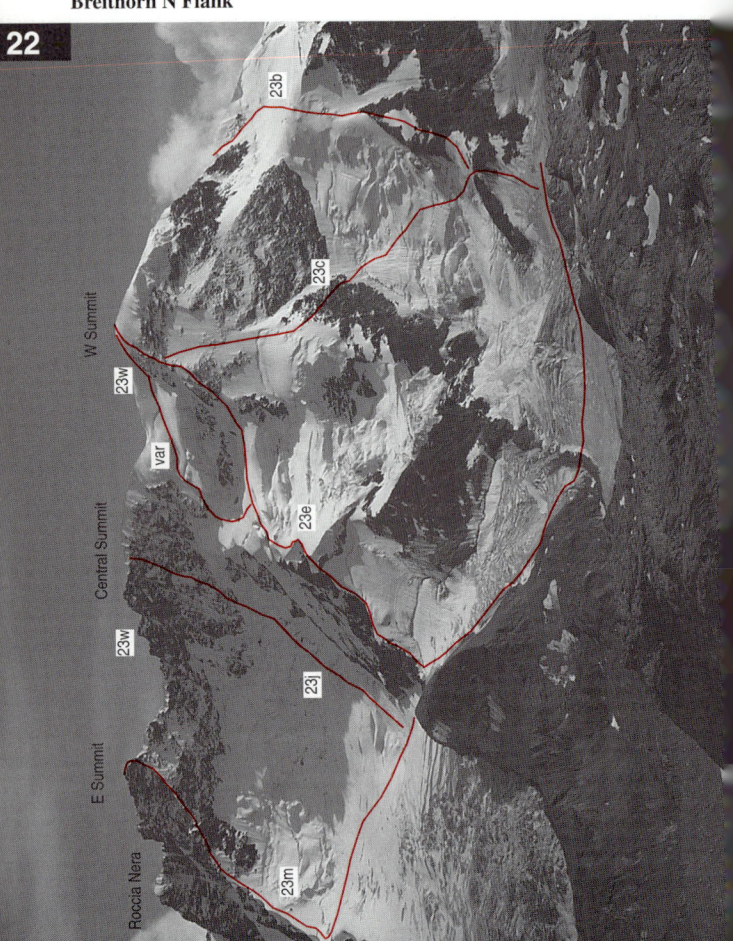

Breithorn N Flank

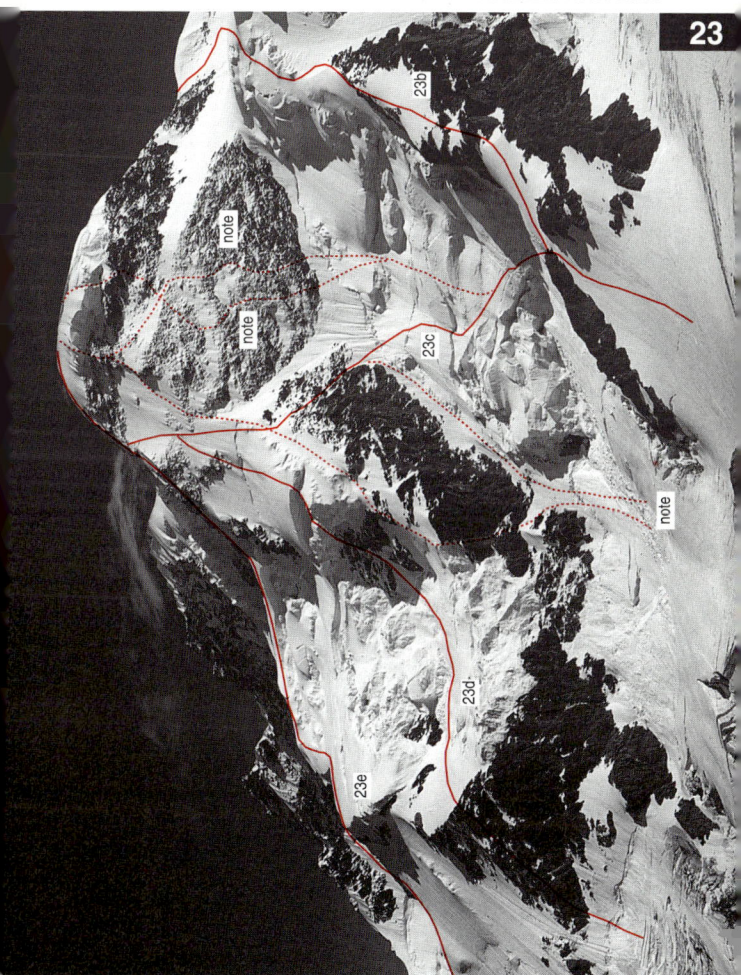

Breithorn W Summit NNW Face

23

Berithorn Central Summit N Flank

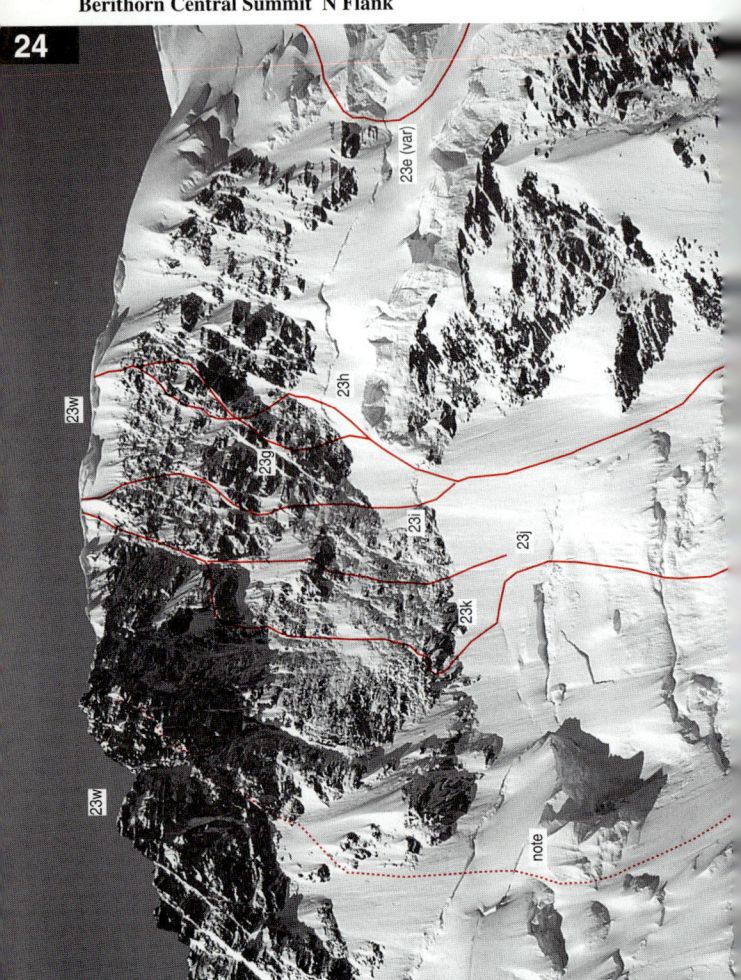

Roccia Nera and Breithorn E Summit N Flanks

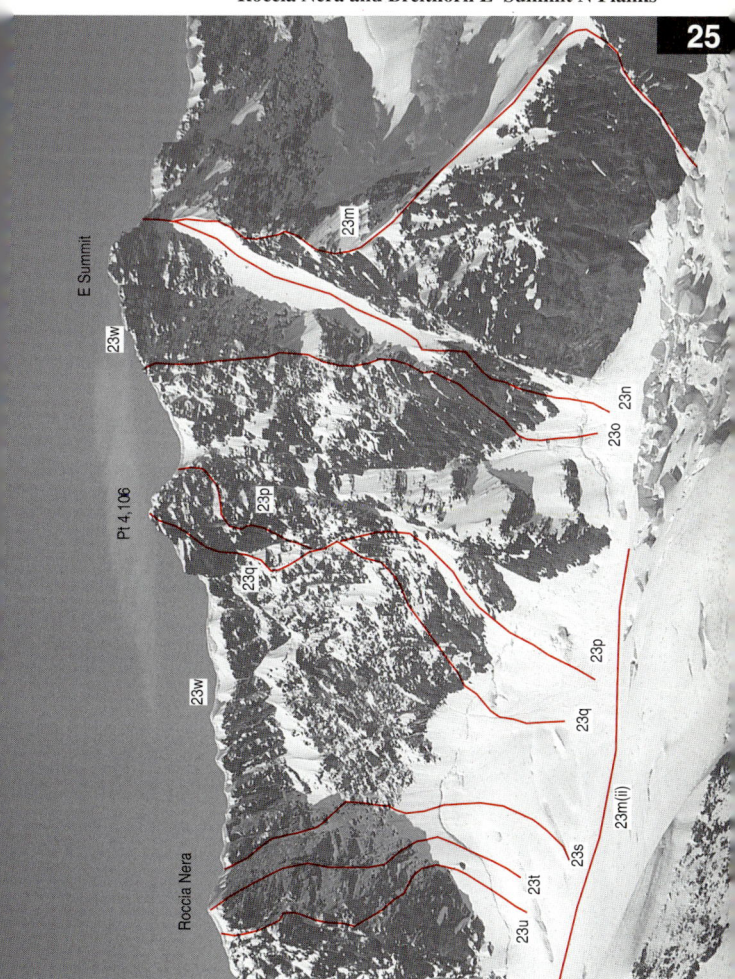

25

Breithorn E Summit and Roccia Nera from the SE

Pollux, Liskamm and Castor from the W

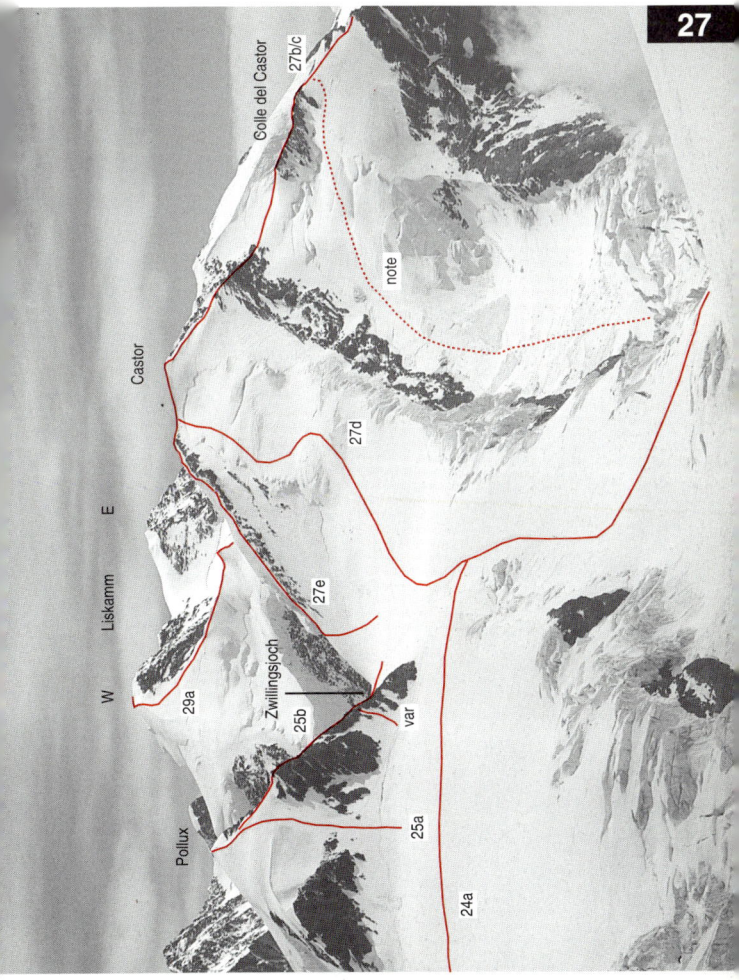

Castor and Pollux N Flanks

28

Liskamm W Summit NNE Face

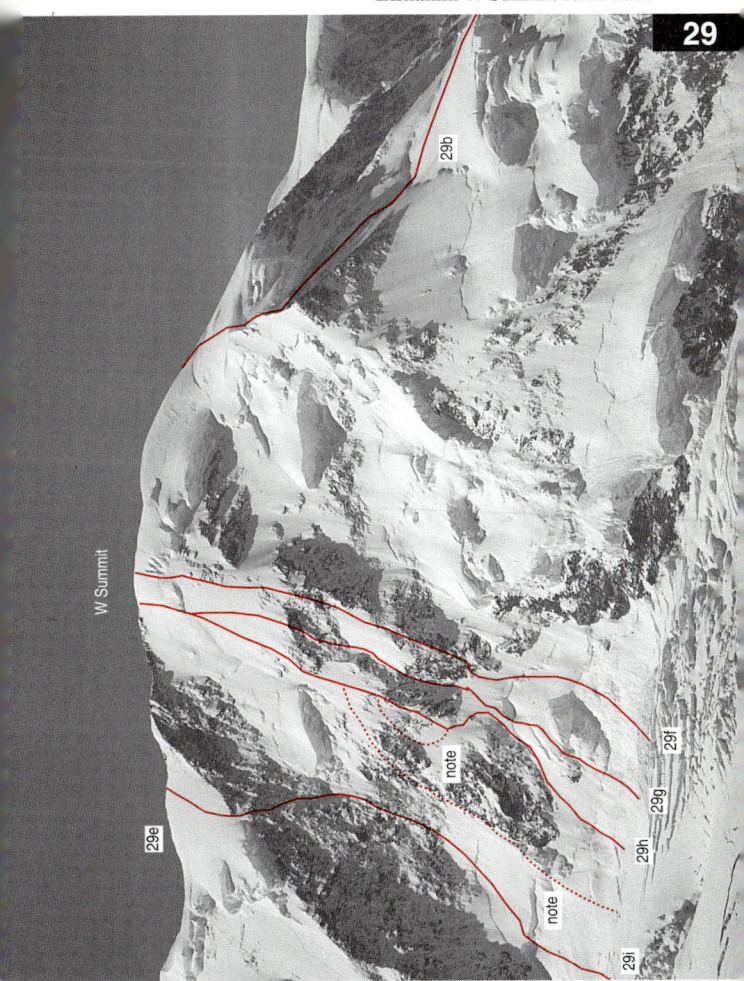

Liskamm E Summit NE Face

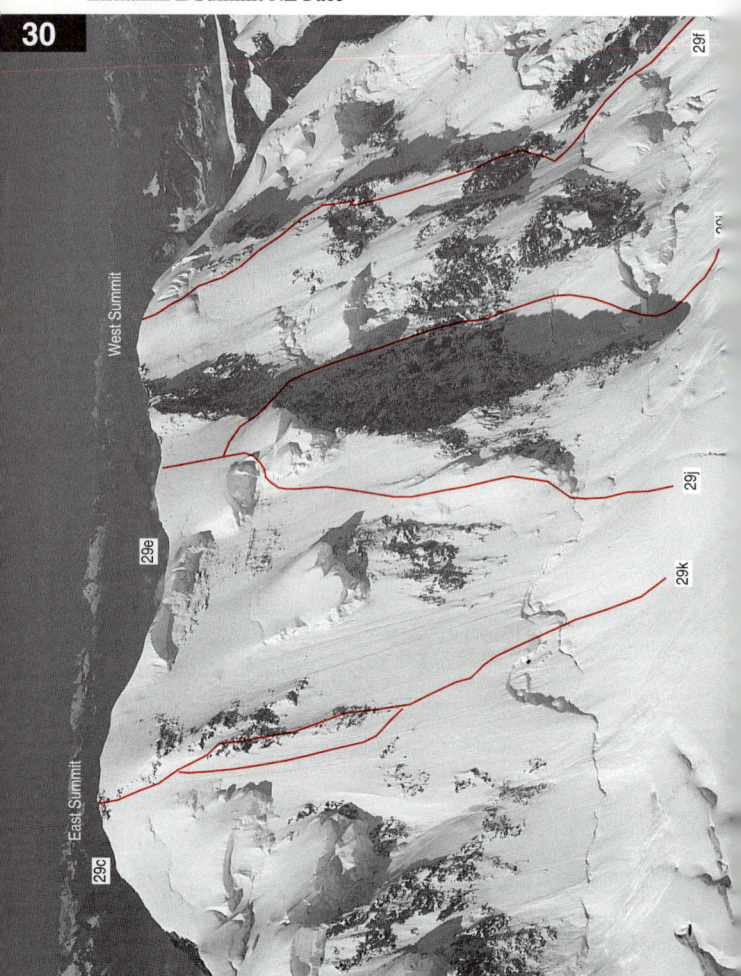

Liskamm S Flank

31

Piramide Vincent and Punta Giordani S Flanks

Piramide Vincent SW Flank

Sperone Vincent

34

Piramide Vincent, Parrotspitze and Signalkuppe E Flanks

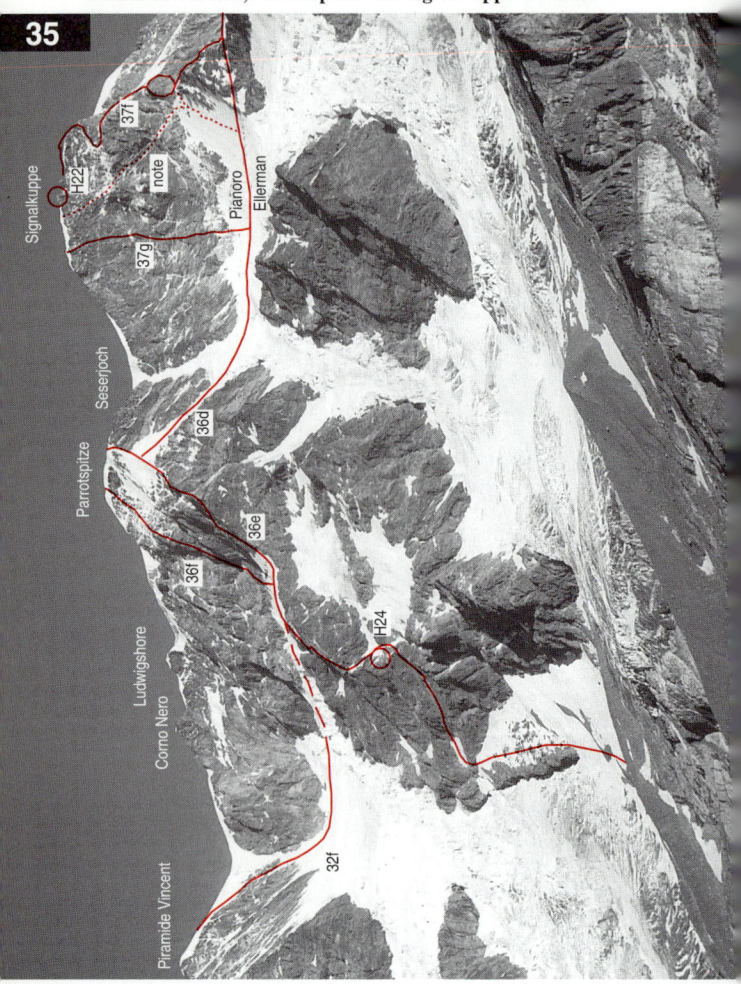

Nordend and Dufourspitze W Flank

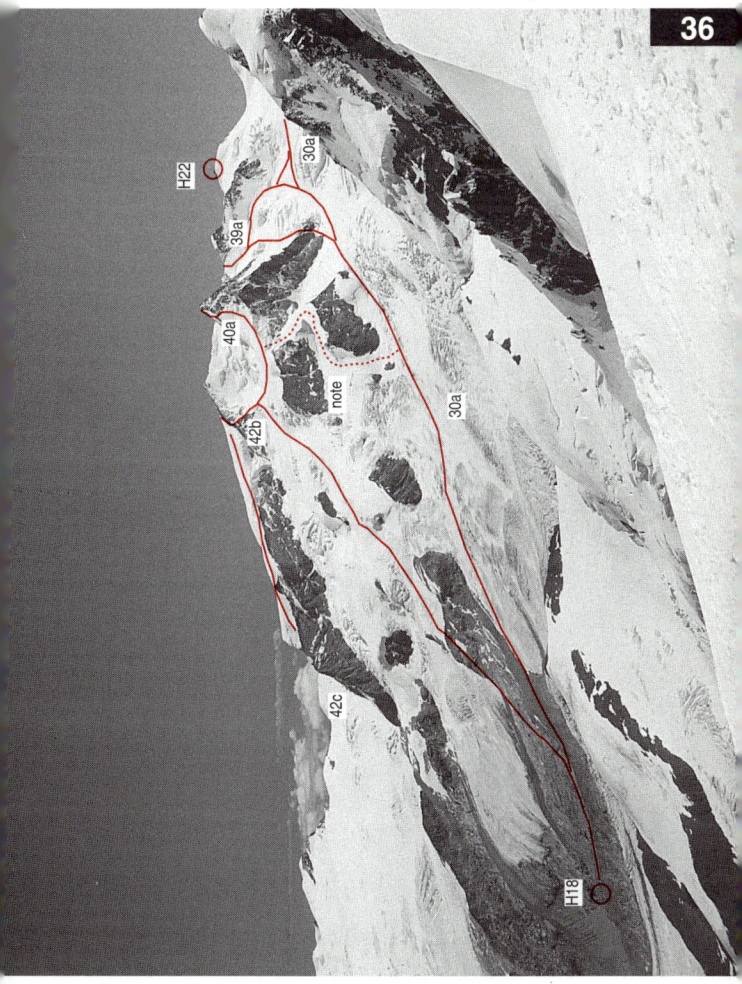

Dufourspitze S Face

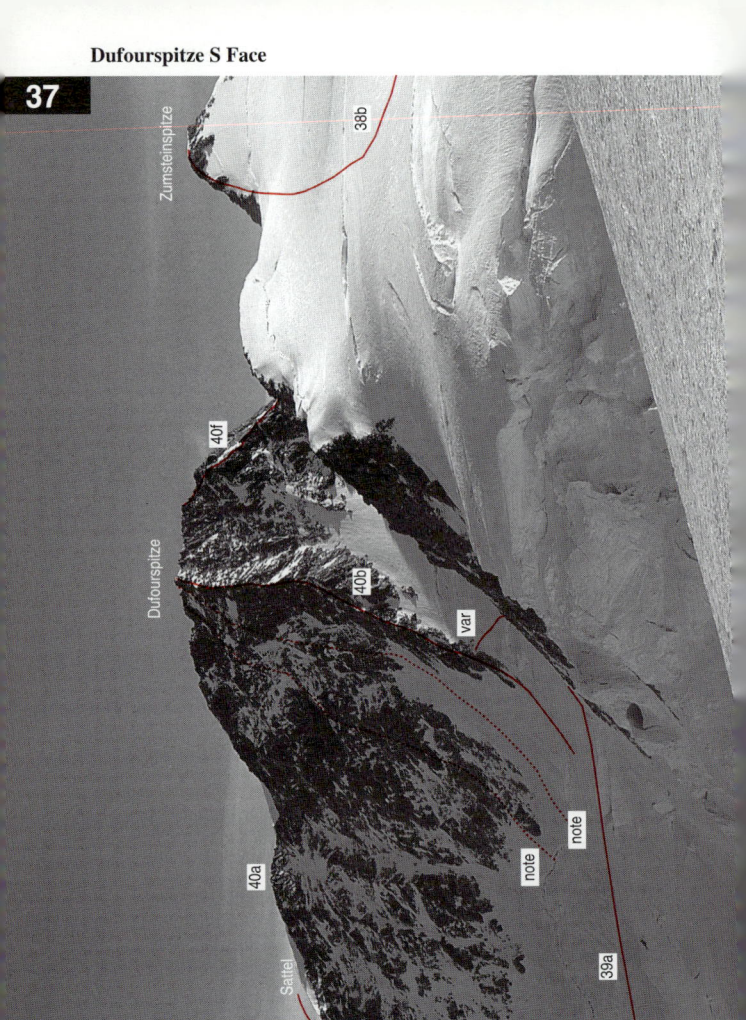

37

Monte Rosa E Face

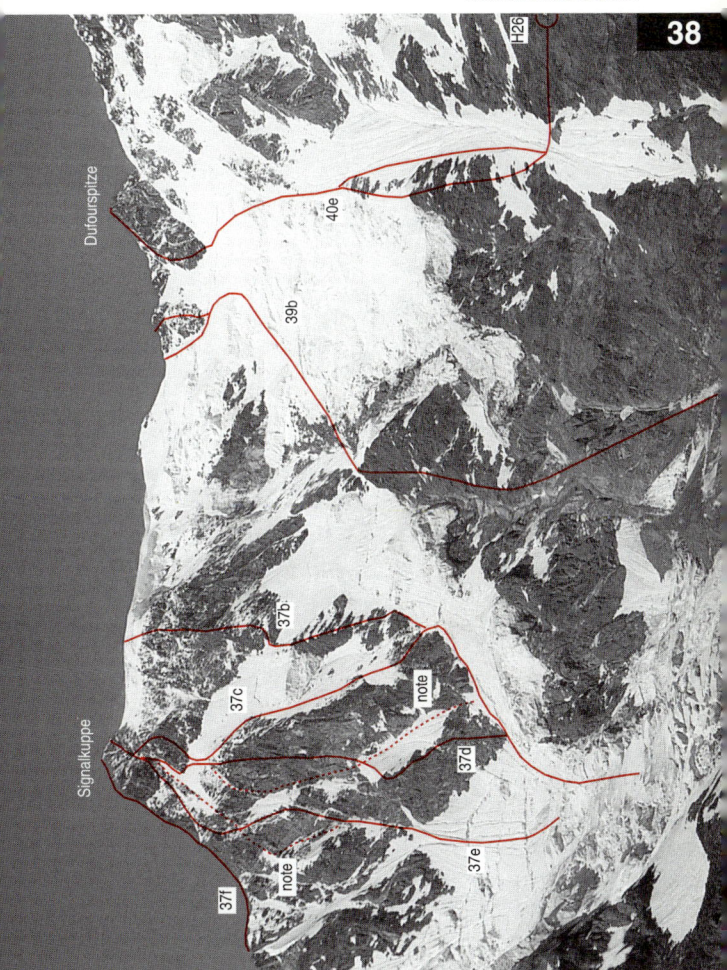

Nordend and Cima di Jazzi from the N

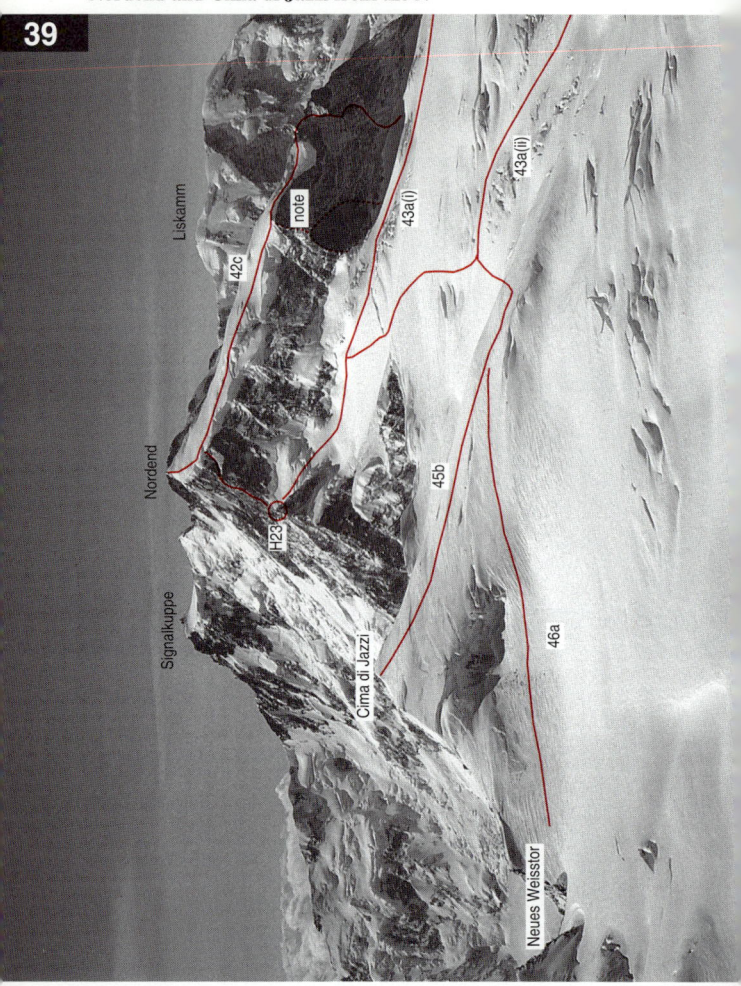

Nordend NW Flank

40

Nordend E Face

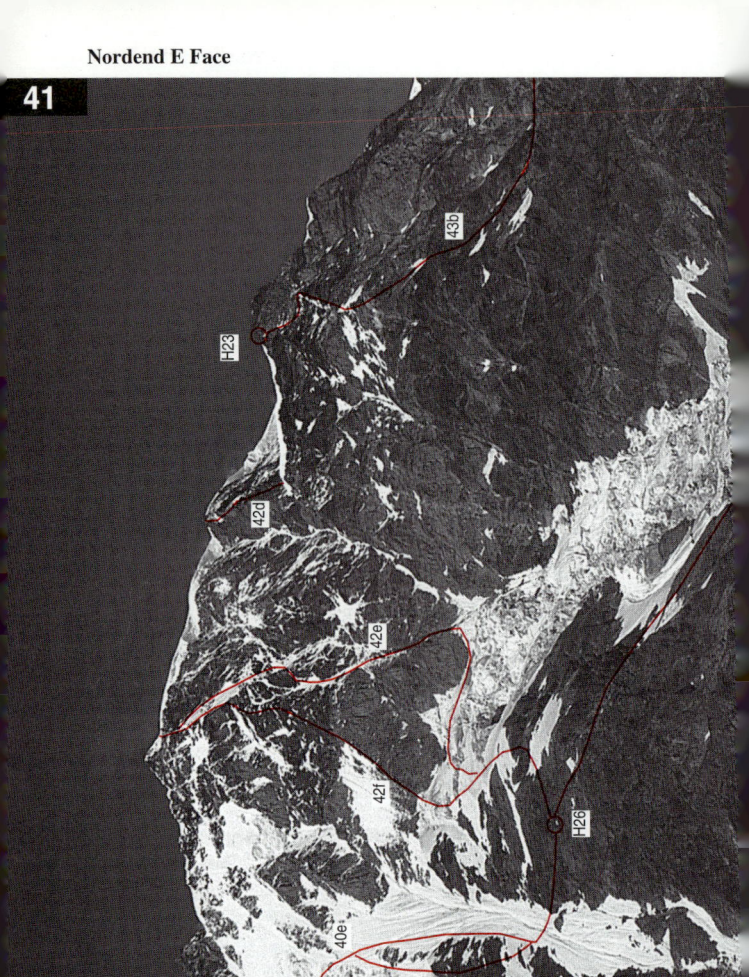

Cima di Jazzi E Flank

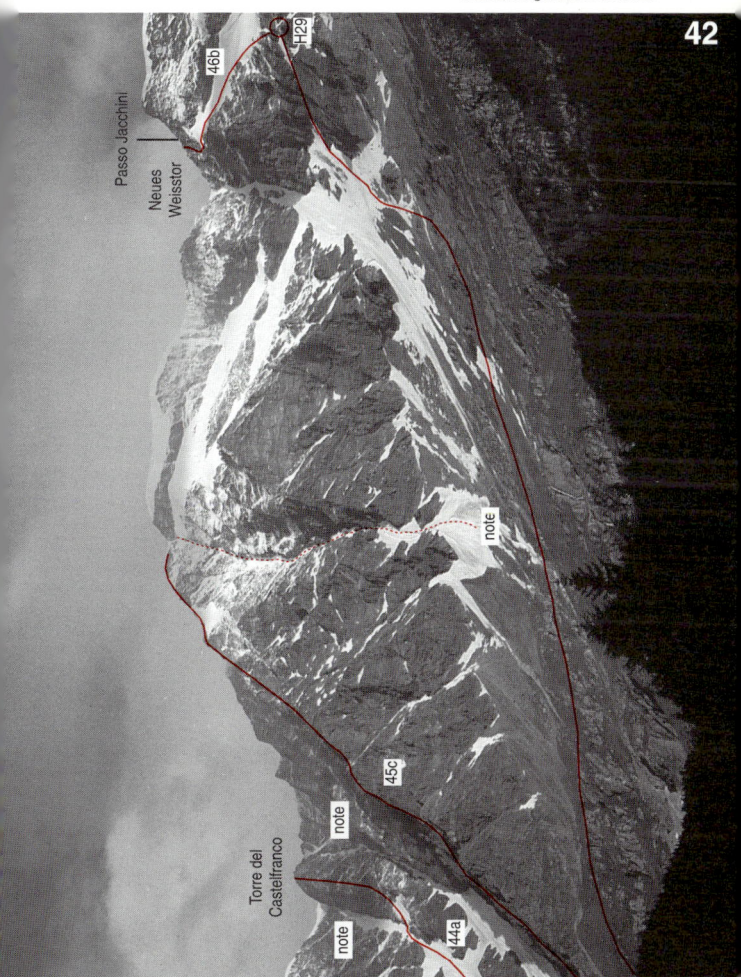

Pizzo Bianco W Flank

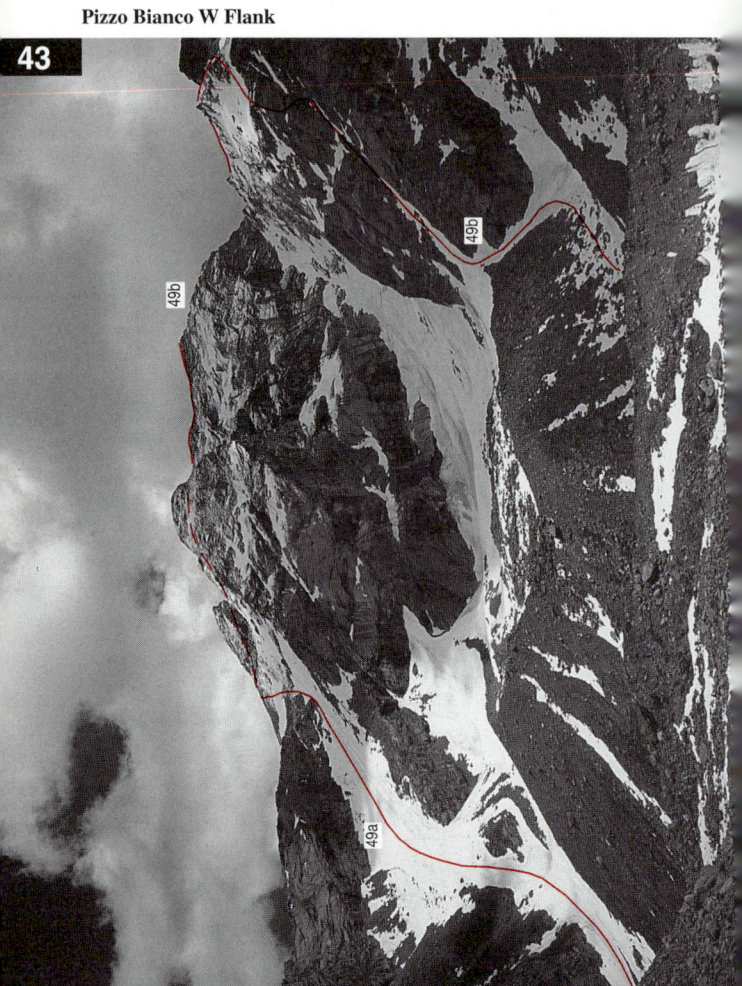

43

Riffelhorn N Side

44

Strahlhorn and Cima di Jazzi from the W

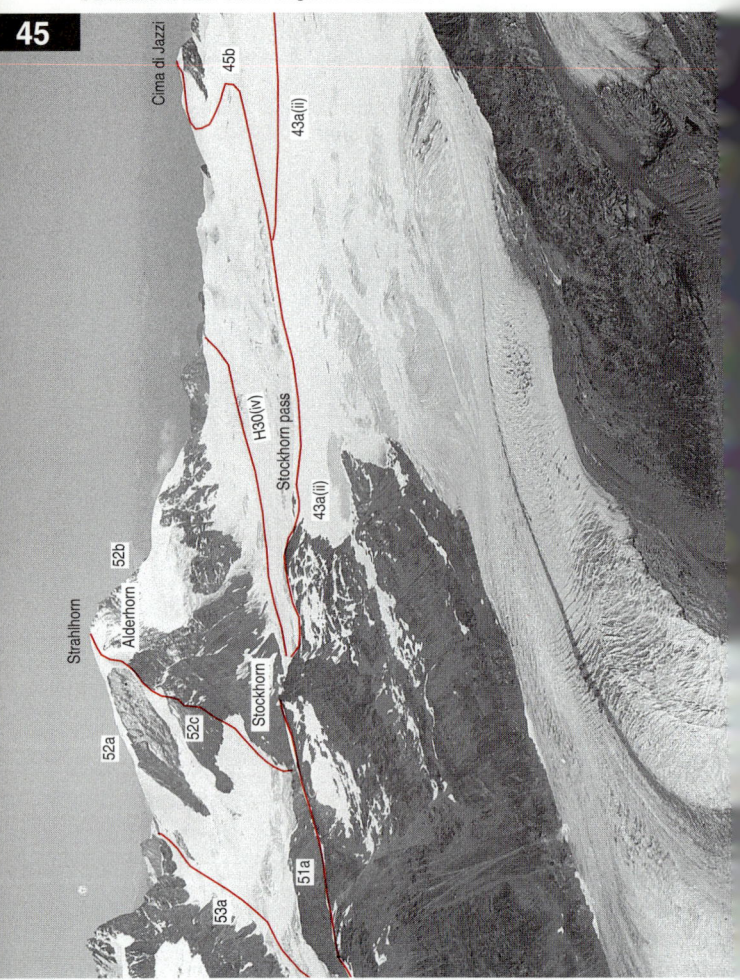

Strahlhorn N Flank

46

Strahlhorn E Face

Rimpfischhorn and Strahlhorn W Flanks

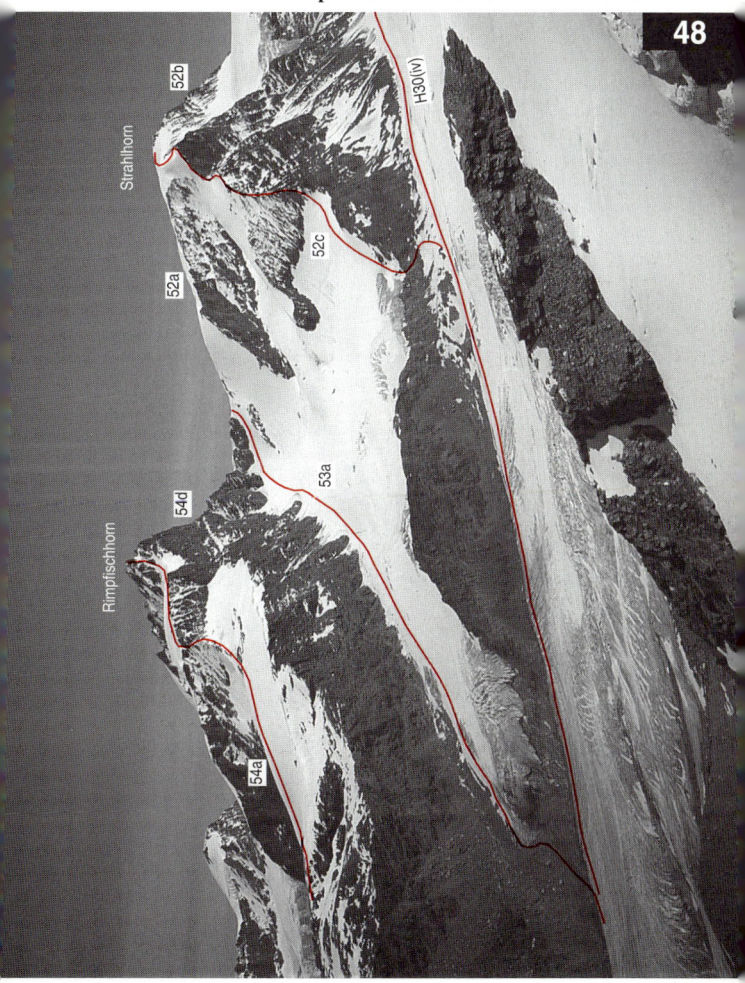

Rimpfischhorn SW Flank

49

Rimpfischhorn W Flank

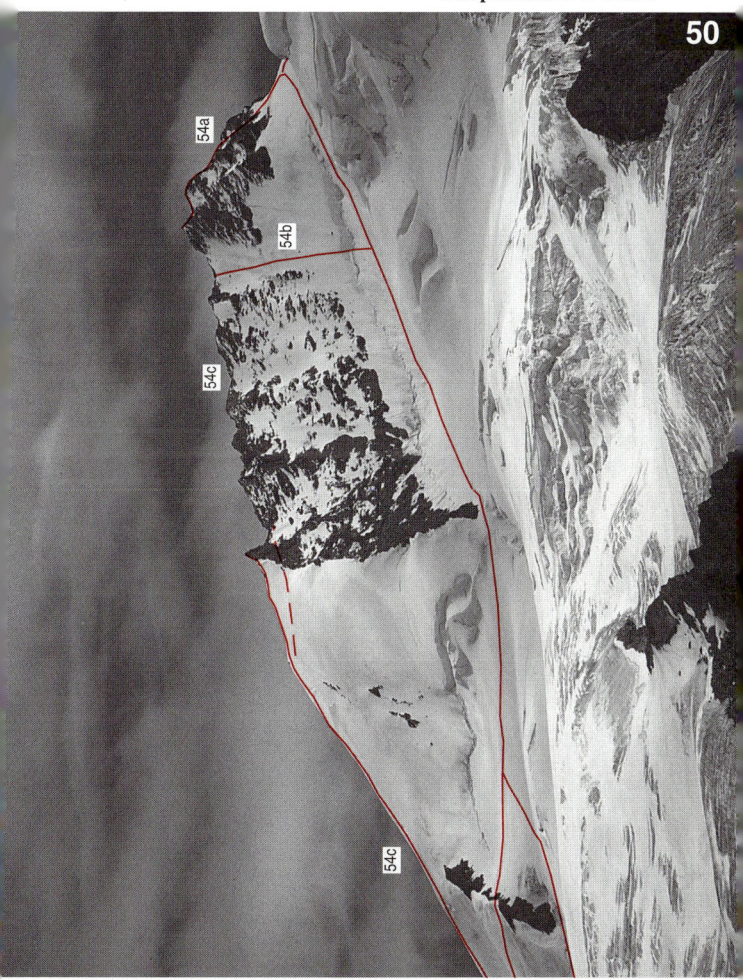

50

Rimpfischhorn and Allalinhorn from the NE

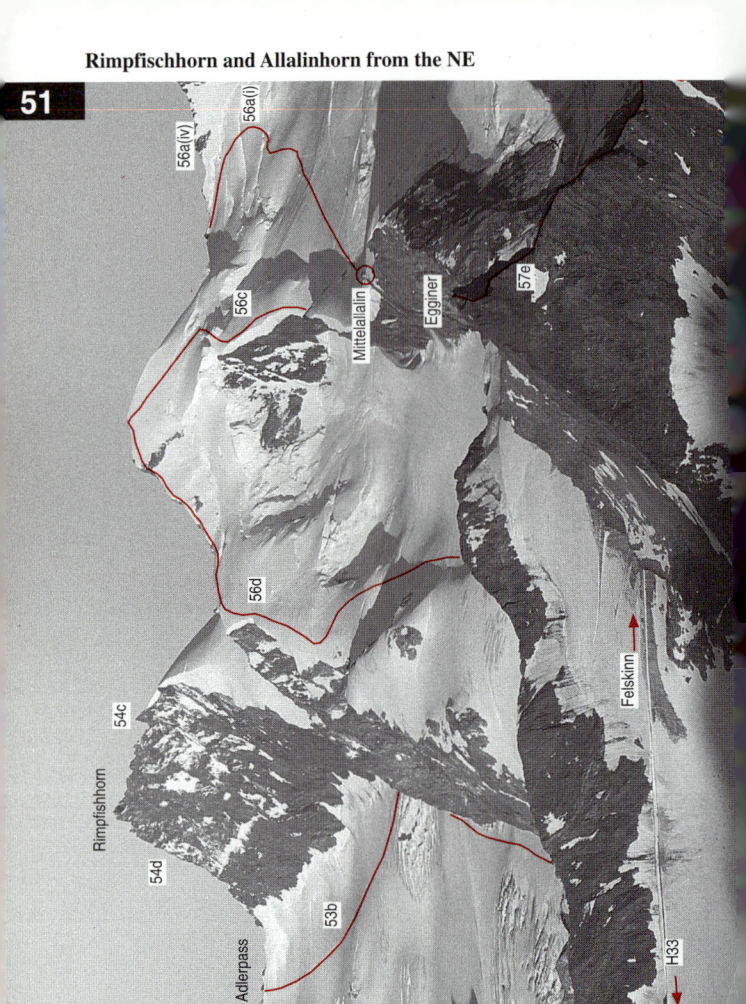

Allalinhorn N Flank

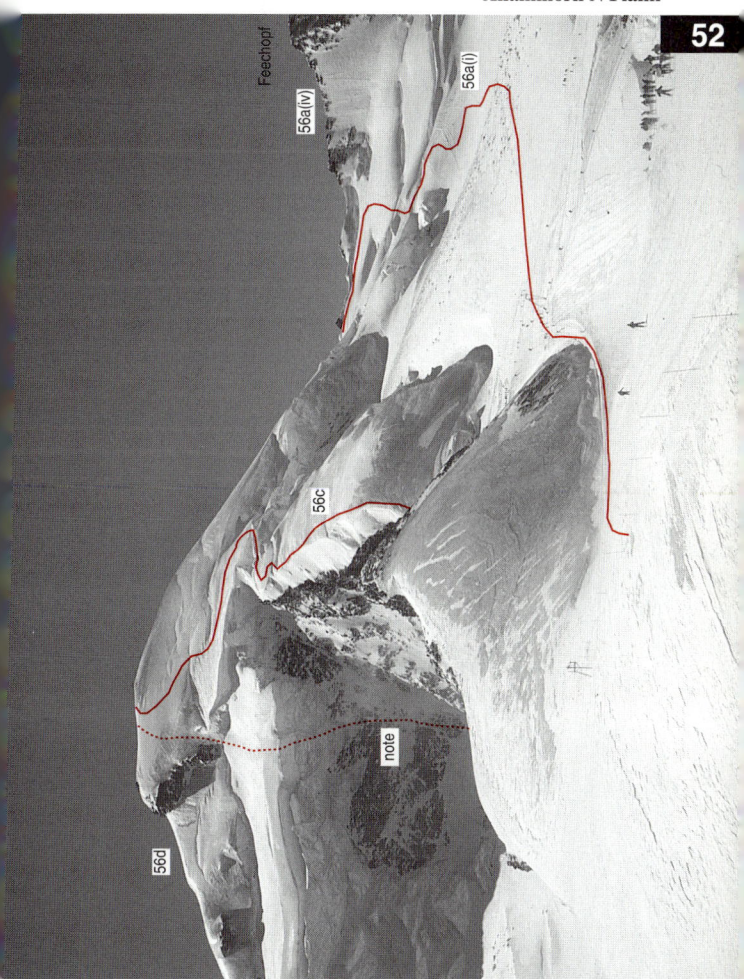

Mittaghorn and Egginer W Flanks

Alphubeljoch and Allalinhorn W Flanks

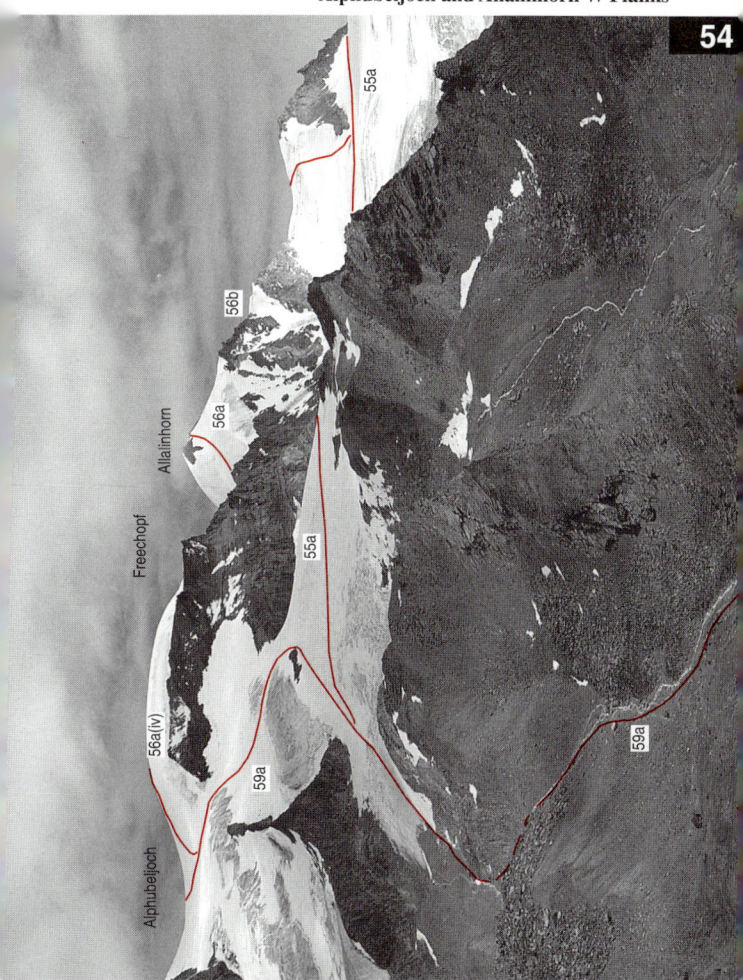

54

Alphubel E Flank

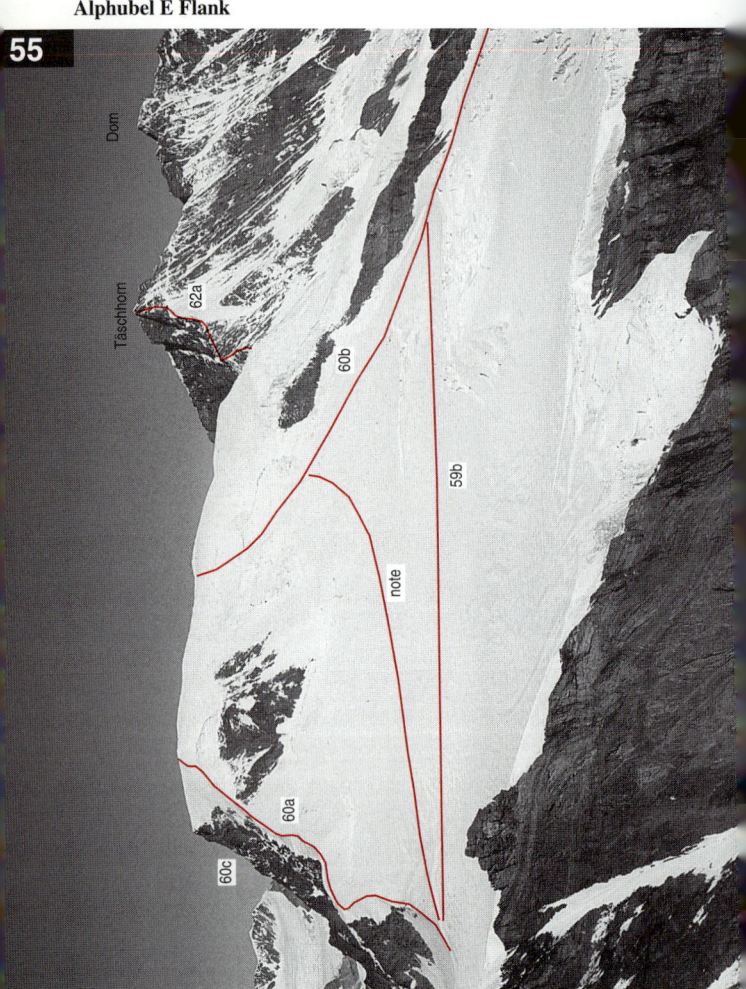

Alphubel W Flank

56

Alphubeljoch

60a

60c

61a

60d

Dom and Täschhorn from the SW

Leiterspitzen S Flank

58

Täschhorn W Flank

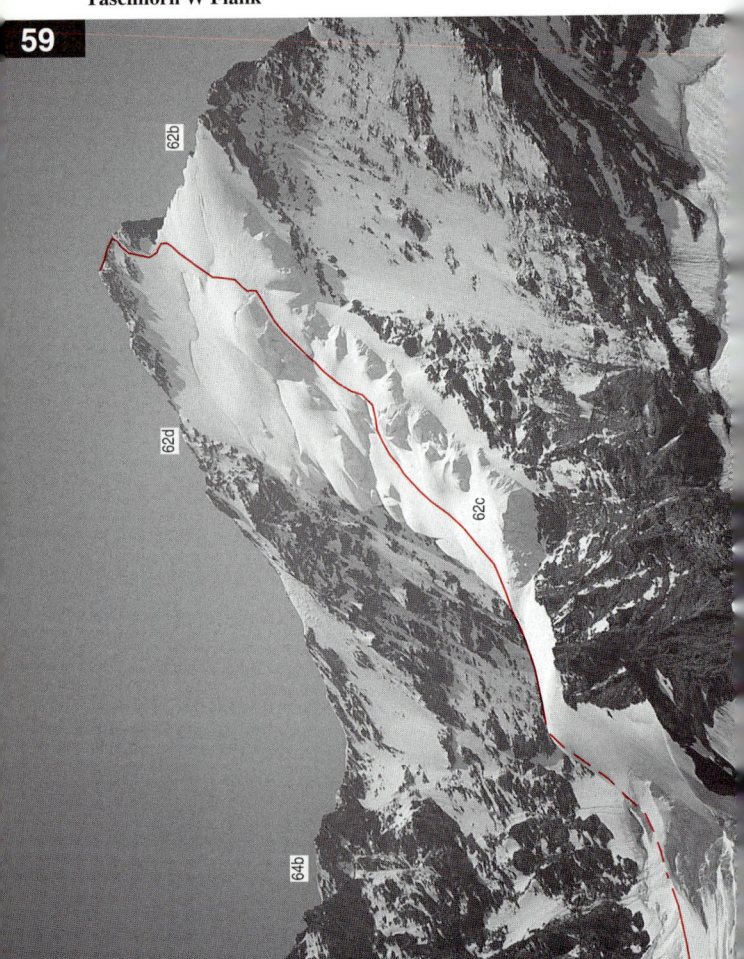

Dom NW Flank

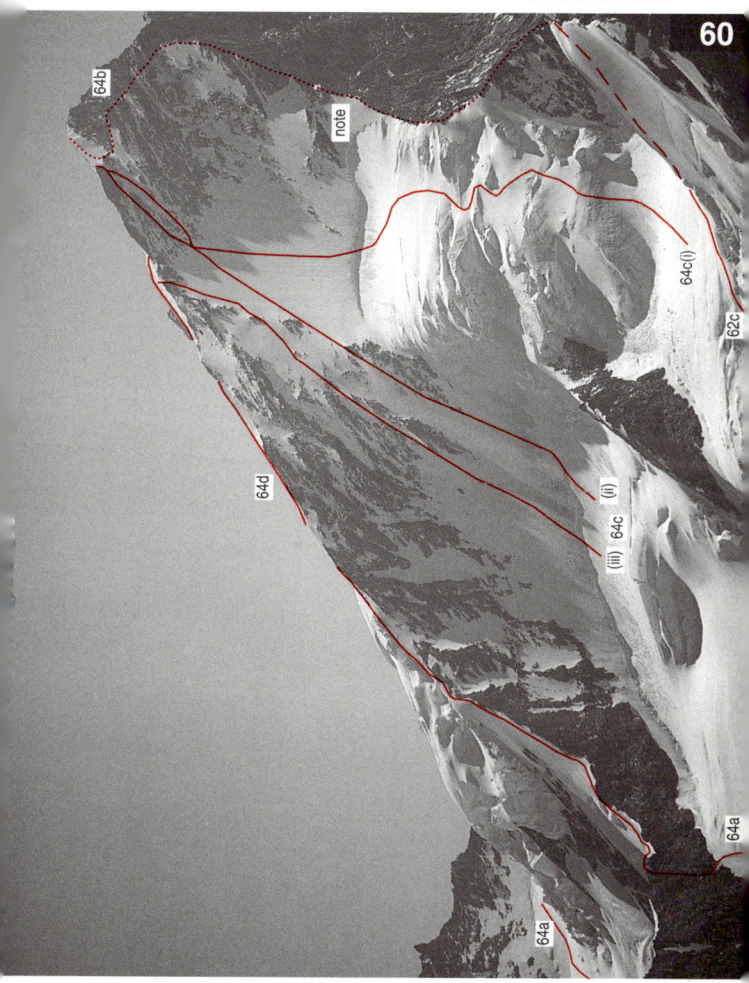

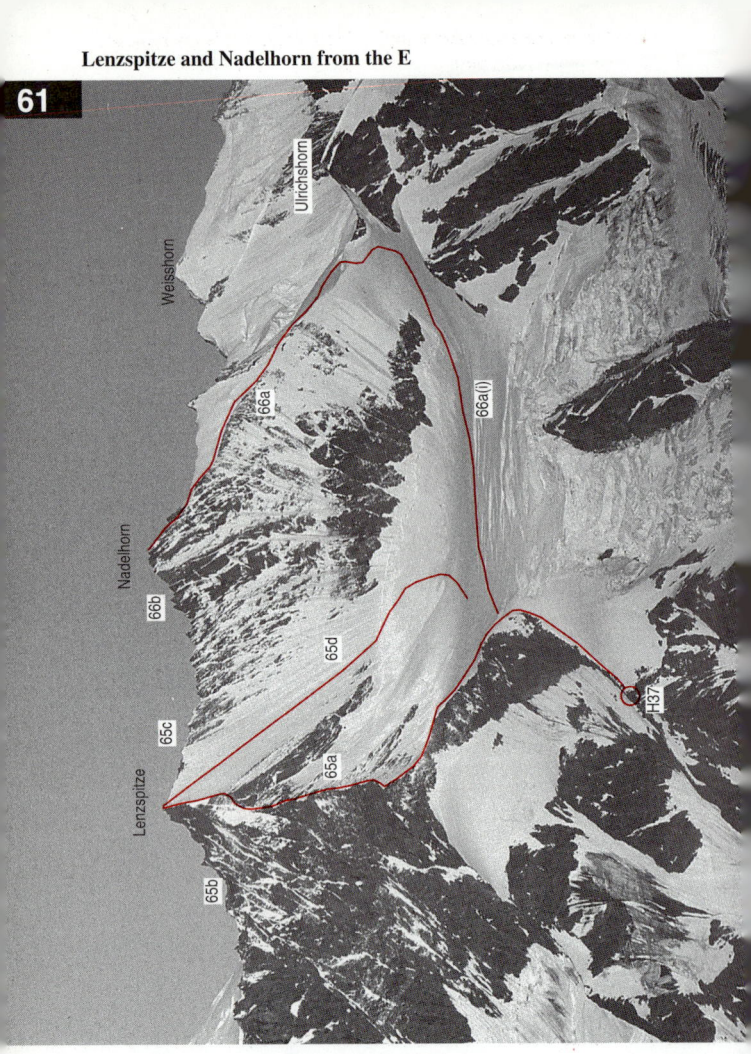

Lenzspitze and Nadelhorn from the E

Nadelhorn, Stecknadelhorn and Hohbärghorn NE Flanks

Hohbärghorn, Nadelhorn and Lenzspitze W Flanks

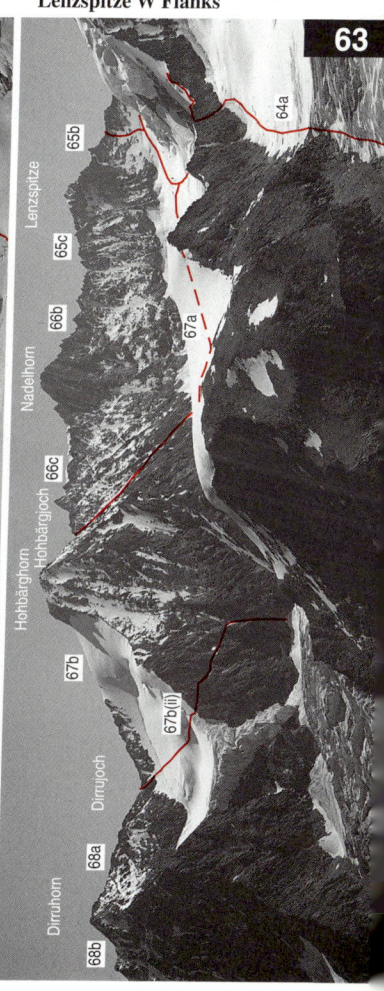

Hohbärghorn and Dirruhorn NE Flanks

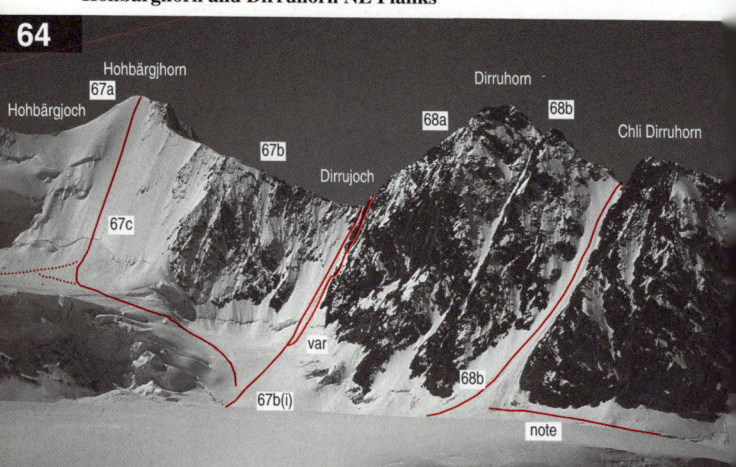

64

Nadelhorn N Side

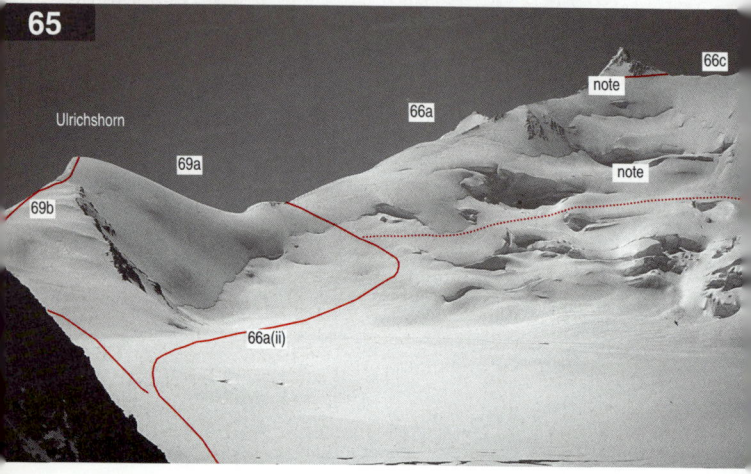

65

Gross Bigerhorn W Flank

66

Joderhorn from the W

67

Joderhorn E Face

68

Sonnighorn N Flank

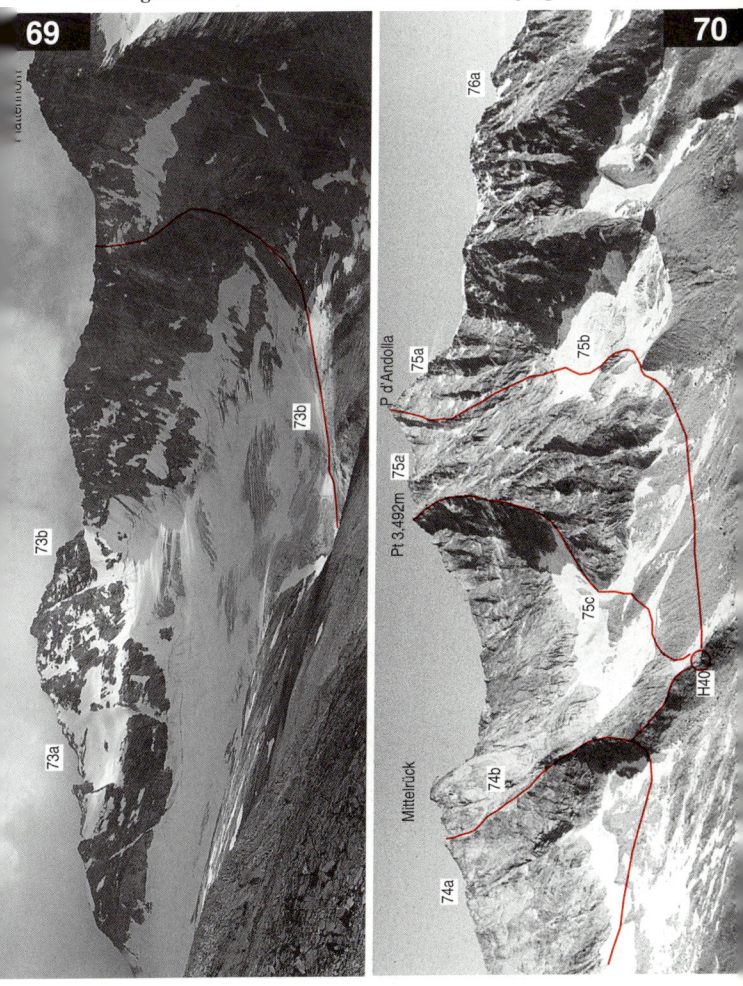

Mittelrück & Portjengrat E Flanks

Portjengrat W Side

Lagginhorn & Fletschhorn
E Flanks

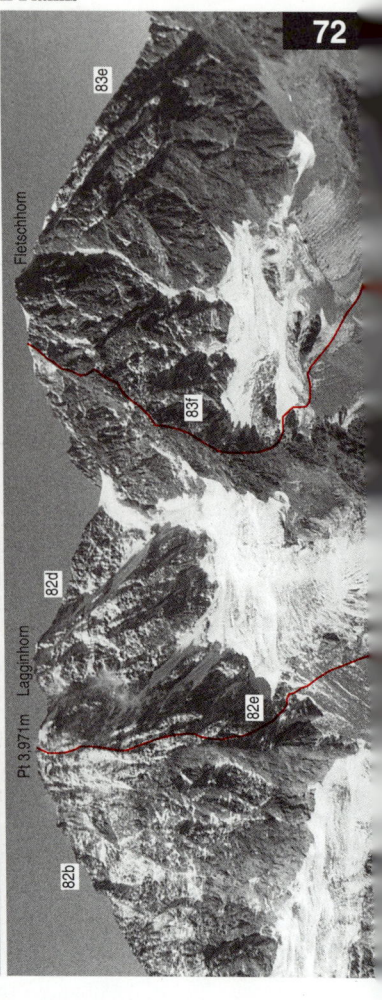

Dri Horlini SE Face SW Sector

73

Dri Horlini SE Face Central Sector

Weissmies W Flank

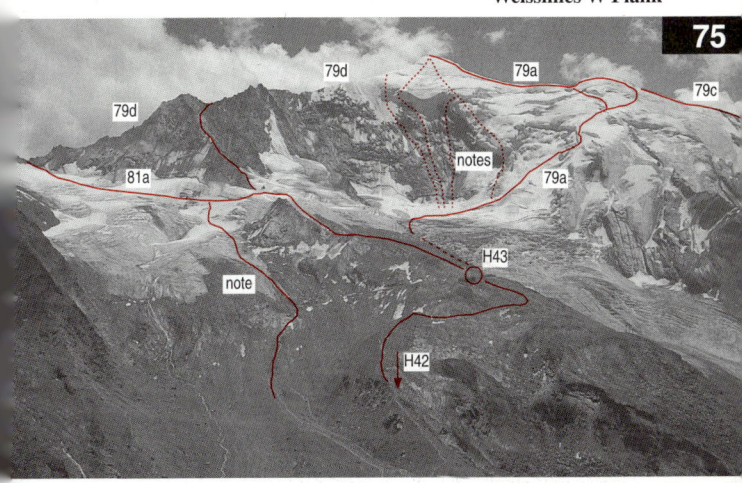

Weissmies from the SW

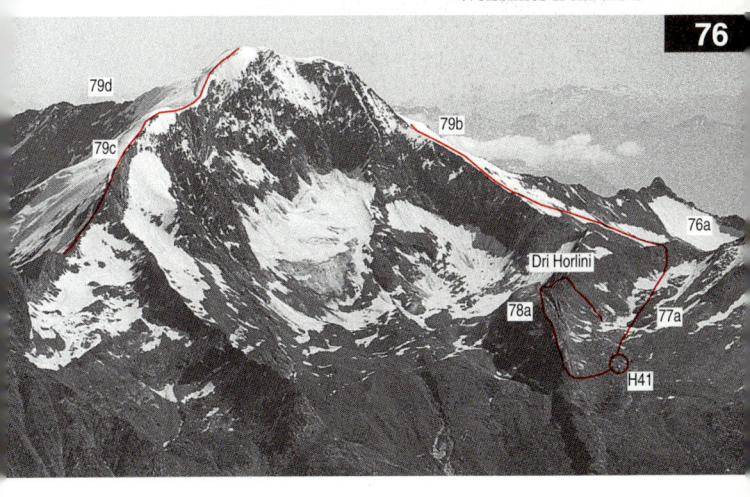

Fletschhorn and Lagginhorn W Flanks

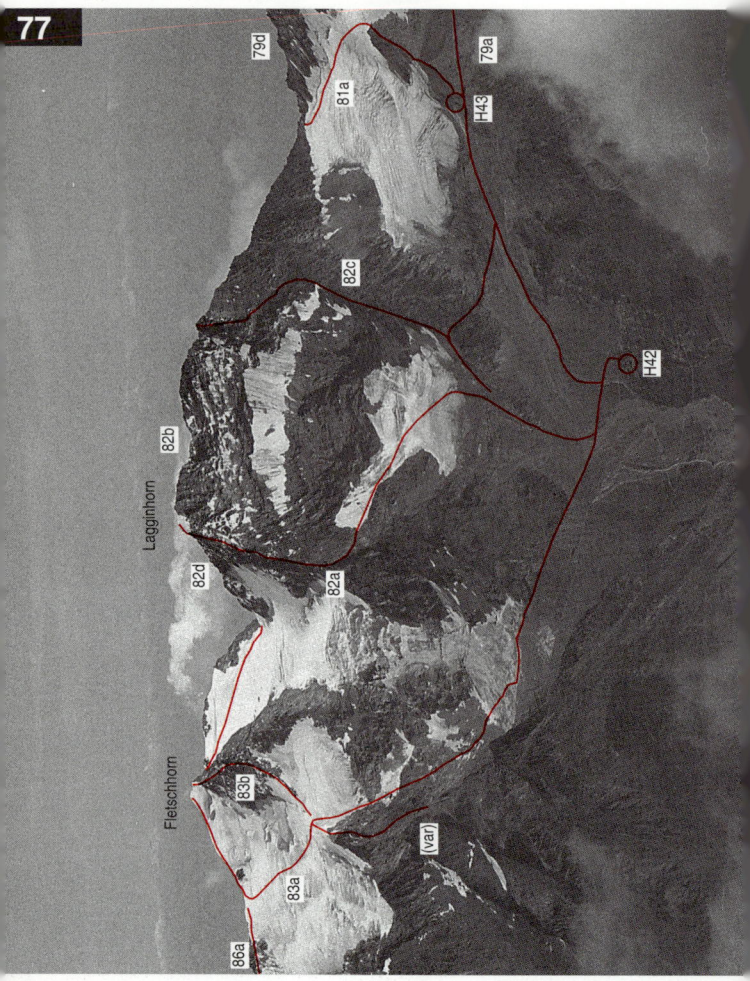

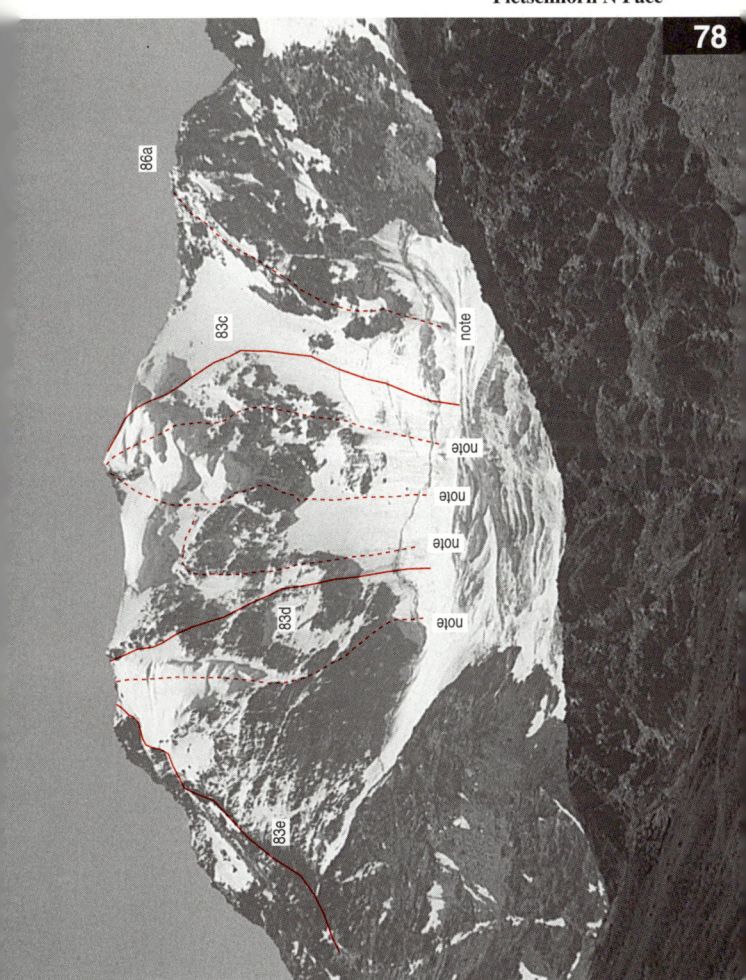

Fletschhorn N Face

Jegihorn S Flank

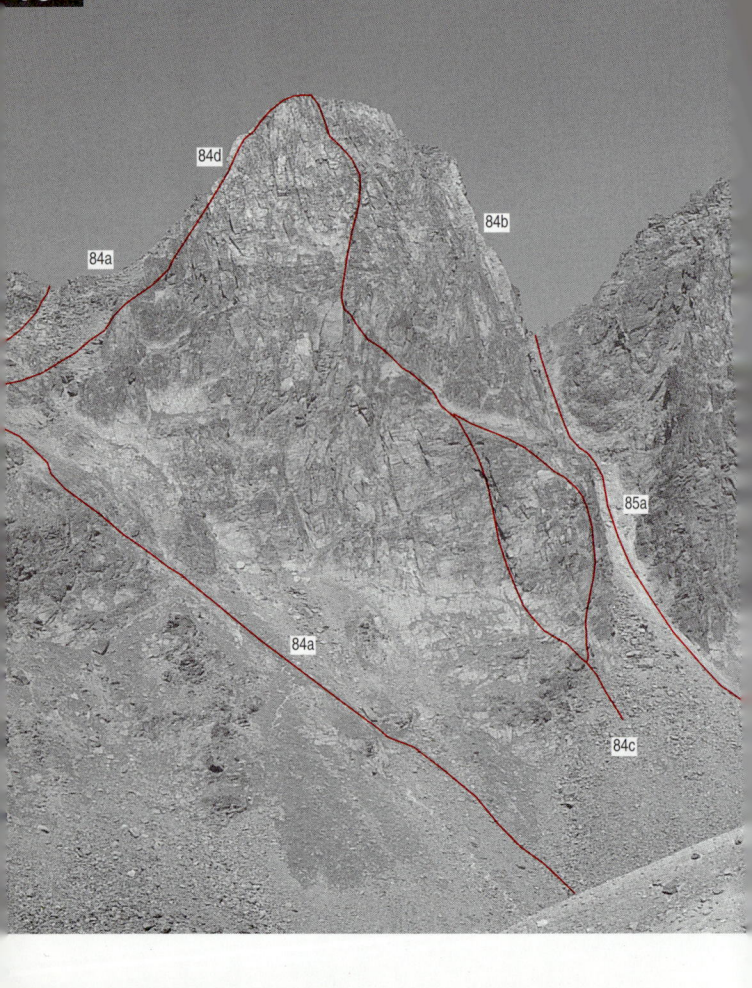

79

Jegigrat

Hubschhorn NW Flank

81

The Alpine Club

The Alpine Club welcomes new members

This guidebook is one of the many services which the Alpine Club offers to the mountaineering community and to its membership in particular. The Alpine Club is the only UK-based mountaineering club catering specifically for those who climb in the Alps and the Greater Ranges of the world. It is an active club, with a **regular programme of events and meets**.

The Alpine Club was founded in 1857 for 'the promotion of good fellowship among mountaineers, of mountain climbing and mountain exploration throughout the world, and of better knowledge of mountains through literature, science and art'. Throughout its existence, the Club has included in its membership many of the leading mountaineers of each generation, and now has members in more than 30 countries worldwide.

The **Alpine Club Library** is one of the foremost collections of mountaineering literature in the world, and is located at the Club premises in London. The **Himalayan Index**, owned and maintained by the Club, is a unique computerised record of climbing activity in the Himalaya.

The membership includes climbers of all abilities, and most active alpine climbers are qualified to join. There are three categories of membership, each with its own entrance requirements, benefits and subscription rates. Full Members are expected to have a record of at least 20 reasonable Alpine routes (or equivalent) over a minimum of three years. Aspirant Member status is for climbers who have some experience of Alpine climbing, and who expect to qualify as Full Members within 5 years. The third category is the Alpine Climbing Group (ACG). Members belonging to the ACG are expected to be active climbers with a record of hard climbs in the Alps and/or Greater Ranges.

Benefits of membership include

- Climbing meets in the UK, Alps and the Greater Ranges
- Reduced rates in many Alpine huts
- BMC affiliation
- Discount on Alpine Club publications, including guidebooks
- Premises in London
- Free access to the Library and Himalayan Index
- Free Alpine Journal
- Regular lectures and symposia

A brochure outlining Club activities and how to join is available from the Assistant Secretary. If you have any queries about the Club, please contact the Assistant Secretary at the Club during office hours, or check out the Alpine Club web site.

The Assistant Secretary, Tel & Fax: 0171 613 0755
Alpine Club, e-mail: asst-sec@alpine-club.org.uk
55/56 Charlotte Road, http://www.alpine-club.org.uk
London EC2A 3QT